S0-CFA-075

THE
FBI FILES

Also by Nicholas Redfern:

A Covert Agenda: The British Government's UFO Top Secrets Exposed

THE FBI FILES

THE FBI's
UFO TOP SECRETS
EXPOSED

by

NICHOLAS REDFERN

SIMON & SCHUSTER
A VIACOM COMPANY

First published by Simon & Schuster, 1998
An imprint of Simon & Schuster Ltd
A Viacom Company

Copyright © Nicholas Redfern, 1998

This book is copyright under the Berne Convention
No reproduction without permission
All rights reserved

The right of Nicholas Redfern to be identified as author of this
work has been asserted in accordance with sections 77 and 78 of
the Copyright Designs and Patents Act 1988

Simon & Schuster
West Garden Place
Kendal Street
London W2 2AQ

Simon & Schuster of Australia Pty Ltd Sydney

A CIP catalogue record for this book is available
from the British Library.

0–684–81938–4

Where possible, permission to quote has been obtained from all
copyright holders.

Typeset in Adobe Garamond by
Palimpsest Book Production Limited,
Polmont, Stirlingshire

Printed and bound by
Butler & Tanner
Frome and London

CONTENTS

Dedication

This book is dedicated to 'Free Spirit'
for the free spirit which she gives to life.

AUTHOR'S NOTE: Since much of the unique and never-before-seen FBI documentation reproduced in this book dates from the late 1940s and early 1950s, several of the papers have inevitably deteriorated with the passage of time. However, you should note that all of the documentation reproduced herein photographically is also cited in full in the text of the book itself.

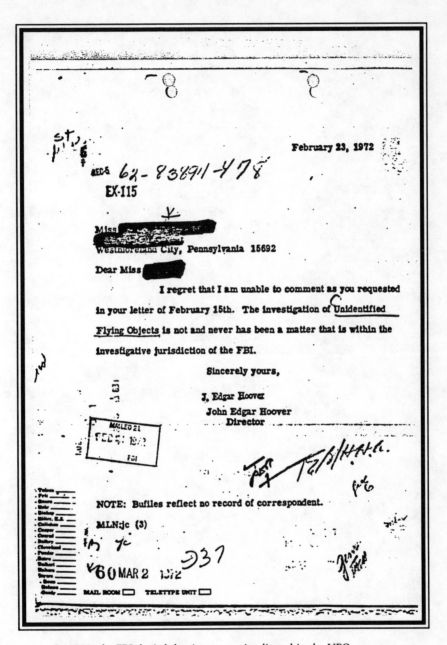

February 23, 1972

REC-5 62-83891-478

EX-115

Miss ████████████
Westmoreland City, Pennsylvania 15692

Dear Miss ████████

      I regret that I am unable to comment as you requested in your letter of February 15th. The investigation of Unidentified Flying Objects is not and never has been a matter that is within the investigative jurisdiction of the FBI.

           Sincerely yours,

           J. Edgar Hoover

           John Edgar Hoover
              Director

MAILED 21
FEB 1972
FBI

NOTE: Bufiles reflect no record of correspondent.

MLN:jc (3)

60 MAR 2 1972

MAIL ROOM ☐   TELETYPE UNIT ☐

In 1972, the FBI denied that it was ever implicated in the UFO mystery.

ACKNOWLEDGEMENTS

I WOULD LIKE TO THANK THE FOLLOWING FOR THEIR CONTRIBUTIONS TO
THIS BOOK:

The Federal Bureau of Investigation, for making available to me its
voluminous files on the subject of unidentified flying objects and related
matters; the US Air Force, for the use of a number of important papers
from its archives; the Public Record Office, for allowing me to cite
once-classified British Air Ministry memoranda; Nick Pope, for his
comments on the UFO issue; Timothy Good, for giving me permission
to make use of material from his book, *George Adamski – the Untold
Story*, and for the use of his photograph of the FBI building; Stanton T.
Friedman; Simon Miller; Christa Tilton, for allowing me to use her
photographs depicting cattle mutilations; the Mutual UFO Network;
Mark Birdsall and everyone at Quest International for the use of most
of the photographs contained within this book; Popperfoto, who supplied the photograph of J. Edgar Hoover; the Central Intelligence
Agency; Bruce G. Hallenbeck; Ron Scherrill, USAF; and Irene Bott,
President of Staffordshire UFO Group and Robert Dean, for granting
me permission to use the photograph of Mr Dean which appears in this
book.

FEDERAL BUREAU OF INVESTIGATION TERMINOLOGY

1. **Airtel:** An intra-FBI communication with highest priority of those sent through the mail. Originally conceived as a teletype sent via airmail, it may be in teletype phraseology.

2. **Cover Page:** The page(s) containing administrative data, leads and informant evaluations not found in LHMs (see below) or reports. Cover page(s) are not disseminated outside the FBI.

3. **Letter:** A communication sent from headquarters to a field office, from a field office to headquarters, or from a field office to any outside agency or person.

4. **Letterhead Memorandum** (LHM): A memorandum on letterhead stationery; it should normally require a cover communication for transmittal.

5. **Memorandum:** A communication on FBI memorandum paper to the Attorney General and other departmental officials; from one official to another at headquarters, or from one employee to another within a field office.

6. **Report:** A written document containing the results of an investigation. It is almost always prepared in a field office.

7. **Teletype:** A communication transmitted by machine.

INTRODUCTION

IN JULY 1908, CHARLES J. BONAPARTE, ATTORNEY GENERAL UNDER UNITED States President Theodore Roosevelt, created a force of special agents within the Department of Justice (DOJ), which ultimately evolved into one of the USA's most efficient and respected organisations – the Federal Bureau of Investigation. With its headquarters in Washington, the FBI has offices in every US state, and employs thousands of personnel, many of whom are hand-picked for their skills.

The primary function of the FBI is law enforcement, something that encompasses organised crime, civil-rights violations, kidnapping, bank robbery, foreign counterintelligence, white-collar crime and drug trafficking.[1]

With the passing of the United States' Freedom of Information Act (FOIA), the FBI was obliged to make available to the general public literally hundreds of thousands of official documents which had previously remained classified and exempt from disclosure. Papers that are now open for study at the Reading Room at the FBI headquarters show that substantial files had been assembled on a wide variety of groups and individuals, including: the American Indian Movement; Albert Einstein; the assassination of Martin Luther King Jr; Marilyn Monroe; Burgess, Philby and Maclean; Lee Harvey Oswald; Errol Flynn; the Chappaquiddick affair; and a host of other topics.

Most startling of all, the Freedom of Information Act has shown that for almost half a century the FBI has been engaged in covertly monitoring one of the most emotive topics of our time – unidentified flying objects. Interestingly, until the FOIA forced the Bureau to relinquish its files, there was a blanket denial on the part of the FBI that it had any interest in the UFO subject. For example, on 23 February 1972, the FBI Director, J. Edgar Hoover, wrote to an enquiring member of the US public: 'The investigation of Unidentified Flying Objects is not and never has been a matter that is within the investigative jurisdiction of the FBI.' A similar comment was made the following year by Hoover's successor, Clarence M. Kelley. We now know, however, those assertions were false.

In the following chapters you will learn of some truly remarkable UFO encounters in which the FBI has been directly implicated since 1947 – encounters involving military and civilian pilots, radar operators, police and security personnel and members of the public.

Also under scrutiny will be the numerous accounts in Bureau files pertaining to actual 'crashed UFOs' and the remains of deceased alien bodies held by the military; the theft and unauthorised release of highly classified official papers relating to unidentified flying objects; the claims of a number of persons (all heavily monitored by the Bureau) who maintained actual face-to-face contact with extraterrestrial beings in the 1950s; repeated UFO encounters in the vicinity of atomic energy installations; and a bizarre alien operation to 'harvest' earthbased life forms for their own needs.

No doubt, there will be those who consider this too fantastic for words. Indeed, it is. However, take note that the astonishing revelations that follow are based on a systematic and in-depth examination of genuine FBI documentation, much of which has been classified for decades. Moreover, the quality of material I have presented wholly belies the notion that the UFO issue is one of no consequence. As will become apparent, even a brief perusal of the facts suggests that something truly extraordinary is taking place on Planet Earth, and that 'something' is directly connected with ongoing visitations by an alien species. Let the evidence speak for itself.

It has long been assumed that the origins of the UFO mystery in the USA can be traced back to 24 June 1947, when a pilot, Kenneth Arnold, viewed nine elliptical vehicles flying over the Cascade Mountains, Washington State. While it is certainly true that Arnold's encounter captured the imagination of the media and public alike, it was simply one of many such encounters that had occurred during the summer months of 1947.

A document called 'Analysis of Flying Object Incidents in the US' (10 December 1948), which originated with the US Air Force and was classified Top Secret, for example, confirms that throughout mid-1947 sightings of unusual aerial vehicles abounded. Commenting on its analysis of a variety of good-quality accounts, the Air Force stated: 'A number of reports on unidentified flying objects come from observers who, because of their technical background and experience, do not appear to be influenced by unfounded sensationalism nor inclined to report explainable phenomena as new types of airborne devices.'

A presentation of selected portions of the evidence collated by the Air Force and related in its Top Secret report follows:

During April 1947, two employees of the Weather Bureau Station at Richmond, Virginia, reported seeing a strange metallic disk on three occasions through the theodolite while making PIBAL observations. One observation was at 15,000 feet when a disk was followed for 15 seconds. The disk appeared metallic, shaped like an ellipse with a flat bottom and a round top. It appeared below the balloon and was much larger in size. The disk appeared to be moving rather rapidly, although it was impossible to estimate its speed.

While flying at 10,000 feet on a course of 300 degrees, 30 miles northwest of Lake Meade, Nevada, an Air Force lieutenant reported seeing five or six white circular objects in close formation and traveling at an estimated speed of 285 miles per hour. This sighting occurred on 28 June 1947.

The following day a party of three, two of them scientists, were motoring along Highway 17 toward the White Sands, New Mexico, V-2 firing grounds and reported seeing a large disk or sphere moving horizontally at a high speed and an estimated altitude of 10,000 feet. It was of uniform shape and had no protruding surfaces such as wings. The object was in sight for about 60 seconds before it disappeared to the northeast. The three observers agreed on the details of the sighting except that one thought he had seen vapor trails.

On 7 July 1947, five Portland, Oregon, police officers reported varying numbers of disks flying over different parts of the city. All observations were made within a minute or two of 1305 hours.

On the same day, William Rhoads of Phoenix, Arizona, allegedly saw a disk circling his locality during sunset and took two photographs. The resulting pictures show a disk-like object with a round front and a square tail in plan form. These photographs have been examined by experts who state they are true photographic images and do not appear to be imperfection [sic] in the emulsion or imperfections in the lens.

On 10 July 1947, Mr Woodruff, a Pan-American Airways mechanic, reported a circular object flying at high velocity, paralleling the earth's surface and leaving a trail which appeared as a 'burning up' of the cloud formation. The sighting occurred near Harmon Field, Newfoundland. Two other persons also saw the trail which remained in the sky for about an hour and was photographed by another PAA employee.[2]

Faced with the possibility that an unidentified, and maybe even hostile, intruder was violating US territory, the military recognized quickly that an immediate investigation and evaluation of the evidence was sorely warranted.

Fifty years on, investigations continue, and documentation declassified under the provisions of the US Freedom of Information Act has disclosed intense interest in the UFO subject as a whole on the part of the CIA, Defense Intelligence Agency, National Security Agency, Department of State and, of course, the Federal Bureau of Investigation.

CHAPTER 1

THE ALIENS ARRIVE

TWO WEEKS AFTER THE KENNETH ARNOLD SIGHTING OVER WASHINGTON
State, Brigadier General George F. Schulgen, Chief of the Requirements
Intelligence Branch of Army Air Corps Intelligence, met with Special
Agent S.W. Reynolds of the Bureau with a view to determining if the
Army Air Force could solicit the assistance of the Bureau on a regular
basis in its investigation of the UFO mystery.

Declassified FBI memoranda show that, at the request of J. Edgar
Hoover, the Bureau had been monitoring aspects of the subject on a
somewhat ad hoc basis since the latter part of June 1947. However, at that
time the Bureau's interest was not directly part of a concerted intelligence-
gathering operation.

General Schulgen advised Reynolds that 'every effort must be undertaken in order to run down and ascertain whether or not the flying discs
are a fact and, if so, to learn all about them'.

As Reynolds listened Schulgen revealed that an Air Corps pilot who
had recently reported sighting a flying-saucer-type craft had been thoroughly
interrogated by both scientists and psychologists and was adamant in his
belief that he had seen something truly anomalous. As a result, orders had
been dispatched to all Air Corps installations to 'obtain all possible data
to assist in this research project'.

It becomes clear that in the weeks following Arnold's encounter of 24
June 1947, the foremost thought within General Schulgen's mind was

that the saucers were Russian in origin, and he confided in Special Agent Reynolds that 'the first reported sightings might have been by individuals of Communist sympathies with the view to causing hysteria and fear of a secret weapon'. And it was on this aspect of the UFO phenomenon that the AAF sought the Bureau's assistance.

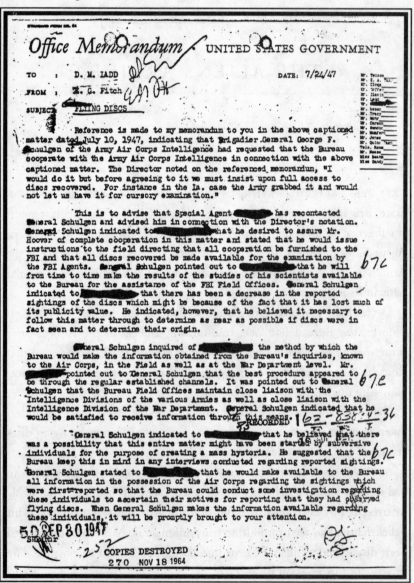

In 1947, Brigadier General George F. Schulgen of the Army Air Corps Intelligence sought the FBI's assistance in investigating UFO encounters.

Assuring Reynolds that he would guarantee the Bureau 'all the facilities of [my] office as to results obtained', General Schulgen outlined a plan which would involve the FBI in both locating and questioning witnesses to ascertain whether they were 'sincere in their statements that they saw these discs, or whether their statements were prompted by personal desire for publicity or political reasons'.

Whatever the perceived origin of the saucers, Schulgen carefully advised Reynolds of one certainty: 'It has been established that the flying disks are not the result of any Army or Navy experiment'. Were the mysterious visitors indeed Russian, or did they have a far stranger origin?

On 24 July 1947, a Bureau official, E.G. Fitch, forwarded to the assistant director of the FBI's Domestic Intelligence Division, D.M. Ladd, a two-page memorandum responding to the concerns of Director Hoover that in one particular instance in early July the Army had denied the Bureau access to a 'recovered' saucer found in Louisiana (see also Chapter 11).

Anxious to resolve matters for Hoover, Fitch directed Special Agent Reynolds to recontact General Schulgen and impress upon him that, if the Bureau was to become involved in investigating aspects of the UFO issue, any involvement would have to be on an equal footing with that of the Army Air Force.

Reynolds responded to Fitch that: 'General Schulgen indicated . . . that he desired to assure Mr Hoover of complete cooperation in this matter and stated that he would issue instructions to the field directing that all cooperation be furnished to the FBI and that all discs recovered be made available for the examination by the FBI Agents.' Later on, we will see that the Bureau has taken more than a passing interest in reports of recovered UFOs . . .

Schulgen continued to express his belief that the entire UFO problem was the work of subversive individuals, although it is hard to reconcile this idea with the testimony of the Air Corps pilot whose account of seeing a circular craft Schulgen was fully aware of.

During the course of the discussion, General Schulgen addressed the issue of how, if it was ultimately to become involved, the FBI would make available its data to the AAF. As Special Agent Reynolds suggested, the most profitable approach would be to go through regular established channels. At the time the Bureau's field offices maintained close liaison with the Intelligence divisions of the Army and the War Department. 'General Schulgen indicated that he would be satisfied to receive information through this means,' Reynolds reported back to Fitch. General Schulgen's plans and assurances evidently satisfied J. Edgar Hoover, and on 30 July the following 'Bureau Bulletin' was dispatched to FBI field offices throughout the USA:

> You should investigate each instance which is brought to your attention of a sighting of a flying disc in order to ascertain whether or not [it] is a bona fide sighting, an imaginary one or a prank. You should also bear in mind that individuals might report seeing flying discs for various reasons. It is conceivable that an individual might be desirous of seeking personal publicity, causing hysteria or playing a prank.
>
> The Bureau should be notified immediately by teletype of all reported sightings and the results of your enquiries. In instances where the report appears to have merit, the teletype should be followed by a letter to the Bureau containing in detail the results of your enquiries. The Army Air Forces have assured the Bureau complete cooperating [sic] in these matters and in any instances where they fail to make information available to you or make the recovered discs available for your examination, it should promptly be brought to the attention of the Bureau.
>
> Any information you develop in connection with these discs should be promptly brought to the attention of the Army through your usual liaison channels.

It is interesting to note that, although General Schulgen had assured the Bureau that the saucers were not US secret weapons, someone in the Army Air Force had been researching the feasibility of constructing circular craft, as a note attached to the 30 July bulletin shows: 'The Air Forces have confidentially advised that it is possible to release three or more discs in odd numbers, attached together by a wire, from an airplane in high altitudes and that these discs would obtain tremendous speed in their descent and would descend to the earth in an arc.'

This is certainly significant, and suggests that factions of the military had determined that UFOs were not solely the result of bogus stories promoted by subversive sources, as postulated by General Schulgen.

Regardless of the veracity of the many theories advanced at the time, the saucers continued to be seen with increasing frequency, and, as a result of Hoover's decision to become involved on an in-depth and pro-active basis, the FBI was inundated with reports of unusual aerial activity, many of which were submitted by the military and predated the 30 July directive, thus allowing the Bureau to obtain a much clearer picture of the UFO mystery from its beginnings in mid-to-late April. A report dated 15 July 1947, submitted to the Bureau for study, makes for eye-opening reading and is of particular note since the witness was a serving member of the armed forces. Classified Confidential, the one-page report states that the witness (whose name is excised on Bureau papers) 'has been in the Army ten years and two months, twenty-six months overseas duty . . . and has been in the Air Corps for about ten months . . . On 8 July 1947, he was going to Base Cleaners from his office and was passing along the sidewalk near the barracks of the ORD when he saw five or six men pointing toward the sky, but as he was use [sic] to this around an Army Air Base, he paid no further attention to it until a lieutenant and a captain ahead of him stopped and pointed in the same direction.' The report continues:

> He stated that on glancing up he saw three objects traveling northeast across the sky. Two seemed to be traveling faster than an ordinary flight of P-80's and he estimated the altitude between 8–10,000 feet and approximately 7–10 miles away. [Witness] stated that the two objects in the lead appeared to be round and of a very light gray color, while the object in the rear seemed to be either rotating or rolling behind the other two . . . from a distance he could not tell exactly the shape of the one which was rolling as it appeared to be turning over and he couldn't tell whether the object was flat. The only means he had of identifying it was the fact that it seemed to get brighter and darker as it appeared to roll. The objects were in sight approximately four seconds . . . it was unlike anything he had ever seen and that he

had been trying to convince himself that it was an optical illusion, and yet at the same time he is certain that he saw the objects as described.

An evaluation by Captain William L. Davidson of the Air Corps put the witness in a very favourable light: '[He] appears to be intelligent and is a reserved sort of person. He was very reluctant to discuss the subject at first and appeared hesitant prompted by the possibility that he might be ridiculed. He seemed to be honest and sincere in what he stated he saw, and said frankly he was puzzled over the matter.'

Nine days later, an equally impressive report caught the Bureau's attention, having been supplied by the Army. In this instance the witness, Byron B. Savage, was a private pilot of Oklahoma City, who had been flying since 1929. In an interview with an Army investigator, Kaiman D. Simon, Savage recalled the events of 23 July, and was willing to 'cooperate in every way possible':

> Savage related that he and his wife had just departed their residence and had started to enter their car in the driveway . . . He judged the time to be between 8.30 p.m. and 9.00 p.m., and the lights from the city of Oklahoma City appeared to be shining on this object when he first saw it. He judged the object to be about 160 degrees in the south when he first saw it, and as it moved toward him he remarked to his wife that 'a big white plane was coming over.'
>
> Savage stated that when this object was at a 45 degree angle from him, he realized it was not a conventional type aircraft, and it appeared elliptical at first and as it moved closer it appeared perfectly round and was flat. Savage advised the object, which appeared to him as a disc, had no appearance of being spherical and had a ratio of diameter to the thickness of approximately 10 to 1, appearing thicker in the center, but this could not be positively ascertained. Savage judged the object to be at an altitude of between 10,000 and 18,000 feet, and it left no trailing effects. Savage related that it appeared to be in bulk as big as the bulk of

six B-29's at an altitude of approximately the same height. Savage advised that the object was in his vision approximately 15 to 20 seconds and traveled at a speed which he judged to be approximately three times that of jet-propelled aircraft . . . Subject further stated that the object appeared to be frosty white in color at all times.

In the latter part of August 1947, a number of UFO sightings were reported in the vicinity of Muroc Air Field, Muroc, California, and copies of the witnesses' affidavits were channelled through to the Bureau, portions of one of which I have reproduced below:

. . . Upon leaving the Post Exchange, I went directly to my Office and before entering heard one of our local aircraft in the traffic pattern. Looking up, as I always do, I observed the aircraft, and looking slightly to the left, whereupon I observed two (2) silver objects of either a spherical or disc-like shape, moving about three hundred (300) miles an hour, or perhaps less, at approximately eight thousand (8,000) feet, heading at about twenty degrees due north.

When I first observed these objects I called [three individuals, whose names are censored by the Bureau] who immediately came to where I was standing. I pointed in the direction of the objects and asked them the question 'Tell me what you see up there.' Whereupon, all the three with sundry comments stated, 'They are Flying Disc' [sic] . . .

I had time to look away several times and renew my vision of the objects to make sure that they were not any results of eye strain, or in any nature an optical illusion. The objects were not, repeat were not aircraft, the objects could not have been weather balloons released from this station, since they were traveling against the prevailing wind, and since the speed at which they were traveling and the horizontal direction in which they were traveling disqualified the fact that they were weather balloons . . .

After the observance of [this] phenomenon . . . I immediately

ran into the dispensary to get personnel who are Medical Officers
to verify, for my own curiosity, the actual observance of these
objects, but by the time I reached the back porch of the dispensary . . . the objects had, by that time, disappeared, due to the
speed with which they were traveling . . .

This statement has been given freely and voluntarily without
any threats or promises under duress . . .

As these three accounts make abundantly clear, throughout the summer
of 1947, quality UFO sightings, frequently reported by highly credible
sources, abounded. But these were simply records forwarded to the
Bureau by the military as part of its agreement to share data. What of
those encounters investigated directly by the FBI itself?

One of the problems that became very apparent to the Bureau in July
1947 was the fact that much of its time was being spent on (a) responding to letters from enquiring members of the public; (b) chasing down
cases that proved to be nothing but outright hoaxes; and (c) investigating
sightings of objects that, having been reported by wholly untrained
observers, could in reality have been anything or nothing.

Added to the fact that factions of the Bureau were still convinced that
the saucer mystery was a highly classified US government project, there
was a belief in some quarters that the FBI should relinquish its involvement in the subject with the utmost haste, as it was becoming clear that
the plans originally envisaged for the Bureau were becoming decidedly
awry.

To illustrate the situation the FBI found itself in, on 11 July it was
forced to deal with a 'landed UFO', which turned out to be nothing more
than a thirty-inch-diameter cymbal on top of which was a plastic dome
surrounded by a number of 'stove bolts'. In other words, a complete hoax.

Similarly, on 13 July, the Bureau received a letter from a resident of Los
Angeles trying to procure donations of $10,000 'for the purpose of my
continuing the collection of field data concerning "discs" while time may
remain in which to do so'!

This understandably infuriated the FBI, and by August there were
repeated calls for it either to get out of the saucer issue, or at least assume
a more positive role, which would extend beyond playing second fiddle to

the military. This is amply summed up in an internal memo to D.M. Ladd:

> It is felt that the situation regarding these flying saucers and flying discs is very similar to the situation which was previously encountered by the Bureau during the past war in handling complaints arising out of the sighting of Japanese balloons. You will recall that at the inception of these complaints the Bureau conducted considerable investigation and located numerous balloons as a cooperative measure for the Army and that after considerable work had been done, the Army then informed that these were military weapons and that they would take over the handling of these completely. This they did and in an extremely short time issued a big press release as to the splendid work of the Army in locating these Japanese balloons. From the information available thus far it does not appear that these discs should be treated other than as a military weapon. Certainly the Bureau has no way to determine what experiments the Army and Navy are conducting and whether such might be arising out of experiments being conducted by them, nor do we have any way of determining how far the Russians have progressed in certain experiments and whether such might be the results of experiments by the Russian Army . . .

It was further argued that 'the Bureau is merely playing bird-dog for the Army by using our manpower to run out these complaints on flying discs'.

Fortunately, as General George F. Schulgen noted, by August the overwhelming hysteria that accompanied the UFO subject had decreased somewhat, and the Bureau's field offices then began to receive more and more credible reports, which contrasted sharply with the situation in June and July, when the Bureau was forced to deal with all manner of hoaxes.

On 7 August an 'Urgent' Teletype for the attention of Hoover was dispatched from the Philadelphia office:

FLYING OBJECT REPORTED OVER PHILA. AUGUST
SIX, NINETEEN FORTY-SEVEN. SABOTAGE. THE

PHILADELPHIA INQUIRER ON AUGUST SEVEN,
NINETEEN FORTY SEVEN, CARRIED ITEM CON-
CERNING FLYING OBJECTS . . . PEOPLE
REPORTED AS OBSERVING SUCH INTERVIEWED BY
PHILA. OFFICE, AND SUBSTANTIALLY FURNISHED
FOLLOWING INFORMATION. AT TEN FORTY-FIVE,
AUGUST SIX . . . A BLUISH WHITE FLAMING
OBJECT WAS OBSERVED AT A HEIGHT OF ONE
THOUSAND FEET OR MORE OVER PHILADELPHIA
PROCEEDING FROM A NORTHEASTERLY TO A
SOUTHEASTERLY DIRECTION. THIS OBJECT LEFT
A TRAIL OF SMOKE WHICH LASTED FOR ABOUT
TWO SECONDS AND [A] HISSING OR BUZZING
SOUND WAS AUDIBLE AFTER THE SIGHT OF SUCH
OBJECT. PEOPLE OBSERVING THE SAME SEEMED
SENSIBLE AND RELIABLE, AND INCLUDE A FOR-
MER ARMY AIR CORPS PILOT. HE DOES NOT
BELIEVE ABOVE MENTIONED OBJECT WAS A JET
PROPELLED PLANE SINCE THE ACCOMPANYING
SOUND WAS NOT AS LOUD AS THAT MADE BY JET
PROPELLED PLANES. HE ESTIMATED ABOVE
OBJECT TRAVELED AT A RATE OF ABOUT FOUR
HUNDRED MILES PER HOUR. INQUIRIES BEING
MADE BY ARMY AND NAVY INTELLIGENCE FORCES,
PHILA. ON THE REQUEST OF THE PHILA. OFFICE
TO DETERMINE IF EITHER ARMY OR NAVY ARE
DOING ANY EXPERIMENTAL WORK ON NEW TYPES
OF PLANES IN VICINITY OF PHILA. THEY WILL
ADVISE PHILA. OFFICE IN NEXT SEVERAL DAYS.
LETTER OF DETAILS WILL FOLLOW. BOARDMAN.

This was undoubtedly the way Hoover wanted matters handled. Here was a believable report, with 'sensible and reliable' witnesses, including a former Army Air Corps pilot, and the Philadelphia FBI office was receiving creditable assistance from both the Army and Navy, as all three sought to determine the nature of the mystery object seen over Philadelphia.

Despite a thorough study of the facts, the case remained frustratingly unresolved, and the Bureau was obliged to turn its attention elsewhere. One week after the encounter over Philadelphia, the Seattle office had an interesting story to tell:

> . . . L.R. Brummett, Box 254, Redmond, Washington, and Sidney Decker, Box 296, Redmond, Washington had sighted two discs at approximately 9.00 a.m. August 13, 1947. Upon interview Decker stated that two very bright objects traveling at an extreme rate of speed were noticed by him as he was standing near the Redmond Post Office. Decker described the objects as having no wings, no tail, and both ends were tapered. Decker added that the objects resembled a belly tank and that they were noiseless.

In a detailed two-page report the Seattle office advised Washington that both objects appeared 'very bright' and were travelling in a northerly direction when seen. During the eight seconds in which the UFOs were in view, Decker formed the opinion that, whatever the origin of the objects, they were travelling at a height in excess of that normally seen in an aeroplane, while Brummett estimated their speed to have been at least three times faster than that of a conventional aircraft.

Fortunately, Brummett and Decker had the opportunity to alert a further person to the objects – a Mrs Mamie English: 'Mrs English stated that when Brummett called her attention to the objects she took a passing glance at the sky and could offer no description other than they looked like two silver balls traveling at a fast rate of speed.'

Again the sighting remained unidentified, but, as the Bureau's report made very clear, there was little doubt that all three witnesses were describing encounters with rationally controlled, high-performance vehicles of unknown origin and intent. Twenty-four hours later, it was the sighting of an unusual flying craft over Idaho that alerted Bureau agents at Butte to dispatch a one-page teletype to Washington:

> Director, FBI. Urgent. On instant date [deleted] of Twin Falls, Idaho, informed local newspaper that at 1.00 p.m. on

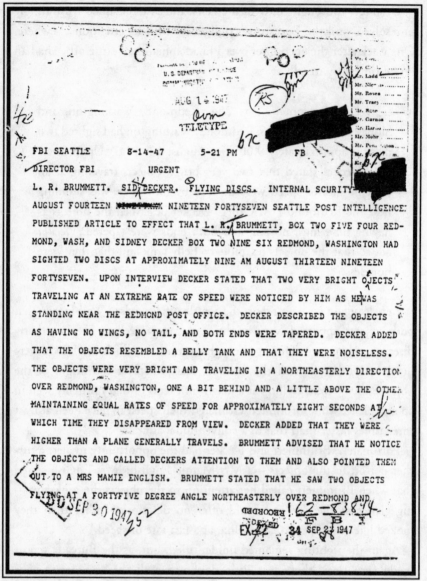

FEDERAL BUREAU OF ... VEST.
U. S. DEPARTMENT ... ICE
COMMUNICATIO... ECT...

AUG 14 1947

TELETYPE

FBI SEATTLE   8-14-47   5-21 PM   FB

DIRECTOR FBI   URGENT

L. R. BRUMMETT. SID DECKER. FLYING DISCS. INTERNAL SCURITY—
AUGUST FOURTEEN ~~NINETY~~ NINETEEN FORTYSEVEN SEATTLE POST INTELLIGENCE:
PUBLISHED ARTICLE TO EFFECT THAT L. R. BRUMMETT, BOX TWO FIVE FOUR RED-
MOND, WASH, AND SIDNEY DECKER BOX TWO NINE SIX REDMOND, WASHINGTON HAD
SIGHTED TWO DISCS AT APPROXIMATELY NINE AM AUGUST THIRTEEN NINETEEN
FORTYSEVEN. UPON INTERVIEW DECKER STATED THAT TWO VERY BRIGHT OJECTS
TRAVELING AT AN EXTREME RATE OF SPEED WERE NOTICED BY HIM AS HE WAS
STANDING NEAR THE REDMOND POST OFFICE. DECKER DESCRIBED THE OBJECTS
AS HAVING NO WINGS, NO TAIL, AND BOTH ENDS WERE TAPERED. DECKER ADDED
THAT THE OBJECTS RESEMBLED A BELLY TANK AND THAT THEY WERE NOISELESS.
THE OBJECTS WERE VERY BRIGHT AND TRAVELING IN A NORTHEASTERLY DIRECTION
OVER REDMOND, WASHINGTON, ONE A BIT BEHIND AND A LITTLE ABOVE THE OTHER
MAINTAINING EQUAL RATES OF SPEED FOR APPROXIMATELY EIGHT SECONDS AT
WHICH TIME THEY DISAPPEARED FROM VIEW. DECKER ADDED THAT THEY WERE
HIGHER THAN A PLANE GENERALLY TRAVELS. BRUMMETT ADVISED THAT HE NOTICE
THE OBJECTS AND CALLED DECKERS ATTENTION TO THEM AND ALSO POINTED THEM
OUT TO A MRS MAMIE ENGLISH. BRUMMETT STATED THAT HE SAW TWO OBJECTS
FLYING AT A FORTYFIVE DEGREE ANGLE NORTHEASTERLY OVER REDMOND AND

SEP 30 1947

RECORDED 162-83874
INDEXED   F B I
EX-   34 SEP 2 1947

An example of one of the earliest UFO incidents in which the FBI played a
direct role.

Wednesday last, August 13, he and two sons Billie, age ten,
Keith, age eight, saw an object nine miles northwest of Twin
Falls, resembling flying disc. [Deleted] stated this object was pro-
ceeding down Salmon River at terrific speed estimated by him at

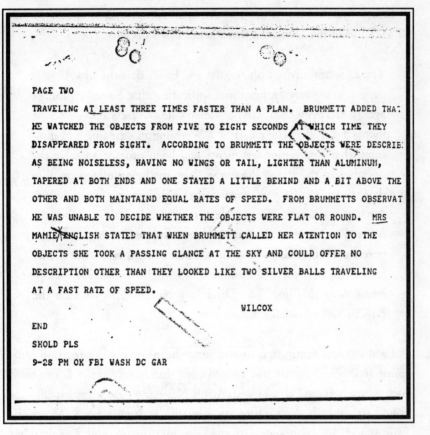

PAGE TWO

TRAVELING AT LEAST THREE TIMES FASTER THAN A PLAN. BRUMMETT ADDED THAT
HE WATCHED THE OBJECTS FROM FIVE TO EIGHT SECONDS AT WHICH TIME THEY
DISAPPEARED FROM SIGHT. ACCORDING TO BRUMMETT THE OBJECTS WERE DESCRIE
AS BEING NOISELESS, HAVING NO WINGS OR TAIL, LIGHTER THAN ALUMINUM,
TAPERED AT BOTH ENDS AND ONE STAYED A LITTLE BEHIND AND A BIT ABOVE THE
OTHER AND BOTH MAINTAIND EQUAL RATES OF SPEED. FROM BRUMMETTS OBSERVAT
HE WAS UNABLE TO DECIDE WHETHER THE OBJECTS WERE FLAT OR ROUND. MRS
MAMIE ENGLISH STATED THAT WHEN BRUMMETT CALLED HER ATENTION TO THE
OBJECTS SHE TOOK A PASSING GLANCE AT THE SKY AND COULD OFFER NO
DESCRIPTION OTHER THAN THEY LOOKED LIKE TWO SILVER BALLS TRAVELING
AT A FAST RATE OF SPEED.

                                        WILCOX

END

SHOLD PLS

9-28 PM OK FBI WASH DC GAR

one thousand miles per hour. [Deleted] and sons described object to newspapers as twenty feet long, ten feet wide and ten feet thick, light sky blue in color and also observed flames emanating from sides of object. At time [deleted] and sons saw object they all heard loud swish when object disappeared from sight. Current efforts being made to interview [deleted] and sons pursuant to Bureau Bulletin 42, Sub-Division B, dated July 30 1947. Bureau will be promptly and fully informed of all pertinent developments. Bannister. End.

In the same week, much of the Bureau's time was taken up investigating a story that was in circulation in the Los Angeles media that Soviet espionage agents were at work in the USA 'under instruction to solve the flying discs'.

In a memorandum to the FBI Assistant Director, Edward A. Tamm, D.M. Ladd of the Domestic Intelligence Division wrote:

The Director advised on August 14, 1947, that the Los Angeles papers were carrying headlines indicating that Soviet espionage agents had been instructed to determine the facts relative to the flying discs. The article carried a Washington date line and indicated that Red espionage agents had been ordered to solve the question of the flying discs, the Russians being of the opinion that this might be some new form of defense perfected by the American military. The article further recalled that during the recent war pieces of tin foil had been dropped in the air for the purpose of off-setting the value of radar being used by the enemy forces and that these aluminum discs might be a new development along this line. The Director inquired as to whether the Bureau had any such information.

Ladd advised Tamm that he had never heard of any information indicating that Soviet agents had indeed been dispatched to the US to fulfil such a function, and checks with Army, Navy and Air Corps Intelligence 'found that they had no information relative to such a story'. Moreover, Ladd stated: 'In accordance with the Director's instructions, I advised Mr Nichols that in the event any inquiries were made concerning such a story, that the story should be flatly denied in so far as the FBI was concerned.'

On 18 August, a further memo was generated, which attributed the source of the media stories to a 'Federal investigative agency', the identity of which remained unknown.

While nothing further was established conclusively at the time, we know now that Soviet agents were indeed present in the US in the summer of 1947, specifically in New Mexico, having been ordered there by the Russian leader Josef Stalin, something that Valeriy Burdakov of the Moscow Aviation Institute has now admitted. More importantly, Burdakov asserts that Soviet studies undertaken at the time had determined that the saucers were not manufactured in the USA, nor were they manufactured by any other country on Earth.[1]

In the 1940s, however, neither Hoover nor anyone else in the Bureau had an awareness of this, and suspecting that, if the Russians were snooping around, the saucers had to be US in origin, Special Agent S.W. Reynolds of the Liaison Section was directed to make further enquiries with the Air Force.

On 19 August, Agent Reynolds met with a colonel (whom I will dub 'X', since all references to his identity are still considered a classified matter by the Bureau) from Air Force Intelligence and the entire 'secret weapon' issue was discussed frankly, as were the possible consequences should the Bureau uncover details of a top-secret research-and-development programme which, presumably, had implications for the national security of the Western world. Following a candid discussion between the two, a remarkable memorandum captioned 'Flying Discs' was drawn up. Here are some pertinent sections.

> Special Agent S.W. Reynolds of the Liaison Section, while discussing the above captioned phenomena with Lieutenant Colonel [X] of the Air Forces Intelligence, expressed the possibility that flying discs were, in fact, a very highly classified experiment of the Army or Navy. Mr Reynolds was very much surprised when Colonel [X] not only agreed that this was a possibility, but confidentially stated it was his personal opinion that such was a probability. Colonel [X] indicated that a Mr [deleted], who is a scientist attached to the Air Forces Intelligence, was of the same opinion.
>
> Colonel [X] stated that he based his assumption on the following: He pointed out that when flying objects were reported seen over Sweden, the 'high brass' of the War Department exerted tremendous pressure on the Air Forces Intelligence to conduct research and collect information in an effort to identify these sightings. Colonel [X] stated that, in contrast to this, we have reported sightings of unknown objects over the United States, and the 'high brass' appeared to be totally unconcerned. He indicated this led him to believe that they knew enough about these objects to express no concern. Colonel [X] pointed out further that the objects in question have been seen by many individuals

who are what he terms 'trained observers' such as airline pilots. He indicated also that several of the individuals are reliable members of the community. He stated it is his conclusion that these individuals saw something. He stated the above has led him to

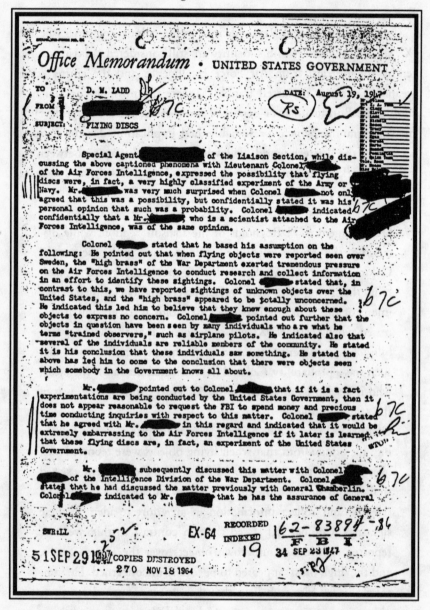

By August 1947, certain elements of the FBI suspected that UFOs were a classified U.S. military project.

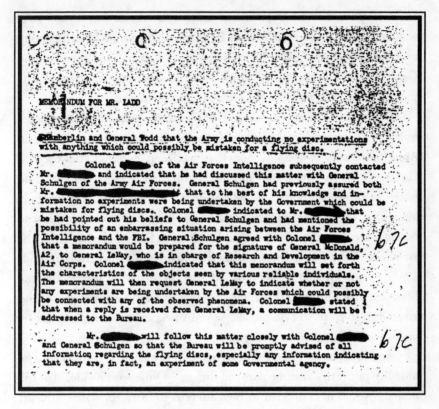

MEMORANDUM FOR MR. LADD

Chamberlin and General Todd that the Army is conducting no experimentations with anything which could possibly be mistaken for a flying disc.

Colonel ▇▇▇ of the Air Forces Intelligence subsequently contacted Mr. ▇▇▇ and indicated that he had discussed this matter with General Schulgen of the Army Air Forces. General Schulgen had previously assured both Mr. ▇▇▇ that to the best of his knowledge and information no experiments were being undertaken by the Government which could be mistaken for flying discs. Colonel ▇▇▇ indicated to Mr. ▇▇▇ that he had pointed out his beliefs to General Schulgen and had mentioned the possibility of an embarrassing situation arising between the Air Forces Intelligence and the FBI. General Schulgen agreed with Colonel ▇▇▇ that a memorandum would be prepared for the signature of General McDonald, A2, to General LeMay, who is in charge of Research and Development in the Air Corps. Colonel ▇▇▇ indicated that this memorandum will set forth the characteristics of the objects seen by various reliable individuals. The memorandum will then request General LeMay to indicate whether or not any experiments are being undertaken by the Air Forces which could possibly be connected with any of the observed phenomena. Colonel ▇▇▇ stated that when a reply is received from General LeMay, a communication will be addressed to the Bureau.

Mr. ▇▇▇ will follow this matter closely with Colonel ▇▇▇ and General Schulgen so that the Bureau will be promptly advised of all information regarding the flying discs, especially any information indicating that they are, in fact, an experiment of some Governmental agency.

the conclusion that there were objects seen which somebody in the Government knows all about.

Special Agent Reynolds then pointed out to the colonel that if UFOs were indeed a highly classified domestic project of the military, then it was wholly unreasonable for the Bureau to be expected to 'spend money and precious time conducting inquiries with respect to this matter'.

The colonel duly concurred with Reynolds, and indicated that it would be 'extremely embarrassing' to Air Force Intelligence if it were shown that the saucers were US in origin.

Perhaps sensing that he was getting close to uncovering the truth behind the UFO puzzle, Reynolds then made enquiries with the Intelligence Division of the War Department to get its opinion on the theory that some shadowy government operation was responsible for the many flying-saucer-type objects seen over North America.

For its part, the War Department issued a flat denial that it was in any way implicated in the UFO issue. In a report written up later, Reynolds noted that he was given 'the assurance of General Chamberlin and General Todd that the Army is conducting no experimentations with anything which could possibly be mistaken for a flying disc'.

The idea that behind the entire UFO mystery there lies some impenetrable governmental conspiracy to conceal the fact that UFOs are an American secret weapon is one that has long endured; however, in Chapter 9, I'll give my argument for why this theory simply does not hold water. For now, two points should be noted. First, if the military was fully aware that UFOs were American, and were by definition of no threat to national security, then there would hardly have been a need to enlist the assistance of the FBI in investigating the phenomenon. Secondly, in mid-1948, Major Donald E. Keyhoe, of the US Naval Academy and the Marine Corps Officers School, spoke with a Pentagon security officer and asked him to comment on the allegations that a classified military experiment was responsible for the saucers.

'Good God, man!' the officer exploded. 'If it was, do you think we'd be ordering pilots to chase the damned things?'[2] Quite so. The idea that the military would have ordered its own aircrews to intercept state-of-the-art experimental aeroforms, which might even have resulted in one being shot down, is, frankly, ludicrous.

Yet, as we shall see in the following chapter, the Bureau continued to suspect that it was being exploited by the military, and took steps to ensure that such action was brought to book.

One day after Special Agent Reynolds's meeting with the mysterious colonel, a painstakingly detailed three-page report reached Hoover, once again having been submitted by Special Agent Bannister at Butte, Idaho.

In this instance the eyewitnesses were a married couple of Twin Falls, Idaho, who along with a family friend viewed a formation of saucers flying at speed at 9.30 p.m. on 19 August 1947:

> [Witnesses] observed an object resembling a flying saucer traveling very rapidly from the southwest to the northeast section of this city. About ten minutes later, all of these individuals saw ten

similar objects proceeding rapidly in the same direction in the form of a triangle. As this group of objects was about to disappear in the overcast sky, three of the objects on the left flank peeled off and proceeded in a northerly direction. The remaining objects in the triangular formation appeared to close ranks and continue in a northeasterly direction. Three to five minutes later these individuals saw another group of three objects proceeding in the same direction, again in the shape of a triangle. Three to five minutes later informants observed another group consisting of from five to six objects, again in triangular formation, proceeding rapidly in a northeasterly direction. A few minutes later a large group of objects estimated at between 35 and 50 flew over the city in a northeasterly direction, again in triangular formation . . .

Quite why there should have been such an incredible number of UFOs over Idaho on that day was never fully ascertained by the Bureau, but it is clear from the report that, with at least fifty craft demonstrating highly advanced technology at their disposal, those piloting the saucers had little to fear from the inferior technology of mid-twentieth-century America. And for his part, Special Agent Bannister had still further data to impart:

Between 20 and 25 minutes after the last group was observed, similar objects were noted coming back over the city very rapidly and proceeding in a southwesterly direction. At this time informants stated the objects appeared in groups of three, five and seven. At this point Mrs [deleted] called [a] Detective [with] the Twin Falls Police Department, a next door neighbor . . . also members of the Twin Falls PD [observed] a group of twelve objects flying in formation over the city in a southwesterly direction. Informants, all reputable citizens this community, unable to estimate height of objects or speed, but claimed they resembled illuminated flying saucers. These individuals were of the opinion that the objects observed were not the landing lights of airplanes nor shooting stars. None of these objects were seen to come to earth near Twin Falls and none appeared to be flying in an arc. None of these observers heard any sound as the above objects passed over the city. Investigation continuing in line with Bureau instructions contained Bureau Bulletin No. 42, paragraph B, dated July 30 last. In event Bureau in possession of any information concerning experimental activities on part of Army Air Forces which may explain these phenomena, advice would be greatly appreciated. It is believed continued appearance of such objects without official explanation may result in hysteria or panic [at] Twin Falls, Idaho. Bannister.

Special Agent Bannister's query to Hoover concerning 'experimental activities on part of Army Air Forces' is notable, and echoes the concerns of General George F. Schulgen of the Army Air Corps and 'Colonel X', both of whom suspected that the saucers were part of a covertly operated US government research-and-development programme. Had Bannister come across similar rumours?

Half a century on, it is difficult to say, but it does seem likely. More important, however, is Bannister's concern that unresolved sightings of the saucers would lead to 'hysteria or panic'. I am certain that, fifty years after the celebrated sighting by Kenneth Arnold, it is the possibility of unchecked overreaction on the part of the public that prevents the US government from confiding in the populace its truly guarded findings on the UFO issue.

On 23 August, Bureau Headquarters received details of a most credible encounter reported by an Oregon-based flying instructor, who, along with his shocked student, viewed a large, spherical UFO in their airspace, which they duly attempted to intercept.

As with many of the accounts already on record, the prime witness had an unimpeachable background, having served as a lieutenant in the US Naval Air Corps for three and a half years, flying on the 'Atlantic submarine patrol'.

'The following investigation was conducted at Canyonville and Myrtle Creek, Oregon, on August 12, 1947,' reported the Bureau at Portland:

... on 8–6–47 at approximately 6:15 PM while instructing a student in a take off at the airport, he noticed an object east of Myrtle Creek which appeared to be from 5,000 to 8,000 feet in the air. The sky was completely clear and visibility was excellent. He stated that the object glistened and appeared to be of aluminum sheeting. Upon noticing it he had immediately taken over the controls of the plane which at that time was at 400 feet, and proceeded East in an attempt to further observe the object.

He advised that the object appeared to be climbing and traveling East at a high rate of speed which he estimated on a computer in his plane as 1,000 miles per hour. He believed the object to be spherical in shape and recalled noticing a darker object to the right the first time he saw it. He observed no vapor trails nor did he hear any noise from the object. After searching the area for approximately 10 minutes [he] returned to the airport and made another landing and take off. In practically the same position at 400 feet altitude, both saw the object in approximately the same position as seen before. He estimated the sphere to be 30 feet in diameter and stated when they first observed it it appeared to be so near he could fly right to it. However, the object sighted the second time disappeared in the same manner as the first had.

The pupil also concurred with his instructor that something truly unknown had intruded upon their airspace: '[Pupil] verified the information stating that the first object sighted had been called to his attention when [the pilot] took over the controls of the plane at about 400 feet following his takeoff, but that they had both sighted the object on the second takeoff at the same time.

'[Pupil] estimated the sphere as being 50 feet in diameter and stated in his opinion the second object appeared to climb straight up. He advised that he did not observe any evidence of motion such as vapor trails, etc. and could hear no noise over the noise of his own ship. Investigation in the vicinity of Myrtle Creek, Oregon, has failed to reveal any other person sighting the objects'.

The Bureau's investigation failed also to reveal whether or not the experience had put the pupil off taking further flying lessons, but that is an entirely separate matter!

With these many reports of mid-1947 in hand, a high percentage of which had been reported by both military and civilian pilots, there was an almost unanimous feeling within the Bureau that continued investigations were of vital importance to the ongoing security of the United States, particularly if the saucers decided to land and make direct contact – and that may have happened, as we shall later see.

CHAPTER 2

ENCOUNTERING THE UNKNOWN

COME THE LATTER PART OF 1947, THE FBI WAS STILL MAINTAINING AN uneasy alliance with the military over its handling of the UFO mystery, and rumours continued to circulate quietly within the Bureau that military intelligence knew far more about the entire UFO subject than it was willing to admit. As a result, Bureau agents, at both field and headquarters level, carefully maintained their screening of all incoming reports. Thanks to the Freedom of Information Act, we can see that many of those reports were of more than passing interest and importance.

On 4 September the Baltimore office of the FBI forwarded to Washington a report concerning its investigation of a UFO sighting initially reported in the 8 July edition of the *Morning News*, of Wilmington, Delaware. According to the press, Forrest Wenyon, a Delaware-based pilot, disclosed that on two occasions in the previous ten months he had seen what the newspaper bizarrely described as 'flying mayonnaise jars' in the Delaware skies: in September 1946 and on 2 June 1947.

It is pertinent to note that Wenyon was quoted as having contacted the FBI, who publicly responded that it was uninterested in the report. However, a copy of the relevant newspaper clipping was supplied to the special agent in charge at Baltimore by the resident agent at Wilmington, and it was determined that an investigation was warranted. Extracts from the final report to Hoover follow:

Mr Wenyon was interviewed and it was determined that his correct name is HORACE P. WENYON. Mr WENYON advised that he had been an airplane pilot approximately thirty years. He stated that in September of 1946, while flying at an altitude of 1,000 feet, two or three miles south of Rehoboth Beach, Delaware, he noticed a projectile approximately fifteen inches in diameter which crossed his course at right angles and was moving in a west-to-east direction. According to Mr WENYON, several jets of flame were spurting from the object and it was traveling at a very high rate of speed, 1,000 to 1,200 miles per hour. He stated that in October of 1946, he observed a similar projectile while flying over Rehoboth Beach at 1,400 feet. This was also traveling from west to east.

Mr WENYON stated that there is little question in his mind but that what he saw was some sort of rocket being tested. He stated that he wished to call the matter to the attention of the appropriate authority inasmuch as he thought that the series of airplane crashes that have occurred recently might in part be explained by what he had observed. He stated that he had reported the information to the Civil Aeronautics Authority and had been telephonically interviewed by a reporter from the Wilmington 'Morning News'.

Mr WENYON stated that what he had seen traveled at such a high rate of speed that it was very difficult to describe it, but the description 'flying mayonnaise jars' was concocted by the newspaper reporter.

The State of Oregon was the site of two separate UFO encounters, which caught the attention of the Bureau in September 1947. Both were the subject of FBI reports, the first of which, dated 13 September, follows:

URGENT. FLYING DISC. [SOURCES NAME], PORTLAND, STATES HE OBSERVED AT ABOUT FIVE FIFTEEN PM ELEVENTH INSTANT, AN OBJECT SIMILAR IN SIZE TO A WEATHER BALLOON, WHICH APPEARED TO BE MADE OF ALUMINUM OR SOME OTHER BRIGHT METAL,

TRAVELING RAPIDLY NORTHWEST TO SOUTHEAST
OVER PORTLAND AT AN ESTIMATED TEN THOUSAND
FEET. OBJECT VEERED TO SOUTH AND DISAPPEARED
IN THE DISTANCE IN APPROXIMATELY ONE MINUTE.
ALSO OBSERVED BY [DELETED], AND POSSIBLY BY
OTHER PORTLAND POLICE OFFICERS. SMALL
ARTICLE IN PORTLAND NEWSPAPER, THE OREGON-
IAN, CONCERNING THIS ON TWELFTH INSTANT.
INVESTIGATION BEING CONDUCTED.

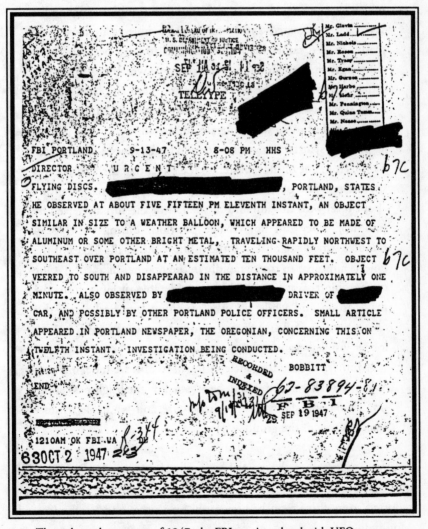

Throughout the summer of 1947, the FBI was inundated with UFO reports.

Most of the accounts discussed so far have involved the sighting of one, or possibly two, UFOs only; from a mother and son in Oswego, Oregon, however, the FBI learned of an incident in which a fleet of unidentified objects were seen manoeuvring over the town. The special agent in charge at Portland recorded in a one-page memo, also dated 13 September, to J. Edgar Hoover that:

> While entertaining her 7 year old son and 10 year old neighbor child on her lawn, at about noon, [mother] and the children noticed approximately two dozen round silver objects high in the sky. [Mother] stated she believed these objects to have been platter shaped rather than spherical and to have been considerably larger than an airplane of the cub type which was flying in a different portion of the sky at the same time. She advised that these objects appeared to her to be at a great distance and constructed of some white metallic material.
>
> [Mother's] attention was first drawn to the objects by an explanation from one of the children to the effect that the airplane was skywriting. The objects were grouped in approximately an arc about level with the sun and to the left of the sun as viewed by [mother]. They did not change positions during the 3 or 4 minutes which she observed them but some of the larger of the objects appeared to rotate rapidly in the manner of a wheel. One of the objects was separated by considerable distance from the main group and while she was watching [mother] states this object began to fall and floated slowly downward until it was no longer visible because of trees on the horizon.
>
> [Mother] advised that she continued to observe the remaining objects until her eyes began to be affected by the brightness of the sky whereupon she went into her house and is unable to state what became of the group.

On 17 September the special agent in charge of the Portland FBI office prepared a summary of his investigation into a UFO sighting reported some three months previously by a prospector in the Cascade Mountains:

[Source] reported without consulting any records that on June
24, 1947, while prospecting at a point in the Cascade Mountains
approximately five thousand feet from sea level, during the afternoon he noticed a reflection, looked up, and saw a disc proceeding in a southeasterly direction. Immediately upon sighting this

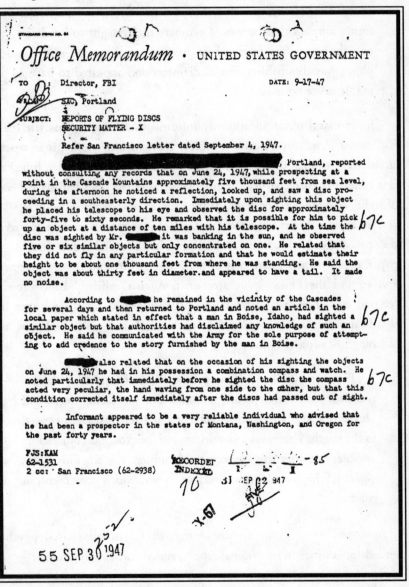

In September 1947, the FBI office at Portland informed J. Edgar Hoover of
a UFO encounter in the Cascade Mountains.

object he placed his telescope to his eye and observed the disc for approximately 45 to 60 seconds. He remarked that it is possible for him to pick up an object at a distance of 10 miles with his telescope. At the time the disc was sighted it was banking in the sun, and he observed 5 or 6 similar objects but only concentrated on one. He related that they did not fly in any particular formation and that he would estimate their height to be about one thousand feet from where he was standing. He said the object was about thirty feet in diameter and appeared to have a tail. It made no noise.

The Portland office additionally informed Washington that the man had noted that, just before the object loomed into view, his compass 'acted very peculiar, the hand waving from one side to the other, but that this condition corrected itself immediately after the discs had passed out of sight'. A side effect, perhaps, of the saucer's unique power source?

Twenty-four hours after the Portland office's report reached Hoover, the special agent in charge at Philadelphia, in a comprehensive three-page paper, detailed the final results of his investigation into the sightings in and around the Philadelphia area on 6 August, which I have already referred to. Since this particular report brought to light a number of significant details not mentioned in the 7 August 1947 Teletype to Washington, extracts follow:

> . . . Between 10:30 and 10:45 p.m. on August 6, 1947, [witness] was sitting on the steps of her home. She was facing north and observed a large white object traveling at a very fast rate of speed to the south. There was a buzzing sound, not too loud but plainly audible, just after this object passed through the air. This white object left in its trail a thin streak of smoke, which was grayish in color . . .

A second witness, the former Army Air Corps pilot cited by the Philadelphia office in its original report, added considerably more:

> He was sitting on the steps of his home around 10:45 p.m. on August 6, 1947, with his wife; and his neighbors were sitting on

their steps next door . . . All of the above parties were facing east [and] noticed at this time an object, emitting a bluish-white flame, passing quickly through the air. The object was traveling from northeast to southwest. Using his experience in the Army Air Corps as a guide, [he] estimated the above object was between 1,000 and 3,000 feet in the air and traveling at a rate of between 400 to 500 miles an hour. This object did not lose elevation as it passed through the air and left either smoke or a condensation trail in its former path, which lasted for about two seconds. A hissing sound accompanied the passing of this object. This sound was moderate and not nearly as loud as the noise accompanying the passage of a rocket ship.

A similar account came form a retired Philadelphia police officer who reported a substantially similar incident, adding only that he thought the object had left a 'fiery trail' which extended for around one hundred feet. Evidently, the combined accounts of the many witnesses impressed the Bureau greatly: 'All of the above persons seem reliable and not the type to seek publicity or to spread rumors.' I concur.

Was the object some form of military device? 'Both the Offices of Naval Intelligence and Army Intelligence in Philadelphia were requested by the Philadelphia [FBI] Office to ascertain if either the Army or the Navy was doing any experimental work on new types of planes or equipment, in the vicinity of Philadelphia,' recorded the special agent in charge. 'Such was done with negative results . . . All logical investigation having been conducted, no further action will be taken . . .' The encounter remained a mystery.

Less than a week later, a highly impressive account of a UFO incident involving two serving members of the military was supplied to the FBI at Anchorage. 'This is to advise that two army officers reported to the Office of the Director of Intelligence headquarters Alaskan Department, at Fort Richardson, Alaska, that they had witnessed an object passing through the air at a tremendous rate of speed which could not be judged as to miles per hour.' Hoover was informed by FBI Anchorage as per standing instructions.

According to the official report, the object was initially sighted by one of the two officers only; but he soon alerted his colleague to the strange sight. 'The object appeared to be shaped like a sphere and did not give the impression of being saucer-like or comparable to a disk,' the report added.

'The first officer stated that it would be impossible to give minute details concerning the object, but that it appeared to be approximately two or three feet in diameter and did not leave any vapor trail in the sky.'

Experienced officer that he was, the first attempted to gauge the altitude of the object, and, from a comparison with cloud formations in the area, it was determined that, whatever the mystery sphere was, it was cruising at a height of more than ten thousand feet. And it should be realised that to be at that height and still be visible, in all probability the object exceeded the initial size estimation of 'two or three feet' by some considerable degree.

'The first officer stated that in his opinion the object appeared to be metallic and was silver in color, much like the color of many airplanes.'

When questioned, the second officer gave a substantially similar account, the only marked difference being that, in his opinion, he considered the object to be approximately ten feet in diameter, and compared it to 'half the size of a full moon on an ordinary night'. This discrepancy was apparently due to the fact that the second officer believed that the object was more likely to have been at a height of three to four thousand feet, as opposed to the estimate of ten thousand feet suggested by his colleague.

The difference of opinion over the altitude of the object may or may not have been significant; the important factor, however, was that both officers agreed that some form of anomalous vehicle had definitely been seen. As the report concluded: '. . . the second officer pointed out that one of the remarkable features of this object was that it was definitely traveling against the wind.'

That the Bureau was immediately supplied with details of the encounter at Fort Richardson suggests that the agreement with the military to routinely share data on the UFO issue was operating with relative smoothness. On 19 September, that all changed.

In 1947 the special agent in charge at the San Francisco FBI office was

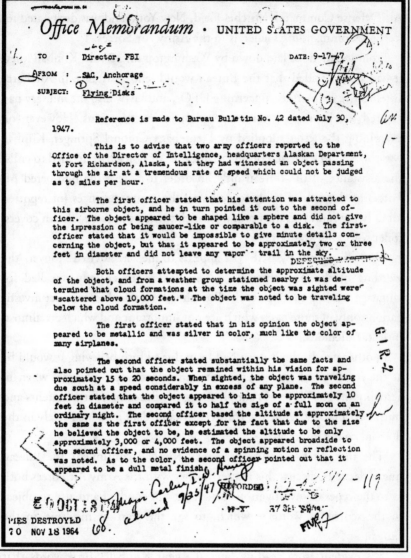

TO   : Director, FBI   DATE: 9-17-47

FROM : SAC, Anchorage

SUBJECT: Flying Disks

Reference is made to Bureau Bulletin No. 42 dated July 30, 1947.

This is to advise that two army officers reported to the Office of the Director of Intelligence, headquarters Alaskan Department, at Fort Richardson, Alaska, that they had witnessed an object passing through the air at a tremendous rate of speed which could not be judged as to miles per hour.

The first officer stated that his attention was attracted to this airborne object, and he in turn pointed it out to the second officer. The object appeared to be shaped like a sphere and did not give the impression of being saucer-like or comparable to a disk. The first-officer stated that it would be impossible to give minute details concerning the object, but that it appeared to be approximately two or three feet in diameter and did not leave any vapor trail in the sky.

Both officers attempted to determine the approximate altitude of the object, and from a weather group stationed nearby it was determined that cloud formations at the time the object was sighted were "scattered above 10,000 feet." The object was noted to be traveling below the cloud formation.

The first officer stated that in his opinion the object appeared to be metallic and was silver in color, much like the color of many airplanes.

The second officer stated substantially the same facts and also pointed out that the object remained within his vision for approximately 15 to 20 seconds. When sighted, the object was traveling due south at a speed considerably in excess of any plane. The second officer stated that the object appeared to him to be approximately 10 feet in diameter and compared it to half the size of a full moon on an ordinary night. The second officer based the altitude at approximately the same as the first officer except for the fact that due to the size he believed the object to be, he estimated the altitude to be only approximately 3,000 or 4,000 feet. The object appeared broadside to the second officer, and no evidence of a spinning motion or reflection was noted. As to the color, the second officer pointed out that it appeared to be a dull metal finish.

COPIES DESTROYED
7 0 NOV 18 1964

Nineteen-forty-seven saw the FBI receive a wealth of quality UFO reports from military sources.

Harry M. Kimball. On 19 September Kimball met with a Lieutenant Colonel Springer of A-2, Armed Forces, Hamilton Field, also in California. During the course of their meeting, Springer supplied Special Agent Kimball with a copy of a 'Restricted' letter dated 3 September 1947. On examination Kimball noted that the letter had been drawn up by Colonel R.H. Smith, the Assistant Chief of Staff-Intelligence, at HQ Air Defense Command, Mitchel Field, New York, and was designated for 'certain Commanding Generals in the Army Air Forces'.

From instructions laid down by Washington on 30 July, Kimball knew it had been decided that the Bureau would lend assistance to Air Force Intelligence on matters concerning UFOs, and knew also the military had assured the Bureau of full cooperation in investigations. However, on examining the letter supplied by Lieutenant Colonel Springer, Kimball was shocked to see that, confidentially, the Air Force had decided to enlist the assistance of the Bureau only 'in order to relieve the numbered Air Forces of the task of tracking down all the many instances [of reported 'discs being found on the ground'] which turned out to be ash can covers, toilet seats and whatnot'.

Kimball was not pleased: '[I]t appears to me,' he advised Hoover, 'the wording of the last sentence . . . is cloaked in entirely uncalled for language tending to indicate the Bureau will be asked to conduct investigations only in those cases which are not important and which are almost, in fact, ridiculous.'

In other words, the Bureau had been duped into believing it would be at the forefront of the government's investigative programme, when in actuality the Air Force was simply using the Bureau as, for all intents and purposes, a lackey, while the truly remarkable data remained solely in the domain of the military.

'The thought has occurred to me,' Kimball continued, 'the Bureau might desire to discuss this matter further with the Army Air Forces both as to the types of investigations which we will conduct and also to object to the scurrilous wordage which, to say the least, is insulting to the Bureau . . .'

It is evident from reading Special Agent Kimball's final words that Lieutenant Colonel Springer had taken a considerable risk in entrusting in Kimball the real reasons why the Air Force had sought the Bureau's assistance:

In the event the Bureau decides to discuss the matter further with the Army Air Forces, it is recommended that no indication whatsoever be given indicating this letter was referred to me by

Lieutenant Colonel Springer inasmuch as it would undoubtedly cause him serious embarrassment and would certainly cause the excellent personal relationship which exists between Lieutenant Colonel Springer and this office to be endangered.

On receipt of this information, Hoover, fiercely proud of the Bureau he had cultivated, moved quickly and in no uncertain terms informed Major General George MacDonald of the Air Staff of his dissatisfaction at the way the Bureau had been treated, adding: 'I am advising the Field Divisions of the Federal Bureau of Investigation to discontinue all investigative activity regarding the reported sightings of flying discs, and am instructing them to refer all complaints received to the appropriate Air Force representative in their area.'

To reiterate this, a bulletin was circulated by Washington to each of the Bureau field offices on 1 October emphasising Hoover's decision.

Hoover's edict has led some commentators to conclude that in the post-October 1947 period, the Bureau had no significant involvement in the UFO issue. An examination of surrounding data, in its full historical context, reveals that this was not the case.

There is little doubt that Hoover's decision to sever the Bureau's direct involvement was due to the 'scurrilous wordage', as FBI Special Agent Harry Kimball put it, of Colonel R.H. Smith's letter of 3 September; however, a sufficient number of convincing UFO reports had been brought to the attention of the FBI, which fully affirmed Hoover's suspicions that something truly unusual was occurring in US skies. Moreover, as we shall see in Chapter 11, there are firm grounds for believing that in the summer of 1947 the Army Air Force retrieved a crashed UFO and crew from the desert of New Mexico, and that the Bureau was purposefully misled over this astonishing find. Since it is all but certain that Hoover was aware that the Bureau had been deceived, and the military was not telling all it knew, it was determined that the UFO issue was of overriding significance to warrant continued FBI surveillance, even if that surveillance was conducted outside of the Air Force's 'inner circle'. To emphasise this, on 14 March 1949, a Bureau official, Howard Fletcher, commented to D.M. Ladd that UFOs were 'of sufficient importance to the internal security of the country that our field offices should secure as much information as possible'.

There is one further matter that warrants comment. Although the military certainly did not entrust in the Bureau its truly spectacular findings concerning UFOs (such as the disc recovered in New Mexico), enough reports did reach the Bureau showing that time and time again UFOs were seen in the vicinity of sensitive facilities, such as Army airfields, and, more importantly, installations under the control of the Atomic Energy Commission (AEC). As Hoover well knew, because of the Bureau's jurisdiction in two areas, 'Espionage' and 'Sabotage', any threats to security that surfaced in and around such AEC installations would be reported automatically to the Bureau. It was largely due to this that the FBI became implicated deeply in the monitoring of anomalous phenomena at a variety of atomic energy research stations in the late 1940s and early 1950s. These matters are spelled out in the next chapter.

Three weeks after Hoover elected to break with the military, the Bureau at Anchorage reported to Hoover that 'we have been able to locate a flyer [who] observed some flying object near Bethel, Alaska, in July, 1947'. Again, there is no doubt in my mind that the pilot's account was a prime example of a genuine encounter with a technologically superior craft of unknown origin, and is proof that the Bureau's interest in the UFO subject did not cease with the termination of its liaison with the military. Let us deliberate on the evidence:

> [Pilot] related that the occasion of seeing the flying object near Bethel was on a July day when the sky was completely clear of clouds, and it being during the early part, it is daylight the entire night. The time of his sighting this flying object was about 10 PM and the sun had just dropped beyond the horizon. Flying weather was extremely good and he . . . was coming into the Bethel Airport with a DC-3 . . .

On approaching the airport the pilot was amazed to see to his left an unidentified craft, 'the size of a C-54 without any fuselage', which seemed to resemble a 'flying wing'. Because of its unique shape, the pilot was initially unable to determine whether the object was heading towards his aircraft or away from it, and elected to make a forty-five-degree turn in an attempt to diffuse any possible chance of collision.

The Bureau noted that the pilot was certain that the craft was free of any external power source, such as a propeller-driven engine, and exhibited no exhaust as it cruised the sky. The report continues:

> He called on his radio to the Civil Aeronautics Administration station at Bethel, asking what aircraft was in the vicinity and they had no reports of any aircraft. The object he sighted was some five or ten miles from the airport before his arrival and [he] stated that the path did not go directly across the airport. He, of course, could not tell whether the object was making any noise and stated that it was flying at a thousand foot altitude and estimated travel at 300 miles per hour. It was traveling in the direction from Bethel to Nome, which is in a northwesterly direction. He noted no radio interference and is unable to describe the color other than it appeared dark but of definite shape and did not blend into the sky but had a definite, concise outline. [He] clearly observed the object at this time . . .

It is interesting to point out that, in addition to interviewing the pilot, the Bureau office at Anchorage learned that Military Intelligence had also taken note of the encounter, which suggests to me the entire affair was considered seriously at all levels.

In 1948, the number of good-quality UFO reports reaching the Bureau dwindled alarmingly, and meaningful liaison with the Air Force was practically nonexistent. However, the Bureau continued to forward copies of incoming UFO data to the Air Force – Hoover certainly had grievances with the military, but he recognised that both the Bureau and the Air Force were working to preserve America's internal and external security – but there is little evidence to show that the Air Force reciprocated to any great degree.

Perhaps the Air Force's silence can be explained by the fact that in August 1948, according to Captain Edward Ruppelt (one-time head of the UFO study programme, Project Blue Book), the Air Technical Intelligence Center had determined that UFOs were indeed extraterrestrial spacecraft, and this alarmed greatly the military establishment, to the extent that ATIC's final report was ordered burned by the Chief of Staff, General Hoyt Vandenberg.[1] We may never know what precisely was contained in the ATIC report (although rumours suggest one copy may have survived the destruction order) but in mid-1948 the Air Force certainly received a number of worthy reports of unexplained aerial phenomena. I quote from a formerly top-secret Air Force report:

> On 1 July 1948, twelve disks were reported over the Rapid City Air Base by Major Hammer. These disks were oval-shaped, about 100 feet long, flying at a speed estimated to be in excess of 500 mph . . .
>
> On 17 July 1948, a report from Kirtland Air Force Base describes a sighting in the vicinity of San Acacia, New Mexico, of seven unidentified objects flying in a 'J' formation at an estimated height of 20,000 feet above the terrain . . . If the reported altitude is correct the speed was estimated at 1,500 miles per hour . . .
>
> On 1 October 1948 at approximately 2030 hours the pilot of a F-51 aircraft . . . flying near Fargo, North Dakota, sighted an intermittent white light about 3,000 feet below his 4,500 feet cruising altitude. The pilot pursued the light which appeared to then take evasive tactics . . .[2]

Since none of these particular 1948 reports were made known to the FBI at the time (the document itself was not declassified until 1985), Hoover's suspicion that the military was not being entirely candid with the Bureau is vindicated.

In 1949, there was an upswing in the number and quality of UFO encounters reported to the Bureau from both official and unofficial sources.

On 5 April, the Salt Lake City FBI office reported: 'Information received at Logan, Utah, 11.00 a.m. today that at 9.00 a.m. a guard at the Army General Supply Depot, Ogden, Utah, observed what appeared to be an explosion in the air accompanied by a flash of light followed by the falling of silver colored object. This was seen at high altitude west of Ogden near the town of Taylor, Utah.'

Other reports of what was considered to be the same object also reached the Bureau:

ABOUT THE SAME TIME LIEUTENANT [DELETED] OF LOGAN, UTAH SAW TWO PUFFS OF SMOKE HIGH IN THE AIR WEST OF LOGAN FOLLOWED BY FALLING OF SILVER COLORED OBJECT. ALSO AT ABOUT SAME TIME UTAH HIGHWAY PATROLMAN AT MANTUA, UTAH, SAW A SILVER COLORED OBJECT HIGH UP APPROACHING THE MOUNTAINS AT SARDINE CANYON BETWEEN LOGAN AND BRIGHAM CITY, UTAH, AND AS OBJECT NEARED THE MOUNTAIN IT APPEARED TO EXPLODE IN A FLASH OF FIRE. SEVERAL RESIDENTS AT TRENTON, UTAH, WHICH IS WEST OF LOGAN, HAVE REPORT- ED SEEING WHAT APPEARED TO BE TWO AERIAL EXPLOSIONS FOLLOWED BY FALLING OBJECT WEST OF TRENTON AT ABOUT 9.20 A.M. TODAY.

Agents from the Salt Lake City FBI office made immediate checks with the Air Force Office of Special Investigations at Hill Field, Utah, and were advised that the sightings were the result of 'two B-29's from Wendover Field which are practice-bombing in the desert'. This may indeed have been the cause of the sightings; however, the overwhelming secrecy on the Air Force's part with respect to the UFO subject suggests that the official explanation may have been treated with a degree of caution by the Bureau.

At around 5.30 p.m. on 16 April, Wade H. Harrison, a special-delivery messenger with the Fort Smith, Arkansas, Post Office Department, was one of a number of people who not only viewed a high-flying UFO over Fort Smith, but also became the topic of a Bureau file of 22 April:

Harrison stated that at 5:25 p.m., Saturday, April 16, 1949, while delivering special delivery mail in Fort Smith, he stopped his automobile at a signal light located at the intersection of North Eleventh Street and Grand Avenue. He glanced up at the stop light and observed a brilliant object moving in a southeastern direction. He presumed the object was approximately 2 miles high.

The report added that, anxious to alert others to the presence of the object, Harrison stopped his car, jumped out and tried to catch the attention of the drivers behind him by pointing skyward. Unfortunately, this did not have the desired effect and Harrison was met with a barrage of honking horns from the furious drivers, angry at Harrison for holding up their journeys! On returning to his car . . .

He watched the object until it was obscured by the line of trees in that section. He estimated he watched it travel some 3 or 4 miles before he lost sight of it. He stated the weather was clear, visibility was good, and there were no clouds near the object. The object made no noise perceptible to Harrison. However, he commented that he was stopped at an intersection where the traffic was heavy and there was considerable noise. He first thought possibly he had seen some type of a reflector on an airplane, but could not locate or hear a plane anywhere.

As he drove to the 1400 Block of North 'C' Street, Harrison observed an Army officer (wearing the insignia of a major or a lieutenant colonel) standing near to the rear of a car. Again wishing to get some corroboration for his sighting, Harrison asked the officer if he had seen anything out of the ordinary in the Fort Smith skies:

The officer, name unknown to [Harrison], answered negatively and then remarked, 'I am glad other people are also reporting seeing flying objects.' The officer then related that the day previous, Friday, April 15, 1949, while the officer was traveling out of Oklahoma City toward Fort Smith, his wife observed a flying object in the sky very similar to that described by Harrison. The officer stated he saw the object, too, but furnished no more information. The interview with Harrison developed he is 52 years of age. He has considerable college training and attended the seminary at Westminister, Maryland, 2½ years . . . The offices of OSI and MID have been notified of the information set out above.

While there was certainly a strained relationship between the Bureau and the Air Force as far as unidentified flying objects were concerned in the late 1940s, the Bureau had more cordial dealings with the Office of Naval Intelligence, who would from time to time send the Bureau copies of reports they deemed noteworthy, including the following, which was directed to Washington from the FBI special agent in charge at New Orleans on 2 June 1949:

> The Bureau is advised that through the Office of Naval Intelligence, New Orleans, Louisiana, this office has been advised that within the past ten days three sightings of flying discs have been reported in the City of New Orleans. The information seems to be that the single discs were in straight flight and traveling in a general direction of North, in late afternoon, about the size of an observation plane, but the shape of a saucer.

ONI additionally informed the FBI that two witnesses described the UFO 'traveling end over end; that weather conditions were good; that sightings were made outdoors by persons who did not wear glasses; that the dates were May 18, 19 and 23, 1949'.

The possibility was discussed that the objects could have been balloons released from a nearby airport, but this was largely discounted since the release times of the balloons did not tally with the reported sightings. The incident remained unresolved.

Within a matter of weeks, an extraordinary report caught the Bureau's attention, once again having been supplied by the Navy. In an internal evaluation of 23 June, the witness, an experienced pilot who had served with the Navy during World War Two, was described as being '. . . married and has three children. He has a BS and BA degree from the University of Southern California, Los Angeles, California; has also had two years of law at the University of Southern California. Source is thirty years of age, but appears to have a background of experience few men his age possess'.

A study of the official report forwarded to Hoover leaves me in no doubt that the witness had an encounter with a number of controlled vehicles which originated with an unknown intelligence:

On Friday, 27 May 1949, source was flying his own SMJ-type aircraft from Red Bluff, California, to Buras, Oregon, a distance of 305 miles. He left Red Bluff at 1332 [Pacific Standard Time] and arrived at Burne at 1458 PST.

At 1423 PST, Friday, 27 May 1949, source observed the sun reflecting on an object or objects at a considerable distance ahead, a few points to the starboard. He continued to watch the course taken by the reflecting material expecting it to materialize into conventional aircraft as the distances lessened between him and the object or objects. As the objects reached the long bluffs which run for a number of miles along the east side of some dry lakes he saw that instead of a single object there were several, which seemed to be flying in formation.

At this point the objects appeared to have changed their course so that they were paralleling his course and were following the bluff's rim at about 1,000 to 1,500 feet below source's altitude, at a distance which he estimates to have been 5½ to 7½ miles. Source is certain that it could not have been as far as 10 miles since the bluffs were less than 10 miles away and he could see the objects outlined against the bluffs.

The objects that source saw are described by him as follows:

Size of each object: Considerably smaller than a fighter plane, probably less than 20 feet in length. All of the separate objects appeared the same in size.

Shape of object: There was no break in the outline. Source is certain he would have recognized conventional aircraft. They had a solid configuration, and no great thickness. They were elongated oval, perhaps twice as long as wide, perhaps five times as long as thick. [T]hey could possibly have been egg-shaped, and could conceivably have been pefectly oval. The objects seemed definitely solid objects as there was nothing ethereal about them.

Source is confident they were traveling at least as fast as source's own plane (212 MPH).

I would refer those who would contend that the pilot had simply misperceived some form of aircraft in flight or a natural phenomenon to the impressive aviation-based background of the witness. According to a 'confidential' report: 'Source holds Naval Aviators certificate plus a senior pilot's rating in the Ferry Wing of the Naval Air Transport Command. He also holds a commercial license, single and multi-engine, and flight instructor's ratings. His flight time began in 1934 and now totals over 5,000 hours, of which 1,300 hours were in the US Navy. Source secured a private license in 1935, and a re-issue commercial pilot's license in 1945. From March 1942 to September 1943 he was flight instructor for the Army Air Force (5 months as primary instructor at Cal-Aero, and the balance of the time as basic instructor at Lancaster, California). From September 1943 to January 1944 he flew for the Superior Oil Company of California.'

In light of the pilot's credentials, there is little wonder that the final evaluation of the encounter read: '. . . the explanation of source's sighting of the strange flying object remains a question mark'.

What was surely the most memorable UFO encounter reported to the Bureau in 1949 had actually occurred some two years previously, and was brought to the attention of the FBI by the columnist and broadcaster Walter Winchell (who was himself the subject of a massive 3,908-page Bureau file) on 9 July 1949.

Early in July, the source of the story (described in FBI memoranda as a 'Mr Jones' of Los Angeles) had contacted Winchell and related the details to him in a letter, a copy of which was turned over to the Bureau. '. . . it was very well written, obviously by a man of intelligence,' Assistant Director Ladd informed J. Edgar Hoover, continuing:

In this letter Jones stated that in August of 1947 he left Los Angeles for the mountains and started hiking through the mountains. About 10.00 A.M. he was lying on the ground when he observed about one-half block away from him a large silver metal [object], greenish in color, shaped like a child's top and about the size of the balloons used at Country Fairs.

He stated that there appeared to be two windows in the object and portions of metal appeared transparent and that he gained the impression that there was some life within this object although he saw no persons. The object appeared as though sealed as a pressure chamber. He stood up and waved toward this object and this so-called Flying Saucer was off the ground in a second, knocking Jones to the ground. In its flight he stated that its power was silent and he raised the question as to whether this was an inter-global landing on our planet. He thought that it might be a device to land [on] our planet because the occupants of another planet had become curious as to the reaction caused by the explosion of the atomic bomb causing trouble in an expanded universe. He asked the question as to whether it was possible that the occupants of another planet might have solved the theory of negative gravity.

A source with whom Ladd spoke asserted that Jones's letter indicated 'a very good knowledge of physics', and that it would be of benefit to the Bureau to 'check into' Jones's background and secure a first-hand interview with him in order to ascertain the full and complete facts.

Curiously, all attempts to find Jones ended in failure, and it was initially suspected that the entire matter was some form of intricate hoax; however, his 1949 story of alien creatures in the California area being concerned by the proliferation of atomic weapons is one that cannot be dismissed, since a rash of almost identical claims surfaced in the same vicinity in the early 1950s, and in a subsequent chapter we'll see evidence of the FBI's deep quest to determine the truth behind this facet of the UFO enigma.

People often ask me, if some UFOs are piloted spacecraft from other worlds, then why are they here? I always answer, honestly, that I do not know. I am convinced, however, that Earth is being visited by a variety of extraterrestrial species, and that, while the majority of those species do not appear to demonstrate a direct threat to the human race (something that indicates they are more interested in simply monitoring our civilisation as it 'develops', if that is the correct word to use!), it would be presumptuous on our part to assume that all of our cosmic visitors are friendly. As we'll see in Chapters 7 and 8, there are indications that at least one breed of extraterrestrial visiting Earth is positively lethal, to man and beast alike.

Concern that the UFOnauts have their dark side was something present in the mind of a doctor in Decatur, Indiana, in September 1949.

On 6 September, a representative of the Air Force Office of Special Investigations at Benjamin Harrison Air Base called at the Bureau office at Indianapolis and spoke with the special agent in charge 'to ascertain if there was any current information on "flying saucers"'.

According to the OSI agent, on 1 July the aforementioned doctor, along with an FBI agent from Omaha, had seen a saucer in the vicinity of Lake of the Woods, Canada, on that same day.

Shocked by what they had seen, the doctor confided in the OSI man that he was convinced that the recent outbreak of a polio epidemic in the vicinity of Decatur, Indiana, was somehow connected with a spate of UFO sightings which had occurred in the same general area in the previous year. He further confided that he was not at all convinced that the sufferers had in fact contracted polio; rather, he suspected uranium poisoning at the hands of the saucers, and made additional checks to try to determine if the outbreak of contagious diseases throughout the USA was in any way connected with UFO encounters.

Whether the doctor was actually on to something here is moot, but the Indianapolis office wasted no time in relating the information to FBI headquarters, and it is interesting to note that the doctor also revealed that 'while in Canada there had been some rather strange events somewhere in the interior with respect to finding what might have been remains of flying saucers'.

Is it theoretically possible that our planet is the unwitting testing ground for extraterrestrial medical research? This may seem an outlandish question to ask, but do we not exploit rats, mice and other animals in a similar fashion?

A further letter directed to J. Edgar Hoover in 1949, by a practicing minister of the church, may offer additional proof that the Earth is a target for alien experimentation:

Dear Mr Hoover:

Here is a bit of information which may be of great significance, or may be merely an observation of a scientific experiment. It may be known by military authorities and the Atomic Energy Commission or only a few may have seen it and none reported it to the right place. Here it is. Can you pass it on to the right persons?

Last May one afternoon I saw four beams in the sky passing from the northwest to the southeast and converging in the Cascade mountains. In those four narrow beams small clouds were forming. And where the beams met apparently against the mountains a great explosion effect was to be seen. I would say that they were visible for at least 10 minutes or longer.

The sight brought to mind an article read before the war about experiments carried on in Europe with various types of radio beams to effect rainfall. I would guess that I had seen the article in the Science Digest.

The Columbia River flood of last summer and the unusual precipitation this winter have forced me to feel that this observation of mine should be sent somewhere in the interest of national security.

I have one son in the Air Corps and another works with the AEC at Hanford which causes me to pray for peace, as well as the fact that as a minister I deplore the waste and tragedy of war. That is one reason that I have refrained from passing on information and ideas that might incite warlike attitudes.

May I add these words to paragraph two. The explosion effect seemed to rise to a height of about ten thousand feet.

The minister did not claim that the activity he witnessed was in any way related to the sightings of unidentified flying objects, but the Bureau evidently knew enough to make a connection, since the minister's letter can now be found on public display in the 'UFO file' at the FBI's Reading Room in Washington, DC.

I would not wish to speculate too wildly on the origin of the 'four narrow beams' seen by the minister, but fifty years on the description of the beams and the resulting damage to the mountainside make it sound uncannily as though a high-powered laser device (not dissimilar to the Star Wars defence project envisaged in the early 1980s by US President Ronald Reagan) was being tested on an unsuspecting Planet Earth. We should consider ourselves fortunate that the intelligences in possession of such technology did not use it for hostile purposes . . .

With the 1940s almost at an end, surely things could not get any stranger? Indeed they could, but before looking in depth at the Federal Bureau of Investigation's involvement in the UFO mystery as a whole in the 1950s, let us first take a brief detour to Los Alamos, New Mexico, and the strange tale of Project Twinkle.

C H A P T E R   3

PROJECT TWINKLE

IN THE LATE 1940S AND EARLY 1950S, A CURIOUS PHENOMENON WAS repeatedly seen in the skies over New Mexico: strange, glowing balls of green light which seemed to take an unhealthy amount of interest in the many military and defence establishments that existed in that area at the time. To fully appreciate the extent to which this was of concern to the US authorities in general, and the FBI in particular, let us travel back in time almost half a century . . .

Lieutenant Colonel Doyle Rees of the USAF Office of Special Investigations at Kirtland Air Force Base, New Mexico, in a 'Confidential' memorandum to Brigadier General Joseph F. Carroll, Director of Special Investigations, USAF, on 25 May 1950, wrote:

> In a liaison meeting with other military and government intelligence and investigative agencies in December 1948, it was determined that the frequency of unexplained aerial phenomena in the New Mexico area was such that an organized plan of reporting these observations should be undertaken.
>
> The organization and physical location of units of this District were most suitable for collecting these data, therefore, since December 1948, this District has assumed the responsibility for collecting and reporting basic information with respect to aerial phenomena occurring in this general area.

The 'aerial phenomena' to which Rees referred fell into three clearly definable categories: (a) 'green fireball phenomena'; (b) 'disc or variation'; and (c) 'probably meteoric'. With regard to category 'a', Rees wrote to Carroll:

> There is attached an analysis of the green fireball occurrences in this area made by Dr Lincoln La Paz. Dr La Paz is the Director of the Institute of Meteoritics and Head of the Department of Mathematics and Astronomy at the University of New Mexico. He was Research Mathematician at the New Mexico Proving Grounds under an OSRD appointment in 1943 and 1944, and Technical Director of the Operations Analysis Section, Headquarters, Second Air Force, 1944–5. Since 1948, Dr La Paz has served on a voluntary basis as a consultant for this district in connection with the green fireball investigations.

Rees added that on 17 February and 14 October 1949 conferences had been convened at Los Alamos, New Mexico, to discuss the green-fireball phenomenon. In attendance were representatives from the US Air Force Office of Special Investigations; the US Atomic Energy Commission; the Armed Forces Special Weapons Project; the Geophysical Research Division Air Materiel Command; and the FBI.

Despite the fact that Rees referred to a conference at Los Alamos held on 17 February 1949, the Bureau had in fact been apprised of elements of the green-fireball mystery as far back as the latter part of December 1948, something that is demonstrated by a 'Confidential' memorandum to J. Edgar Hoover from the FBI office at San Antonio. Titled 'Protection of Vital Installations', and dated 31 January 1949, it reveals:

> At recent Weekly Intelligence Conferences of G-2 [Army Intelligence], ONI [Office of Naval Intelligence], OSI [Office of Special Investigations] and FBI, in the Fourth Army area, Officers of G-2 have discussed the matter of 'Unidentified Aircraft' or 'Unidentified Aerial Phenomena' otherwise known as 'Flying Discs', 'Flying Saucers', and 'Balls of Fire'. This matter is

considered top secret by intelligence Officers of both the Army and the Air Forces . . .

In July 1948 an unidentified aircraft was 'seen' by an Eastern Airlines pilot and co-pilot and one or more passengers of the

A three-page FBI memorandum concerning Project Twinkle and the 'green fireball' mystery.

Office Memorandum · UNITED STATES GOVERNMENT

TO   DIRECTOR, FBI
DATE: January 31, 1949

FROM SAC, SAN ANTONIO

SUBJECT: PROTECTION OF VITAL INSTALLATIONS
BUREAU FILE # 65-58300

CONFIDENTIAL declassified 2010 8/31/77

At recent Weekly Intelligence Conferences of G-2, ONI, OSI, and F.B.I., in the Fourth Army Area, Officers of G-2, Fourth Army have discussed the matter of "Unidentified Aircraft" or "Unidentified Aerial Phenomena" otherwise known as "Flying Discs", "Flying Saucers", and "Balls of Fire". This matter is considered top secret by Intelligence Officers of both the Army and the Air Forces.

It is well known that there have been during the past two years reports from the various parts of the country of the sighting of unidentified aerial objects which have been called in newspaper parlance "flying discs" and "flying saucers". The first such sightings were reported from Sweden, and it was thought that the objects, the nature of which was unknown, might have originated in Russia.

In July 1948 an unidentified aircraft was "seen" by an Eastern Airlines Pilot and Co-Pilot and one or more passengers of the Eastern Airlines Plane over Montgomery, Alabama. This aircraft was reported to be of an unconventional type without wings and resembled generally a "rocket ship" of the type depicted in comic strips. It was reported to have had windows; to have been larger than the Eastern Airlines plane, and to have been traveling at an estimated speed of 2700 miles an hour. It appeared out of a thunderhead ahead of the Eastern Airlines plane and immediately disappeared in another cloud narrowly missing a collision with the Eastern Airlines plane. No sound or air disturbance was noted in connection with this appearance.

During the past two months various sightings of unexplained phenomena have been reported in the vicinity of the A.E.C. Installation at Los Alamos, New Mexico, where these phenomena now appear to be concentrated. During December 1948 on the 5th, 6th, 7th, 8th, 11th, 13, 14th, 20th and 28th sightings of unexplained phenomena were made near Los Alamos by Special Agents of the Office of Special Investigation; Airline Pilots; Military Pilots, Los Alamos Security Inspectors, and private citizens. On January 6, 1949, another similar object was sighted in the same area.

b7c [REDACTED] a Meteorologist of some note, has been generally in charge of the observations near Los Alamos, attempting to learn characteristics of the unexplained phenomena.

Up to this time little concrete information has been obtained.

JEJ:md
S-100-7545
El Paso (2)
Dallas (2)
Houston (2)
Little Rock (2)
Oklahoma City (2)

RECORDED

F B I
43 MAR 16 1949

Eastern Airlines Plane over Montgomery, Alabama. This aircraft was reported to be of an unconventional type without wings and resembled generally a 'rocket ship' of the type depicted in comic strips. It was reported to have had windows; to have been larger than the Eastern Airlines plane; and to have been traveling at an estimated speed of 2,700 miles an hour. It appeared out of a thunderhead ahead of the Eastern Airlines plane and immediately

DIRECTOR, FBI   1/31/49

There have been day time sightings which are tentatively considered to possibly resemble the exhaust of some type of jet propelled object. Night-time sightings have taken the form of lights usually described as brilliant green, similar to a green traffic signal or green neon light. Some reports indicated that the light began and ended with a red or orange flash. Other reports have given the color as red, white, blu-white, and yellowish green. Trailing lights sometimes observed are said to be red. The spectrum analysis of one light indicates that it may be a copper compound of the type known to be used in rocket experiments and which completely disintegrates upon explosion, leaving no debris. It is noted that no debris has ever been known to be located anywhere resulting from the unexplained phenomena.

Recent observations have indicated that the unidentified phenomena travel at a rate of speed estimated at a minimum of three miles per second and a maximum of twelve miles per second, or a mean calculated speed of seven and one-half miles a second, or 27,000 miles an hour. Their reported course indicates that they travel on an East - West line with probability that they approach from the Northern quadrant, which would be the last stage of the great circle route if they originated in Russia. When observed they seem to be in level flight at a height of six to ten miles and thus traveling on a tangent to the earth's surface. They occasionally dip at the end of the path and on two occasions a definite vertical change in path was indicated. These phenomena have not been known to have been sighted, however, at any intermediate point between Russia and Los Alamos, but only at the end of the flight toward the apparent "target", namely, Los Alamos.

In every case but one the shape of the objects has been reported as round in a point of light with a definite area to the light's source. One report gives a diamond shape; another indicates that trailing lights are elongated. The size is usually compared to one-fourth the diameter of the full moon, and they have also been compared in size to a basketball with trailing lights the size of a baseball.

On no occasion has sound been associated directly with the phenomena, but unexplained sounds have been reported from Los Alamos. On two occasions reports have been received of the sighting of multiple units.

Some nine scientific reasons are stated to exist which indicated that the phenomena observed are not due to meteorites. The only conclusions reached thus far are that they are either hitherto unobserved natural phenomena or that they are man made. No scientific experiments are known to exist in this country which could give rise to such phenomena.

- 2 -

DIRECTOR, FBI   1/31/49

████████████████████ was the subject of a letter from the Atlanta office
to the Bureau dated August 10, 1948, entitled, ██████████████   b7C
INFORMATION CONCERNING."

She has written many letters to Military Authorities concerning her theories
regarding Atomic Energy. She has generally been considered unreliable and
possibly mentally unbalanced. She, however, has submitted to Military
authorities the only theory thus far known that has any credibility at all,
namely, that the lights are manifestations of cosmic rays which are directed
toward a specific point. She further theorizes that such rays may interfere
with the ignition of motors and may account for various unexplained air crashes.

The above is submitted for the confidential information of the Bureau and
offices to which copies of this letter are directed so that these offices may
evaluate any such reports they may have received or may receive in the future.

It is noted that the Fourth Army has the responsibility of protecting vital
installations at Los Alamos, New Mexico, Sandia Base, New Mexico, and Camp
Hood, Texas. Any information developed should be expeditiously transmitted to
G-2, Fourth Army.

It is further noted that G-2 and O.S.I. are actively engaged in investigating
this matter. No investigation is being conducted by this office.

-3-

disappeared in another cloud narrowly missing a collision with
the Eastern Airlines plane. No sound or air disturbance was
noted in connection with this appearance.

During the past two months various sightings of unexplained
phenomena have been reported in the vicinity of the Atomic
Energy Commission Installation at Los Alamos, New Mexico,

where these phenomena now appear to be concentrated. During December 1948 on the 5th, 6th, 7th, 8th, 11th, 13th, 14th, 20th, and 28th sightings of unexplained phenomena were made near Los Alamos by Special Agents of the Office of Special Investigations; Airline Pilots; Military Pilots; Los Alamos Security Inspectors, and private citizens. On January 6, 1949, another similar object was sighted in the same area.

Although the sceptics would have us believe that the bulk of all UFO sightings are made by wholly untrained observers whose testimony is suspect at best, these revelations show that, in reality, the exact opposite is the case. And as far as the green fireballs were concerned, there was more to come. Here are extracts from the FBI memorandum of 31 January 1949:

There have been daytime sightings which are tentatively considered to possibly resemble the exhaust of some type of jet-propelled object. Night-time sightings have taken the form of lights usually described as brilliant green, similar to a green traffic signal or green neon light. Some reports indicated that the light began and ended with a red or orange flash. Other reports have given the color as red, white, blue-white, and yellowish-green. Trailing lights sometimes observed are said to be red. The spectrum analysis of one light indicates that it may be a copper compound of the type known to be used in rocket experiments and which completely disintegrates upon explosion, leaving no debris. It is noted that no debris has ever been known to be located anywhere resulting from the unexplained phenomena.

The San Antonio office memorandum continued:

Recent observations have indicated that the unidentified phenomena travel at a rate of speed estimated at a minimum of three miles per second and a maximum of twelve miles per second, or a mean calculated speed of one-half miles a second, or 27,000 miles an hour. Their reported course indicates that they travel on an East-West line with probability that they approach from the Northern Quadrant, which would be the last stage of the great circle route if they orginated in Russia.

Unidentified aerial objects travelling at 27,000 miles per hour over sensitive defence establishments? And their point of origin was possibly Russia? One can easily imagine the concern that such reports would have generated in US military and government circles, particularly in the light of the fact that, at the time, the Atomic Energy Commission Installation at Los Alamos was perhaps the most highly significant defence facility in the Western world. It was at Los Alamos that just a few years earlier scientists attached to the Manhattan Project had succeeded in creating one of the most awesome weapons of the twentieth century: the atomic bomb.

J. Edgar Hoover was further advised by the San Antonio office:

> In every case but one the shape of the objects has been reported as round in a point of light with a definite area to the light's source. One report gives a diamond shape; another indicates that trailing lights are elongated. The size is usually compared to one-fourth the diameter of the full moon, and they have also been compared in size to a basketball with trailing lights the size of a baseball . . . Some nine scientific reasons are stated to exist which indicated that the phenomena observed are not due to meteorites. The only conclusions reached thus far are that they are either hitherto unobserved natural phenomena or that they are man made. No scientific experiments are known to exist in this country which could give rise to such phenomena.

The 'nine scientific reasons' that effectively ruled out the green fireballs as being a manifestation of natural phenomena had been advanced by the aforementioned Dr Lincoln La Paz. In a five-page 'Confidential' report made available to me by the FBI, La Paz listed some of those nine reasons:

> . . . the horizontal nature of the paths of most of the December fireballs is most unusual. Genuine meteors are rarely observed to move in horizontal paths . . .

[T]he very low height of the December fireball . . . sets it off in sharp contrast from the genuine meteors for which heights of the order of 40 or more miles are normally observed . . .

[T]he remarkably vivid green color reported for most of the

A Confidential memorandum of 1949 relating to the FBI's findings on the 'green fireballs' seen near sensitive defence installations in the United States.

Office Memorandum • UNITED STATES GOVERNMENT

TO   : DIRECTOR, FBI   DATE: March 22, 1949

FROM   : SAC, SAN ANTONIO

SUBJECT: PROTECTION OF VITAL INSTALLATIONS
         BUREAU FILE 65-58300   CONFIDENTIAL

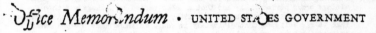

Re San Antonio letter to the Director dated January 31, 1949, which outlined discussion had at recent weekly Intelligence Conferences of G-2, ONI, OSI and FBI in the Fourth Army Area concerning "Unidentified Aircraft" or "Unidentified Areial Phenomena" otherwise known as "flying discs", "Flying saucers" and "balls of fire". It is repeated that this matter is considered secret by Intelligence Officers of both the Army and the Air Force.

G-2, 4th Army, has now advised that the above matter is now termed "Unconventional Aircraft" and investigations concerning such matters have been given the name "Project Grudge".

G-2, 4th Army, advised on February 16, 1949, a conference was held at Los Alamos, New Mexico, to consider the so-called "Green fire ball phenomena" which began about December 5, 1948. It was brought out this question has been classified "secret" and that investigation is now the primary responsibility of the U.S. Air Force, Air Materiel Command, T-2.

Dr. LINCOLN LA PAZ of the University of New Mexico, discussed one siting which he himself had made which was termed the "Starvation peak incident" and described the following characteristics which indicated that the phenomenon could not be classified as a normal meteorite fall.

1. There was an initial bright light (no period of intensity increase) and constant intensity during the duration of the phenomenon.

2. Yellow green color about 5200 Angstroms.

3. Essentially horizontal path.

4. Trajectory traversed at constant angular velocity.

5. Duration about two seconds.

6. No accompanying noise.

RECORDED

15 Apr. 4·1949

JEJ:md
2 cc: El Paso (100-4562)
   2 cc: Dallas
     " ": Houston
     " " Little Rock
     " " Oklahoma City

-1-

DIRECTOR, FBI   March 22, 1949

It was brought out that since December 5, 1948 there have been more than
ten incidents analogous to the "green fireball" above described and some
twenty others with minor deviations from the above. It is also pointed out
that the only sitings which had occurred seemed to have been confined to the
Los Alamos, Las Vegas, and West Texas triangle.

G-2 also advised that as of November 1, 1948, information had been received
from higher Military authorities that the Air Force had advised that such
sitings occur periodically and that another period of sitings was then
imminent. Further, on February 14, 1949, higher Military authorities advised
that it was believed that ultimately it would be found that the phenomena
in question have a natural explanation.

It is further noted that about 7:30 p.m., March 6, 1949, what was at first
thought to be a flare was seen approximately one-half mile north of Killeen
Base in the area of the Vital Installation at Camp Hood, Texas, and a second
flare was noticed at 1:45 a.m., March 7, 1949, approximately three miles from
Killeen Base. It has since been concluded that the flares seen near Killeen
are probably similar to the phenomena previously noted in the Los Almos,
Sandia Base Area although those are the first sitings of such phenomena near
Camp Hood.

There appears to be reason to believe that the above-mentioned phenomena may
be connected with secret experiments being conducted by some U.S. Government
Agency as it is believed that the United States is farther advanced in guided
missile development than any foreign power.

Although the primary responsibility for investigating such matters is now
with the U.S. A.F. Air Material Command, G-2, 4th Army is still interested
in being advised of any further sitings of such phenomena which might be
observed.

- 2 -

December fireballs is rarely observed in the case of genuine
meteors . . .

[D]uration estimates of between 2 and 3 seconds reported for
the green fireballs are considerably longer than those for the
ordinary visual meteors . . .

In the year and a half since this list was prepared, many additional observations have been made, the total number of objects now accepted as belonging in the green fireball category being 72 . . .

La Paz also made another most interesting observation about the phenomenon: 'It is a curious and fairly well-established fact that there has been a distinct decline in the number of green fireball sightings during the last two months, within which the number of so-called "flying saucer" incidents in this region has attained an all-time high.'

La Paz added that, in his opinion, at least some of the green fireballs were: 'US guided missiles undergoing tests in the neighborhoods of the sensitive installations they are designed to defend . . .' He did, however, qualify this statement with the following: '. . . if I am wrong in interpreting the guided missiles as of US origin, then certainly, intensive, systematic investigation of these objects should not be delayed until the termination of the present academic year. Recent international developments compel one to sense the imperative necessity of immediate investigation of the unconventional green fireballs, in case you are in possession of information proving that they are not US missiles.'

Barely a week after the San Antonio office advised Hoover of the latest developments in the fireball mystery, a further event occurred, this time near Roswell, New Mexico. A Bureau memorandum from the FBI special agent in charge (SAC) at EL Paso, dated 10 February 1949, gives us the following:

> On 2/6/49 [6 February] PAUL RYAN, Office of Special Investigations, Roswell, New Mexico, advised the resident agent at Roswell that he had just left a conference with Dr LINCOLN LA PAZ, Meteorologist, who has written a letter summarizing the search for the 'Unidentified Aerial Phenomena'.
>
> RYAN advised that Dr LA PAZ came to Rosewell after one of these objects had been observed by several persons in the Roswell area the night of January 30, 1949, at approximately 6:00 P.M. One of these persons who witnessed the object was an OSI Investigator who stated the object appeared to explode or

disintegrate near the Walker Air Force Base at Roswell, New Mexico.

RYAN informed that all of his agents had been searching the area around Roswell, Artesia, Tatum, and Kenna, New Mexico; Amherst, Brownfield, and Lamesa, Texas, where the phenomena had recently been observed. These searches all met with negative results.

Dr LA PAZ advanced the theory to RYAN that the objects were controlled missiles traveling around the earth at an altitude of approximately 25 miles and at a speed of approximately 15 miles per second. The missile was probably controlled by agents stationed at various intervals who are able to bring the missile down over a designated area and explode it. He stated that Dr LA PAZ added that he believed the Russians or some other country was practicing with these weapons which carried no warhead and were being exploded at an altitude of approximately 10 miles. After the practice periods LA PAZ assumed the weapons would be loaded with an atomic warhead.

As alarming as this most certainly was, throughout March 1949 sightings of the elusive fireballs proliferated. Witness the following memo to Hoover, dated 22 March 1949:

'. . . about 7.30 p.m., March 6, 1949, what was at first thought to be a flare was seen . . . in the area of the Vital Installation at Camp Hood, Texas, and a second flare was noticed at 1:45 a.m., March 7, 1949 . . . It has since been concluded that the flares seen are probably similar to the phenomena previously noted in the Los Alamos, Sandia Base Area although these are the first sightings of such phenomena near Camp Hood. There apears to be reason to believe that the above-mentioned phenomena may be connected with secret experiments being conducted by some US Government Agency as it is believed that the United States is farther advanced in guided missile development than any foreign power.

Three weeks later, Camp Hood once again played host to a mysterious visitor. An 'Air Mail Special Delivery' memo, dated 4 April 1949, from the San Antonio FBI Office to Washington disclosed:

> The Office of the Assistant Chief of Staff, G-2, 4th Army, has advised that at 11:50 P.M. March 31, 1949, a lighted object about the size of a basketball, reddish white in color, followed by a fire trail, was observed southwest of Killeen Base, adjacent to Camp Hood, Texas. The observation was made by 1st Lieutenant FREDERICK W. DAVIS, who was in charge of a platoon, Company C, 12th Armored Infantry Battalion, which is assigned as a part of an alert force (called force Abel) from Camp Hood, whose function is to protect the installation at Killeen Base.
>
> Lt DAVIS advised that the object was at an altitude estimated at 6,000 feet, was traveling parallel to the ground and passed directly over him at a rapid rate of speed. It was in view 10 to 15 seconds and suddenly disappeared high in the sky without having descended. No sound or odor was detected. The night was clear and visibility good. The object passed almost directly over the airstrip at Killeen Base.
>
> When Lt DAVIS attempted to advise his headquarters by telephone immediately after the sighting, he heard static or electrical interference on the telephone line which he stated might be possible radio interference.
>
> G-2 has advised that other lights of unknown origin were observed on March 6, 7, 8 and 17, 1949, by military personnel of the alert force stationed approximately 1,000 yards east of the fences which surround Killeen Base.

A 36-page report prepared by the US Air Force's 17th District Office of Special Investigations and sent to the FBI for information purposes shows that, throughout the remainder of 1949 and 1950, literally dozens of similar sightings were recorded throughout New Mexico. And in a still partly censored FBI memorandum of 1950, it was stated that: 'The Air Force together with Land-Air, Inc., have established a number of observation posts in the vicinity of Vaughn, New Mexico, for the purpose of photographing and determining the speed, height and nature of the unusual phenomena referred to as green fireballs and discs. On 24 May 1950, personnel of [censored] sighted 8 to 10 objects of aerial phenomena. A 24-hour day watch is being maintained and has been designated "Project Twinkle".'

In 1947, D.M. 'Mickey' Ladd was the assistant director of the Domestic Intelligence Division of the FBI, and shortly thereafter became head of all investigative operations undertaken by the Bureau. On taking early retirement at age 50 in 1954, Ladd was succeeded by Alan H. Belmont, subsequently acknowledged as 'number three man' in the FBI.[1] Four years previously, on 23 August 1950, Belmont sent Ladd a memorandum which advised that the Air Force Office of Special Investigations was still expressing 'concern' in connection with 'the continued appearance of unexplained phenomena described as green fireballs, discs and meteors in the vicinity of sensitive installations in New Mexico'.

Belmont added: 'Since 1948, approximately 150 observations of aerial phenomena referred to above have been recorded in the vicinity of installations in New Mexico.'

On 9 October 1950, Ladd wrote to Hoover:

> You will recall that on August 23, 1950, I furnished to you a memorandum regarding Project Twinkle set up by the Department of the Air Force, with the assistance of Land-Air, Inc. at Vaughn, New Mexico, for the purpose of obtaining data regarding these unusual aerial phenomena which have been seen in the vicinity of sensitive installations in New Mexico . . .
>
> You will recall the investigation to obtain information concerning these aerial phenomena is the jurisdiction of the Department of the Air Force. The Department of the Air Force is aware of our jurisdiction in matters relating to espionage, sabotage and internal security, and we have contacted OSI and requested them to advise us of any developments in connection with these phenomena which would be of interest to us as a result of our jurisdiction.

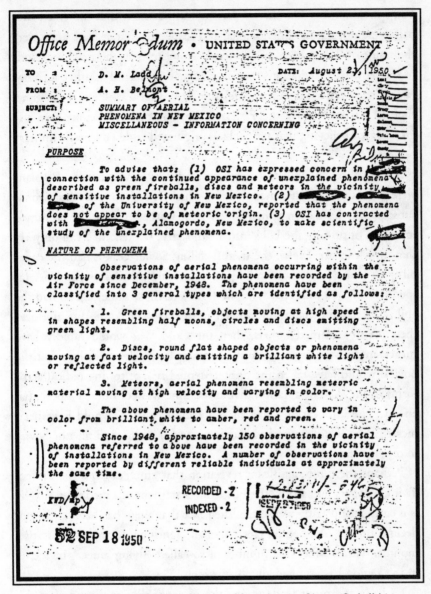

A 1950 FBI paper confirming more than fifty sightings of 'green fireballs' in New Mexico.

Ladd also added that the Air Force's investigation 'fails to indicate that the sightings involved space ships or missiles from any other planet or country'. This in itself is curious.

Let us examine why.

You will recall that Dr Lincoln La Paz was adamant that the green fireballs were not natural phenomena, and suspected that at least some were the result of 'US guided missiles undergoing tests in the neighborhoods of the sensitive installations they are designed to defend'. Suffice it to say, of the many official documents relating to Project Twinkle and the green fireballs declassified by the FBI and the US Air Force, none give any grounds for believing that the fireballs originated with a domestic military project.

What of the possibility, as once mooted by La Paz, that the Russians were practising with unarmed missiles, which, if proven successful, would subsequently have been armed with atomic warheads, with the presumed intention of turning the USA into a radioactive wasteland? I can only say that if, in the late 1940s, the then fledgling Soviet Union had the capability to launch dozens of fully primed atomic missiles at the USA (at speeds of 27,000 miles per hour, no less!) and those same objects had the ability to remain practically unseen until they were quite literally over their preprogrammed targets, then the Cold War would rapidly have turned into a very hot one! And I consider it wholly unfeasible that the Soviets would have taken the unprecedented risk of testing radical aeroforms in the skies of a nation that at the time was considered a potential enemy. The implications, had such a vehicle crashed, would have been incalculable. If not natural phenomena, and if not American nor Soviet in origin, what remains?

Perhaps the most significant revelation that emerges from the Project Twinkle papers released by the FBI is the statement of Lincoln La Paz: 'It is a curious and fairly well-established fact that there has been a distinct decline in the number of green fireball sightings during the last two months, within which the number of so-called "flying saucer" incidents in this region has attained an all-time high.'

La Paz's comment leads me to the inescapable conclusion that the two phenomena were inextricably linked. Moreover, a previously classified document dated 28 October 1947, which originated with the US Air Force's Intelligence Requirements Division, reveals that it was the considered opinion of some elements of the Air Force that 'Flying Saucers' and 'Flying Discs' represented 'interplanetary craft of some kind'.

Although reports continued to flow into Project Twinkle, by 1951 it was recommended that the project be disbanded owing to the fact that, 'the gist of the findings is essentially negative'. I find this decidedly odd since, as Lincoln La Paz recognised, many of the reports simply did not fit in with accepted meteor activity.

There are also indications that, despite D.M. Ladd's assertion that the Air Force would keep the FBI informed of any developments concerning the fireballs, the Air Force did not adhere to this policy. For example, the Final Report on Project Twinkle states that on two occasions at Holloman Air Force Base, specifically on 30 and 31 August 1950, green-fireball activity was seen shortly after missiles had been launched from the base.

That the fireball sightings continued to be taken seriously by the Air Force is something supported by the following statement found within Project Twinkle records: 'On 11 September [1950], arrangements were made by Holloman AFB for Major Glover, Commander 93rd Fighter Squadron at Kirtland AFB, to be on call so that aerial objects might be pursued. This would make possible more intimate visual observation and photography at close range. Major Glover was not authorized to shoot at the phenomenon.' Needless to say, none of these facts were related to the FBI.

These incidents seem to suggest that there was an accepted belief that the fireball phenomenon existed, so why was Project Twinkle ultimately cancelled? A study of the Final Report suggests that a lack of firm evidence pertaining to the mystery was the main reason. Even so, a once 'Secret' memo, prepared by Lieutenant Colonel John H. Clayton of the USAF, and Albert E. Lombard, Jnr, of the Directorate of Research and Development Division, on 19 February 1952, revealed that: 'The Scientific Advisory Board Secretariat has suggested that this project not be declassified for a variety of reasons, chief among which is that no scientific explanation for any of the "fireballs" and other phenomena was revealed by the report and that some reputable scientists still believe that the observed phenomena are man-made.'[2]

Nevertheless, Project Twinkle was cancelled, and both it and the green fireballs fell into obscurity and became part of the ever-growing UFO lore. However, I remain firmly convinced that the fireballs were some form of anomalous phenomena, primarily because of the high concentration of reports that emanated from, as the FBI so succinctly put it, 'vital installations' such as Los Alamos, birthplace of the atomic bomb. Furthermore, incidents practically identical to those reported in New Mexico in the late 1940s still surface to this very day. Since such reports are now occurring on a worldwide scale, the possibility that they are the result of some obscure fifty-year-old governmental project becomes ever more remote as time goes by.

In the mid-1980s, for example, another facility connected to the nuclear industry, the Indian Point reactor complex at Buchanan, New York, was plagued with visitations from numerous unidentified aerial craft, many of a boomerang or 'ice-cream cone' configuration. One investigator, Philip Imbrogno, states: 'I'm sure there's an incredible story here. I am still being given information about certain things going on [at the complex]. In the nighttime, people seeing little creatures coming through the walls of the casing on the reactor, and military personnel indicating "we're aware of these creatures and we don't care if they're from outer space – shoot 'em!"'[3]

Across the Atlantic in early 1994 Britain's Ministry of Defence released to me two files of UFO reports, totalling some 600 pages, which had been investigated by the Air Ministry between 1961 and 1963. An examination of those files shows that Britain, too, has been targeted by the green fireballs. A 'Loose Minute' dated 29 December 1962, from Squadron Leader J.G. Mejor of the Air Ministry Operations Centre, states:

> A civilian pilot, call sign GASCX, name and company unknown, flying from Renfrew to Manchester, was over Morecambe Bay at 7,000 feet on 28th December, 1962, when he saw approx 1,000 feet below him a bright light, three times brighter than a star, travelling East to West at approx 800 m.p.h. At exactly the same time a motorist, reporting via the Morecambe Police and Crosby Coastguard, said he saw a green flare. He was at Levens Bridge, near Barrow, looking South.

A similar report of 17 January 1963 states:

West of Lyneham, Sevenoaks area, 3 controllers at Lyneham report seeing a green light. Midland Control also report that a pilot had seen a green light that he could not identify. Pilot landed at Upper Heyford [and] reported that at 0330 he was in Sevenoak area at FL100 when he and other aircraft saw a foreign body believed entering the earth's atmosphere at a very great height and commencing to burn with a green light.[4]

And, to demonstrate that sightings of the green fireballs over Britain postdate the early 1960s, I present the following account, details of which were related to me by one of the prime witnesses, Simon Miller, in December 1995. The time was approximately 9 p.m., and the date was 17 October 1995.

My son and two other girls had been swimming at a village called Street in Somerset, and after their swimming training session had finished, we set off back home through Glastonbury and out across the peat moors towards a village called Mark.

The sky on this particular night was clear and most of the stars could be seen and the air was still with no breeze. As we drove out of Glastonbury, I saw a green light in the top right hand corner of my windscreen which at first I thought was a reflection. But as we drove for about another half mile, this green light then appeared at the rear of us, and I can best describe it as being shaped like a spinning top; colour was a blurred green, and the formation of the shape changed again. This then followed us for approximately five miles darting above us, to the left and right and tracked us along this country road.

There were no other vehicles on the road except for ourselves. I actually wanted to stop and get out to investigate if there was any noise from this object; unfortunately, the two girls in the rear of the car had by then become very frightened and the one was very hysterical and could not understand what it was. They are thirteen and fourteen years of age and my son is fifteen, and he watched it follow us most of the time.

At one point we came to a 'T-Junction' and when we stopped

it also stopped; it also stopped and hovered in the field to the left-hand-side of us. Its size was approximately ten metres high by six metres in width. It hovered above the ground by about three to four metres; as I said, it was a still night, but there must have been air turbulence from it because the straw in the field for the cattle was blowing towards us through the air.

We only stopped for about thirty seconds, and then I drove on until the motorway. When it finally stopped following us, we were getting nearer an area which was well lit up with lights from the motorway service area.

When I arrived back home I rang the local RAF camp at Locking just outside Weston to find out if they had any strange objects appear on their radar screen that night, but was told that the radar was not operated after 5.00 p.m. that day. Also, I have a friend who spoke about this to someone else who lives at Cheddar and they have also had a similar experience but on this occasion, the lights on their car went out.[5]

Having heard Mr Miller's report, and had the opportunity to speak with him in person, I am persuaded that the evidence for a truly anomalous event is overwhelming. Given the remarkable similarity between the object seen by Mr Miller and those detailed in FBI memoranda of the 1940s and 1950s, I have to wonder: were those same elusive objects seen in the USA nearly half a century ago and that reported in southern England in 1995 of like provenance? It is a possibility we would be wise to consider.

Having examined the facts surrounding the green-fireball phenomenon, there seems little doubt that the bulk of the work undertaken concerning the mystery fell to the US Air Force; however, if and when the full story of Project Twinkle ultimately surfaces, those FBI papers released into the public domain will play an important part in determining who or what was infiltrating US airspace with such unnerving ease some fifty years ago.

Were alien visitors, infinitely far from home, monitoring the United States' most prized defence and atomic installations in the post-World War Two era? And, if so, where are they now? Do they continue to maintain surveillance over us, watching as our technology advances at a dizzying rate? The experiences at Indian Point, New York, seem to suggest so; as does the encounter of Simon Miller in Somerset, on 17 October 1995.

I feel sure we have not heard the last of this enigma, and, as more and more developing nations venture into the atomic age, is it asking too much to suggest that they, too, will be blessed, if that is an appropriate word, with visitations from the green fireballs?

Whatever the future brings, perhaps we should be grateful to the Federal Bureau of Investigation for entrusting in us its files on Project Twinkle, for revealing its role in this enduring, decades-old mystery, and for paving the way for the release of what could turn out to be the story of the millennium.

CHAPTER 4

THE OAK RIDGE INVASION

AS THE 1940S DREW TO A CLOSE AND A NEW DECADE BEGAN, THE FBI continued to receive and log high-quality UFO reports on a regular basis. Of those, one of the more credible relates to an astonishing series of encounters which occurred in Alaskan airspace over the course of two days in early 1950.

Forwarded to the Bureau by an official US Navy source, the 'Confidential' three-page intelligence report paints a startling picture of multiple UFO encounters involving the US military. Titled 'Unidentified phenomena in vicinity of Kodiak, Alaska', the report concerns 'A report of sightings of unidentified airborne objects, by various naval personnel, on 22 and 23 January 1950'.

The report confirms:

> . . . at 220240W January Lt. Smith, USN, patrol plane commander of P2V3 No. 4 of Patrol Squadron One reported an unidentified radar contact 20 miles north of the Naval Air Station, Kodiak, Alaska. When this contact was first made, Lt. Smith was flying the Kodiak Security Patrol. At 0243W, 8 minutes later a radar contact was made on an object 10 miles southeast of NAS Kodiak. Lt. Smith checked with the control tower to determine known traffic in the area, and was informed that there was none. During this period, the radar operator, Gaskey, ALC,

USN, reported intermittent radar interference of a type never before experienced. Contact was lost at this time, but intermittent interference continued.

Smith and Gaskey were not the only two to report that unidentified vehicles had intruded upon US military airspace: At the time of the above encounters, the USS *Tilbrook* was anchored in the vicinity of 'buoy 19' in the nearby main ship channel. On board the *Tillbrook* was a seaman named Morgan (first name unknown) who was standing watch. At some point between 0200 and 0300 hours, Morgan reported that a 'very fast moving red light, which appeared to be of exhaust nature, seemed to come from the southeast, moved clockwise in a large circle in the direction of, and around Kodiak and returned out in a generally southeast direction'.

Perhaps not quite believing what he was seeing, Morgan alerted one of his shipmates, Carver, to the strange spectacle, and both watched as the UFO made a 'return flight'. According to Morgan and Carver's testimony: 'The object was in sight for an estimated 30 seconds. No odor or sound was detected, and the object was described to have the appearance of a ball of fire about one foot in diameter.' A further extract from the report records yet another encounter with the mystery visitor:

At 220440W, conducting routine Kodiak security patrol, Lt Smith reported a visual sighting of an unidentified airborne object at a radar range of 5 miles, on the starboard bow. This object showed indications of great speed on the radar scope. (The trailing edge of the blip gave a tail like indication.)

Lieutenant Smith quickly advised the rest of the crew of PV23 No. 24 that the UFO was in sight, and all watched fascinated as the strange vehicle soared overhead at a speed estimated to be 1,800 m.p.h. Smith climbed to intercept the UFO, and vainly tried to circle it. Needless to say, its high speed and remarkable manoeuvrability ensured that Smith's actions resulted in failure. However, neither Lieutenant Smith nor his crew were quite prepared for what happened next: 'Subsequently the object appeared to be opening the range,' the official report reads, 'and Smith attempted to close the range. The object was observed to open out somewhat, then to turn to the left and come up on Smith's quarter. Smith considered this to be a highly threatening gesture, and turned out all lights in the aircraft. Four minutes later the object disappeared from view in a southeasterly direction.'

At 0435 hours on the following day, Lieutenants Barco and Causer of Patrol Squadron One were conducting the Kodiak Security Patrol when they, too, sighted an unidentified aerial vehicle. At the time of their encounter the aircraft in which the officers were flying was approximately 62 miles south of Kodiak. For ten minutes, Barco and Causer, along with the pilot, Captain Paulson, watched stunned as the mystery object twisted and turned in the Alaskan sky. An assessment of these particular reports follows:

> (1) To Lt. Smith and crew it appeared as two orange lights rotating about a common center, 'like two jet aircraft making slow rolls in tight formation'. It had a wide speed range.
>
> (2) To Morgan [illegible] and Carver, it appeared as a reddish orange ball of fire about one foot in diameter, traveling at a high rate of speed.
>
> (3) To Causer, Barco, and Paulson, it appeared to be a pulsating orange yellow projectile shaped flame, with regular periods of pulsation on 3 to 5 seconds. Later, as the object increased the range, the pulsations appeared to increase to on 7 to 8 seconds and off 7 to 8 seconds.

The final 'Comment' on these encounters reads: 'In view of the fact that no weather balloons were known to have been released within a reasonable time before the sightings, it appears that the object or objects were not balloons. If not balloons the objects must be regarded as phenomena (possibly meteorites), the exact nature of which could not be determined by this office.'

The 'meteorite' theory for this encounter is something I find decidedly puzzling. It goes without saying that meteorites do not stay in sight for 'an estimated 30 seconds'; meteorites do not close in on military aircraft in what is deemed to be a 'highly threatening gesture'; and they do not appear as 'two orange lights rotating about a common center'. So I can only conclude that this was a poorly executed attempt to dismiss the importance of the events. An examination of the evidence, however, leads me to believe that anomalous phenomena were indeed viewed over Kodiak, Alaska, on 22–23 January 1950.

In the weeks that followed the sightings at Kodiak, the Bureau found itself further embroiled in the UFO puzzle when more and more credible reports poured into its offices. Consider the following 'Confidential' report of 2 March 1950:

A. There is a radar station near Knoxville which has been in operation about 3 weeks. This radar station is being operated by station WROL of Knoxville.

B. On 1 March at 2135 hours the station picked up an object 340 degrees and 18 miles from Knoxville altitude 40,000 feet. Direction and distance put the object directly over Oak Ridge. AEC Security Division Chief at Oak Ridge checked with Smyrna Air Base Nashville which reported it had no flight plan for any plane being in that vicinity and altitude.

C. On 2 March at 1105 station picked up object at 335 degrees and 18 miles from Knoxville altitude 40,000 feet. AEC Security Division Chief checked with Smyrna Air Base with negative results.

On the following day, 3 March 1950, a further report surfaced: 'At 2130 hours on 2nd March, radar station picked up two objects 310 degrees, altitude 80,000 feet, approximately 18 miles from Knoxville in general direction of Oak Ridge, moving in circular motion but in opposite directions . . . At 2230 hours 2nd March, and again at 0030 hours 3rd March, station picked up object, moving same direction, locality and altitude . . . Density of object similar to DC-3 airplane, speed not established but report as "terrific" . . . CIA Radar Technician reportedly arrives Knoxville today to check radar set and operation.'

* * *

Faced with the evidence that something truly out of the ordinary had taken place over Alaska and Oak Ridge in the early part of 1950, J. Edgar Hoover requested an updated briefing from the Air Force on its latest UFO findings.

On 28 March 1950, FBI Special Agent S.W. Reynolds met with two Air Force Intelligence operatives, Lieutenant Colonel J.V. Hearn and Major Jerry Boggs. Despite the fact that we now know that in the late 1940s and 1950s the US Air Force was concerned greatly by the UFO phenomenon, a memorandum drawn up by Reynolds for the attention of Hoover reveals that the Air Force was more than reluctant to entrust in the FBI its findings on the subject: 'Major Boggs and Lieutenant Colonel Hearn made the observation that many of the reported sightings of flying saucers at this time appear to be an outgrowth of recent magazine articles,' recorded Reynolds. 'They reiterated that the Air Force is conducting no active investigation to determine whether flying saucers exist or what they might happen to be.' Boggs and Hearn made no mention of the Oak Ridge and Kodiak sightings; they did, however advise Special Agent Reynolds that: 'The Air Force discontinued their intelligence project to determine what flying saucers are [in] the latter part of last year. They publicly announced to the press in December, 1949, that the project had been discontinued.'

Interestingly enough, this public announcement followed swiftly in the footsteps of a *True* magazine article by Donald E. Keyhoe, a graduate of the US Naval Academy, who asserted that confidential informants within the US military had quietly advised him that UFOs were indeed extraterrestrial spacecraft.

Of greater significance is the fact that, while researching the Air Force's role in the UFO mystery, Keyhoe had the opportunity to conduct a first-hand interview with Major Jerry Boggs in the Washington office of one General Sory Smith, Deputy Director for Air Information. After having discussed a number of UFO cases with Boggs, and having received answers which he felt to be unsatisfactory, Keyhoe remarked: 'I was sure now why Major Jerry Boggs had been chosen for his job, the all-important connecting link with the project at Wright-Field. No one would ever catch this man off guard, no matter what secret was given him to conceal.'[1] And as the researcher and nuclear physicist Stanton

Friedman and the aviation writer Don Berliner have stated: 'In fact, the official investigation was not discontinued but merely deemphasised.'[2]

In view of this, I have to wonder if Hoover was truly satisfied with the information related to Special Agent Reynolds on his behalf. Did Hoover suspect that the Air Force was being less than candid with the Bureau? I do not know, but there can be no doubt that the FBI continued to monitor carefully all subsequent incoming UFO reports, of which there were quite literally dozens.

On 30 June 1950, an 'Urgent' teletype was sent to the Bureau headquarters from the Phoenix, Arizona, office, which detailed a UFO encounter over the city:

> At 5.45 p.m. June 29th last, an object in sky was observed by many citizens of Phoenix including FBI personnel. Matter immediately reported to [censored] Office of Special Investigations, Williams AFB, Arizona. [Censored] advised today object was picked up by radar scope at 6.00 p.m., June 29th, at which time it was estimated object was thirty to thirty five thousand feet in air. A B-29 from 509th Bomb Group, Roswell, New Mexico, was assigned to follow object and pilot reported that while traveling at 25,000 feet he estimated object to be additional 10 to 20,000 feet above him. Plane was traveling at 290 MPH and was able to circle beneath object. Object was moving in westwardly direction in absence of wind. It was last sighted at 8.55 p.m. at a point about 20 miles north of Blythe, California, when it was lost due to heavy thunderstorm in area. [Censored] estimated size of object to be very large, inasmuch as with use of binoculars he could easily see the object. Nevertheless, the B-29 could not be observed with binoculars. OSI will submit full report after consultation with airplane crew and further study.

Over the space of one week in July 1950 the FBI secured the details of two UFO reports. The first came from an Illinois-based meteorologist with United Airlines, who brought to the attention of the Chicago Office that 'at 9:38 PM on July 4, 1950, he observed a large, bright, silvery object moving at an approximate altitude of 10,000 feet in a north, north-westerly direction over Downers Grove. [The witness] said that his wife also observed this object. He stated that he estimated the speed of the object at 700 to 800 miles [per hour] by comparing its rate of movement with that of commercial airplanes.'

The second report is rather more substantial, and relates to the sighting of a small, missile-shaped object, also seen over Illinois. The source of the data, described in Bureau memoranda as being of 'known reliability', reported that:

. . . at 1:00 a.m. July 1, 1950, at North Chicago, Illinois, east intersection of 22nd Street and the Chicago, North Shore and Milwaukee Railroad and Chicago Northwestern Railroad tracks, atop the watchman's tower, which is approximately fifteen feet in the air, he observed one cigar-shaped object, about five feet in appearance from his viewpoint, traveling from northwestern to southeastern direction at an excessive rate of speed over the Great Lakes Naval Training Center, Great Lakes, Illinois. According to the informant, this object appeared almost directly overhead at an altitude which he estimated to be about 15,000 to 20,000 feet, and it remained in sight for about twenty to twenty-five seconds until it disappeared over the horizon.

This informant advised the object did not appear like any falling star or meteor he had ever seen, and that it proceeded in a straight and level flight. The informant continued that the front two-thirds of the object was a constant glow about the coloring of a burning kerosene lamp, and that the rear third was dark. He continued that the object left a bluish-white trail behind it, appearing to be about four inches in width, and about three times the length of the object. The informant advised that there were no wings or other type of support visible to him, and that the propulsion, control and stability were unknown to him. He advised that the speed of this object was much faster than any conventional type of aircraft he had ever seen, although it did not travel as fast as a falling star . . . his attention was drawn to this object while he was watching for an approaching train. It is to be noted that he advised there were no other witnesses who saw the aforementioned object.

This informant has furnished reliable information to the Chicago Division in the past, is of average intelligence, and considered of good character and reputation.

An interesting report, involving what was alleged to be a reel of movie film showing a UFO in flight, caught the attention of the FBI in August 1950. 'On June 28, 1950,' reported the Louisville Bureau office, 'the *Louisville Times*, a newspaper of general circulation published at Louisville, Kentucky, carried a two column cut showing three frames of a movie camera film of what purported to be a moving picture of a flying saucer. The photographs, taken by Alf (A1) Hixenbaugh, *Times* staff photographer, were taken, Hixenbaugh said, on a 16mm magazine-loading movie camera'.

The memo went on to record that Hixenbaugh succeeded in shooting 50 feet of film in which 'the bright flying object shows clearly'. At the time of the encounter Hixenbaugh had been at home, when at 4.15 p.m. on 27 June 1950 he 'suddenly heard the roar of a big plane – a twin-motored DC-3 – and glanced overhead. At first he thought it was a jet plane[;] then he looked to the west of the plane, which was flying south-west toward Standiford Field – and saw the large disk. It had a slight corona around it and seemed to be lower than the plane.'

As Hixenbaugh watched, the UFO remained motionless for around ten seconds, then 'began to get smaller, finally vanishing into the west'. The Bureau noted that 'military officers' at Godman Field were advised, who in turn notified flight headquarters at Wright-Patterson.

The Louisville memo continued: 'A subsequent newspaper article stated that representatives of the military would fly to Louisville to examine the films.' As the available records show, this greatly concerned Al Hixenbaugh:

On July 28, 1950, Hixenbaugh telephonically communicated with the Louisville [FBI] Division stating that he had been advised that a representative of one of the Army Intelligence Agencies would be in Louisville on Saturday, July 29, 1950, to view the film. He expressed fear that the persons who might be contacting him might be unauthorized individuals and asked if he could bring the film to the FBI office for clearance. Hixenbaugh was advised that the Bureau did not clear employees of other agencies and if he had doubt as to their authenticity he should check with the agency they professed to represent. Hixenbaugh was advised that in the event [that] they were not representatives of the agency they professed to represent, the information should be furnished [to] this office and appropriate action would be taken under the Impersonation Statute.

Curiously, the remainder of this report was censored in its entirety prior to its release; yet it is quite clear that the Bureau took Hixenbaugh's concerns about bogus officials seriously. At the time (as we shall later learn) numerous rumours were in circulation in the 1950s that shadowy persons who may or may not have been connected with the US government were actively threatening and silencing witnesses to UFO encounters.

You will have noted that most of the cases investigated by the Bureau thus far were conducted largely behind a wall of secrecy. Despite this, rumours that the Bureau was involved in determining the origin of the saucers did leak outside of official channels, something that prompted the following letter of 29 August 1950 from a resident of Toronto:

It has come to my attention that one of the Departments of the FBI is collecting information from eyewitnesses of the phenomenon commonly termed 'Flying Saucers' and with this in view I have the following incident to relate. On July 19th at 10:30 I was looking over my farm facing west. The moon was fairly full and there was a low ceiling of light clouds. Much to my amazement I saw through the clouds a hazy object of light coming toward the farmhouse with incredible speed. It circled before reaching the farmhouse and continued to do so, neither the height or the orbit of which I could determine. I could not distinguish its shape, as it was above the clouds and I could only see a filter of light.

This was an entity in itself or within itself. It did not come from a beam either above or below. At times it seemed to retard its speed and then would circle in the opposite direction. I continued to watch it in all for about 35 minutes, from 10:30 p.m. to 11.05 p.m. when it disappeared in a westerly direction.

When UFOs returned in force to the Atomic Energy Commission complex at Oak Ridge, Tennessee, in the latter part of 1950 and early 1951, the Bureau took immediate steps to ensure that it remained fully conversant with the facts surrounding the encounters. As shown by a study of the unique documentation drawn up in response to these bizarre events, there can be little doubt that FBI concern over unidentified flying objects reached an all-time high.

To demonstrate, a Bureau teletype of 13 October 1950 refers to the detection of a veritable squadron of unknown objects tracked over the Oak Ridge installation at 11.25 p.m. on 12 October. 'USAF radar installation at Knoxville . . . picked up indications of eleven objects and perhaps more traveling across controlled area of Atomic Energy installation at Oak Ridge,' reported the FBI special agent in charge at Knoxville.

'Altitude of objects varied from one thousand to five thousand feet, courses from south south east to southeast, and density from reading made by light aircraft to aircraft equal in size to C-47, speed from one hundred to one hundred twenty-five miles per hour . . .

'No reasonable explanation for radar readings yet developed although operators are experienced reliable personnel and radar set is in perfect operating condition. Bureau will be advised of further developments.'

Four days later, the Bureau received details of yet another incident, this time involving the visual sighting of a structured UFO over Oak Ridge by a trio of military witnesses. In a report of 16 October, signed by Troopers Lendelle Clark and Hank N. Briggs, it was reported: '. . . at approximately 2:55 P.M. Trooper [John L.] Isabell stopped us at this Installation and showed us an object in the north that was traveling toward the northwest. It looked to be about 2,000 feet in the air and a white-silverish looking color, rotating in a counter clockwise manner. It was round in shape and going in a rather fast motion. This object was at a high altitude and

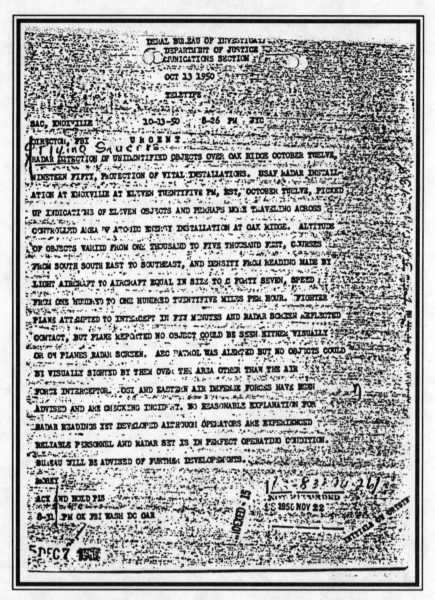

In October 1950, J. Edgar Hoover was informed that a fleet of UFOs had
been tracked overflying the atomic energy installation at Oak Ridge.

seemed to come in sight and then disappear. It looked about the size of a
ball and round at every angle we looked at it.'

Trooper Isabell added further details: 'This object was slowly circling in
a wide circle and spinning very fast, that is, the object was spinning

around and around. The object drifted toward the southwest and in just a few minutes it reappeared at a very high altitude going back into the northeast and going very fast . . .

'About fifteen minutes after the object disappeared into the northeast, an F-82 Fighter plane showed up in the area where the object was last seen but appeared to be thousands of feet lower than the object which Troopers Clark, Briggs, [and I] saw and reported.'

I do not propose to detail all of the many such encounters at Oak Ridge reported to the Bureau throughout the latter part of 1950 and early 1951, but do wish to call your attention to three sightings which in my opinion fully demonstrate that unknown vehicles from elsewhere were taking far more than a mere passing interest in the affairs at the Atomic Energy Commission installation. Consider the report of Trooper E.D. Rymer, who, along with Captain J.J. Zarzecki, sighted an unusual vehicle in mid-October 1950:

> . . . the size [of the UFO] appeared to be about the size of a four or five passenger plane. The object had a smoke trail the same cross-sectional size of its body and about one quarter of a mile long. The smoke was grayish in color. The color of the body of the object was silver metallic. The object gave off no reflection. It was dull in appearance. When first observed, it was describing an arc toward the ground. When the object failed to complete the outside loop, I went into the gate house to report its appearance . . .
>
> While I was making the phone call, Captain Zarzecki watched the object continue downward to 1,500 feet. At that altitude, a second object was noticed alongside the smoke trail. The second object was the same size and shape and was about 50 feet behind the first object . . .
>
> At this altitude, both objects changed from a bullet shape to a bladder shape . . . From 1,500 feet, the angle of descent was about 45 degrees. At about 500 feet, the second or trailing object disappeared. The object continued downward to a point north of the perimeter fence over the roadway about 60 yards from the gatehouse toward Solway bridge. This was where the object was when I came out of the gatehouse.

As he continued to watch, Rymer recalled that the UFO came alarmingly close to the ground:

> The object was hovering about 5 or 6 feet above the road in a completely stationary position. I went toward the object and the object started moving southward as I moved toward it . . . It moved straight up to about 12 feet then described a horizontal movement southward across the fence, then it again moved straight up at about sixty feet where it again moved south over a light pole and a willow tree . . .
>
> The object was now ascending at an angle of about 45 degrees in a southeast direction. As it moved away, it got larger in size and again assumed a pear or bladder shape. The object continued in this manner until it had passed over the ridge south of Solway road and disappeared.

That this sighting was taken seriously by the authorities is evident from the fact that William B. Gray, special agent in charge of the Counter Intelligence Corps at Knoxville, personally signed the official report pertaining to the encounter. And it should not go without comment that a significant passage from the report, which details Gray's 'Notes' on the case, remains classified to this day.

One of the things that have long persuaded me that the UFO mystery is a genuine one deserving intense study is the simple yet compelling fact that many reports of unusual aerial phenomena are made by highly competent observers, as we have now seen time and time again. And with respect to the Oak Ridge sightings, consider the following report, filed with the FBI by a US Air Force major on 27 October 1950:

> On the evening of 24 October 1950 at approximately 1855 I heard a plane fly over my home in the woodland area. Being a curious individual I went outdoors to watch it with my binoculars. While looking for the plane I saw an object in the western sky which appeared at first to be a star but upon closer observation I noticed that it was rapidly changing colors from red to blue

to white. When first seen it appeared over a telephone pole about 100 yards from my house and seemed to be moving very slowly in a northwest direction. It was moving relative to the other stars. The object was too small to be able to see any details even with the glasses. It disappeared from sight about 1920. During this period of time my wife also observed the object.

Finally, a statement dated 15 November 1950 reports:

A light emanating in the shape of a circle, of an intensity much greater than that of a bright moon, giving the impression of form

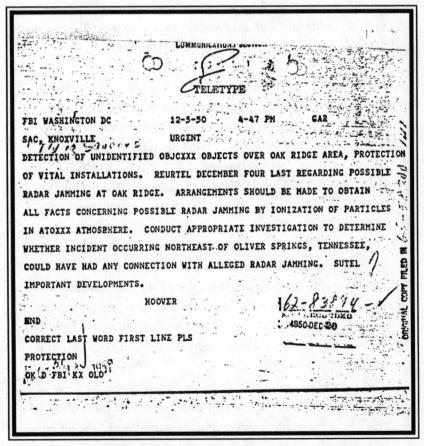

In December 1950, the FBI learned that UFOs had returned to the Oak Ridge area.

in connection with the light. The light was white in appearance
and did not show any signs of refraction into a band or continuous spectrum. This object was traveling in a north-westerly direction, 15 to 30 degrees elevation above the horizon, and appeared
to diminish considerable [sic] in size during thirty seconds of
observation. To another group, the object appeared only as a
bright reflection of the sun from an apparently metal surface. No
accurate estimate of the object's size or range could be made from
the observation.

Although it can be argued convincingly that the US Air Force gave a
somewhat guarded statement to the FBI following J. Edgar Hoover's
request for an official updating of the Air Force's findings concerning the
UFO subject in March 1950, the conclusions related to the Bureau on the
Oak Ridge incidents make for highly interesting reading:

> The opinions of the Security Division, AEC Oak Ridge;
> Security Branch, NEPA Division, Oak Ridge; AEC Security
> Patrol, Oak Ridge; FBI Knoxville; Air Force Radar and Fighter
> Squadrons, Knoxville; and the OSI, Knoxville, Tennessee, fail to
> evolve an adequate explanation for OBJECTS SIGHTED
> OVER OAK RIDGE, TENNESSEE; however the possibilities
> of practical jokers, mass hysteria, balloons of any description,
> flights of birds, falling leaves, insect swarms, peculiar weather
> conditions, reflections, flying kites, objects thrown from the
> ground, windblown objects, insanity, and many other natural
> happenings have been rejected because of the simultaneous wit-
> nessing of the objects with the reported radar sightings; because
> of the reliability of the witnesses; because of the detailed, simi-
> lar description of the objects seen by different persons; and
> because of impossibility . . .
>
> The trend of opinions seem to follow three patterns of
> thought. The first is that the objects are a physical phenomenon
> which have a scientific explanation; the second is that the objects
> are experimental objects (from an undetermined source) guided
> by electronics; and the third is similar to the second except that

an intended demoralization or harassment is involved. The fantastic is generally rejected.

Presumably this final sentence was a reference to the UFO phenomenon; however, the many credible reports which I have cited almost certainly preclude the involvement of conventional terrestrial technology. And it should not be forgotten that the UFO sightings over the Oak Ridge installation in 1950 mirrored those at the Los Alamos facility in the late 1940s. Did both phenomena have a common point of origin? Personally, I suspect so.

Of the reports detailed so far, the majority with which the FBI was tasked originated with military and governmental sources. One interesting exception is a report filed by a husband and wife in the latter part of 1950.

According to the FBI's records on the case: '[O]n October 20, 1950, [witness] and his wife and daughter went out of the back door of their home at New Haven to the back yard at approximately 6:15 P.M. His little daughter called his attention to a star in the sky that was moving.'

As the family scanned the sky, the father noticed a 'sphere-like object directly overhead which gave a steady golden orange glow . . . this object was very high between ten to twenty thousand feet, possibly higher'.

For twenty seconds the whole family watched as the object travelled in a westerly direction towards New York City, after which time it suddenly veered towards the Long Island area. An experienced pilot, the father estimated that the mystery craft was 'approximately ten times the diameter of Venus'.

It is also worth noting that according to the FBI agent at New Haven who interviewed the father: 'Mr [deleted] appeared to be a very reliable and sincere individual and evidences considerable technical knowledge and experience in reporting the above incident.'

In the final weeks of 1950 a flurry of good accounts detailing encounters with unusual objects over US airspace reached the Bureau. To demonstrate, a report of 15 December 1950 describes an actual 'UFO pursuit' undertaken by the military. While flying over Weeks International Field at around 8,000 feet, a number of military jet pilots 'observed a flash of light, yellow in color at an altitude between 25,000 and 30,000 feet.'

As the pilots maintained watch over the area from which the flash of light emanated, a dark-brown pillar of smoke suddenly appeared to rise at an angle of some 40 degrees, from the leading edge of which suddenly appeared 'an object either cigar-shaped or a fuselage without wings traveling at terrific speed'. Amazed by what they were seeing, '[the] pilots started pursuit on heading of 210 degrees, indicating 380 at a very steep climb'.

Unfortunately, it was all to no avail: 'Pursuit continued until pilots reached village and lost sight of the object. Meantime object gained altitude and speed and disappeared because of distance of approx. 50 to 55,000 feet. Color of smoke brown, color of object dark and no reflection from sunlight. Pilots assured of shape because of perfect silhouette against the sun. One pilot had object in view 4½ mins.'

An analysis of UFO sightings reported over the course of the twentieth century shows that encounters with cigar- and fuselage-shaped objects are surprisingly common. In the late 1940s a wealth of such reports surfaced in the Scandinavian countries; while in 1991 a 'missile'-like object came perilously close to colliding with an Alitalia MD80 jet airliner over Kent.

Curiously enough, a 'leaked' document (the authenticity of which has not yet been established), which was supplied to the researcher Don Berliner in March 1994, shows that by 1954 the US authorities were aware that this particular type of UFO was a reality. A part of the document states:

> b. Fuselage or cigar shape. Documented reports of this type of craft are extremely rare. Air Force radar reports indicate they are approximately 2 thousand feet long and 95 feet thick, and apparently they do not operate in the lower atmosphere. Very little information is available on the performance of these craft, but radar reports have indicated speeds in excess of 7,000 miles per hour. They do not appear to engage in the violent and erratic maneuvers associated with the smaller types.[3]

Although there can be no doubt that the object cited in the report of 15 December 1950 and that seen over Kent in 1991 were much smaller than those referred to in the above document, their basic design and capacity for high speed suggest a possible connection.

In 1951 the number of good-quality reports reaching the Bureau waned considerably, but one report in my possession, I am convinced,

The FBI office at Newark advised Bureau headquarters of a 1951 event in which a fast-moving UFO was tracked on military radar screens.

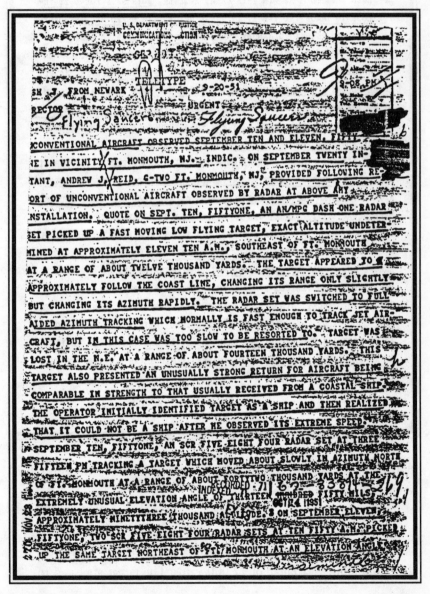

PAGE TWO

OF THREE HUNDRED FIFTY TO THREE HUNDRED MILS AT A RANGE OF APPROXI-
MATELY THIRTY THOUSAND YARDS, APPROXIMATE ALTITUDE THIRTYONE THOUSAND
FEET. THE SET TRACK AUTOMATICALLY IS AZIMUTH AND ELEVATION AND WAS
AIDED RANGE TRACKING AND CAPABLE OF TRACKING TARGETS UP TO A SPEED
OF SEVEN HUNDRED MPH. IN THIS CASE, HOWEVER, BOTH SETS FOUND IT IM-
POSSIBLE TO TRACK THE TARGET IN RANGE DUE TO ITS SPEED AND THE OPER-
ATORS HAD TO RESORT TO MANUAL RANGE TRACKING IN ORDER TO HOLD THE
TARGET. THE TARGET WAS TRACKED IN THIS MANNER TO THE MAXIMUM TRACK-
ING RANGE OF THIRTYTWO THOUSAND YARDS. THE OPERATOR SAID THE TARGET
TO BE MOVING AT A SPEED SEVERAL HUNDRED MPH HIGHER THAN THE MAXIMUM
AIDED TRACKING ABILITY OF THE RADAR SETS. THIS TARGET PROVIDED AN EX-
TREMELY STRONG RETURN ECHO AT TIMES EVEN THOUGH IT WAS THE MAXIMUM
RANGE, HOWEVER, ECHO SIGNAL OCCASIONALLY FELL OFF TO A LEVEL BELOW
NORMAL RETURN. THESE CHANGES COINCIDED WITH MANEUVERS OF THE TARGET.
ON SEPTEMBER ELEVEN, FIFTYONE AT ABOUT ONE THIRTY P.M. THE TARGET WAS
PICKED UP ON AN SCR FIVE EIGHT FOUR RADAR SET THAT DISPLAYED UNUSUAL
MANEUVERABILITY. TARGET WAS APPROXIMATELY OVER NAVESINK, NJ., AS IN-
DICATED BY HIS TEN THOUSAND RANGE, SIX THOUSAND FEET ALTITUDE AND DUE
NORTH AZIMUTH. THE TARGET REMAINED PRACTICALLY STATIONARY ON THE
SCHOPE AND APPEARED TO BE HOVERING. THE OPERATOR LOOKED OUT OF THE
VAN PAREND THE VEHICLE HOUSING THE RADAR SETX PAREND IN AN ATTEMPT
TO SEE THE TARGET, SINCE IT WAS AT SUCH A SHORT RANGE, HOWEVER, OVER-
CAST CONDITIONS PREVENTED SUCH OBSERVATION. RETURNING TO THEIR OPER-
ATING POSITION THE TARGET WAS OBSERVED TO BE CHANGING IN ELEVATION
AT AN EXTREMELY RAPID RATE, BUT CHANGE IN RANGE WAS SO SLOW THE OPER-
END OF PAGE TWO

fully demonstrates that some UFOs are tangible, intelligently controlled vehicles. Consider the evidence:

On 10 September 1951 as AN/MPG-1 radar set picked up a fast moving low flying target at approximately 1110 hours SE of Fort Monmouth at a range of 12,000 yards. The target appeared to

PAGE THREE

ATOR BELIEVED THE TARGET MUST HAVE RISEN NEARLY VERTICALLY. TARGET
FIXED ITS RISE IN ELEVATION AT AN ELEVATION ANGLE OF APPROX. FIFTEEN
HUNDRED MILS, AT WHICH TIME IT PROCEEDED TO MOVE AT AN EXTREMELY RAPID
RATE IN RANGE IN A SOUTHERLY DIRECTION. ONCE AGAIN THE SPEED OF THE
TARGET EXCEEDED THE AIDED TRACKING ABILITY OF THE SCR FIVE EIGHT FOUR
SET SO THAT MANUAL TRACKING BECAME NECESSARY. RADAR TRACKED THE TAR-
GET MAXIMUM RANGE OF THIRTYTWO THOUSAND YARDS AT WHICH TIME TARGET
WAS AT AN ELEVATION ANGLE THREE HUNDRED MILS. THE OPERATOR DID NOT
ATTEMPT TO JUDGE THE SPEED IN EXCESS OF THE AIDED TRACKING RATE OF SEVEN
HUNDRED MPH. THE WEATHER WAS FAIR WHEN THE OBSERVATION WAS MADE SEPT-
EMBER TENTH AND CLOUDY FOR THE SEPTEMBER ELEVENTH REPORT. UNQUOTE.
ABOVE INCIDENT OBSERVED BY THREE WITNESSES WITH EXCEPTION OF FIRST
INCIDENT ON SEPTEMBER TEN. ABOVE INFO FURNISHED BY REID AFTER AP-
PROVAL OF G-TWO, GOVERNORS ISLAND, NY, WITH REQUEST THAT INFO BE CO-
ORDINATED WITH AIR FORCE. REID ALSO ADVISED IN CONFIDENCE THAT ABOVE
REPORT RECEIVED BY HIM AFTER CONSIDERABLE UNACCOUNTABLE DELAY.

MC KEE

END AAD PLS

NK R 7 WA AS

DISC

approximately follow the coast line changing its range only
slightly but changing its azimuth rapidly. The radar set was
switched to full aided azimuth tracking which normally is fast
enough to track jet aircraft, but in this case was too slow to be
resorted to. The target was lost in the NE at a range of about
14,000 yards. This target also presented an unusually strong
return for an aircraft being comparable in strength to that usually received from a coastal ship. The operator initially identified
the target as a ship and then realized that it could not be a ship
after he observed its extreme speed.

As the report also shows, further anomalous targets were recorded in the vicinity of Fort Monmouth. Four hours after the encounter described above took place, a slow-moving object was tracked at an altitude of 93,000 feet; while on the following day, what was reported to be 'the same target' was once again tracked flying at fantastic speeds: '[B]oth sets found it impossible to track the target in range due to its speed and the operators had to resort to manual range tracking in order to hold the target . . . The operators judged the target to be moving at a speed several hundred miles per hour higher than the maximum aided tracking ability of the radar sets . . .'

When the full and unexpurgated facts surrounding the UFO issue are finally revealed to the public (and I, for one, suspect that time is coming), the events of 1952 will have a tremendously significant place in history. In that year, Britain's Royal Air Force was finally forced to concede that UFOs presented a serious risk to the defence of the realm when numerous UFO encounters were reported throughout Exercise Mainbrace, a NATO operation held in the North Sea and Northeast Atlantic.[4] Also in that year, as CIA records now reveal: 'During 1952 alone, official reports totaled 250. Of the 1,500 reports, Air Force carries 20 per cent as unexplained and of those received from January through July 1952 it carries 28 per cent unexplained.' And as I will now demonstrate, there were considerable surprises in store for the FBI, too.

CHAPTER 5

THE UFOs TARGET WASHINGTON

IN JULY 1952, THE SKIES OF WASHINGTON, DC WERE SATURATED WITH unidentified aerial objects, which ultimately led to a high-level exchange of data between the Bureau and the US Air Force. As records show, however, the encounters reported throughout the summer of 1952 were merely the final link in a chain of events that had begun several months before.

To begin with, reports began to trickle slowly into FBI field offices, including the following, which was filed by a lieutenant commander with the US Navy. For reasons of personal privacy, the identity of the commander has been deleted from the report.

Lt [censored] stated that approximately 10:20 p.m. on March 13, 1952, while standing in the backyard of 1900 Graybar Lane and looking toward the moon, which was then in the southwest section of the sky, he observed an object which appeared 20 degrees above the horizon. [He] described the object as being circular in shape, approximately one-half the size of the moon, deep bright blue in color, very vivid blue. He stated the object appeared to be moving from the northwest to the southeast . . . [Witness] stated that the only way he could describe it was that it appeared to be a very high powered spotlight on a cloud, but he did not believe this could have been the cause of that which he had seen because he had not seen any spotlight or any strong searchlights there during the evening.

While I am convinced that many UFOs are indeed piloted space vehicles which originate with an intelligence from beyond Earth, there are a number of reports in existence that suggest some UFOs are unmanned probes, perhaps undertaking operations deemed too risky for a fully crewed vessel. In many such instances the UFOs are described as relatively compact objects, perhaps the size of a family car or smaller. If remotely controlled UFOs are being used to conduct investigations in our environment, then perhaps the following report, filed with the FBI by a Chicago-based artist, can be considered relevant. As a one-page memorandum of 21 March 1952 tells us, at 9.00 a.m. on 11 March the witness was casually looking out of a south-facing window at his Chicago home when his attention was attracted to a 'flying disc' moving at a height of around 7,000 feet. 'The disc came out of a cloud in the east, stopped and hung motionless in mid-air for a split second, then flew due south at great speed.'

Additional portions of the report reveal:

> He described the disc as approximately six feet in diameter, circular, white in color with a bluish tinge. The disc, he said, appeared to have been constructed out of a metal similar to aluminum. He also stated that he saw no exhaust, lights or heard no sound connected with its movements. He noted nothing on it as to how it could maintain its even flight and believed it to have been radio controlled. He said it disappeared out of sight in approximately three seconds, estimating the speed at 600–700 miles per hour or more. He said it went so fast it appeared to flutter. When the disc disappeared from sight it was about the size of a golf ball on the southern horizon.

The peculiar 'fluttering' motion of the UFO described by the witness is typical in many encounters: six months after the sighting at Chicago a UFO was seen manoeuvring over RAF Topcliffe, Yorkshire, where, according to witness accounts, the object was 'swinging in pendular motion like a falling sycamore leaf'.

* * *

If J. Edgar Hoover was concerned by the UFO encounters at Los Alamos
in the 1940s and at Oak Ridge in 1950, then the following teletype from
the Bureau office at Savannah would most definitely not have gone un-
noticed:

SAVANNAH RIVER PLANT. ATOMIC ENERGY COMMISSION.
FLYING DISC. AT APPROXIMATELY TEN FORTYFIVE
P.M., MAY TEN LAST FOUR EMPLOYEES OF DUPONT CO.,
EMPLOYED ON SAVANNAH RIVER PLANT NEAR ELLEN-
TION, S.C. SAW FOUR DISC SHAPED OBJECTS
APPROACHING THE FOUR HUNDRED AREA FROM THE
SOUTH, DISAPPEARING IN NORTHERLY DIRECTION. AT
APPROXIMATELY ELEVEN FIVE P.M., ABOVE-MENTIONED
EMPLOYEES SAW TWO SIMILAR OBJECTS APPROACH FROM
SOUTH AND DISAPPEARED IN SOUTHWESTERLY DIREC-
TION. ONE MORE OBJECT SIGHTED ABOUT ELEVEN FIF-
TEEN P.M. TRAVELING FROM SOUTH TO NORTH. EMPLOY-
EES DESCRIBED OBJECTS AS BEING ABOUT FIFTEEN
INCHES IN DIAMETER, HAVING YELLOW TO GOLD COLOR.
ALL OF THESE OBJECTS WERE TRAVELING AT HIGH RATE
OF SPEED AT HIGH ALTITUDE WITHOUT ANY NOISE.
EIGHTH OBJECT WHICH APPROACHED THE FOUR HUNDRED
AREA FROM N.E. WAS TRAVELING AT ALTITUDE SO LOW
IT HAD TO RISE TO PASS OVER SOME SMALL TANKS IN
FOUR HUNDRED AREA. THIS OBJECT WAS ALSO FLYING
AT HIGH RATE OF SPEED AND WAS NOISELESS. WIT-
NESSES STATED OBSERVED OBJECTS WEAVING FROM
LEFT TO RIGHT BUT SEEMED TO HOLD GENERAL COURSE.
ALSO STATED DUE TO SPEED AND ALTITUDE THEY WERE
ONLY VISIBLE FOR FEW SECONDS. SAVANNAH OFFICE
IS NOT ACTIVELY CONDUCTING INVESTIGATION IN
THIS MATTER AND IS FURNISHING THIS INFO TO
BUREAU FOR WHATEVER THEY DEEM ADVISABLE.

It is interesting to note that this report refers to the sighting of 'objects
as being about fifteen inches in diameter, having yellow to gold color'.

This sounds astonishingly like a seldom-discussed report filed by the pilot Kenneth Arnold on 29 July 1947, who described seeing at least two dozen small, brass-coloured objects while flying over La Grande Valley, Oregon. Arnold was the subject of a lengthy Bureau file following his historic encounter of 24 June 1947 over the Cascade Mountains, Washington State.[1]

In any event, the Bureau was quick to advise Army Intelligence, Naval Intelligence, and Captain John A. Waters, Director of Security for the Atomic Energy Commission, of the encounter at the Savannah River Plant.

Two weeks after the sightings at Savannah came the following report from Louisville. Directed to Hoover, it reads:

> Re Flying Saucers, information concerning. Three women saw a strange objects [sic] floating in sky over Ashland, Kentucky, at 8.55 p.m. eastern standard time, May 25 last for two or three minutes. Objects described as looking like large oysters with fish-tails floating low like a cloud. They were oval in shape and according to observers could have been balloons. They came in over Ashland from the north, circled and went back in the opposite direction.

Balloons? Perhaps, but the fact that their movements appeared to be intelligently controlled suggests otherwise.

As we saw at the beginning of this chapter, it was largely the series of UFO encounters reported during July 1952 that led to additional Bureau interest in the UFO subject. Faced with the evidence, this is not surprising.

On 19 and 20 July there were repeated sightings of unknown objects in Washington airspace, something that, on 24 July, led Major General John A. Samford, USAF, to state in a 'Secret' memorandum for the Deputy Chief of Staff, Operations: 'We are interested in these reports in that we must be always on the alert for any threat or indication of a threat to the United States. We cannot ignore these reports but the mild hysteria subsequent to publicity given this subject causes an influx of reports which since the 19th of July has almost saturated our "Emergency" procedures.'

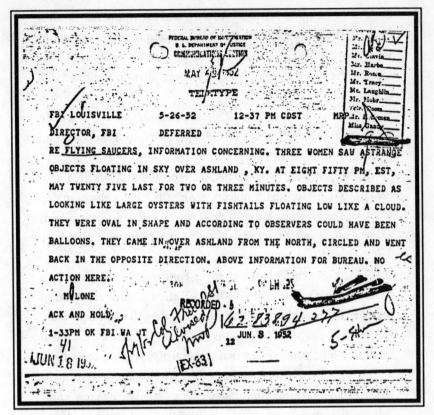

In May 1952, UFOs targeted Ashland, Kentucky. Once again, the FBI was fully conversant with the evidence.

While I would agree that localised 'UFO flaps' can on occasion induce a degree of hysteria, it is a demonstrable fact that the initial reports of UFO activity in July 1952 originated with military and civil aviation sources – people not usually recognised for displaying 'mild hysteria'. And on 26 July, one week later, the UFOs were once again out in force over Washington.

To illustrate that many of the reports filed during that time span were deemed highly disturbing, consider the following two-page USAF document outlining what occurred on 26–27 July 1952:

This incident involved unidentified targets observed on the radar scopes at the Air Route Traffic Control Center and the tower, both at Washington National Airport, and the Approach Control Radar at Andrews Air Force Base. In addition, visual observations were reported to Andrews and Bolling AFB and to ARTC Center, the latter by pilots of commercial aircraft and one CAA aircraft . . .

Varying numbers (up to 12 simultaneously) of u/i targets on ARTC radar scope. Termed by CAA personnel as 'generally, solid returns', similar to a/c except slower . . .

Mr Bill Schreve, flying a/c NC-12 reported at 2246 EDT that he had visually spotted 5 objects giving off a light glow ranging from orange to white; his altitude at time was 2,200´. Some commercial pilots reported visuals ranging from 'cigarette glow' to a 'light' . . .

ARTC crew commented that, as compared with u/i returns picked up in early hours of 20 July 52, these returns appeared to be more haphazard in their actions, i.e. they did not follow a/c around nor did they cross scope consistently on same general heading. Some commented that the returns appeared to be from objects 'capable of dropping out of the pattern at will'. Also that returns had 'creeping appearance'. One member of crew commented that one object to which F-94 was vectored just 'disappeared from Scope' shortly after F-94 started pursuing. All crew members emphatic that most u/i returns have been picked up from time to time over the past few months but never before had they appeared in such quantities over such a prolonged period and with such definition as was experienced on the nights of 19/20 and 26/27 July 52.

Although the portions cited from this report speak for themselves, let us now look at some fascinating extracts from a transcript of a conversation, of 26 July, between staff at Washington National Airport and Andrews Air Force Base at the time of the sightings:

Wash: Andrews Tower, do you read? Did you have an airplane in sight west-northwest or east of your airport eastbound?

Andr: No, but we just got a call from the Center. We're looking for it.

Wash: We've got a big target showing up on our scope. He's just coming in on the west edge of your airport – the northwest edge of it eastbound. He'll be passing right through the northern portion of your field on an east heading. He's about a quarter of a mile from the northwest runway – right over the edge of your runway now.

The conversation continues:

Andr: This is Andrews. Our radar tracking says he's got a big fat target out here northeast of Andrews. He says he's got two more south of the field.

Wash: Yes, well the Center has about four or five around the Andrews Range Station. The Center is working a National Airlines – the Center is working him and vectoring him around his target. He went around Andrews. He saw one of them – looks like a meteor. (Garbled) . . . went by him . . . or something. He said he's got one about three miles off his right wing right now. There are so many targets around here it is hard to tell as they are not moving very fast.[2]

That J. Edgar Hoover was greatly concerned by the Washington sightings is something I am now able to show. Within a matter of hours of hearing of the events of 26–27 July, Hoover instructed N.W. Philcox, the Bureau's Air Force liaison representative, to determine what had taken place and to ascertain the Air Force's then current opinions on the UFO subject as a whole.

On 29 July, Philcox made arrangements through the office of the Director of Air Intelligence, Major General John A. Samford, to meet with Commander Randall Boyd of the Current Intelligence Branch, Estimates Division, Air Intelligence, regarding 'the present status of Air Intelligence research into the numerous reports regarding flying saucers and flying discs'.

Although the Air Force was publicly playing down the possibility that

UFOs were anything truly extraordinary, Philcox was advised that: 'at the present time the Air Force has failed to arrive at any satisfactory conclusion in its research regarding numerous reports of flying saucers and flying discs sighted throughout the United States'.

Philcox was further advised that Air Intelligence had set up at Wright-Patterson Air Force Base, Ohio, the Air Technical Intelligence Center, which had been established for the purpose of 'coordinating, correlating and making research into all reports regarding flying saucers and flying discs'. It is somewhat illuminating to note that Commander Boyd also added, 'Air Force research has indicated that the sightings of flying saucers goes back several centuries and that the number of sightings reported varies with the amount of publicity . . . immediately if publicity appears in newspapers, the number of sightings reported increases considerably and that citizens immediately call in reporting sightings which occurred several months previously.'

Having studied the UFO issue for more than fifteen years, I am aware that good-quality sightings invariably prompt other people, who had previously remained silent, to report their encounters; however, this in no way implies that the subsequent reports are hoaxes or delusions: it simply demonstrates the adage that there is safety in numbers. If one person speaks openly, more often than not others will feel a degree of camaraderie which overcomes the fear of being labelled a crank – as still happens, I regret to say.

As Philcox listened carefully to what Boyd had to say, he noted that the Air Force had lumped their UFO reports into three definable categories. In the first instance there were those sightings 'which are reported by citizens who claim they have seen flying saucers from the ground. These sightings vary in description, color and speeds. Very little credence is given to these sightings inasmuch as in most instances they are believed to be imaginative or some explainable object which actually crossed through the sky.'

As Philcox then learned, the second category of encounters proved to be of far greater significance:

(2) Sightings reported by commercial or military pilots. These

sightings are considered more credible by the Air Force inasmuch as commercial or military pilots are experienced in the air and are not expected to see objects which are entirely imaginative. In each of these instances, the individual who reports the sightings

Following a series of stunning UFO encounters over Washington, DC in July 1952, the FBI received an updated briefing on the UFO issue from the US Air Force.

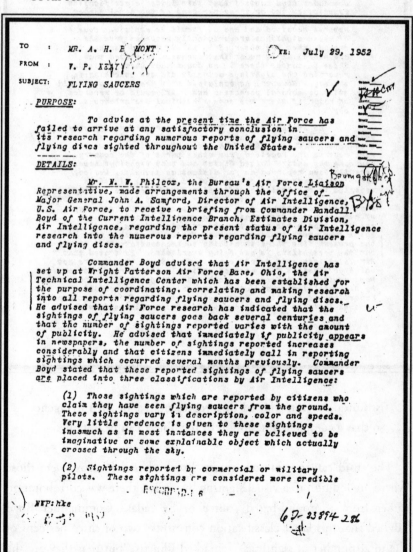

TO   :   MR. A. H. BELMONT   DATE: July 29, 1952

FROM   :   V. P. KEAY

SUBJECT: FLYING SAUCERS

PURPOSE:

           To advise at the present time the Air Force has failed to arrive at any satisfactory conclusion in its research regarding numerous reports of flying saucers and flying discs sighted throughout the United States.

DETAILS:

           Mr. N. W. Philcox, the Bureau's Air Force Liaison Representative, made arrangements through the office of Major General John A. Samford, Director of Air Intelligence, U.S. Air Force, to receive a briefing from Commander Randall Boyd of the Current Intelligence Branch, Estimates Division, Air Intelligence, regarding the present status of Air Intelligence research into the numerous reports regarding flying saucers and flying discs.

           Commander Boyd advised that Air Intelligence has set up at Wright Patterson Air Force Base, Ohio, the Air Technical Intelligence Center which has been established for the purpose of coordinating, correlating and making research into all reports regarding flying saucers and flying discs. He advised that Air Force research has indicated that the sightings of flying saucers goes back several centuries and that the number of sightings reported varies with the amount of publicity. He advised that immediately if publicity appears in newspapers, the number of sightings reported increases considerably and that citizens immediately call in reporting sightings which occurred several months previously. Commander Boyd stated that these reported sightings of flying saucers are placed into three classifications by Air Intelligence:

          (1) Those sightings which are reported by citizens who claim they have seen flying saucers from the ground. These sightings vary in description, color and speeds. Very little credence is given to these sightings inasmuch as in most instances they are believed to be imaginative or some explainable object which actually crossed through the sky.

          (2) Sightings reported by commercial or military pilots. These sightings are considered more credible

NVP:hke

67-23894-286

by the Air Force inasmuch as commercial or military
pilots are experienced in the air and are not
expected to see objects which are entirely imaginative.
In each of these instances, the individual who reports
the sighting is thoroughly interviewed by a representative
of Air Intelligence so that a complete description of
the object sighted can be obtained.

(3) Those sightings which are reported by pilots and
for which there is additional corroboration, such as
recording by radar or sighting from the ground.
Commander Boyd advised that this latter classification
constitutes two or three per cent of the total number
of sightings, but that they are the most credible
reports received and are difficult to explain. Some
of these sightings are originally reported from the
ground, then are observed by pilots in the air and then
are picked up by radar instruments. He stated that in
these instances there is no doubt that these individuals
reporting the sightings actually did see something in
the sky. However, he explained that these objects could
still be natural phenomena and still could be recorded
on radar if there was some electrical disturbance in the
sky.

He stated that the flying saucers are most frequently
observed in areas where there is heavy air traffic, such as
Washington, D.C., and New York City. He advised, however, that
some reports are received from other parts of the country
covering the entire United States and that sightings have also
recently been reported as far distant as Acapulco, Mexico;
Korea and French Morocco. He advised that the sightings
reported in the last classification have never been satisfactorily
explained. He pointed out, however, that it is still possible
that these objects may be a natural phenomenon or some type
of atmospherical disturbance. He advised that it is not
entirely impossible that the objects sighted may possibly be
ships from another planet such as Mars. He advised that at
the present time there is nothing to substantiate this theory
but the possibility is not being overlooked. He stated that
Air Intelligence is fairly certain that these objects are not
ships or missiles from another nation in this world. Commander
Boyd advised that intense research is being carried on presently
by Air Intelligence, and at the present time when credible
reportings of sightings are received, the Air Force is attempting
in each instance to send up jet interceptor planes in order to

- 2 -

is thoroughly interviewed by a representative of Air Intelligence
so that a complete description of the object can be obtained.

The third category of encounters, Boyd advised Philcox, were those
where, in addition to a visual sighting by a pilot, there was corroboration
either from a ground-based source or by radar. 'Commander Boyd
advised that this latter classification constitutes two or three per cent of
the total number of sightings,' remarked Philcox, 'but that they are the
most credible reports received and are difficult to explain.'

obtain a better view of these objects. However, recent attempts in this regard have indicated that when the pilot in the jet approaches the object it invariably fades from view.

RECOMMENDATION:

None. The foregoing is for your information.

- 3 -

'In these instances,' Philcox was told, 'there is no doubt that these individuals reporting the sightings actually did see something in the sky.' Ever cautious, however, Boyd qualified this statement with the following: '. . . these objects could still be natural phenomena and still could be recorded on radar if there was some electrical disturbance in the sky.' Quite so. But let us not forget that, with the encounters at Oak Ridge in 1950, the possibility that the sightings were due to some from of natural phenomena was summarily dismissed.

To demonstrate that Boyd was well acquainted with the UFO issue on a worldwide scale, he confided in Philcox that: 'sightings have also recently been reported as far distant as Acapulco, Mexico; Korea and French Morocco . . . the sightings reported in the last classification have never been satisfactorily explained'.

Boyd then came out with a true bombshell, as Philcox noted in his report on their meeting: '[Boyd] advised that it is not entirely impossible that the objects sighted may possibly be ships from another planet such as Mars.' Of course, history has shown that, today at least, Mars is a barren and hostile world almost certainly incapable of maintaining an indigenous life form. However, Boyd's assertion that some UFOs were possibly spacecraft from another world is eye-opening to say the least.

In support of the spacecraft theory, Boyd admitted: 'Air Intelligence is fairly certain that these objects are not ships or missiles from another nation in this world.' And as Philcox noted in the final passage of his three-page report to Hoover:

> Commander Boyd advised that intense research is being carried on presently by Air Intelligence, and at the present time when credible reportings of sightings are received, the Air Force is attempting in each instance to send up jet interceptor planes in order to obtain a better view of these objects. However, recent attempts in this regard have indicated that when the pilot in the jet approaches the object it invariably fades from view.

Philcox's final comment is rather intriguing and does not preclude the possibility that those piloting the UFOs are somehow automatically forewarned of the presence of potentially aggressive military aircraft. This was something noted decades ago by the late Donald Keyhoe. Following the outstanding UFO sightings over Washington in 1952, Jim Ritchey, a veteran traffic controller at Washington International Airport, told Keyhoe that he had once attempted to vector a Capital Airlines plane on to a UFO; however, as soon as the order was given, the UFO 'shot straight up, accelerating from 130 to 500 miles an hour in four seconds'.

Keyhoe was also informed that Senior Controller Harry Barnes had noted the same results on at least two occasions, something that convinced Barnes that 'the unknown visitors' were listening to his instructions.[3] It is a sobering thought that perhaps in the upper reaches of the atmosphere alien creatures are monitoring the radio transmissions of military and civilian aircraft, ever watchful in case one should attempt a hostile interception.

On 31 July, the Bureau learned of another incident, which had occurred on 27 July; in this case, however, the eyewitness may have inadvertently viewed a classified government experiment designed to replicate the actions of the saucers. Quoting the testimony of a doctor based in Kokomo, Indiana, the Bureau special agent in charge at Indianapolis wrote to J. Edgar Hoover:

> On July 30, 1952, [the witness] advised . . . that on July 27, 1952, at approximately 10:00 A.M. while fishing in the back waters of Thessalon Lake, Ontario, Canada, he noticed a formation of bombing planes, sixteen to twenty in number, in two groups flying south at a height estimated by him to be four or five miles.
>
> Dr [deleted] stated that the planes went over the lake, suddenly dropped objects at first thought by him to be parachutes. He continued that these objects fell straight down for a short time, then suddenly spurted vapor and at a high rate of speed flew off in a southwesterly direction.
>
> Dr [deleted] was unable to identify the nationality of the planes, but stated that they had twin trails of bluish smoke . . . [He] had no further information concerning instant planes or the objects dropped by them.
>
> [The doctor] was referred to the FBI by the President of the First National Bank of Kokomo, Indiana, who advised [the doctor] enjoyed a good reputation in Kokomo.

Following the 29 July meeting between N.W. Philcox of the Bureau and Air Intelligence Commander Randall Boyd, the working relationship between the FBI and the Air Force, which had declined drastically in September 1947, improved a little. As evidence of this, on 18 August 1952, the Air Force expressed its concerns to the Bureau that the saucer problem was one of mounting anxiety, and once again enquired if a more compatible liaison between the two could be formulated. Particularly looking to enlist the assistance of the FBI were elements of the Air Force's Office of Special Investigations, as is shown in a memo to Alan Belmont displayed below:

> PURPOSE: To advise all Supervisors engaged on night duty of instructions concerning the referral of flying disc information to OSI.
>
> BACKGROUND: Captain [deleted], OSI, 4th Air Force Base, Bowling Field, has requested that any information concerning the sighting of flying discs (saucers, etc.) be telephonically furnished immediately to his office, day or night, by dialling Code 1261, and asking for Extension 509. Captain [deleted] advised [that] the Air Force is greatly concerned about the captioned matter, and would appreciate the Bureau's cooperation in immediately advising of details received concerning such complaints.

The Bureau was apparently not disagreeable to this request, despite what had occurred in the past, and copies of incoming UFO reports were duly passed on to the Air Force for scrutiny.

Almost three months to the day after four disc-shaped UFOs were seen in the vicinity of the AEC-run Savannah River Plant, a second event occurred. A teletype to Hoover read:

> FLYING SAUCERS, SAVANNAH RIVER PLANT, AEC. SECURITY OFFICE OF AEC ADVISED THIS DATE THAT TWO EMPLOYEES OF THE E.I. DU PONT COMPANY SAW A BLUE LIGHT WITH AN ORANGE FRINGE SHAPED LIKE A SAUCER FLY OVER THE FOUR HUNDRED AREA OF THE SAVANNAH RIVER PLANT AT APPROXIMATELY NINE THIRTY PM AUGUST EIGHT, FIFTY TWO. OBJECT FLYING AT A HIGH RATE OF SPEED AND TRAVELING IN A NORTHEASTERN DIRECTION.

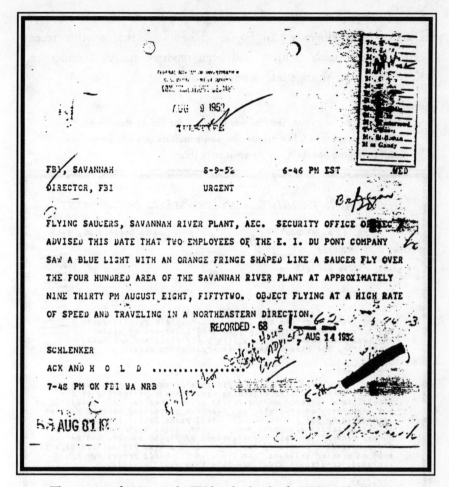

The summer of 1952 saw the FBI log the details of a UFO incident near
the atomic-energy installation at Savannah.

With this information in hand, steps were taken by Hoover to
ensure that the Bureau was kept informed by the Air Force of any further potentially important encounters. He would not have to wait
long . . .

An internal Bureau memorandum to Alan Belmont, dated 27 October
1952, reveals: 'Air Intelligence advised of another creditable and unexplainable sighting of flying saucers . . . some military officials are seriously considering the possibility of interplanetary ships.'

A Bureau official, V.P. Keay, was informed on 23 October: 'Colonel

C.M. Young, Executive Officer to Major General John A. Samford, Director of Intelligence, Air Force, advised . . . that another recent extremely creditable sighting had been reported to Air Intelligence.' Keay's report on Young's information follows:

As 1952 drew to a close, the FBI was quietly informed by the US Air Force that, with respect to UFO encounters, 'some military officials are seriously considering the possibility of interplanetary ships'.

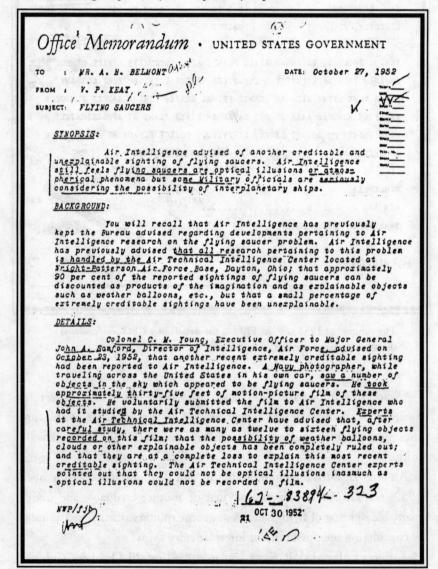

Office Memorandum • UNITED STATES GOVERNMENT

TO : MR. A. H. BELMONT   DATE: *October 27, 1952*

FROM : *V. P. KEAY*

SUBJECT: *FLYING SAUCERS*

SYNOPSIS:

Air Intelligence advised of another creditable and unexplainable sighting of flying saucers. Air Intelligence still feels flying saucers are optical illusions or atmospherical phenomena but some Military officials are seriously considering the possibility of interplanetary ships.

BACKGROUND:

You will recall that Air Intelligence has previously kept the Bureau advised regarding developments pertaining to Air Intelligence research on the flying saucer problem. Air Intelligence has previously advised that all research pertaining to this problem is handled by the Air Technical Intelligence Center located at Wright-Patterson Air Force Base, Dayton, Ohio; that approximately 90 per cent of the reported sightings of flying saucers can be discounted as products of the imagination and as explainable objects such as weather balloons, etc., but that a small percentage of extremely creditable sightings have been unexplainable.

DETAILS:

Colonel C. M. Young, Executive Officer to Major General John A. Samford, Director of Intelligence, Air Force, advised on October 23, 1952, that another recent extremely creditable sighting had been reported to Air Intelligence. A Navy photographer, while traveling across the United States in his own car, saw a number of objects in the sky which appeared to be flying saucers. He took approximately thirty-five feet of motion-picture film of these objects. He voluntarily submitted the film to Air Intelligence who had it studied by the Air Technical Intelligence Center. Experts at the Air Technical Intelligence Center have advised that, after careful study, there were as many as twelve to sixteen flying objects recorded on this film; that the possibility of weather balloons, clouds or other explainable objects has been completely ruled out; and that they are at a complete loss to explain this most recent creditable sighting. The Air Technical Intelligence Center experts pointed out that they could not be optical illusions inasmuch as optical illusions could not be recorded on film.

162 - 83894 - 323

21   OCT 30 1952

NWP/jjy

Memo to Mr. A. H. Belmont   *RE: FLYING SAUCERS*
from V. P. Keay

     Colonel Young advised that Air Intelligence still feels that the so-called flying saucers are either optical illusions or atmospherical phenomena. He pointed out, however, that some Military officials are seriously considering the possibility of interplanetary ships.

ACTION:

     None. This is for your information.

A Navy photographer, while traveling across the United States in his own car, saw a number of objects in the sky which appeared to be flying saucers. He took approximately thirty-five feet of motion-picture film of these objects. He voluntarily submitted the film to Air Intelligence who had it studied by the Air Technical Intelligence Center. Experts at the ATIC have advised that, after careful study, there were as many as twelve to sixteen flying objects recorded on this film; that the possibility of weather balloons, clouds or other explainable objects has been completely ruled out; and that they are at a complete loss to explain this most recent creditable sighting. The Air Technical Intelligence Center experts pointed out that they could not be optical illusions inasmuch as optical illusions could not be recorded on film.

The last decade has seen a tremendous amount of UFO activity, quite literally on a scale unparalleled, in Puerto Rico. Encounters with nonhuman entities, sometimes of an aggressive nature, are becoming more commonplace, and sightings of unidentified flying craft abound. Moreover, a leading Puerto Rican investigator, Jorge Martin, has compiled an astonishing amount of data, which suggests strongly that some form of alien intelligence is present on the island.

Perhaps of relevance to the events of the 1980s and 1990s, is the following report from the San Juan FBI office: 'Five persons observed an unidentified flying object at 11:30 AM on 4/8/53 [8 April] at Fort Buchanan, Puerto Rico. Statements were taken from all of the witnesses, among whom were three Captains and a Sergeant of the US Army, as well as a civilian. They described the object as a bright star or a bright ball of fire at a great height, and it was moving rapidly at the time it was observed.' Jorge Martin has learned also that the FBI may still be implicated in the monitoring of UFO encounters on the island to this day. Commenting on the overwhelming number of reports relating to both structured craft of an unusual design and unearthly-looking creatures seen throughout Puerto Rico during the 1990s, Freddie Cruz, Director of the Civil Defence Agency of Lajas, informed Martin that: 'There are UFOs in the Laguna Cartegena, and something weird is going on at the aerostat radar facility . . . To me, there's an alien base around here and the authorities know about it, but don't want anyone else to . . .'

In addition, a high-ranking police officer on the island told Martin in confidence that police personnel selected to stand guard at the radar facility were debriefed by American federal agents (rumoured to be with the FBI), and were deluged with a variety of questions relating to UFOs and contact with alien beings.[4] Is the Bureau aware that extraterrestrial creatures have taken up residence somewhere on Puerto Rico? And, if so, who has the upper hand? Should an official announcement confirming the above be forthcoming, let us hope that the news is good . . .

Throughout 1954 and 1955 much of the Bureau's time was expended investigating the claims of numerous persons who asserted that they were in direct contact with alien beings much like ourselves. In due course I will elaborate on this, but let us now jump forward to 1956.

One of the most memorable UFO encounters in which the FBI was involved occurred in April of that year, and is particularly notable for the fact that, of the two witnesses, one was actually employed by the Bureau!

Before the release of the relevant documentation surrounding the case, the FBI sought to delete any mention of the names of the two witnesses; however, one passage of the report was overlooked, and reveals the prime informant to be a 'Miss Richards' in the employ of the FBI at the Washington, DC headquarters.

On 6 April 1956, Miss Richards and her fiancé left Washington by car with the intention of travelling to Morven, North Carolina, for a family get-together. At around 5 a.m. on the following morning, something truly eye-opening occurred, as now declassified documentation shows: '. . . while driving on Route 1 north of Henderson, North Carolina, the pair was startled by what appeared to be a round low-flying object coming directly toward the car. The object appeared to pass over the car and Miss Richards turned to see it appear to speed up and then veer off out of sight. She and [her fiancé] both felt they had seen something unusual which was difficult to explain and certainly did not appear to be an optical illusion.'

In a debriefing with Bureau agents, Miss Richards recalled that the object was definitely circular in shape, was spinning, and 'was bright as though containing a series of lights in a zig-zag pattern'. The debriefing report continued: 'The object appeared to be flying very low as it came toward them, moving at great speed and gave off no particular sound. The object, to the best of her belief, was at least as wide as the highway and appeared no more than two to four feet in thickness.'

The apparent lack of depth associated with this particular object suggests to me that it was most probably remotely piloted (much like that

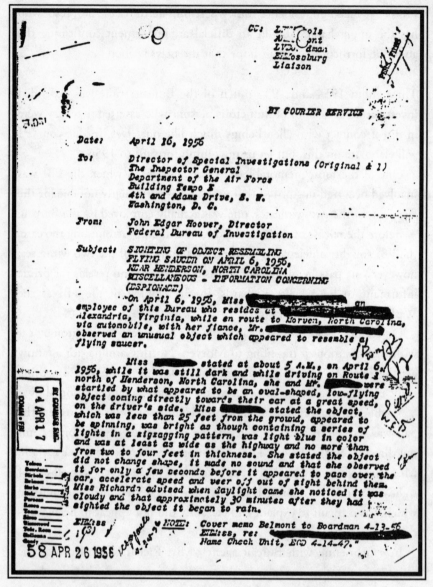

CC: L... ols
N... ont
LVD.. dma..
Ellosburg
Liaison

BY COURIER SERVICE

Date:		April 16, 1956

To:		Director of Special Investigations (Original & 1)
		The Inspector General
		Department of the Air Force
		Building Tempo E
		4th and Adams Drive, S. W.
		Washington, D. C.

From:		John Edgar Hoover, Director
		Federal Bureau of Investigation

Subject:	SIGHTING OF OBJECT RESEMBLING
		FLYING SAUCER ON APRIL 6, 1956,
		NEAR HENDERSON, NORTH CAROLINA
		MISCELLANEOUS - INFORMATION CONCERNING
		(ESPIONAGE)

On April 6, 1956, Miss _____ an employee of this Bureau who resides at Alexandria, Virginia, while en route to Norven, North Carolina, via automobile, with her fiance, Mr. _____ observed an unusual object which appeared to resemble a flying saucer.

Miss _____ stated at about 5 A.M., on April 6, 1956, while it was still dark and while driving on Route 1 north of Henderson, North Carolina, she and Mr. _____ were startled by what appeared to be an oval-shaped, low-flying object coming directly towards their car at a great speed, on the driver's side. Miss _____ stated the object, which was less than 25 feet from the ground, appeared to be spinning, was bright as though containing a series of lights in a zigzagging pattern, was light blue in color and was at least as wide as the highway and no more than from two to four feet in thickness. She stated the object did not change shape, it made no sound and that she observed it for only a few seconds before it appeared to pass over the car, accelerate speed and veer off out of sight behind them. Miss Richards advised when daylight came she noticed it was cloudy and that approximately 30 minutes after they had sighted the object it began to rain.

EX.ss		NOTE:	Cover memo Belmont to Boardman 4-13-56
(3)			EX.ss, re:
				Name Check Unit, ECO 4-14-47.

58 APR 26 1956

A 1956 UFO encounter involving a then-serving member of the FBI.

seen over Chicago on 11 March 1952), rather than a manned vehicle. Unless, of course, some of our otherworldly visitors are exceedingly slight in stature!

It is also interesting to note that Miss Richards was subsequently described as being: 'one of our best employees, [and] stated heretofore she has placed little credence in "flying saucer" stories and felt that had she and her boyfriend not seen the same object she would be inclined to think she had imagined something.'

From my own research, I know that many people find it difficult to accept the reality of the UFO phenomenon without having had first-hand experience; however, it is safe to say that when faced with something truly bizarre (as by definition the UFO mystery is), many discover that their lives are for ever changed.

Subsequent to the encounter, on 10 April 1956 a memorandum was drawn up for the attention of the Air Force, which Miss Richards carefully scanned for accuracy. A memo of 13 April adds:

[Miss Richards] advised she had seen the object for only a few seconds, that it was still dark when she observed it, although it was near daylight on April 6, 1956. She stated when daylight came she observed the sky to be cloudy and it started raining approximately 30 minutes after she had observed the object. She recalled the object approached their car on the driver's side straight ahead at a height which she thought to be less than 25 feet. She was unable to estimate the speed of the object. She described it as being oval shaped, being very bright and having a light blue color. It made no sound that she could hear. She advised her fiance would be able to state exactly where they had observed the object in North Carolina, inasmuch as he was familiar with that area.

As an examination of the documentation shows, a recommendation was made that all the papers pertaining to the case be forwarded to the FBI's Domestic Intelligence Division for possible liaison with 'interested military agencies'. While there is indeed evidence to show that the matter was discussed with the Air Force's Office of Special Investigations, who would presumably have informed the Bureau of its opinions, the FBI has chosen not to reveal any further data on this particular encounter.

On 20 September 1957, an impressive incident occurred which was brought to the attention of the Bureau, the CIA and the US Air Defense

Command. At a special joint meeting of the Intelligence Advisory Committee and the Watch Committee on 21 September 1957, an FBI liaison supervisor, M.W. Kuhrtz, was apprised of the details. In a comprehensive report sent to Alan Belmont, it was related that '. . . the initial report in this matter was given by the US Air Defence Command to the White House'.

According to the data given to Kuhrtz, a UFO was picked up on radar at the tracking station at Montauk Point, Long Island, New York, at 4 p.m. in the afternoon, travelling in a westerly direction at an altitude of 50,000 feet and a speed of 2,000 knots (or 2,300 miles per hour). Montauk maintained a continuous track of the object for about a minute, after which time it was monitored by a radar tracking facility at Benton, Pennsylvania, where it was monitored for no less than nine minutes. 'Thereafter,' the report continues, 'jamming was reported by several stations westward as far as Chicago.'

Kuhrtz was informed additionally that a decision had been taken to down grade the original reports, since there had been an eleven-minute break in the tracking by the various radar stations, and further that weather stations in the area were of the type that had 'in the past produced false radar "pips" and electronic information'. Nevertheless, the possibility that the target had been a structured object was not dismissed, although the theory that it was Soviet in origin was considered unlikely:

> The Watch Committee concluded that, 'It is highly improbable that a Soviet operation is responsible for the unidentified flying object reports of September, 1957.' The Watch Committee in considering this matter also concluded that there is no intelligence on Soviet activities which can be related to a missile launching of this type over the US.

Kuhrtz noted that the Watch Committee deemed it most unlikely that the Russians had the capability to dispatch an aircraft over US soil at such speed and altitude, and thereafter make a safe return to the Soviet Union. 'The Soviets are given credit for the capability of a "submarine launched cruise-type missile of low supersonic performance" and a range of about

'500 nautical miles,' Kuhrtz reported; 'however, there is no evidence of the existence of such a missile by the Soviets.'

Since it was determined that the Air Defense Command had yet to come to a completely satisfactory conclusion, Kuhrtz advised Belmont

A two-page paper describing a fast-moving UFO tracked over the United States.

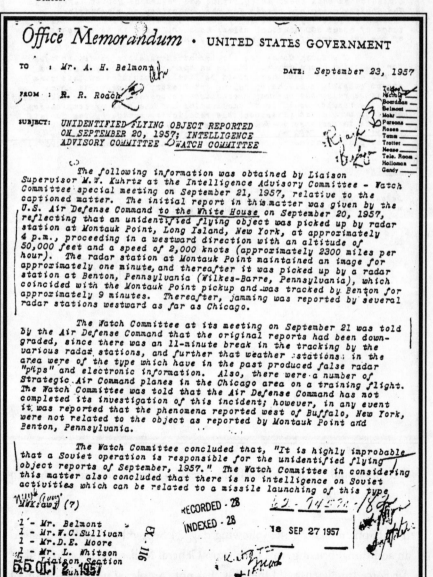

Office Memorandum • UNITED STATES GOVERNMENT

TO : Mr. A. H. Belmont

FROM : R. R. Roach

DATE: September 23, 1957

SUBJECT: UNIDENTIFIED FLYING OBJECT REPORTED ON SEPTEMBER 20, 1957; INTELLIGENCE ADVISORY COMMITTEE WATCH COMMITTEE

Tolson
Nichols
Boardman
Belmont
Mohr
Parsons
Rosen
Tamm
Trotter
Nease
Tele. Room
Holloman
Gandy

The following information was obtained by Liaison Supervisor M.W. Kuhrtz at the Intelligence Advisory Committee - Watch Committee special meeting on September 21, 1957, relative to the captioned matter. The initial report in this matter was given by the U.S. Air Defense Command to the White House on September 20, 1957, reflecting that an unidentified flying object was picked up by radar station at Montauk Point, Long Island, New York, at approximately 4 p.m., proceeding in a westward direction with an altitude of 50,000 feet and a speed of 2,000 knots (approximately 2300 miles per hour). The radar station at Montauk Point maintained an image for approximately one minute, and thereafter it was picked up by a radar station at Benton, Pennsylvania (Wilkes-Barre, Pennsylvania), which coincided with the Montauk Point pickup and was tracked by Benton for approximately 9 minutes. Thereafter, jamming was reported by several radar stations westward as far as Chicago.

The Watch Committee at its meeting on September 21 was told by the Air Defense Command that the original reports had been downgraded, since there was an 11-minute break in the tracking by the various radar stations, and further that weather stations in the area were of the type which have in the past produced false radar "pips" and electronic information. Also, there were a number of Strategic Air Command planes in the Chicago area on a training flight. The Watch Committee was told that the Air Defense Command has not completed its investigation of this incident; however, in any event it was reported that the phenomena reported west of Buffalo, New York, were not related to the object as reported by Montauk Point and Benton, Pennsylvania.

The Watch Committee concluded that, "It is highly improbable that a Soviet operation is responsible for the unidentified flying object reports of September, 1957." The Watch Committee in considering this matter also concluded that there is no intelligence on Soviet activities which can be related to a missile launching of this type.

MWK:aw (7)

1 - Mr. Belmont
1 - Mr. W.C. Sullivan
1 - Mr. D.E. Moore
1 - Mr. L. Whitson
1 - Liaison Section

RECORDED - 28
INDEXED - 28

18 SEP 27 1957

55 OCT 2 1957

Memorandum Roach to Belmont
UNIDENTIFIED FLYING OBJECT REPORTED
ON SEPTEMBER 20, 1957; INTELLIGENCE
ADVISORY COMMITTEE - WATCH COMMITTEE

over the U.S. It is unlikely that a Soviet aircraft could conduct
a mission at this speed and altitude and return to Soviet territory.
The Soviets are given credit for the capability of a "submarine
launched cruise-type missile of low supersonic performance" and a
range of about 500 nautical miles; however, there is no evidence
of the existence of such a missile by the Soviets.

The Watch Committee also examined possible Soviet motives
for launching a one way missile on an operation over the U.S., and
it was concluded that there would be little motivation at this time
except possibly a psychological or retaliatory motive. The Watch
Committee ruled out one way reconnaissance operations on the likelihood
that the results would be of small value and the risk of compromise
would be very great. (This possible retaliatory motive by the Soviets
could be in response to U.S. flights to a U.S. "Project Aquatone"
flight over the USSR which was detected on September 9, 1956, by
Soviet planes and mentioned in my memorandum of September 19, 1957.)

ACTION:

The above is submitted for information. Since the Air
Defense Command is still investigating this report, further information
will be reported as a more conclusive evaluation can be made.

- 2 -

that he would inform him of any breaking details as and when such
became available.

It so happens that on the following day, 24 September, the FBI received
an additional briefing, this time from General Millard Lewis, Director of
Air Force Intelligence. '[T]he ADC has not completed its investigation of

the evidence on this matter,' Assistant-to-the-Director Belmont was told; 'there are continuing indications that the object detected was an atmospheric phenomenon. The radar pickups now reflect speed variations in the object's course, ranging from 1,500 miles per hour to 4,500 miles per hour. This latter speed is improbable according to US scientific theory for any type [of] flying object which this could conceivably be. General Lewis added that the present sun spots are associated with the peculiar radar activity throughout the globe and that this could have some cause for the captioned report.'

Of course, the Air Defense Command could have noted (but didn't) that the 'improbable' speed of the target was based on estimates of then current terrestrial technology. If some UFOs are extraterrestrial in origin, it is almost certain that they have the capability to outperform our most advanced aircraft today, never mind forty years ago!

Although a note attached to this report stated: 'Liaison will report further information on this matter as quickly as it is developed,' the FBI were apparently not tasked further, and accepted the findings of the Air Defense Command. Or did they? A study of the internal distribution list attached to the Bureau's memorandum of 24 September shows that copies were forwarded to, among others, Lish Whitson and William C. Sullivan. For his part, Whitson was a highly regarded Bureau expert on the Soviets, who, as an Espionage Section man, had served on numerous inter-agency committees; while Sullivan was later involved intimately in the FBI's counterintelligence programme, COINTELPRO.[5] If the Bureau wished to shed further light on the events of 20 September 1957, they could not have turned to two better-qualified individuals.

Two months later, the high-level discussions between the Bureau and Air Force Intelligence continued. Following the launch of the Russian Sputnik satellite in October 1957, there was a sudden increase in the number of UFO sightings reported over the US. There is a possibility that some sightings were the result of overexcitement and concern that, at the height of the Cold War, the Soviets were venturing into space, but other cases cannot be dismissed so easily. A Bureau report of 12 November 1957 reads:

Within the past two weeks reports . . . have increased tremendously and some of the more serious have been described as follows: An object had landed in Nebraska with six people aboard, the persons had talked to a Nebraska farmer and then sped off into space; a fiery object was seen flashing across the southern skies from Albany, Georgia, to Miami, Florida; a Coast Guard cutter had sighted a huge object flying over the Gulf of Mexico, and persons in the Southwestern states while driving their cars have allegedly seen UFOs that caused the engines in their automobiles to stop . . .

The Air Force is following these sightings closely and all reports are submitted to the Air Technical and Intelligence Center, at Wright-Patterson Air Force Base in Ohio where they are evaluated and analyzed. In the event any of the future reports appear to be authentic, the Air Force will immediately notify the Bureau, keeping in mind our particular interest in matters concerning espionage and sabotage.

The Bureau's comment on witnesses' malfunctioning cars is worthy of note, and actually parallels a number of classic cases reported in England. As I mentioned in my previous book, *A Covert Agenda* (Simon & Schuster, 1997), in 1962 the RAF Police conducted an investigation into a report filed by one Ronald Wildman, whose car was rendered inoperative when he came face to face with an oval-shaped UFO on a lonely road in the early hours of a February morning.[6] Is it asking too much to suspect that the same UFO had also been operating in US skies five years previously?

Before closing this chapter, I want to make mention of two UFO encounters reported to the Bureau in late 1957. In a memorandum headed REPORTS OF FLYING DISKS FOREIGN MISCELLANEOUS, and prepared by the Legal Attaché at Havana, Cuba, it was related: 'The Havana daily newspaper "Diario de la Marina", November 12, 1957, carried a dispatch datelined November 11, 1957, at Pinar del Rio, Cuba, reporting that [two witnesses] who had just arrived in that town from the Matahambre Mines in Pinar del Rio Province, claimed that they had seen a flying disc in the shape of a man's hat hovering over the general area of Matahambre for several minutes.'

The report continued: 'They claimed that this disc was larger than ordinary airplanes normally seen in that area and that it was completely silent in its flight. They said that it disappeared at a very high speed toward the sea. There was no further descriptive information furnished in this newspaper article. It is noted that Matahambre is located approximately 90 miles to the west of Havana.'

It may not be a coincidence that the sighting over Cuba had been preceded by a further report of a hovering UFO seen in early November, this time over the New York village of Old Brookville. In this particular case, the object was seen by members of both the public and serving law-enforcement officers, and such was the alarm generated by the encounter that, as well as the FBI, the intelligence divisions of both the Army and the Air Force took note of the entire affair. As evidence of this, a Bureau teletype of 7 November from the special agent in charge at New York city reads:

> Unidentified flying objects over incorporated village of Old Brookville, Li, NY. Evening of 11/6/57 [6 November]. Info. concerning. [Source] of Inc. village of Old Brookville advised several residents of that area and member of Police Department have reported sighting two red lights hovering in air that vicinity. Lights appear to be an even distance apart and to be joined together. At one time these lights lit up and seemed to cast a red dust or fog in surrounding air. [Source] advised he reported above info to Mitchell Air Force Base and Roselyn Airfield. Both advised receiving numerous reports re above and Roselyn Air Field said aircraft are investigating matter. [Source] advised above info broadcast on news program local radio station. OSI, G-2, CAA in area advised. End.

Of those both past and present who have attempted to force the US government to reveal the full extent of its knowledge surrounding the UFO mystery, one name stands out – Donald E. Keyhoe. Prior to his death on 29 November 1988 at the age of 91, Keyhoe had worked relentlessly to break down the barriers of secrecy constructed by the American military and intelligence community, and as Director of the National

Investigations Committee on Aerial Phenomena succeeded in uncovering the details of a wealth of UFO encounters involving, primarily, the US Air Force.

The author of five highly regarded books on the subject, Keyhoe graduated from the US Naval Academy in 1919 and for five years served with the Marine Corps. Following his retirement from the Corps (the unfortunate result of injuries sustained in a plane crash), Keyhoe worked as an editor with the *Coast and Geodetic Survey*, and was later employed as an aide to the renowned aviator Charles Lindbergh. During the 1930s and 1940s he turned his hand to freelance writing and ultimately went on to become one of the most respected and famed UFO researchers of the 1950s.

On 22 September 1958, Keyhoe wrote to the Bureau requesting that its position on the UFO subject be made clear. 'Have FBI Agents told witnesses not to talk about UFO sightings?' asked Keyhoe. 'Does the Bureau make character investigations of UFO witnesses in some cases?'

This concerned the Bureau somewhat, and a memorandum was drawn up on 26 September which addressed the issues raised by Keyhoe:

> Subject [Donald E. Keyhoe], Director of National Investigations Committee on Aerial Phenomena, by letter of 9/22/58 requested particulars of Bureau's participation concerning unidentified flying objects. The committee he heads is described on letterhead as 'A privately supported fact finding civilian committee serving the public interests' and he lists several prominent individuals among 'our Board members and Special Advisers.' He is a retired Marine . . .
>
> Keyhoe has been known to the Bureau since 1935 and was, and may still be, a free-lance writer . . .

The Bureau was not at all happy about having to answer Keyhoe's direct questioning, and did its utmost to avoid having to do so: 'The answers which have been furnished are designed to avoid the charge we have not answered questions yet they are broad in nature to avoid his apparent pointed inquiries. His request for an interview with a Bureau official concerning our policy concerning unidentified flying objects has been side-stepped since there appears to be no point in discussing this matter further with him.' And the answers the Bureau furnished to Keyhoe were indeed 'broad in nature':

> . . . This Bureau does not have information on unidentified fly-ing objects which can be released. This does not imply that this Bureau has information concerning unidentified flying objects which cannot be released . . .
>
> Possible communication with extraterrestrial vehicles from another planet, should the unidentified flying objects prove to be extraterrestrial, is not a function of the Federal Bureau of Investigation. This Bureau is, of course, interested in any aspect of any development which would affect the internal security of the United States . . .
>
> Since this Bureau's policy in connection with unidentified fly-ing objects has been fully set forth above, you may feel that the requested interview is not now necessary . . .

During the remaining fifteen months of the 1950s the FBI's involve-ment in the UFO subject tailed off somewhat, but a new decade was dawning and it would not be long before the Bureau found itself once again caught up in the mystery of the saucers . . .

CHAPTER 6

SOCORRO AND BEYOND

ONE OF THE MORE UNUSUAL UFO CASES BROUGHT TO THE ATTENTION OF the Bureau in the 1960s was that involving Joseph Perry of Grand Blanc, Michigan, who was interviewed by agents of the Detroit FBI office on 5 March 1960, and four days later became the subject of the following memorandum:

> Mr Perry advised that he operates a Pizza House at 3075 Edwards Street, Grand Blanc, and that he has been a professional photographer for thirty years. He explained that he has a hobby of taking photographs of the moon through a home-made telescope. At about 1.00 a.m. on February 21, 1960, he took some photographs of the moon and after developing same, he put them in his viewer and in one photograph he observed what appears to be a flying object somewhere between the end of his telescope and the surface of the moon. He said that when blown up, this object is flat on the bottom, is oval shaped, and appears to have a fluorescent glow around the entire object, and that it is apparently moving as it has a vapor trail running behind it. He has taken over one thousand pictures of the moon and has never seen anything resembling this object.

Certain that he had photographed something truly anomalous, Perry duly furnished the FBI with the relevant photograph for expert analysis.

As a teletype message of 9 March 1960 shows, the FBI in turn contacted the Air Force Office of Special Investigations at Selfridge Air Force Base, who assumed custody of Perry's picture. However, the Bureau continued to monitor aspects of the case, particularly in light of the fact that Perry's

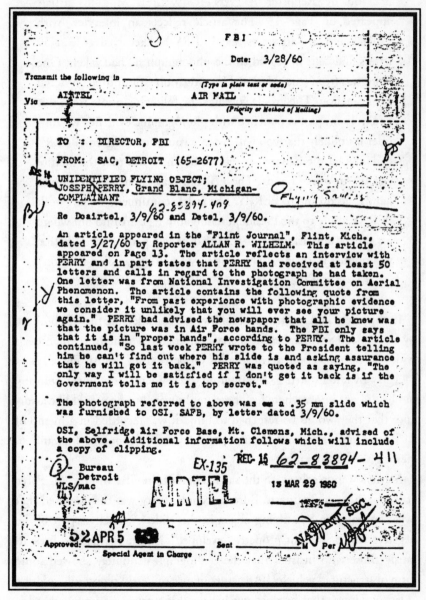

In 1960, the Detroit office of the FBI monitored the activities of UFO witness Joseph Perry.

photograph had caught the attention of the media. A Bureau Airtel of 28
March to the FBI Director, J. Edgar Hoover, reveals:

> An article appeared in the 'Flint Journal', Flint, Michigan, dated
> 3/27/60 by Reporter ALLAN R. WILHELM. This article
> appeared on Page 13. The article reflects an interview with
> PERRY and in part states that PERRY had received at least 50
> letters and calls in regard to the photograph he had taken. One
> letter was from [the] National Investigation Committee on Aerial
> Phenomenon. The article contains the following quote from this
> letter, 'From past experience with photographic evidence we con-
> sider it unlikely that you will ever see your picture again.' PERRY
> had advised the newspaper that all he knew was that the picture
> was in Air Force hands. The FBI only says that it is in 'proper
> hands', according to PERRY. The article continued, 'So last week
> PERRY wrote to the President telling him he can't find out where
> his slide is and asking assurance that he will get it back.' PERRY
> was quoted as saying, 'The only way I will be satisfied if I don't
> get it back is if the Government tells me it is top secret.'

In the weeks and months that followed, a considerable file was built up
by the Bureau with respect to Perry's photograph, much of which dealt
with his concerns about retrieving his property from the Air Force.

'Perry by letter dated 3-21-60 wrote to President Eisenhower pointing
out he did not know where his photographs were but he would like assurance that they would be returned to him,' it was recorded in a memo of
21 April 1960. 'He pointed out that "thousands are looking forward" to
viewing the photographs.'

Matters were resolved, to the satisfaction of the FBI and the Air Force
at least, when, according to Bureau records, Perry was duly advised that
'what appeared to be a flying object in this slide is actually a part of the
negative which was not properly developed'. Naturally, this did little to
satisfy those who insisted that the photograph genuinely showed some
form of structured vehicle: '[An acquaintance of Perry] reportedly told the
"Detroit Times" that he does not believe this story as he knows that Joe
Perry is very meticulous when he develops pictures; therefore he feels the

slide actually does contain a picture of a flying object,' reported the FBI Michigan office.

Possibly recognising that the controversy surrounding this particular case was likely to run and run, the FBI insisted to all enquirers that this was a matter for the Air Force, not the Bureau, and steered all letters in the Air Force's direction. Indeed, such was the interest in the Perry case that six years later, the Bureau was still receiving correspondence from interested members of the American public: 'Inasmuch as your communication is of interest to another governmental agency, I am referring a copy of it to the Office of Special Investigations, Department of the Air Force,' wrote J. Edgar Hoover on 15 April 1966 to an enquirer asking about the status of the FBI's investigation of Perry's photographs.

Interestingly, Hoover's final comment on the case refers to a local newspaper (possibly the aforementioned *Flint Journal*), which reported that the FBI had had involvement in the Perry affair. As Hoover ominously stated, 'it was necessary for this Bureau to straighten the record with that newspaper . . .'

On 24 April 1964, the FBI found itself implicated in the investigation of what is now considered one of the most credible UFO cases on record. Although there is evidence to suggest that there were a number of witnesses to the encounter, the prime participant was one Lonnie Zamora, a sergeant with the Socorro, New Mexico, Police Department.[1]

At approximately 5.45 p.m. on 24 April, 31-year-old Zamora was pursuing a car which was flagrantly flouting the speed limits on US Highway 85. While still in hot pursuit, Zamora was suddenly startled by a loud roar and brilliant blue 'cone of flame' which emanated from an area to the southwest, some 2,400 feet away.

Realising that this was not an everyday occurrence, Zamora broke off chasing the speeding car and drove his white 1964 Pontiac patrol car in the direction from which the flames and roar surfaced. In order to reach the area in question Zamora was obliged to travel along a little-used road which passed over a number of hills and gullies.

After two or three attempts to drive his car up a gravel-covered incline, Zamora reached a crest, got out of his patrol car and was astonished by the sight that confronted him. Sitting on girder-like legs was a strange 'egg-

'shaped' object, unlike anything Zamora had ever seen before. But that was not all, as Zamora acutely recalled: 'I saw two small figures in what resembled white coveralls, pretty close to the object on its northwest side, as if inspecting it . . . One of the figures seemed to turn as if it heard or saw my car coming. It must have seen me, 'cause when it turned and looked straight at my car, it seemed startled – almost seemed to jump somewhat.'

FBI files on the famous UFO landing at Socorro, New Mexico, in 1964.

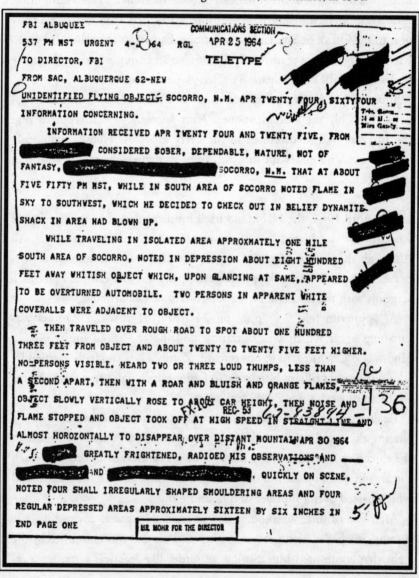

This proved too much for Zamora, who was totally unprepared for the encounter. As an official CIA report on the case reveals:

> Thinking that the object was going to explode [Zamora] became frightened. He turned, ran back to get behind the police car, bumping his leg and losing his glasses on the way. He crouched down, shielding his eyes with his arm while the noise continued

RECTANGULAR TYPE PATTERN AVERAGING ABOUT TWELVE FEET APART.

████ STATES OBJECT WAS OVAL SHAPED, SIMILAR TO FOOTBALL, POSSIBLY TWENTY FEET LONG, AND HAD A RED INSIGNIA ABOUT THIRTY INCHES HIGH AND TWO FEET WIDE, CENTERED ON OBJECT. NO OTHER WITNESSES KNOWN TO NOISE, FLAME OR OBJECT.

████████████ COMMANDER, STALLION RANGE CENTER, SOCORRO, N.M., ADVISED AT ONCE APRIL TWENTY FOUR AND IS HANDLING.

MILITARY PRESENTLY CONDUCTING OPERATION KNOWN AS CLOUD GAP WHICH IS JOINT OPERATION DEPARTMENT OF DEFENSE AND ARMY CONTROL, DISARMAMENT AGENCY IN SOUTHWEST STATES INCLUDING NEW MEXICO. NOT KNOWN IF ABOVE INCIDENT RELATES TO CLOUD GAP.

CONSIDERABLE INTEREST OF PRESS IN MATTER. ALBUQUERQUE CONDUCTING NO INVESTIGATION, IS MAINTAINING LIAISON WITH MILITARY. BUREAU WILL BE ADVISED OF ANY PERTINENT DEVELOPMENTS.

END

WA NHH

FBI WASH DC

TUP

cc Dr Roach

for another 10 seconds. At this time the noise stopped and he looked up. The object had risen to a point about 15–20 feet above the ground and the flame and smoke had ceased to come from the object . . . The object had a red marking about 1 ft or maybe 16 inches in height, shaped like a crescent with a vertical arrow and horizontal line underneath.

The object hovered in this spot for several seconds and then flew off in a SW direction following the contour of the gully. It cleared the dynamite shack by not more than 3 ft. He watched the object disappear in the distance over a point on Highway 85 about 6 miles from where he was standing. The object took about 3 minutes to travel that far. Disappearance was by fading in the distance and at no time did he observe the object to rise more than 20 feet off the ground.[2]

Since Zamora had maintained radio communication with his head-quarters while en route to the landing site, the New Mexico State Police, who operated on the same radio frequency, also realised that something out of the ordinary had occurred.

As luck would have it, at the time of the encounter an FBI agent, J. Arthur Byrnes, was actually at the State Police office in Socorro when Zamora's call came through, as is demonstrated in an FBI report of 8 May 1964:

Special Agent J. Arthur Byrnes, Jr., Federal Bureau of Investigation, stationed at New Mexico, was at Socorro, New Mexico, and at the State Police Office there on business late afternoon of April 24, 1964.

At approximately 5:45 p.m. to 5:50 p.m., Nep Lopez, radio operator in the Socorro County Sheriff's Office, located about thirty feet down the hall from the State Police Office, came into the State Police Office.

Nep Lopez advised Samuel Chavez, New Mexico State Police, that he had just received a radio call from Officer Lonnie Zamora to come to an area about one mile southwest of Socorro. The call was in relation to some unknown object which 'landed and has taken off.' Agent Byrnes finished his work in the State Police Office at Socorro at approximately 6:00 p.m., April 24, 1964, and thereafter proceeded to the site where Officer Zamora, Socorro County Undersheriff James Luckie, Sergeant Samuel Chavez, and Officer Ted Jordan, New Mexico State Police, were assembled.

It may be noted that it has been the observation of Agent Byrnes that Officer Zamora, known intimately for approximately five years, is well regarded as a sober, industrious, and conscientious officer and not given to fantasy.

Officer Zamora was noted to be perfectly sober and somewhat agitated over his experience.

Special Agent Byrnes noted four indentations in the rough ground at the 'site' of the object described by Officer Zamora. These depressions appeared regular in shape, approximately sixteen by six inches rectangular. Each depression seemed to have been made by an object going into the earth at an angle from a center line. Each depression was approximately two inches deep and pushed some earth to the side.

Inside the four depressions were three burned patches of clumps of grass. Other clumps of grass in the same area appeared not to be disturbed. One burned area was outside the four depressions.

There were three circular marks in the earth which were smooth, approximately four inches in diameter and [illegible] in the sandy earth approximately one-eighth of an inch as if a jar lid had been pushed into the sand.

No other person was noted in the area the night of April 24, 1964. No other objects were noted in the area possibly connected with the incident related by Officer Zamora.

So far as could be noted, there were no houses or inhabited dwellings in the area or in sight of the area.

And the FBI's involvement in the encounter does not end there. As the author and researcher Ray Stanford noted in his authoritative book on the case, *Socorro Saucer*, the Bureau went to great lengths to ensure that its involvement in the incident remained classified. In a report on Zamora's sighting prepared by Captain Richard T. Holder of the US Army, it was remarked: 'NOTE: By request of agent J. Arthur Byrnes, Jr., please do not refer to the Federal Bureau of Investigation as participating in any fashion – use of local law enforcement authorities is acceptable.'

More intriguing, with respect to Zamora's assertion that 'two small figures' accompanied the UFO, Byrnes advised Zamora: 'It will be better if you don't publicly mention seeing the two small figures in white. No one will believe you anyhow.' Was there an official desire on the Bureau's part to ensure that any discussion of the 'humanoid' angle was kept to a minimum? And if so, why?

Documentation shows that the Zamora encounter was not a one-off. For example, a Bureau teletype of 27 April 1964 refers to a similar incident which occurred at La Maderia, New Mexico, during the same few days. According to the FBI Albuquerque Office, the witness, described as 'age thirty-five, sober and frightened' was tending some 'noisy horses at about 1:00 a.m., and located about three hundred feet from house, something shaped like a butane tank, possibly twelve to fourteen feet high, and [as] long as a telephone pole. Apparently on the ground and surrounded with blue white flame, which appeared to come from port holes.' The document continues:

> He watched scene for about one minute, when flame went out. Object not noted to move, was silent at all times. [Witness] went into house, told father, who laughed at him. Next morning he visited site, saw smoldering area. Later in day saw a state police officer and related incident to him.
>
> [Censored] continued that he checked site at seven thirty p.m. four twenty-six last, noted scorched circular area about thirty to forty feet in diameter. He noted one rectangular, V-shaped indentation in ground, eight by twelve inches, and about three to four inches deep.

In addition to the above, a further Bureau report remarks that: 'Liaison will be maintained with [censored] who advised he has received several more reported incidents to which he will give attention.'

Indeed, it now appears that the landing at Socorro was a relatively minor event which pales into insignificance when examined in its full context. In 1983, the Emmy award-winning producer, director, writer and editor of documentary films, Linda Howe, secured an interview with Richard Doty, who at the time was serving with the US Air Force. The sighting by Zamora, said Doty, was a mistake: 'We, or they . . . someone blew the time and coordinates. That was an advanced military scout ship. We got it corrected and they came back to where they were supposed to be at Holloman [Air Force Base] the next morning at 6 a.m., April 25, 1964.'[3]

In 1996, the investigator Dan Pinchas received some amazing information from a former government source who was conversant with what lay behind the Holloman landing. According to the informant, an alien spacecraft crashed near Roswell, New Mexico, in July 1947 (we'll hear more on this later). From the wreckage, one live and five dead extraterrestrial creatures were recovered. Pinchas's source further added that the creature that survived the initial crash went on to remain in captivity for some three years before it died.

More astonishing is the claim that in April 1964, at the pre-arranged Holloman landing, the bodies of the six 'crew members' recovered at Roswell in 1947 were returned to their newly-arrived comrades! As Pinchas was told:

> 'Regarding the landing of a UFO at Holloman on April 25, 1964, yes, it did happen. The only exchange that occurred was us giving back six alien bodies. In an exchange of good will, the aliens provided us with several 'items' of advanced technology. No further comment on that . . . To the best of my knowledge, these aliens have not returned . . . Regarding the alleged cover-up, I don't know the government's reason. I am no longer employed by the government nor am I a spokesman for the government. I really don't know. As far as the government's alleged effort to hide information, there was a disinformation operation, but that's all I can say.'[4]

Is it possible that during the course of looking into the sighting reported by Officer Lonnie Zamora, the FBI uncovered details pertaining to the information related by Doty? If that was the case, it would go some way towards explaining Agent J. Arthur Byrnes's comment to Zamora that: 'It will be better if you don't publicly mention seeing the two small figures in white.'

If a meeting between representatives of the human race and an alien species did occur back in April 1964, and the incident at Socorro was indirectly related to that event, then it is clear why there should have been such intense interest in the case on the part of the FBI, CIA, Army and Air Force. I leave the final words to Hector J. Quintanilla, USAF (retired): 'There is no doubt that Lonnie Zamora saw an object which left quite an impression on him. There is also no question about Zamora's reliability . . . This is the best documented case on record . . .'[5]

When in 1964 a UFO researcher and US Army employee, Larry Bryant, wrote an article, 'Let's Challenge the UFO Censors', which addressed his UFO-related dealings with elements of the American military, the Bureau was apprised quickly of the nature of the article. A report dated 23 May 1964, to Cartha DeLoach, the former assistant director of the Federal Bureau of Investigation, states:

> On 5–21–64 the Department of Defense delivered at the Bureau a manuscript by [Larry Bryant] entitled 'Let's Challenge the UFO (Unidentified Flying Objects) Censors.' The Department of the Army, according to the transmittal form from the Department of Defense, has no objection to the publication of the article. The FBI's attention was directed to page 6. Also included with the manuscript was a copy of the author's transmittal letter to the Department of the Army stating he would like to know the name, rank/grade, title and office of each person who actually conducts the review of Bryant's article. A review of the article revealed it is a criticism of the Department of Defense's policy with regard to issuing clearances of articles relative to Unidentified Flying Objects (UFO), particularly when the author is employed by the US Army as in the case of Bryant. The article is in essence a history of Bryant's problems in getting articles published on UFO.

References to the FBI are as follows: On page 2, Bryant indicates he will reveal the role played by the FBI in monitoring UFO research activities of Army civilian employees. On page 6, Bryant refers to his being interviewed on 9–17–63 by Special Agent [deleted] of our Norfolk Office. Bryant states [the] Special Agent contacted him in response to Bryant's letter of 7–23–63 to the Sheriff of Sussex County, Virginia, requesting UFO sighting data . . .

Bryant claims he asked SA [deleted] if it was customary for the FBI to question people who expressed an interest in UFO. SA [deleted] replied in the negative and added that 'Since his office was queried . . . he was just seeking information on which he could write a "memorandum for the files."' Bryant also states that SA [deleted] volunteered the following: 'If the FBI has any such data (on UFO sightings), it is probably of an intelligence nature and thus would be unavailable to the public and to private individuals.'

It transpired that the Bureau office had been brought into the picture because 'Bryant has directed a voluminous amount of correspondence to military officials in the area and as Bryant was employed by the Department of the Army, Fort Eustis, Virginia, the G-2 Section of the Second Army, Fort Meade, Maryland, was conducting a background check of Bryant . . . Bryant was interviewed on 9/7/63 [7 September] by SA [deleted] in order to obtain background information concerning him in order to reply to the correspondence from the [agency name deleted] and the US Naval Base, Norfolk, Virginia.'

The Bureau added that: '. . . the reference to the FBI on page 6 of Bryant's manuscript is not completely true. However, it has the effect of leaving the wrong impression; the FBI was not investigating Bryant but was merely interviewing him in order to respond to inquiries directed to us from other agencies.'

Here we see the undeniable proof that as a result of Bryant's 'voluminous amount of correspondence to military officials' on the UFO subject, the authorities responded by having him checked out by the Bureau. If the US government has nothing to hide, then why the need for such extraordinary actions on its part? And surveillance of Bryant's activities in the UFO field did not end there, as Bryant noted in 1990:

> Back in the winter of 1971–72, when I was employed by the Industrial College of the Armed Forces in Washington, DC, two of my superiors there, USAF Col. Samuel B. Adams and Army Col. Patrick J. Kenney, called me into their office to discuss their role in the College's decision not to process my immediate supervisor's recommendation that I be granted a Top Secret security clearance. They explained to me that the College's secretary, Army Col. John S. Sullivan, had expressed reluctance to process the recommendation because of the vigor and determination by which I had been pursuing UFO research during the past dozen years or so.[6]

Although US intelligence agencies such as the CIA, Defense Intelligence Agency, and National Security Agency have, in recent years, released into the public domain a wealth of hitherto-unseen documents on the UFO issue, I am firmly convinced that many more pages of material remain exempt from public disclosure, primarily for reasons affecting national security. For example, Bruce Maccabee, a US Navy physicist, has confirmed that the one-time custodian of the CIA's UFO files, Dr Christopher Green, admitted to him that, in addition to the publicly acknowledged one thousand or so UFO documents held by the CIA, the Agency had in its possession considerably more papers: 'From what I recall,' said Maccabee, 'Green probably said there were many more documents, maybe as many as 15,000 documents.'[7] Needless to say, on the record, the CIA will neither confirm nor deny that this is the case.

In light of the above, I am certain that it is an ongoing concern of the US intelligence community that someone with high-level clearance, and perhaps sympathetic to the views of researchers such as myself, will take it upon themselves to breach security and leak into the public domain highly classified UFO information that would otherwise never have seen the light of day. Perhaps something of that nature occurred in 1965.

A heavily censored Bureau memorandum of 2 September 1965 gives an indication that a source within the National Aeronautics and Space

Administration (NASA) had access to incredible UFO data, and furthermore that the same individual was covertly passing it on to persons without official clearance.

According to the memorandum, 'a source' had advised the FBI office at

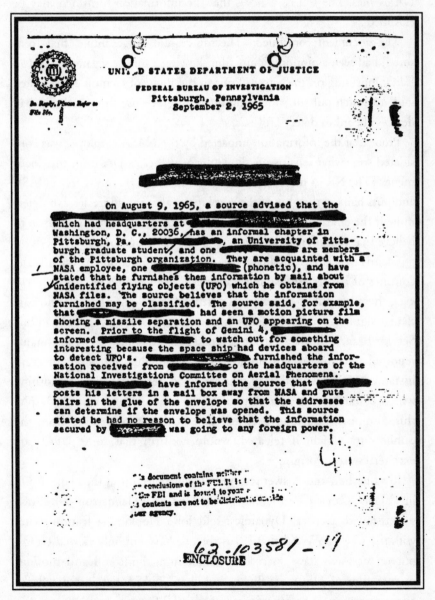

According to a 1965 FBI paper, NASA had at its disposal sensitive data relating to UFO encounters involving US astronauts.

Pittsburgh, Pennsylvania, that two people (one of whom was a graduate student at Pittsburgh University) were 'acquainted with a NASA employee, [name censored], and have stated that he furnishes them information by mail about unidentified flying objects (UFO) which he obtains from NASA files. The source believes that the information furnished may be classified'.

The document continued: 'The source said, for example, that [censored] had seen a motion picture film showing a missile separation and an UFO appearing on the screen. Prior to the flight of Gemini 4, [censored said] to watch out for something interesting because the space ship had devices aboard to detect UFOs.'

Proof that the information imparted by the NASA employee was considered somewhat sensitive is shown by a further extract from the document: '[The NASA mole] posts his letters in a mail box away from NASA and puts hairs in the glue of the envelope so that the addressee can determine if the envelope was opened. This source stated he had no reason to believe that the information was going to any foreign power.'

Claims that US astronauts have seen unusual phenomena outside the confines of Earth's atmosphere have never been denied by NASA; however, there is a public belief on its part that such sightings are of no particular significance, as the following statement issued by NASA's Public Service Branch shows: 'During several space missions NASA astronauts reported phenomena not immediately explainable. However, in every instance NASA satisfied itself that what had been observed was nothing which could be termed abnormal in the space environment.' Despite this, rumours have long persisted that NASA is concealing from the public data which, if released, would confirm that some UFOs are extraterrestrial in origin.

In a question-and-answer session following a lecture at the planetarium in Calgary, Canada, in the late 1960s, Dr Garry Henderson, a research scientist with General Dynamics, told John Hopkins, a feature writer with the *Calgary Herald*, that US astronauts have not only viewed UFOs, but on occasion have succeeded in obtaining both still and motion-picture film of UFOs in flight, and that, 'NASA has instructed the astronauts never to breathe a word of their UFO encounters'.[8]

Henderson's revelations that NASA has in its possession actual movie footage of UFOs lend a great deal of credence to the claims of the NASA individual cited by the FBI in September 1965.

I do not know what became of the NASA source, but there can be no doubt from reading the relevant FBI records that his name was known to the Bureau. Presumably, therefore, the FBI would have informed NASA that one of its employees was talking out of turn. That the FBI was apparently not tasked with this matter again (at least, this is the inference one gets from reading the available papers) suggests that, whoever the source was, he was swiftly and effectively silenced.

Although not widely known, at various times since 1947 the FBI has taken more than a passing interest in monitoring publications on the UFO subject, much like the one you are reading at this very moment! To illustrate, June 1966 saw the first printing by Lyle Stuart publishers of Frank Edwards's book, *Flying Saucers – Serious Business*. By October of that year Edwards's book was in its third printing and was also available in paperback. On 16 October it was announced in the 'This World' supplement of San Francisco-based newspaper, the *Examiner & Chronicle*, that the Congressional Representative of Michigan (and later US President), Gerald Ford, was pressing for Congress to look into the UFO matter. It was also announced that the US Air Force had commissioned a University of Colorado physics professor, Edward U. Condon, to conduct an in-depth study of unidentified flying objects.

An FBI memo of 19 October 1966 stated: 'The ["This World"] article also points out that since last summer pressure has been mounting for the establishment of an independent, civilian controlled investigative agency to look into the UFO problem.' The Bureau added: '[Edwards's book] is probably a contributing factor to the current controversy.'

That both Edwards and his book were of interest to the FBI is something spelled out further in the three-page 19 October document:

> In [*Flying Saucers – Serious Business*] Edwards points out that
> flying saucers were observed in the spring of 1946, in
> Scandinavia and Russia (which he points out is about a year
> from the date of the testing of the Alamogordo atomic bomb),
> and the book documents many reports throughout the world of

UFOs since that date, and claims that 1965 was the year of the greatest number of UFO sightings and that these were observed by multiple witnesses. It is author Edwards' contention that UFOs are space vehicles sent to observe activities on earth and

Frank Edwards's 1966 book, *Flying Saucers – Serious Business*, was the subject of a detailed three-page FBI memorandum.

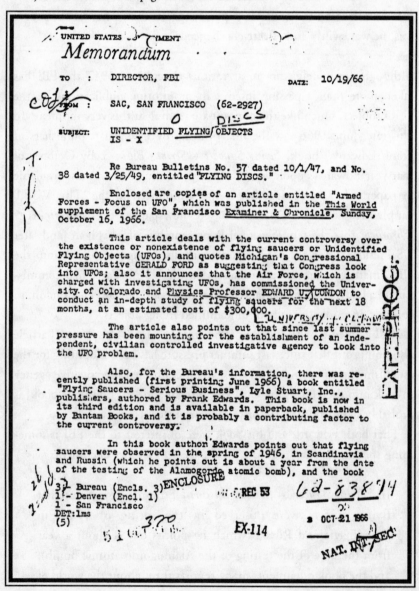

UNITED STATES DEPARTMENT

Memorandum

TO : DIRECTOR, FBI   DATE: 10/19/66

FROM : SAC, SAN FRANCISCO (62-2927)

SUBJECT: UNIDENTIFIED FLYING OBJECTS
IS - X

    Re Bureau Bulletins No. 57 dated 10/1/47, and No. 38 dated 3/25/49, entitled "FLYING DISCS."

    Enclosed are copies of an article entitled "Armed Forces - Focus on UFO", which was published in the This World supplement of the San Francisco Examiner & Chronicle, Sunday, October 16, 1966.

    This article deals with the current controversy over the existence or nonexistence of flying saucers or Unidentified Flying Objects (UFOs), and quotes Michigan's Congressional Representative GERALD FORD as suggesting that Congress look into UFOs; also it announces that the Air Force, which is charged with investigating UFOs, has commissioned the University of Colorado and Physics Professor EDWARD U. CONDON to conduct an in-depth study of flying saucers for the next 18 months, at an estimated cost of $300,000.

    The article also points out that since last summer pressure has been mounting for the establishment of an independent, civilian controlled investigative agency to look into the UFO problem.

    Also, for the Bureau's information, there was recently published (first printing June 1966) a book entitled "Flying Saucers - Serious Business", Lyle Stuart, Inc., publishers, authored by Frank Edwards. This book is now in its third edition and is available in paperback, published by Bantam Books, and it is probably a contributing factor to the current controversy.

    In this book author Edwards points out that flying saucers were observed in the spring of 1946, in Scandinavia and Russia (which he points out is about a year from the date of the testing of the Alamogordo atomic bomb), and the book

3 - Bureau (Encls. 3) ENCLOSURE
1 - Denver (Encl. 1)
1 - San Francisco
DET:lms
(5)

REC 53   62-83874

EX-114   OCT 21 1966

the Air Force, which is charged with the responsibility of investigating UFOs, has deliberately withheld information and given misleading explanations because it fears a mass panic by the public if the public were told the truth.

The book describes UFOs as polished metal objects, radiating heat and light (sufficient to have burned witnesses who were too

SF 62-2927
DET:lms

documents many reports throughout the world of UFOs since that date, and claims that 1965 was the year of the greatest number of UFO sightings and that these were observed by multiple witnesses. It is author Edwards' contention that UFOs are space vehicles sent to observe activities on earth and the Air Force, which is charged with the responsibility of investigating UFOs, has deliberately withheld information and given misleading explanations because it fears a mass panic by the public if the public were told the truth.

The book describes UFOs as polished metal objects, radiating heat and light (sufficient to have burned witnesses who were too near), and emitting some force field that interferes with electromagnetic instruments and power sources. Colors range from brilliant white to dull reds and brilliant orange. Some objects have carried blinking lights. There are three basic shapes: 1) zeppelin-shaped ships up to 300 feet long; 2) disk-shaped objects ranging from a few feet in diameter to 100 feet, with many reported at about 30 feet diameter; and 3) egg-shaped objects, which according to the author are the ones most recently sighted.

According to the book, the objects move silently and attain fantastic speeds, yet can hover motionless in mid-air; they have been reported to land and to take off with great speed, usually with a burst of light from the underside, which in some cases has left the ground beneath them scorched.

Many of the persons named in the book who have reported them are reliable individuals, including law enforcement officers, military personnel on official duty, military pilots, commercial airline pilots, civilian defense officials, etc. A number of photographs of the objects have been reproduced in the book, some reportedly taken by reputable persons. Many reported sightings are from atomic and missile research areas.

Wreckage of crashed saucers has been reportedly recovered on at least three occasions, in one case described as a magnesium alloy, in another as pure magnesium, and in a third case, attributed to an official of the Canadian government, the material was described as an exceptionally hard unknown metal, actually a matrix of magnesium orthosilicate which contained thousands of 15-micron metal spheres throughout, and showing evidence of micro-meteorites on its surface.

- 2 -

SF 62-2927
DET:lms

A few witnesses have reported seeing crewmen who
hand landed from the objects, who are described as three and
a half to four feet tall, wearing what appear to be space suits
and helmets.

Author Edwards concludes this book with a prediction
that in the near future UFOs will make an "overt landing" or
deliberate contact with earth.

A copy of this letter is being directed to Denver,
in view of the contract awarded to Dr. EDWARD U. CONDON.

The above is being called to the Bureau's attention
in view of the press report of mounting pressure for a civilian
controlled investigative agency to handle UFO matters.

- 3 -

near), and emitting some force field that interferes with electromagnetic instruments and power sources. Colors range from brilliant white to dull reds and brilliant orange. Some objects have
carried blinking lights. There are three basic shapes: 1) Zeppelin-
shaped ships up to 300 feet long; 2) disk-shaped objects ranging
from a few feet in diameter to 100 feet, with many reported at

about 30 feet diameter; and 3) egg-shaped objects, which according to the author are the ones most recently sighted.

According to the book, the objects move silently and attain fantastic speeds, yet can hover motionless in mid-air; they have been reported to land and to take off with great speed, usually with a burst of light from the underside, which in some cases has left the ground beneath them scorched.

Many of the persons named in the book who have reported them are reliable individuals, including law enforcement officers, military personnel on official duty, military pilots, commercial airline pilots, civilian defense officials, etc. A number of photographs of the objects have been reproduced in the book, some reportedly taken by reputable persons. Many reported sightings are from atomic and missile research areas.

Wreckage of crashed saucers has been reportedly recovered on at least three occasions, in one case described as a magnesium alloy, in another as pure magnesium, and in a third case, attributed to an official of the Canadian government, the material was described as an exceptionally hard unknown metal, actually a matrix of magnesium orthosilicate which contained thousands of 15-micron metal spheres throughout, and showing evidence of micro-meteorites on its surface.

A few witnesses have reported seeing crewmen who had landed from the objects, who are described as three and a half to four feet tall, wearing what appear to be space suits and helmets.

Author Edwards concludes this book with a prediction that in the near future UFOs will make an 'overt landing' or deliberate contact with earth.

A copy of this letter is being directed to Denver, in view of the contract awarded to Dr Edward U. Condon.

The above is being called to the Bureau's attention in view of the press report of mounting pressure for a civilian controlled investigative agency to handle UFO matters.

Having discussed the issue of unidentified flying objects with a number of journalists, I know that many view the hypothesis that government and intelligence agencies are taking an interest in the activities of civilian UFO researchers as little more than rank paranoia. Yet, as the remarkably detailed document we saw above shows, those of us who enter into the world of the UFO can expect to soon attract the attention of officialdom.

A further report found in Bureau archives, this time dating from January 1967, relates additional details of the proposed Air Force-sponsored 'Condon investigation':

DR EDWARD CONDON, HEAD OF A GOVERNMENT-FINANCED SCIENTIFIC STUDY OF UNIDENTIFIED FLYING OBJECTS (UFO), SAID TODAY HE HAD RECEIVED A LETTER TELLING HIM WHEN AND WHERE A FLYING SAUCER WOULD LAND ON EARTH.

CONDON, PROFESSOR OF PHYSICS AT THE UNIVERSITY OF COLORADO, SAID HE WOULD WRITE TO THE MAN AND ASK HIM ON WHAT BASIS HE MADE THE PREDICTION.

'HE GAVE ME THE EXACT DATE AND THE EXACT LOCATION THE SAUCER WOULD LAND [AND] SAID IT WOULD BE MANNED BY PERSONS FROM ANOTHER PLANET,' CONDON SAID.

'HE SUGGESTED WE CONTACT THE SPACE TRAVELERS AND MAKE FRIENDS WITH THEM,' THE UNIVERSITY OF COLORADO PROFESSOR SAID. CONDON WOULD NOT DISCLOSE THE NAME OF THE PERSON WHO WROTE THE LETTER, SAY WHERE THE PREDICTED LANDING WOULD TAKE PLACE OR THE DATE. HE DID SAY IT WOULD BE SOME TIME THIS SPRING.

'I'M GOING TO ANSWER THE LETTER TO TRY AND FIND OUT WHAT THE BASIS IS FOR THE MAN'S PREDICTION,' CONDON SAID.

The Bureau seemed none too impressed by Condon's comments, as is shown by the following handwritten note at the base of the document: 'Condon is a publicity hound.' An examination of the handwriting confirms that this brief character assessment of the good professor was written by none other than J. Edgar Hoover himself. This is perhaps not surprising: on 29 May 1946, Hoover had sent to the White House various reports suggesting that an enormous Soviet spy ring in Washington was attempting to obtain information about US atomic energy research. Among the people Hoover believed involved, and 'noted for their pro-Soviet leanings' was none other than Edward U. Condon. According to one of Hoover's sources, Condon was 'nothing more or less than an espionage agent in disguise'.[9] In 1967, apparently, Hoover's feelings towards Condon had not improved.

Almost three years later, on 17 December 1969, the Secretary of the Air Force announced the termination of the US Air Force's only publicly acknowledged UFO research body, Project Blue Book. 'The decision to discontinue UFO investigations was based on an evaluation of a report prepared by the University of Colorado entitled, "Scientific Study of Unidentified Flying Objects"; a review of the University of Colorado's report by the National Academy of Sciences; past UFO studies; and the Air Force's two decades of experience investigating UFO reports,' stated the Air Force.

The salient points of the report were that (a) UFOs demonstrated no threat to national security; (b) UFOs were not a manifestation of advanced technology; and (c) there was no evidence to suggest that any UFOs were extraterrestrial in origin.

Although the available UFO files declassified by the FBI do not reflect Hoover's personal opinions on Condon's work with the Colorado University project, given his suspicions about Condon in the 1940s, I find it inconceivable that Hoover would not have monitored intimately Condon's work for the Air Force in the 1966–9 period. And as history has shown, in its final years Blue Book was little more than a public-relations exercise, with the truly important work undertaken by the US intelligence community. This has led a number of researchers to conclude that the 'Condon Report', as the Colorado University report is generally called, was specifically designed to absolve the Air Force (and by definition, the entire US government) of any further involvement in the UFO subject.

As we have seen, FBI files on Condon's UFO-related work with the Air Force are scant; it should be noted, however, that after Hoover's death on

1 May 1972, his 'Personal and Confidential' files were almost all destroyed by his secretary, Helen Gandy, and the associate director of the Bureau, Clyde Tolson. It has to be said that we simply do not know what, if anything, was contained within those files relating to the UFO mystery.

As public interest in, and media comment on, unidentified flying objects increases, there can be few people who are not at least aware of the term 'alien abduction'. Although something barely acknowledged thirty years ago, as we approach the twenty-first century, more and more seemingly responsible people throughout the planet are reporting bizarre interactions with alien entities.

Examined in the cold light of day, the alien-abduction scenario presents us with a shocking possibility: highly advanced creatures from other worlds are systematically abducting human beings and subjecting them to a variety of medical procedures with the intent of creating a half-human, half-alien race. In the majority of cases where alien abduction has been suspected, the victims (and I do not shirk from portraying them thus) describe hazily remembered encounters with diminutive, insect-like creatures, periods of missing time, feelings of bodily violation, and the distinct impression of having been 'transported' to some form of craft where they are treated, for all intents and purposes, like laboratory rats.

Publicly, the US government professes to having no interest in the abduction mystery; however, some people suggest otherwise. In a 1987 paper, John Lear, a skilled pilot who has previously worked with the CIA, revealed that the American authorities were aware of the abduction issue, and had been since the 1960s. More alarming is that, according to Lear's information, since 1979 there has been increasing concern on the part of the American administration that more and more people are now being routinely abducted, and that the situation is essentially out of control. 'Next time you see a flying saucer and are awed by its obvious display of technology and gorgeous lights of pure colour,' said Lear, 'run like hell!'[10]

At the time of its publication, Lear's paper provoked a high degree of controversy, with many suggesting Lear's claims that the US government was monitoring the 'abductees' were totally without foundation. And yet this is not strictly the case. It so happens that as far back as the 1960s the FBI had in its files actual details of alien abduction incidents. I quote from a Bureau report dated 18 January 1967:

> At 4.10 a.m., January 18 1967, [witness] advised that he desired
> to report that he had observed a large oblong-shaped object

A rare example of an FBI report detailing a 1967 'alien abduction' event.

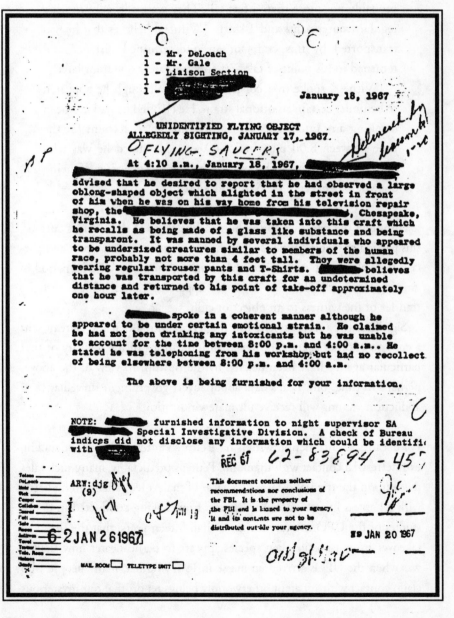

1 - Mr. DeLoach
1 - Mr. Gale
1 - Liaison Section
1 -
1 -

January 18, 1967

UNIDENTIFIED FLYING OBJECT
ALLEGEDLY SIGHTING, JANUARY 17, 1967.

O FLYING SAUCERS

At 4:10 a.m., January 18, 1967,

advised that he desired to report that he had observed a large
oblong-shaped object which alighted in the street in front
of him when he was on his way home from his television repair
shop, the   , Chesapeake,
Virginia. He believes that he was taken into this craft which
he recalls as being made of a glass like substance and being
transparent. It was manned by several individuals who appeared
to be undersized creatures similar to members of the human
race, probably not more than 4 feet tall. They were allegedly
wearing regular trouser pants and T-Shirts.   believes
that he was transported by this craft for an undetermined
distance and returned to his point of take-off approximately
one hour later.

          spoke in a coherent manner although he
appeared to be under certain emotional strain. He claimed
he had not been drinking any intoxicants but he was unable
to account for the time between 8:00 p.m. and 4:00 a.m.. He
stated he was telephoning from his workshop but had no recollect.
of being elsewhere between 8:00 p.m. and 4:00 a.m.

          The above is being furnished for your information.

NOTE: furnished information to night supervisor SA
          Special Investigative Division. A check of Bureau
indices did not disclose any information which could be identifi
with

REC 61 62-83894-45

ARW:djg
(9)

62 JAN 26 1967

This document contains neither
recommendations nor conclusions of
the FBI. It is the property of
the FBI and is loaned to your agency.
It and its contents are not to be
distributed outside your agency.

19 JAN 20 1967

MAIL ROOM ☐ TELETYPE UNIT ☐

which alighted in the street in front of him when he was on his way home from his television repair shop [at] Chesapeake, Virginia. He believes that he was taken into this craft which he recalls as being made of a glass like substance and being transparent. It was manned by several individuals who appeared to be undersized creatures similar to members of the human race, probably not more than 4 feet tall. They were allegedly wearing regular trouser pants and T-shirts. [Witness] believes that he was transported by this craft for an undetermined distance and returned to his point of take-off approximately one hour later.

[Witness] spoke in a coherent manner although he appeared to be under certain emotional strain. He claimed he had not been drinking any intoxicants but he was unable to account for the time between 8:00 p.m. and 4:00 a.m. He stated he was telephoning from his workshop but had no recollection of being elsewhere between 8:00 p.m. and 4:00 a.m.

Although the reference to the human-like attire of the aliens is curious, this particular report contains all of the key elements that are part and parcel of the abduction experience: the initial sighting of a UFO; a period of 'missing time'; recollections of small, apparently alien beings; and the transfer of the witness to an object or craft.

Significantly, a note attached to the report shows that the Bureau sent a copy to another agency; however, all indications of the identity of that particular agency have been deleted by the Bureau. In view of the above, perhaps in time John Lear's data about covert government surveillance of abduction victims will receive ultimate vindication.

For decades science-fiction writers have created entertaining tales detailing extraterrestrial contact with mankind. Perhaps predictably, many such tales dwell upon the tried-and-tested scenario of malevolent aliens doing battle with a hapless human race. Yet I know, from having conducted in-depth studies of the UFO mystery for more than fifteen years, that the threat of takeover from a hostile alien species appears to be no nearer now than it was when the UFOs arrived en masse in 1947. Rather, many people who claim contact with apparent otherworldly beings report that our mysterious visitors want little more than to impart information to us, albeit on a clandestine basis.[11] Perhaps the following account, dated 10 October 1967, from the Dallas, Texas, office of the FBI, falls into that category:

A young white female, who refused to give her name, appeared at the Dallas FBI Office on October 9, 1967. She stated she is interested in Unidentified Flying Objects (UFOs) and has received a quantity of information concerning beings from outer space. She stated she will not reveal her identity as she would feel like a fool if the information is not true. She stated if it is true, however, she will meet with interested officials and furnish all the information she has, provided nothing is done to endanger her safety.

She stated in July 1967, she met a being from another planet who had assumed earthly form. He gave her certain information, then he was picked up and departed from the earth on August 21, 1967. She stated she then received messages from non-earthly sources in a manner she refused to discuss. She stated these sources told her of the following:

(1) An anti-missile missile was fired at a UFO over Africa on May 22, 1962, but the UFO was protected by its 'force field'.

(2) A UFO was detected 22,000 miles from earth by radar about August 6, 1967.

(3) A UFO was detected over Antarctica August 20, 1967.

(4) A UFO was detected over the 'Dewline' in the past week and was shot down, and beings from outer space are trying to recover it.

Informant would furnish no further details. She stated if this information is true, she will know other information she received is true, and will furnish full details. This will include information regarding the destruction of a moon explorer vehicle by beings from outer space, and how those beings shot down the Russian Cosmonaut.

She stated she fears for her life if it becomes known she contacted officials, as persons who saw UFOs have died mysteriously in the past. She stated if Air Force officials want to contact her she can be reached by a message to a telephone number she has

Nineteen sixty-seven saw the FBI office at Dallas, Texas, receive some illuminating UFO data from a witness who claimed contact with alien intelligences.

UNITED STATES DEPARTMENT OF JUSTICE

FEDERAL BUREAU OF INVESTIGATION

Dallas, Texas
October 10, 1967

In Reply, Please Refer to File No.

Re: UNIDENTIFIED FLYING OBJECTS;
ANONYMOUS INFORMANT
DALLAS, TEXAS
OCTOBER 9, 1967

A young white female, who refused to give her name, appeared at the Dallas FBI Office on October 9, 1967. She stated she is interested in Unidentified Flying Objects (UFOs) and has received a quantity of information concerning beings from outer space. She stated she will not reveal her identity as she would feel like a fool if this information is not true. She stated if it is true, however, she will meet with interested officials and furnish all the information she has, provided nothing is done to endanger her safety.

She stated in July, 1967, she met a being from another planet who had assumed earthly form. He gave her certain information, then he was picked up and departed from the earth on August 21, 1967. She stated she then received messages from non-earthly sources in a manner she refused to discuss. She stated these sources told her of the following:

(1) An antimissile missile was fired at a UFO over Africa on May 22, 1962, but the UFO was protected by its "force field."

(2) A UFO was detected 22,000 miles from earth by radar about August 6, 1967.

(3) A UFO was detected over Antartica August 20, 1967.

(4) A UFO was detected over the "Dewline" in the past week and was shot down, and beings from outer space are trying to recover it.

Informant would furnish no further details. She stated if this information is true, she will know other information

This document contains neither recommendations nor conclusions of the FBI. It is the property of the FBI and is loaned to your agency. It and its contents are not to be distributed outside your agency.

62-8??1 — 461

ENCLOSURE

given an FBI agent, and she will meet officials at the Dallas FBI Office only.

A one-page memorandum referring the above details to the Air Force Office of Special Investigations aside, Dallas FBI files reflect no further contact with the unnamed woman, which is perhaps not surprising.

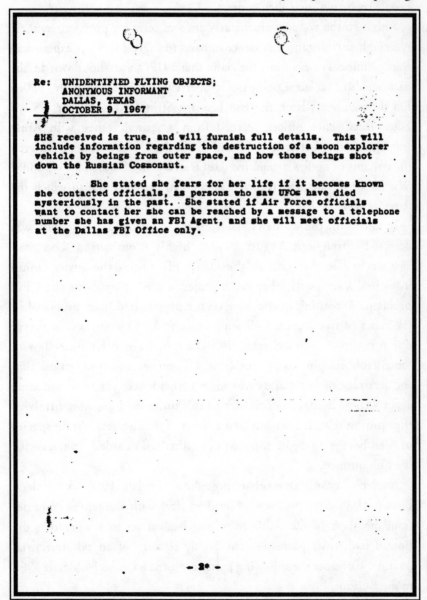

Re: UNIDENTIFIED FLYING OBJECTS;
ANONYMOUS INFORMANT
DALLAS, TEXAS
OCTOBER 9, 1967

she received is true, and will furnish full details. This will include information regarding the destruction of a moon explorer vehicle by beings from outer space, and how those beings shot down the Russian Cosmonaut.

She stated she fears for her life if it becomes known she contacted officials, as persons who saw UFOs have died mysteriously in the past. She stated if Air Force officials want to contact her she can be reached by a message to a telephone number she has given an FBI Agent, and she will meet officials at the Dallas FBI Office only.

- 2* -

Having spoken with a number of people who have found themselves in similar situations, I know that many view their experiences as intensely personal matters, which more often than not generates a reluctance to speak openly. I should stress, however, that accounts of surreptitious communications with human-like extraterrestrials abound, and, as I will later reveal, the Federal Bureau of Investigation maintains a close watch on people reporting such alien contact.

Although the young woman's account was certainly provocative, there is enough circumstantial evidence in hand to suggest that her experiences were genuine. For example, the claim that a UFO was 'shot down' in 'the past week' (i.e. at some point in October 1967) is interesting. In 1980, a full thirteen years later, the late Leonard Stringfield, a former US Air Force Intelligence officer, learned from a retired source with Army Intelligence that between 1966 and 1968, the US government retrieved the remains of no fewer than five UFOs which had crashed on US soil.[12] Was the 1967 incident reported to the FBI one of those to which the Army officer alluded?

In addition, the woman's assertion that unusual aerial activity was detected throughout August 1967 is highly illuminating. Less than two weeks after her visit to the Dallas FBI office, the Soviet Union instigated a semi-official research project aimed at resolving the UFO problem. According to the Soviets, the project had been proposed in the wake of five recent, well-authenticated UFO sightings. Whoever our mysterious woman was, she seems to have been blessed with remarkable insight, to say the least! Of course, one could argue that the accuracy of her claims was mere coincidence; yet time and time again I come across cases similar to this one, and I am now firmly of the opinion that, for reasons best known to themselves, certain species of alien beings do desire some form of direct, if guarded, contact with the human race.

Available records show that throughout the late 1960s the Federal Bureau of Investigation was obliged to deal with numerous enquiries from members of the public who had latched on to a story that the Bureau had in its possession the bodily remains of an extraterrestrial creature. Consider the following partly censored letter of 14 March 1968 to the Bureau:

My name is [deleted]. I work for the United Saucer Hunter Organization. I am writing this in regard to a report that the FBI had captured a saucer occupant. This was published in a flying saucer mag. along with a photo of two alleged FBI agents and a saucer occupant. Is this true? Does the FBI really have a saucer man?

A similar letter to the Bureau from a UFO research group based in Ontario, Canada, states:

Our club is very interested in the study of Unidentified Flying Objects. We were studying a magazine called 'UFO's A Pictorial' and on one of the pages there was a picture of a supposedly [sic.] man from outer space who was being held by two men. Above the picture it stated [that] the two men were FBI agents who had captured this man and were walking down an American street. It had also stated that the picture had first been published in a German newspaper. There was no other additional information. We would appreciate it if you would send us a letter telling us whether this is true or untrue.

'I can assure you the photograph you mentioned does not represent employees of this Bureau,' wrote Hoover in a response of 13 October 1969, adding in a 'Note' for FBI eyes only: 'The photograph in question has previously come to the Bureau's attention and is known to have appeared in a publication in Europe concerning unidentified flying objects. A caption under the photograph alleges two FBI Agents are leading a person from outer space down the street.'

Subsequent research has shown the photograph in question to be bogus, and nothing more than a good-humoured April Fools' Day hoax. However, as the FBI well knew, other accounts of alien bodies being in the possession of the US government could not be dismissed so readily. As we shall see in a subsequent chapter, the Bureau has built up an impressive number of files relating to apparently crashed UFOs and their deceased unearthly occupants.

Midway through 1971, a cryptic letter was sent anonymously to the

Pentagon by a source who claimed that sensitive UFO data originating with the US government was to be turned over to elements of the media. This provoked some concern on the part of the military, and a copy of the letter was made available to the FBI for action. The letter revealed:

> In approximately seven months or January, 1972, certain copies of top-secret documents shall be sent to the New York Times as well as two other newspapers. These documents are related to and will be an ostentation of the involvement of the Pentagon in the controversial 'Unidentified Flying Objects' or 'Flying Saucer' subject. It will show that not only the US Air Force was involved in UFO research but the other military branches as well.
>
> Analysis and the actual conclusions of the classic UFO cases shall be revealed. This shall be accomplished by zeroxed documents and photographs that General Wolfe had reviewed when he was head of the Army's UFO support program in the Pentagon during the Eisenhower years.
>
> Sorry, but it is concluded here that this is the best course to take because we feel that the secret UFO investigations are parallel in nature to the Times–Pentagon–Vietnam controversy. If we are wrong in taking this action, time will tell.

With little evidence to go on, the Bureau simply filed the curious letter, but it is worth noting that in the early to mid-1970s, rumours were rife that the American government was contemplating the release of sensational hitherto-unseen UFO data. The investigator Leonard Stringfield recalled one such occasion in 1974:

> I knew that a report was quietly circulating among responsible researchers in late 1974 anticipating such an announcement, perhaps jointly by the US and France . . . I was alerted by Walter Andrus, Director of [the Mutual UFO Network], to be prepared as Public Relations Director, to rush to Chicago, joining he and Dr [J. Allen] Hynek of CUFOS in a press conference if official word was released.

On the suggestion of Andrus, I prepared a tentative press release, got both his and Hynek's approval, and we waited. In my UFOlog entry for December 16, 1974, I noted, 'Wonder what President Ford and Giscard d'Estaing, President of France, are discussing in Martinique beside the oil problem?'

If UFOs were on the agenda we can only guess. The Martinique meeting ended with nothing said about UFOs. The biggest story ever, was never told.[13]

The 'biggest story ever' may not have been told; however, a decidedly unsettling, even macabre, issue was waiting in the wings to task the FBI, as we will see in the following chapters.

Documentation generated by the Bureau in 1977 suggests at first glance that meaningful involvement in the UFO subject on its part was by that time practically nonexistent.

On 14 June 1977, Jay Cochran Jnr, Assistant Director, FBI, Technical Services Division, was contacted by Stanley Schneider of the Office of Science and Technology at the White House and asked about the Bureau's procedures for handling information received which related to UFOs. In a memorandum generated for internal use, Cochran wrote:

> [Schneider] advised that Jody Powell of the President's staff has raised the question as to whether or not there is any coordination within the Executive Branch relating to information concerning [the UFO] subject. He stated that the US Air Force had closed their investigation of these matters several years ago and currently does nothing but refer such information to appropriate local authorities.
>
> I advised him that as far as the FBI is concerned there appears to be no conceivable jurisdiction for us to conduct any inquiries upon receipt of information relating to a UFO sighting and, in the absence of some investigative jurisdiction based upon the information furnished, that information would be referred to the Department of the Air Force without any action being taken by the Bureau.

He thanked me for the information and stated that if any further contact was necessary he would call back.

Has the Bureau been out of the UFO field since 1977, as this letter would seem to imply? No. Between 1974 and 1980 the Bureau was deeply involved in collating and examining data on the subject of so-called 'cattle mutilations' – a subject that many researchers of the phenomenon believe is linked directly to the mystery of unidentified flying objects, and which will be discussed shortly.

Moreover, two investigators, Lawrence Fawcett and Barry Greenwood, have learned that, beginning in 1978 (only one year after the White House queried the Bureau), the FBI Academy at Quantico, Virginia, began monitoring and collecting newspaper clippings that dealt with the UFO subject, and that to this day are stored on reels of microfilm at the Academy under the curious file reference of TRANSPORTATION. It may not be entirely coincidental that one of the earliest clippings collected by the Academy came from the 12 January 1979 edition of the *Arizona Republic* newspaper, and concerned the then recent release into the public domain of hundreds of pages of previously classified UFO data which originated with the CIA.[14]

Nineteen seventy-eight was also the year that the investigator Robert Todd found himself the subject of FBI enquiries when he began looking – a little too closely for his own good – into a UFO encounter which occurred in Cuban airspace in the 1960s.[15] And in 1982, in conjunction with the US Air Force, the Bureau was involved heavily in an investigation of Simone Mendez, a telecommunications specialist at Nellis Air Force Base in Nevada.

In connection with her work, Mendez was routinely involved with the dispatching and receiving of high-security telecommunication messages, and in the latter part of 1981 was given access to what appeared to be a top-secret message concerning the detection by the North American Aerospace Defense Command (NORAD) of a group of unknown objects which entered Earth's atmosphere from deep space, and headed towards Moscow.[16]

As a result of her viewing this particular document (which the authorities declared was bogus), Mendez was interrogated deeply to the extent that the combined files generated by the Air Force and the Bureau amount to almost two hundred pages! An FBI document dated 27 January 1982, for example, states:

> Investigation has determined that the subject Mendez has access to crypotographic keys and routinely sends and receives crypto-graphic messages. On a daily basis, Mendez handles classified communications up to and including Top Secret. This informa-tion was previously provided to the Bureau and Dallas via Las Vegas Teletype dated January 12, 1982.

A Bureau cable of 25 March 1982 adds: 'The communication related to three UFOs over the Soviet Union and the Air Force was attempting to identify them.'

Although the Air Force ultimately determined that the message was not genuine (but had presumably been constructed by persons unknown who knew enough for it to appear legitimate), to this day much of the paper-work generated by the Bureau and the Air Force on this investigation remains classified, and the USAF now claims that the 'document' itself cannot be located . . .[17]

Come 1988, the Bureau was still delving into the hidden world of the UFO, and found itself caught up in the saga of the notorious MJ-12 doc-uments, which purported to be official US government papers relating to the recovery of an alien spacecraft found crash-landed in the desert of New Mexico in July 1947. As the story of MJ-12 is a complex one, I will not elaborate further here, but refer you to Chapter 11 for a full account.

During the course of my research I have spoken with a number of people who have made claims that some of the more advanced species of aliens visiting Earth are able to manipulate the human mind to the extent that the free will of the individual at issue is essentially lost.

One such source (whom I am regrettably unable to name) was employed in the early 1980s with a computer-software company which had close ties with Britain's Ministry of Defence. According to the infor-mation imparted to me, a person attached to the British government's Electronic Security Committee (which deals with the protection of classified data held on computer by the MOD and other government departments) had confided in my source that one particular division of the MOD had on its files the names of a number of persons, all members of the British public, who were designated 'Black Sleepers' – a term used to describe people who the government had reason to believe had been (a) abducted by alien beings; and (b) 'programmed' for some future task which it was suspected would not be in the best interests of Britain's security.

This is certainly a fantastic story, and without official confirmation it should be considered merely as an interesting aside; however, in 1993, the FBI was tangentially involved in something not dissimilar.

When in 1993 US Federal law-enforcement officials were attempting to end the siege at Waco, Texas, involving the Branch Davidian group led by the cultist David Koresh, the FBI turned to Dr Igor Smirnov of the Moscow Medical Academy, who had had some measure of success in the field of mind control. In a series of closed meetings which began on 17 March, the Bureau was briefed on Dr Smirnov's decade-long research into a computerised acoustic device which was allegedly capable of 'implanting thoughts in a person's mind without that person being aware of the source of the thought'. One presumes that the utilisation of such a device would have ended the siege in record time.

After some discussion, it was finally decided that the entire plan was too risky, and it was abandoned; however, in the July 1993 issue of *Defense Electronics*, it was reported that in addition to the Bureau, representatives of the CIA and the Defense Intelligence Agency were present at the meetings, as was Dr Christopher Green, director of the biomedical research department of General Motors, and, according to Dr Bruce Maccabee of the US Navy, a previous custodian of thousands of pages of classified UFO data at the CIA . . .[18]

Do I think this is merely coincidence? No, I do not: it simply reinforces my strongly held opinion that the Bureau's involvement in UFO-related matters is ongoing to this very day.

In addition, in 1996 I received from the US Defense Intelligence Agency a package of official documentation detailing UFO encounters reported to the DIA in the 1990's.

Contained amongst those reports was a two-page document (formerly classified Secret) which concerned a UFO encounter over China in 1988. Interestingly enough, a copy of the report (which was made available to me by the DIA in a heavily censored format) was circulated to FBI headquarters at Washington, DC! The released part of the document (titled 'Dome of Light') reads thus:

A STRANGE LIGHT OCCURRED IN THE NORTHWEST-
ERN SIDE AT 9.06 ON AUGUST 28, 1988. IT WAS
TAKEN FROM THE UTMOST WESTERN WINDOW OF
THE NUMBER 5 BUILDING OF THE TECHNICAL
COLLEGE. AT FIRST, IT (THE LIGHT)
[APPEARED] AS A LIGHT SPOT WITH TAIL. IT
ALSO SPINS. IT RISES RAPIDLY. AFTER RISING
INTO THE SKY THE TAIL REVOLVES AROUND
LIGHT SPOT. IN THE MEANTIME, THE CIRCLE
EXPANDS QUICKLY. THIS LASTS FOR ABOUT 4
MINUTES. THEN IT BECAME A LARGE CIRCLE,
COVERING THE NORTHWESTERN SKY. THERE IS A
BLUE LIGHT SPOT WITH A TADPOLE SHAPE, NEAR
LEFT, WHERE THE ORIGINAL LIGHT ROSE.

Quite why the FBI should be briefed on UFO encounters over China remains unclear; however, I remain confident that the future will see yet more startling disclosures from the files of the Bureau.

CHAPTER 7

COSMIC PREDATORS

FOR THIRTY YEARS, RURAL AMERICA HAS PLAYED HOST TO AN UNINVITED, and most definitely unwelcome, guest. With remarkable stealth, it prowls the length and breadth of the country, committing atrocious acts of mutilation on innocent cattle: blood, bodily organs, fluids and glands are removed with disturbing speed and precision, giving every impression that a superior technology, far exceeding that of twentieth-century science, is at work.

Moreover, in many instances of mutilation strange aerial lights are seen in the same area suggesting that the two phenomena, whatever their ultimate nature, have a common point of origin. And it is not just unidentified airborne objects that are seen. In a number of cases, the cattle mutilators have been witnessed committing their savage acts of slaughter, and those responsible are not predators such as foxes and coyotes; they are not livestock rustlers; and they are not mentally deranged persons seeking macabre thrills. No, all the evidence suggests that North America has in its midst a silent and deadly breed of extraterrestrial which is literally harvesting cattle on a massive scale, and the authorites are fully aware of what is taking place.

And there is some evidence, fantastic as it may be, that suggests that elements of the US military and intelligence community are actually lending assistance to, and providing cover for, the mutilators. Before addressing the issue of FBI involvement in the mutilations, however, let us examine what lies behind this strange and elusive mystery.

* * *

For the majority of investigators, the premier mutilation event was that of September 1967, when Lady, a three-year-old horse belonging to Nellie Lewis, was found killed and mutilated under shocking circumstances on the ranch of her brother, Harry King, in southern Colorado. While the body of Lady was left essentially intact, the flesh from her neck and head had been completely removed in what seemed to be a surgical-like procedure.

From his Alamosa home, Nellie Lewis's husband, Berle, commenting on the sudden increase in UFO sightings which accompanied Lady's death, said: 'We see something – I won't say what it is – every night.' A further account came one month after the events at the King ranch from two witnesses who caught sight of a pair of high-flying, cigar-shaped objects – each about half the size of a football field – on a course that would have taken them over the southern Colorado area.[1]

The case of Lady has now been well documented, and the most comprehensive account can be found in Linda Howe's excellent 1989 book, *An Alien Harvest*.[2] For the purpose of this review of the evidence, however, I will cite a number of lesser-known events, which offer support for my belief that the truly unexplained animal mutilations are the work of some otherworldly force.

In mid-1974, at least five cattle were found slain and mutilated in Madison County, Nebraska. In all cases the genitalia of the animals were removed, and in one instance the cow was reported to be minus one ear and eye, as well as its nose, mouth and tongue.

Again, UFOs were reported. One witness, Harold Kester, described seeing an object which 'looked as if it had a little bluish-green light on each side with a glow surrounding it. It was behind a tree and moved from one side of the tree to the other. We couldn't tell how close it was or how fast it was moving.'[3]

In July 1975, six heads of cattle were found mutilated forty miles north of Council, Idaho. Again, tongues, genitalia, and in these instances, the udders of the animals were removed. In a series of similar findings in Colorado, the cattle had been entirely drained of blood.

'We didn't find any [blood] at all,' commented Sheriff Jim Hileman of Adams County. 'It could have been washed away by rain, but I'd have to say that not finding any blood in this sort of a case is highly unusual.'[4]

'I'm not scared, just uneasy,' reported a citizen of Elsberry, Missouri, following a series of mutilations which hit the town in June 1978. As in Madison County, Nebraska, in 1974, and Council, Idaho in 1975, the animals were missing vital organs and body parts including teeth, eyes, tongues and ears. And, more baffling, the animals were once again drained of blood in some vampiric-type fashion.

Needless to say, during this time period UFOs were ever present. On 18 June, a bright, saucer-shaped light was seen in the southern sky by Manford, Maurice and Aprile Hammond and a Mr and Mrs Melvin Parker. Prior to the sighting, Mr Hammond had been listening on a 'police scanner' and heard that a woman in the Kings Lake area had reported a bright light over her home. Going outside, Hammond searched the sky and saw it: a huge light blazing in the night sky.[5]

Greeley, Colorado, was the target of the mutilators in September 1980. A Briggsdale rancher, Roland Ball, commenting on two cattle found slaughtered, said: 'That's the first one I've ever seen this way. We found another west of the one that had been dead for about two days, but it had been dead for quite a while. But it had one ear gone and I could tell it wasn't a predator.'

In addition to the removed organs, one of the cattle had a four-inch-diameter circle of hide removed from the area of its navel. '[T]hey had just taken the navel out and everything around it. It was just as neat a cut as could be,' said Ball.[6]

Eight years after the killings at Greeley, a variety of animals were mutilated and killed in the North Bellport area of New York, including sheep, dogs and goats. Again, a number were drained of blood and had been subjected to surgical procedures, something confirmed by the Brookhaven Department of Public Safety Commissioner, Thomas Liguori.

When Tuscon, Arizona, was singled out for attack in 1991, Detective Mike Rafferty of the Cochise County Sheriff's Office commented: 'Nine animals, that's the official number, but we know there are a lot more out there. These [mutilations] are happening all over the state – and country –

but we seem to have had our fair share lately in Cochise County. We don't know why.

'The signs are distinct. For example, the animal has been totally drained of its blood, and the sexual parts of its body have been cut off.'[7]

At 9.45 p.m. on 13 December 1993, Christopher O'Brien, a journalist of southern Colorado, received a telephone call from a Crestone resident 'house-sitting' in the Baca Grants, who reported that a 'glowing white object' had fallen to the ground south of the Baca, north of Hooper.

The next day, a 1,700-pound bull was found dead on the Dale and Clarence Vigil ranch in the nearby Costilla County. In addition to the usual signs of mutilation, broken tree branches were found where the animal lay, and, six feet up, red hair and blood were found on the tips of other branches, giving the impression that the bull had been physically lifted off the ground.[8]

Having now established that the cattle-mutilation mystery is genuine and appears to be linked with the sighting of anomalous flying objects, what evidence is their to suggest that this is the work of extraterrestrials?

There are now a number of valid accounts in hand which give every indication that the killing and mutilation of animals in the USA is indeed the work of an alien force.

In May 1973, Judy Doraty was driving home with her family after an evening in Houston, Texas, when they actually came across alien entities in the process of conducting just such a procedure on a calf. In a 1989 interview on 21st Century Radio, Linda Howe divulged what had been learned from the experience of Judy Doraty: 'Judy described . . . in a pale beam of yellow light, a small brown and white calf being taken up into a craft. Then, in an extraordinary way, [Judy] was inside the craft, and she watches the calf have pieces of it excised: the tongue, the sex organs, the eyes . . .

'When Leo Sprinkle [of the University of Wyoming] asked her "Is there anyone around you?", there was this long, almost forty-five-second pause, and then she said: "Two little men."

'[The two beings] were about three and a half to four feet tall; grey creatures with large egg-shaped heads.'

* * *

In June 1990, Ralph Steiner, an award-winning radio producer who lives in Berkeley, California, conducted an interview with Linda Howe, during which Howe discussed the testimony of a Waco, Texas, rancher who in 1980 had a practically identical encounter with two four-foot-tall creatures, with oversized, oval heads and 'long, solid' black eyes carrying the body of a calf near a small hill on his ranch.

'That rancher was petrified,' said Howe. 'He ran away, and it took him three days to get up the courage to go back. When he did, he took his wife and his son with him . . . There they found the calf, completely eviscerated of skeleton and organs.'[9]

A number of other similar reports exist, and I am convinced of their veracity, even if they do stretch our credulity to the maximum. One such case involves the abduction of a woman and her son by alien entities in May 1980 at Cimarron, New Mexico, and the mother's recollection of seeing a cow mutilated within some form of room or chamber by creatures variously described as 'Bony . . . skinny . . . almost skeletal . . . They have burning eyes, like the devil.'

But if these macabre killings are the work of alien predators, what is the nature of their agenda? Do they consider the Earth to be some form of 'cosmic supermarket' which they can liberally exploit at will? And if so, what is our relationship with these beings?

A former pilot for the CIA, John Lear, has said that the extra-terrestrials responsible for the cattle mutilations have a genetic disorder which has destroyed their digestive system, and, in order to sustain themselves, they use an enzyme or hormonal secretion obtained from the tissue extracted not just from cattle, but humans also – which has highly disturbing implications.

Lear says: 'The cattle mutilations that were prevalent throughout the period from 1973 to 1983 . . . were for the collection of these tissues by the aliens.'

If Lear's information is accurate, what, if anything, does the US government know about this? On repeated occasions since the 1970s there have been an untold number of sightings of unmarked helicopters in the vicinity of cattle mutilation sites, which almost certainly confirms that they are somehow implicated in the events.

Inevitably, it has been postulated that the mutilations are the work of some clandestine arm of government which is exploiting the cattle, possibly in tests for germ-warfare weapons, and the helicopters are the means by which those involved move from site to site. This is not an impossible scenario, but no one connected to such a project has ever spoken publicly to confirm their involvement, and nothing substantial has surfaced to support this hypothesis. Far more likely, in my opinion, is that the helicopters are piloted by military or intelligence sources specifically to monitor the activities of the real mutilators.

In January 1994, when cattle mutilations were rife in the southern Colorado area, a local journalist, Christopher O'Brien, informed the researcher John Grace that over the course of the previous one and a half months, the San Luis Valley area had played host to a variety of unusual and unexplained phenomena. Almost nightly, O'Brien advised Grace, formations of helicopters had been viewed in the vicinity of the valley perimeter, as if waiting for 'something' to make its presence felt; and more disturbingly, the local cattle population was also suffering adversely at the hands of unknown forces.

Further proof that some arm of the US military has more than a passing knowledge of the cattle mutilations comes from the researcher Christa Tilton of Oklahoma. Having had a number of striking UFO encounters herself, Tilton takes more than a passing interest in the subject, and has conducted an in-depth study of the 1980 abduction and cattle-mutilation event at Cimarron, New Mexico. Most notable of all, many of Tilton's experiences mirror closely those reported in the Cimarron case.

During the course of her enquiries, Tilton had a period of communication with Richard Doty, formerly a counterintelligence agent with the US Air Force Office of Special Investigations. In November 1989, Christa Tilton was informed by Doty that the mother and son at Cimarron had 'a very real encounter with something very strange'.

What particularly struck Doty was the woman's description of the place she was taken to. According to Doty, the description sounded very much like an underground weapons facility. Admitting to having been 'taken aback' by what he heard, Doty felt that both the woman and her child had accidentally stumbled across a highly classified government project, which resulted in their being drugged and detained, before being removed from the area.[10]

If the sequence of events suggested by Doty was correct, and the woman had inadvertently intruded upon some covert government operation, what role was played by the 'Bony . . . skinny . . . almost skeletal' creatures which were also in attendance?

Perhaps in time, this particular incident will serve to prove that not only are aliens mutilating and exploiting numerous heads of cattle, but that the US government is also deeply enmeshed. One question we would do well to consider, however: who is in control?

Before I turn to the Federal Bureau of Investigation's knowledge of the cattle mutilations, a final statement from Christa Tilton with respect to her first-hand knowledge of underground facilities, the abduction of human beings by extraterrestrial entities, and alien – human interaction with respect to the livestock killings:

> Strange things to prove and the reasoning behind such experiments is unclear . . . I have reason to believe I was taken against my will to some base that was underground. Where it was is not clear now . . . I still hold out some belief that I may have been taken to somewhere in the Catalina Mountains . . . It was a frightening experience because of the fact I realised that our military was in charge of some covert operation that was taking place underground. The experiments have been going on for decades . . . No one knows truly what is going on for what reason. The operation is so covert that I fear we may never find out the whole story behind these underground bases.[11]

All the available evidence suggests that FBI knowledge of the cattle-mutilation mystery dates back to the early part of 1973, when a cluster of reports surfaced in Iowa. Later that year, yet further incidents occurred in at least a dozen counties in Kansas, with more still extending into Nebraska. In common with the cases I have cited already, many of the reports referred to sightings of unidentified lights, unmarked helicopters, not to mention the absolute lack of any incriminating evidence to suggest who was perpetrating these distressing crimes.

With public anxiety rising, rumours began to circulate to the effect that the mutilations were the work of a powerful and extraordinarily well-equipped band of devil-worshippers who were presumably killing the unfortunate cattle and excising various body parts for use in their satanic ceremonies. A number of individuals came forward claiming knowledge of such a cult, although it has to be said that if the cattle mutilations are in some way connected with occult sacrificial ceremonies, then those involved have been very lucky, since no person has ever been apprehended in the act of carrying out a mutilation, despite the fact that incidents have been reported the length and breadth of the USA.

To illustrate that the 'cult' theory was in favour in the mid-1970s, and that the Bureau had an awareness of this, I cite the letter of US Senator Carl T. Curtis to the FBI Director, Clarence M. Kelley, dated 4 September 1974: 'This will refer to my previous letter of August 21 to you regarding the series of incidents stretching from Oklahoma to Nebraska in which cattle have been dismembered in some kind of strange witchcraft cult.' Curtis further informed Kelley:

> Enclosed is a newspaper article which appeared in the Hastings, Nebraska, Daily Tribune concerning these weird events. Articles similar to this one have appeared in many of the Nebraska newspapers. I thought you would want to see this article in order to substantiate the claims which have been made.
>
> I am wondering if your good offices have instigated an investigation into this situation either in Nebraska or any of the other states experiencing similar acts of mutilation to livestock. I will appreciate hearing from you.

The *Daily Tribune* article to which Curtis referred made an intriguing revelation: 'Cattle killings aren't the only strange happenings in northeast Nebraska. There have been numerous reports of unidentified flying objects in both Antelope and Knox counties.' This was something expanded upon by Sheriff Herbert Thompson: 'We don't know if they are helicopters or strange lights for the most part. There were several reported over the weekend. The people who reported them called them strange lights. Previously we had two positive identifications of helicopters.'

Despite the phenomenal number of mutilations and the repeated sightings of anomalous aerial lights, all of which suggested that some form of coordinated operation was under way, the Bureau was curiously reluctant to become involved: '. . . it appears that no Federal Law within the investigative jurisdiction of the FBI has been violated, inasmuch as there is no indication of interstate transportation of the maimed or killed animals,' Clarence Kelley advised Senator Curtis.

Four months later, an Airtel was sent from the Bureau office at Minneapolis to the FBI laboratory, which played down the theory that the mutilations were the work of some unidentified source, and asserted that, in all probability, they were the work of 'other animals or varmints, believed to be foxes'. A report citing the testimony of Richard Hilde, Chief Agent with the North Dakota Crime Bureau, stated: '[Hilde] said the dead animals in North Dakota had been found in scattered locations, and the Bureau believed they died of natural causes and then small animals such as foxes had eaten the soft part of the animals.'

This is all well and good; however, it does not account for the mystery helicopters, nor the many unidentifed flying objects reported time and time again in the areas of mutilation sites. Nor does it explain why there was a total lack of similar reports prior to the late 1960s.

And when there was an alarming outbreak of mutilations in Colorado in 1974 and 1975, it became more than apparent that this was the work of something far stranger than the local animal population.

On 29 August 1975, Floyd K. Haskell, Senator for the State of Colorado, wrote an impassioned letter to Theodore P. Rosack, special agent in charge of the FBI at Denver, Colorado, imploring the Bureau to make a full investigation into the cattle mutilations, in an attempt to resolve the matter once and for all.

'At least 130 cases in Colorado alone have been reported to local officials and the Colorado Bureau of Investigation (CBI) has verified that the incidents have occurred for the last two years in nine states,' said Haskell. He continued: 'The ranchers and rural residents of Colorado are concerned and frightened by these incidents. The bizarre mutilations are frightening in themselves: in virtually all the cases, the left ear, left eye, rectum and sex organ of each animal has been cut away and the blood drained from the carcass, but with no traces of blood left on the ground and no footprints.'

Our old friend, the unmarked helicopter, was also out in force in Colorado, as Haskell was only too well aware. 'In Colorado's Morgan County area,' he elaborated, 'there has [sic] also been reports that a helicopter was used by those who mutilated the carcasses of the cattle, and

Following a series of grisly 'cattle mutilations' in the USA, Senator Floyd K. Haskell asked the FBI to conduct an investigation.

FLOYD K. HASKELL
COLORADO

( ) ( )

𝕌𝕟𝕚𝕥𝕖𝕕 𝕊𝕥𝕒𝕥𝕖𝕤 𝕊𝕖𝕟𝕒𝕥𝕖
WASHINGTON, D.C. 20510
August 29, 1975

Theodore P. Rosack
Special Agent In Charge
Denver Federal Building
1961 Stout Street
Denver, Colorado 80202

Dear Mr. Rosack:

For several months my office has been receiving reports of cattle mutilations throughout Colorado and other western states. At least 130 cases in Colorado alone have been reported to local officials and the Colorado Bureau of Investigation (CBI); the CBI has verified that the incidents have occured for the last two years in nine states.

The ranchers and rural residents of Colorado are concerned and frightened by these incidents. The bizarre mutilations are frightening in themselves: in virtually all the cases, the left ear, left eye, rectum and sex organ of each animal has been cut away and the blood drained from the carcass, but with no traces of blood left on the ground and no footprints.

In Colorado's Morgan County area, there has also been reports that a helicopter was used by those who mutilated the carcasses of the cattle, and several persons have reported being chased by a similar helicopter.

Because I am gravely concerned by this situation, I am asking that the Federal Bureau of Investigation enter the case. Although the CBI has been investigating the incidents, and local officials also have been involved, the lack of a central unified direction has frustrated the investigation. It seems to have progressed little, except for the recognition at long last that the incidents must be taken seriously.

Now it appears that ranchers are arming themselves to protect their livestock, as well as their families and themselves, because they are frustrated by the unsuccessful investigation. Clearly something must be done before someone gets hurt.

Page 2

The fact that allegations have been made of the loss of livestock
in 21 states under similar circumstances strongly suggests the very
real possibility that the crossing of state lines is involved and, this
alone, I feel, should justify the participation of the FBI in this case.

I urge you to begin your investigation as soon as possible, and to
contact my office to discuss in more detail the incidents I have described.
We stand ready to give you all possible assistance.

Sincerely,

Floyd K. Haskell
United States Senator

FKH:enw

several persons have reported being chased by a similar helicopter. Because I am gravely concerned by this situation, I am asking that the Federal Bureau of Investigation enter the case . . . Now it appears that ranchers are arming themselves to protect their livestock, as well as their families and themselves, because they are frustrated by the unsuccessful investigation. Clearly something must be done before someone gets hurt.'

Stressing that the loss of livestock in at least 21 states under similar circumstances suggested an interstate operation was being coordinated, Senator Haskell closed his letter to Agent Rosack thus: 'I urge you to begin your investigation as soon as possible, and to contact my office to discuss in more detail the incidents I have described. We stand ready to give you all possible assistance.'

In addition to contacting Agent Rosack, Senator Haskell also issued a press release, informing the media that he had asked the Bureau to investigate the mutilations. This caused the *Denver Post* to comment on 3 September: 'If the Bureau will not enter the investigation of mysterious livestock deaths in Colorado and some adjacent states then Senator Floyd Haskell should take the matter to Congress for resolution.'

Aware of previous Bureau statements that there was nothing to indicate that the killings were within the FBI's jurisdiction, the *Denver Post* stated firmly: 'The incidents are too widespread – and potentially too dangerous to public order – to ignore. Narrow interpretations of what the FBI's role is vis-à-vis state authority are not adequate to the need.'

The issue of possible disregard for the law should the Bureau not wish to become involved was also something high on the *Post*'s agenda:

> There is already federal involvement. Consider this: Because of the gun-happy frame of mind developing in eastern Colorado (where most of the incidents have been occurring), the US Bureau of Land Management (BLM) has had to cancel a helicopter inventory of its lands in six counties. BLM officials are simply afraid their helicopters might be shot down by ranchers and others frightened by cattle deaths.

This certainly concerned the Bureau, and on the day after publication, Special Agents Rosack and Sebesta of the Colorado FBI made a visit to the offices of the *Denver Post*, where, in a meeting with three *Post* representatives, Charles R. Buxton, Lee Olson and Robert Pattridge, the Bureau's position with respect to the mutilations was laid out: '. . . unless the FBI has investigative jurisdiction under Federal statute, we cannot enter any investigation'.

One week later, on 11 September, Senator Haskell telephoned Clarence M. Kelley at the FBI to discuss the entire issue of cattle mutilation and the possibility of the Bureau's becoming involved in determining who exactly was responsible. Again, the Bureau asserted that this was a matter outside of its jurisdiction. 'Senator Haskell [said] he understood our statutory limitations . . . but he wished there was something we could do,' reported a Bureau official, R.J. Gallagher.

Haskell had additional reasons for wanting the mutilation issue resolved swiftly, as Gallagher recorded in an internal memorandum of 12 September:

> Senator Haskell recontacted me this afternoon and said that he had received a call from Dane Edwards, editor of the paper in

Brush, Colorado, who furnished information that US Army helicopters had been seen in the vicinity of where some of the cattle
were mutilated and that he, Edwards, had been threatened but
Senator Haskell did not know what sort of threats Edwards had
received or by whom. He was advised that this information
would be furnished to our Denver Office and that Denver would
closely follow the situation. Senator Haskell expressed his appre-
ciation.

The Bureau ultimately determined that the helicopter issue was also
outside its jurisdiction, and that on this matter it was unable to proceed
further. Curiously, however, during this same time frame, numerous
reports of UFOs and unidentified helicopters surfaced in the immediate
vicinity of strategic military installations around the USA, and there is
evidence to show that someone in the Bureau was fully aware of this, and
was taking more than a cursory interest in these sightings.

Proof of this comes in a number of Air Force reports forwarded to the
FBI only weeks after its contact with Senator Haskell. Selected extracts
from those reports follow:

On 7 Nov 75 . . . an off duty missile launch officer reported that
unidentified aircraft resembling a helicopter had approached and
hovered near a USAF missile launch control facility, near
Lewistown. Source explained that at about 0020, 7 Nov 75,
source and his deputy officer had just retired for crew rest in the
Soft Support Building (SSB) at the LCF, when both heard the
sound of a helicopter rotor above the SSB . . . The Deputy
observed two red-and-white lights on the front of the aircraft, a
white light on the bottom, and a white light on the rear . . .

On 7 Nov 75, Roscoe E. Moulthrop III, Captain, 341
Strategic Missile Wing, advised that during the evening hours of
6–7 Nov 75, two adjacent LCFs, approximately 50 miles south
of aforementioned LCF, reported moving lights as unidentified
flying objects (UFO). During this period there were no reports
of helicopter noises from personnel at these LCFs . . .

This office was recently notified of a message received by

security police MAFB, MT., detailing a similar nocturnal approach by a helicopter at a USAF weapons storage area located at another USAF base in the Northern Tier states. Local authorities denied the use of their helicopters during the period 6–7 Nov 75 . . .[12]

That these particular reports should have been of interest to the FBI is perplexing, given the statements made to Senator Haskell that the unidentified helicopter sightings reported in Colorado were outside of the Bureau's jurisdiction. One might be forgiven for wondering if a directive had come from on high in the US government, ordering the Bureau to steer clear of the mutilation issue . . .

It is also perhaps notable that a currently unauthenticated document, leaked to the researcher William Moore, refers to the 'Northern Tier' helicopter and UFO sightings of 1975, and expresses concern that, in view of the fact that the media had picked up on the stories, there was a need on the part of some authority to develop an effective disinformation plan, presumably to counter the developing interest that was surrounding the sightings.[13] Could this perhaps be why the Bureau professed no interest in the Colorado helicopter encounters?

Moving on from the mutilations of 1975, we see that the next indication of Bureau involvement in the subject came in the final months of 1976. In September of that year, *Oui* magazine published a large and comprehensive article outlining the history of the cattle mutilations, the theories surrounding who or what was responsible, and the opinions of numerous persons one way or another implicated in the whole affair. Under the cover of the following memorandum, a copy of the article was sent to Washington by the special agent in charge at the Springfield, Illinois, Bureau office:

Enclosed for the Bureau is one copy of an article entitled 'The Mutilation Mystery', which allegedly appeared in Oui Magazine, September 1976 issue.

For the information of the Bureau, Sheriff Russell Crews, Illinois, on 9/30/76, furnished enclosed article to SA Donald R.

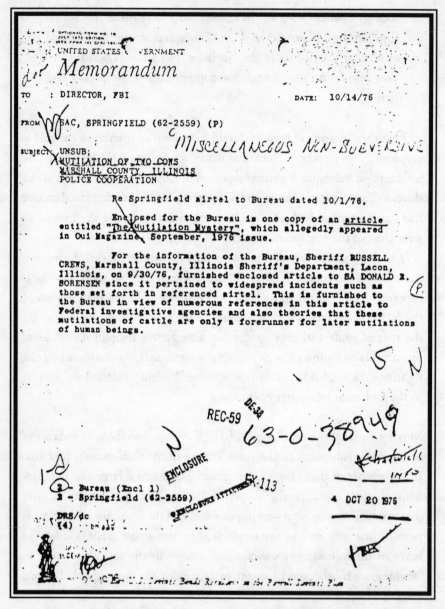

OPTIONAL FORM NO. 10
JULY 1973 EDITION
GSA FPMR (41 CFR) 101-11

UNITED STATES GOVERNMENT

Memorandum

TO : DIRECTOR, FBI   DATE: 10/14/76

FROM : SAC, SPRINGFIELD (62-2559) (P)

SUBJECT: UNSUB;   MISCELLANEOUS NON-SUBVERSIVE
MUTILATION OF TWO COWS
MARSHALL COUNTY, ILLINOIS
POLICE COOPERATION

    Re Springfield airtel to Bureau dated 10/1/76.

    Enclosed for the Bureau is one copy of an article
entitled "The Mutilation Mystery", which allegedly appeared
in Oui Magazine, September, 1976 issue.

    For the information of the Bureau, Sheriff RUSSELL
CREWS, Marshall County, Illinois Sheriff's Department, Lacon,
Illinois, on 9/30/76, furnished enclosed article to SA DONALD R.
SORENSEN since it pertained to widespread incidents such as
those set forth in referenced airtel. This is furnished to
the Bureau in view of numerous references in this article to
Federal investigative agencies and also theories that these
mutilations of cattle are only a forerunner for later mutilations
of human beings.

REC-59   63-0-38949

ENCLOSURE   EX-113

③ - Bureau (Encl 1)   4 OCT 20 1976
2 - Springfield (62-2559)
DRS/dc
(4)

Buy U.S. Savings Bonds Regularly on the Payroll Savings Plan

FBI records of 1976 revealed that the Bureau had learned: 'these mutilations
of cattle are only a forerunner for later mutilations of human beings'.

Sorensen since it pertained to widespread incidents such as those
set forth in referenced airtel. [Author's note: The 'referenced
airtel' has yet to be declassified by the FBI.] This is furnished to

the Bureau in view of numerous references in this article to Federal investigative agencies and also theories that these mutilations of cattle are only a forerunner for later mutilations of human beings.

Between September 1976 and early 1978, the Bureau had no further significant involvement in the mutilation issue, but by mid-1978 it had become clear that this was something that the Bureau could afford to ignore no longer. With the assistance of local police authorities, medical sources and concerned ranchers, the Bureau came to accept slowly that this sickening mystery was all too real, even if the perpetrators remained disturbingly anonymous and free to continue their butchery on a country-wide scale.

CHAPTER 8

OPERATION ANIMAL MUTILATION

WHEN THE MUTILATORS FOCUSED THEIR ATTENTION ON RIO ARRIBA COUNTY, New Mexico, it marked the turning point in convincing the FBI that, whoever was responsible for the strange killings, they were here to stay.

Following a series of mutilations between 1976 and 1978, Manuel S. Gomez, a rancher who had himself lost a number of cattle, approached the Senator for New Mexico (and a former US astronaut) Harrison Schmitt, and requested that enquiries be made to determine if, finally, some form of investigation could be instigated to settle the problem.

Schmitt duly complied, and on 10 July 1978 wrote to Chief Martin E. Vigil of the New Mexico State Police and informed him of the concerns of Manuel Gomez and other ranchers in the area, many of whom were also losing livestock to the elusive mutilators with worrying regularity.

Aware that Police Officer Gabe Valdez of Espanola had investigated a number of such cases, Vigil asked Captain Charlie P. Anaya of the Espanola Police to forward him copies of all relevant paperwork, which could in turn be made available to Senator Schmitt, should he wish to take matters further. As a result, by October 1978, Schmitt was in receipt of Valdez's files and, armed with the evidence that something truly mind-blowing was taking place, mailed a letter voicing his concern to the Attorney General of the Department of Justice, Griffin B. Bell.

During the past several years, [wrote Schmitt] ranchers throughout the West, including my home state of New Mexico, have
been victimized by a series of cattle mutilations. As a result, these
ranchers have as a group and individually suffered serious eco-
nomic losses . . .

While an individual cattle mutilation may not be a federal
offense, I am very concerned at what appears to be a continued
pattern of an organized interstate criminal activity. Therefore, I
am requesting that the Justice Department re-examine its juris-

---

MEMORANDUM

January 31, 1979

TO: Senator, John Ryan

FROM: SFDOM

SUBJECT: Steer mutilation, January 29, 1979,
Torrance County, NM

Sergeant O'Dell of the Torrance County Sheriff's Department called the
Albuquerque Office early in the afternoon of January 29, 1979, to report
that he had discovered the first reported cattle mutilation in Torrance
County, and wanted information on whom he should report it to. SFDOM called
O'Dell and was told the following:

In response to a telephone call from Samuel N. Hindi, O'Dell arrived
at a location near the village of Duran, NM, at approximately 11 a.m. on
January 29, 1979, and found the carcass of a six month old steer that had
apparently been recently mutilated. O'Dell said the carcass was still warm
enough to melt the snow around it. O'Dell indicated that he had been following
news reports of previous mutilations in Rio Arriba County and believed that
the Torrance County mutilation was the "freshest" ever discovered. He called
because he thought it would be helpful for investigators to have a fresh mutilation to examine and subject to tests.
    O'Dell said the steer's scrotum and penis had been removed with surgical
precision -- a feature common to all previous mutilations -- and indicated
that patches of hair around the carcass seemed to indicate that the steer
had been dropped or bounced -- another feature common to all previous mutilations.
The steer's intestines had been removed through the hole where the scrotum had
been cut out, but were not disturbed. O'Dell felt that an animal would have
gone directly to the intestines. The steer's tongue was <u>not</u> removed as in
previous mutilations, but the insides of the ears appeared to have been
"beveled" out with a sharp instrument.
    O'Dell notified the state Game and Fish Department, the State Police Crime
Lab in Santa Fe, and the New Mexico Livestock Board. The State Police Crime
Lab apparently notified State Police Officer Gabe Valdez of Chama, the officer
who has investigated most of the mutilations over the past 18 months. In the
interim, the Livestock Board removed the carcass and apparently froze it. Valdez
later contacted the Torrance County Sheriff and was to have gone to Torrance
County on January 30 to investigate.

    *** In response to your question about whether any of the mutilations
have occurred on federal land, Officer Valdez informs me that eight mutilations
were discovered on the Jicarilla Apache Reservation, and seven on the Santa
Clara Pueblo. There have been a total of 68 cattle mutilations, and six
horse mutilations, reported in New Mexico since 1975. Forty-five of the
cattle mutilations and four of the horse mutilations occurred in 1978.

A macabre cattle-mutilation report forwarded to the FBI in 1979.

diction in this area with respect to the possible reopening of this investigation.

Attorney General Bell responded with speed and assured Senator Schmitt: 'I have asked Philip Heymann, head of the Criminal Division, to look into our jurisdiction over the cattle mutilation problem with which you are concerned,' adding: 'I must say that the materials sent me indicate the existence of one of the strangest phenomenons in my memory.' That Bell took all of this seriously is evident from the following note attached to a letter to Heymann: 'Please have someone look into this matter at an early date. Senator Schmitt is our friend and there have been about 60 mutilations in New Mexico in recent months.'

For his part, on 2 March 1979, Assistant Attorney General Heymann wrote a one-page memorandum for the attention of the FBI, under the cover of which were sent copies of Officer Gabe Valdez's files. 'For several years the Criminal Division has been aware of the phenomenon of animals being mutilated in a manner that could indicate that such acts are performed by persons as part of a ritual or ceremony. The report that some of the mutilations have occurred in Indian country is our first indication that Federal Law may have been violated.

'It is requested that the Federal Bureau of Investigation conduct an appropriate investigation of the 15 mutilations and any others that occur in Indian country as a possible crime on an Indian reservation.' And so the FBI's involvement in the mutilation issue began . . .

For the men and women of the Bureau assigned to deal with the cattle mutilations, the first step was to review the files of Police Officer Gabe Valdez. And none, I am quite sure, were prepared for the horrifying, and painstakingly detailed, facts contained within.

Between August 1975 and the summer of 1978, almost 30 cases of animal mutilation had been recorded in the Rio Arriba area, with many indicating that the attacks were the work of some well-equipped intelligence. One report that stands out, and demonstrates that the genuine mutilations are not the work of predators, was filed by Valdez in June 1976.

At 8 p.m. on 13 June, Valdez was contacted by the rancher Manuel

Gomez and advised that he had found a three-year-old cow on his ranch which bore all the classic signs of mutilation. As Valdez listened, Gomez stated that the cow's left ear, tongue, udder and rectum had been removed with what appeared to be a sharp instrument. Yet there was absolutely no blood in the immediate vicinity of the cow, nor were there any footprints in evidence; however, there were marks of some sort: marks that gave every impression that some form of aerial object had landed and carried out a grisly attack on the unfortunate animal . . .

At 5 a.m. on the following day, Valdez set off for the Gomez ranch along with Paul Riley of the New Mexico Cattle Sanitary Board, where both intended examining the evidence for themselves. On arrival, Officer Valdez and Riley were confronted by a scene of carnage. There was the cow, just as Gomez had described: three years old, lying on its right side, vital body parts having been removed with the utmost precision. But that was not all. There were also the strange 'landing marks'. In a two-page report written up shortly afterwards, Valdez recorded the details:

Investigations continued around the area and revealed that a suspected aircraft of some type had landed twice, leaving three pod marks positioned in a triangular shape. The diameter of each pod part was 14″ . . . Emanating from the two landings were smaller triangular shaped tripods 28″ apart and 4″ in diameter. Investigation at the scene showed that these small tripods had followed the cow for approximately 600′. Tracks of the cow showed where she had struggled and fallen. The small tripod tracks were all around the cow. Other evidence showed that grass around the tripods, as they followed the cow, had been scorched. Also a yellow oily substance was located in two places under the small tripods. This substance was submitted to the State Police Lab. The Lab was unable to detect the content of the substance.

A sample of the substance was submitted to a private lab and they were unable to analyze the substance due to the fact that it disappeared or disintegrated. Skin samples were analyzed by the State Police Lab and the Medical Examiner's office. It was reported that the skin had been cut with a sharp instrument.

Three days after, Valdez contacted Dr Howard Burgess, a retired Sandia
Laboratories scientist, and asked him to conduct a radiation test at the
scene. The results were astounding. All around the tripod marks and in
the immediate tracks, the radiation count was found to be twice that of
normal. Valdez came up with an intriguing hypothesis as to why this
should have been so: 'It is the opinion of this writer that radiation findings are deliberately being left at the scene to confuse investigators.'

Valdez discovered something else. In the days between his first visit to
the Gomez ranch and the second visit with Dr Howard Burgess, the
mystery object had returned. 'There was also evidence that the tripod
marks had returned and removed the left ear,' said Officer Valdez.
'Tripod marks were found over Mr Gomez's tire tracks of his original
visit. The left ear was intact when Mr Gomez first found the cow.'

Most distressing of all: 'The cow had a 3 month old calf which has not
been located since the incident. This appears strange since a small calf
normally stays around the mother even though the cow is dead.'

Valdez also noted in his report that this particular incident was typical
of those he had investigated over the course of a sixteen-month period.
'They all carry the same pattern,' he asserted. Perhaps most pertinent,
Valdez had been able to determine that in at least one case, the animal in
question was found to have a high dose of atropine in its blood system.
'This substance is a tranquilizing drug,' reported Valdez.

There was also concern on Valdez's part that 'government associated
laboratories are not reporting complete findings', and for that reason samples from the slain cattle were later submitted to private chemists for
analysis.

Fully aware of the theories that all the mutilations were the work of
either satanic cults or natural predators, Valdez stated:

> Both [theories] have been ruled out due to expertise and precise-
> ness and the cost involved to conduct such a sophisticated and
> secretive operation. It should also be noted that during the
> spring of 1974 when a tremendous amount of cattle were lost
> due to heavy snowfalls, the carcasses had been eaten by predators.
> These carcasses did not resemble the carcasses of the mutilated
> cows.

Valdez concluded his remarkable report with a statement that had far-reaching implications: 'Investigation has narrowed down to these theories which involve (1) Experimental use of Vitamin B12 and (2) The testing of the lymph node system. During this investigation an intensive study has been made of (3) What is involved in germ warfare testing, and the possible correlation of these 3 factors (germ warfare testing, use of Vitamin B12, testing of the lymph node system).'

Lest you should deem this a once-in-a-lifetime occurrence, consider the following report of May 1978, also from the files of Officer Valdez:

> This four year old cross Hereford and Black Angus native cow was found lying on left side with rectum, sex organs, tongue, and ears removed. Pinkish blood from [illegible] was visible, and after two days the blood still had not coagulated. Left front and left rear leg were pulled out of their sockets apparently from the weight of the cow which indicates that it was lifted and dropped back to the ground. The ground around and under the cow was soft and showed indentations where the cow had been dropped. 600 yards away from the cow were the 4″ circular indentations similar to the ones found at the Manuel Gomez ranch on 4-24-78. This cow had been dead approximately [illegible] hours and was too decomposed to extract samples. This is the first in a series of mutilations in which the cows legs are broken. Previously the animals had been lifted from the brisket with a strap. These mutilated animals all dehydrate rapidly (in one or two days).

A final document, also of 1978, refers to another incident where abnormal radiation traces were found:

> It is believed that this type of radiation is not harmful to humans, although approximately 7 people who visited the mutilation site complained of nausea and headaches. However, this writer has had no such symptoms after checking approximately 11 mutilations in the past 4 months . . . Identical mutilations have been

taking place all over the Southwest. It is strange that no eye witnesses have come forward or that no accidents [have] occurred. One has to admit that whoever is responsible for the mutilations is very well organized with boundless financing and secrecy. Writer is presently getting equipment through the efforts of Mr Howard Burgess, Albuquerque, N.M. to detect substances on the cattle which might mark them and be picked up by infra-red rays but not visible to the naked eye . . .

A four-page Airtel, dated 16 February 1979, from Forrest S. Putman, FBI special agent in charge at Albuquerque, to Washington, makes it very clear that Officer Valdez's case histories had been digested thoroughly by the Bureau and were being treated very seriously. A number of extracts from Putman's Airtel follow:

. . . the animals are being shot with some type of paralyzing drug and the blood is being drawn from the animal after an injection of an anti-coagulant. It appears that in some instances the cattle's legs have been broken and helicopters without any identifying numbers have reportedly been seen in the vicinity of these mutilations . . .

[C]lamps are being placed on the cow's legs and they are being lifted by helicopter to some remote area where the mutilations are taking place and then the animal is returned to its original pasture . . .

Officer Valdez stated that Colorado probably has the most mutilations occurring within their State and that over the past four years approximately 30 have occurred in New Mexico . . . of these 15 have occurred on Indian Reservations but he did know that many mutilations have gone unreported which have occurred on the Indian reservations because the Indians, particularly in the Pueblos, are extremely superstitious and will not even allow officers in to investigate in some instances . . .

[S]ince the outset of these mutilations there have been an estimated 8,000 animals mutilated which would place the loss at approximately $1,000,000.

J. Edgar Hoover, Director of the Federal Bureau of Investigation from 1924 to 1972.

February 23, 1972

REC-6 62-83891-478
EX-115

Miss ████████
Westmoreland City, Pennsylvania 15692

Dear Miss ████████

I regret that I am unable to comment as you requested in your letter of February 15th. The investigation of Unidentified Flying Objects is not and never has been a matter that is within the investigative jurisdiction of the FBI.

Sincerely yours,

J. Edgar Hoover

John Edgar Hoover
Director

NOTE: Bufiles reflect no record of correspondent.

MLN:jc (3)

FBI Headquarters, Washington DC.

In 1972, J. Edgar Hoover categorically denied that the FBI had ever had any involvement in the investigation of the UFO sightings.

Dr. Lincoln La Paz who was heavily involved in the mystery of Project Twinkle and the green fireballs.

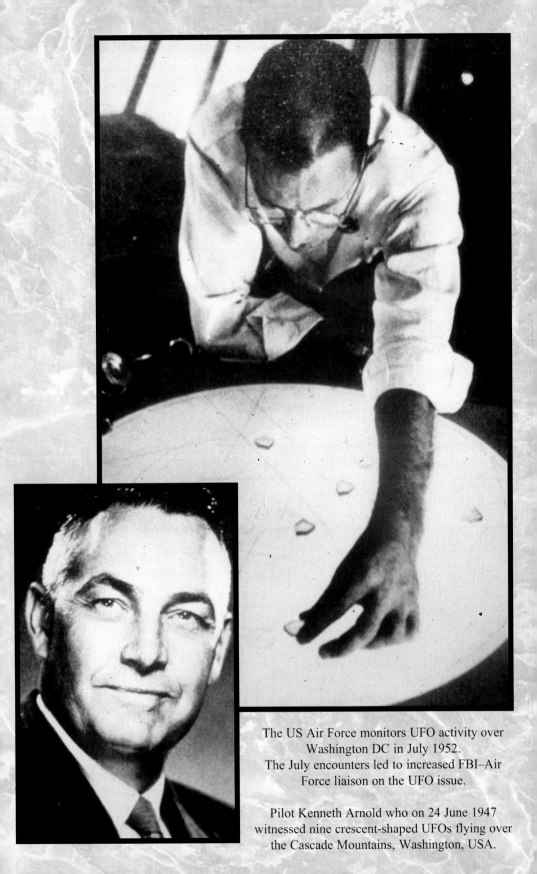

The US Air Force monitors UFO activity over
Washington DC in July 1952.
The July encounters led to increased FBI–Air
Force liaison on the UFO issue.

Pilot Kenneth Arnold who on 24 June 1947
witnessed nine crescent-shaped UFOs flying over
the Cascade Mountains, Washington, USA.

George Adamski, whose contacts with human-like aliens were the subject of a lengthy FBI file.

A drawing of one of the green fireballs as seen by Dr. La Paz and his wife.

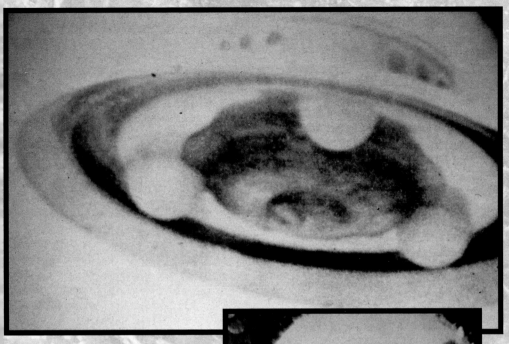

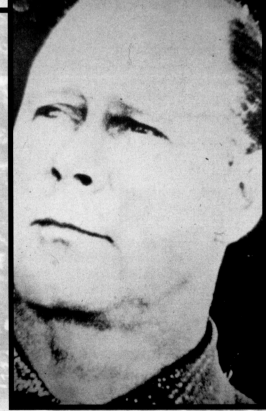

George Adamski's famous 1952 photograph of an alien spacecraft.

Like George Adamski, George Van Tassel was deeply monitored by the FBI as a result of his meetings with extra-terrestrials. In 1960, FBI agents attended a public lecture on UFOs given by Van Tassel.

Support for the claims of both Adamski and Van Tassel that there are human-like aliens visiting the Earth comes from retired US Army Command sergeant-major, Robert Dean.

Famed UFO investigator Donald Keyhoe, Director of the civilian UFO group, National Investigations Committee on Aerial Phenomena. Declassified FBI documents show that the Bureau was well acquainted with Keyhoe's activities.

Sergeant Lonnie Zamora of the New Mexico Police Department, who in April 1964 reported seeing a landed UFO and crew at Socorro, New Mexico.

The landing site of the UFO seen by Zamora at Socorro.

Throughout the 1970s the FBI was heavily involved in the country-wide
cattle mutilation mystery.

On 6 October 1994 a mutilated cow was discovered at Mt. Dora, New Mexico.
The cow's left rear hip was broken, as if the animal had been dropped from the air.

Special Agent Putman continued by saying that on the previous day, 15 February, he had met with Officer Gabe Valdez, Senator Harrison Schmitt, US Attorney R.E. Thompson and Bureau Special Agent Samuel Jones, and it had been decided that the best course of action was for a

In February 1979, the FBI prepared an in-depth, four-page Airtel concerning cattle-mutilation data compiled by New Mexican police officer, Gabe Valdez.

FD-36 (Rev. 5-22-78)

FBI

TRANSMIT VIA:
- ☐ Teletype
- ☐ Facsimile
- ☐ AIRTEL

PRECEDENCE:
- ☐ Immediate
- ☐ Priority
- ☐ Routine

CLASSIFICATION:
- ☐ TOP SECRET
- ☐ SECRET
- ☐ CONFIDENTIAL
- ☐ UNCLAS E F T O
- ☐ UNCLAS

Date _____ 2/16/79

TO: DIRECTOR, FBI

FROM: SAC, ALBUQUERQUE

UNSUBS;
CATTLE MUTILATIONS OCCURRING
IN WESTERN STATES
CIR - MISCELLANEOUS

For the past seven or eight years mysterious cattle mutilations have been occurring throughout the United States and for the past four years have been occurring within the State of New Mexico. Officer GABE VALDEZ, New Mexico State Police, has been handling investigations of these mutilations within New Mexico. Information furnished to this office by Officer VALDEZ indicates that the animals are being shot with some type of paralyzing drug and the blood is being drawn from the animal after an injection of an anti-coagulant. It appears that in some instances the cattle's legs have been broken and helicopters without any identifying numbers have reportedly been seen in the vicinity of these mutilations. Officer VALDEZ theorizes that clamps are being placed on the cow's legs and they are being lifted by helicopter to some remote area where the mutilations are taking place and then the animal is returned to its original pasture. The mutilations primarily consist of removal of the tongue, the lymph gland, lower lip and the sexual organs of the animal. Much mystery has surrounded these mutilations, but according to witnesses they give the appearance of being very professionally done with a surgical instrument, and according to VALDEZ, as the years progress, each surgical procedure appears to be more professional. Officer VALDEZ has advised that in no instance, to his knowledge, have these carcasses ever attacked by predator or scavenger animals, although there are tracks which would indicate that coyotes have been circling the carcass from a distance. He also advised that he has requested Los Alamos Scientific Laboratory to conduct investigations for him but until just recently has always been advised that the mutilations were done by predatory animals. Officer VALDEZ stated that just recently he has been told by two assistants at Los Alamos Scientific Laboratory that they were able to determine

2 - Bureau
1 - Albuquerque

AQ

the type of tranquilizer and blood anti-coagulant that
have been utilized.

Officer VALDEZ stated that Colorado probably has the
most mutilations occurring within their State and that over
the past four years approximately 30 have occurred in New
Mexico. He stated of these 30, 15 have occurred on Indian
Reservations but he did know that many mutilations have gone
unreported which have occurred on the Indian reservations
because the Indians, particularly in the Pueblos, are extremely
superstitious and will not even allow officers in to investigate
in some instances. Officer VALDEZ stated since the outset
of these mutilations there have been an estimated 8,000 animals
mutilated which would place the loss at approximately $1,000,000.

R. E. THOMPSON, United States Attorney, advised that he
had received an urgent call from the head of the Criminal
Division, Department of Justice, advising him that he would be
contacted by Senator HARRISON SCHMITT of New Mexico, who had
been in contact with Attorney General GRIFFIN BELL in an effort
to obtain Federal assistance in seeking to solve these cattle
mutilations.

Bureau telephone call of 2/13/79 advised that a letter
was forthcoming from the Department to the Bureau requesting
our assistance in the investigation based on the fact that 15
of these animals had been mutilated on Indian reservation
land.

On 2/15/79 / Senator HARRISON SCHMITT, USA R. E. THOMPSON,
SA SAMUEL W. JONES and myself met to discuss this matter.
It was agreed that a conference should be held in April of
this year in Albuquerque involving New Mexico and the surrounding
States who have suffered cattle mutilation cases in an effort
to fully discuss this matter to determine what has been
developed to date and to recommend further steps to be taken
to solve this ongoing problem. The role of the FBI was
discussed but was not established since it was not resolved
whether the FBI would act in a coordinating capacity,
an investigating capacity or both. It was decided however
that it would be most beneficial if all this available information could be placed in a computer bank so that appropriate
printouts could be made and an analysis made in an effort to
determine a trend or pattern of these mutilations.

It is obvious if mutilations are to be solved there is
a need for a coordinated effort so that all material available
can be gathered and analyzed and further efforts synchronized.
Whether the FBI should assume this role is a matter to be

conference to be convened in Albuquerque, no later than April, where
those 'who have suffered cattle mutilation [can] discuss this matter to
determine what has been developed to date and to recommend further
steps to be taken to solve this ongoing problem'.

Of the Bureau itself, Putman elaborated: 'It is obvious if mutilations are
to be solved there is a need for a coordinated effort so that all material

AQ

decided. If we are merely to investigate and direct our
efforts toward the 15 mutilated cattle on the Indian reservation we, I believe, will be in the same position as the
other law enforcement agencies at this time and would be seeking
to achieve an almost impossible task. It is my belief that
if we are to participate in any manner that we should do so
fully, although this office and the USA's office are at a loss
to determine what statute our investigative jurisdiction would
be in this matter. If we are to act solely as a coordinator
or in any other official capacity the sooner we can place
this information in the computer bank, the better off we
would be and in this regard it would be my recommendation that
an expert in the computer field at the Bureau travel to
Albuquerque in the very near future so that we can determine
what type of information will be needed so that when the
invitation for the April conference is submitted from Senator
SCHMITT's Office that the surrounding States will be aware
of the information that is needed to place in the computer. It
should be noted that Senator SCHMITT's Office is coordinating the
April conference and will submit the appropriate invitations
and with the cooperation of the USA, Mr. THOMPSON will chair
this conference. The FBI will act only as a participant.

Since this has not been investigated by the FBI in any
manner we have no theories whatsoever as to why or what is
responsible for these cattle mutilations. Officer GABE
VALDEZ is very adamant in his opinion that these mutilations
are the work of the U. S. Government and that it is some
clandestine operation either by the CIA or the Department of
Energy and in all probability is connected with some type of
research into biological warfare. His main reason for these
beliefs is that he feels that he was given the "run around"
by Los Alamos Scientific Laboratory and they are attempting to
cover up this situation. There are also theories that these are
cults (religious) or some type of Indian rituals resulting in
these mutilations and the wildest theory advanced is that they
have some connection with unidentified flying objects.

If we are to assume an investigative posture into this
area, the matter of manpower, of course, becomes a consideration
and I an umable to determine at this time the amount of manpower
that would be needed to give this our full attention so that
a rapid conclusion could be reached.

The Bureau is requested to furnish its comments and
guidance on this whole situation including, if desired, the
Legal Counsel's assessment of jurisdictional question. An
early response would be needed however, so that we might
properly, if requested to do so, obtain the data bank
information. If it appears that we are going to become
-3-

AQ

involved in this matter, it is obvious that there would be a
large amount of correspondence necessary and Albuquerque would
suggest a code name be established of BOVMUT.

available can be gathered and analyzed and further efforts synchronized. Whether the FBI should assume this role is a matter to be decided.'

Concerning the various theories mooted, Putman noted:

> Valdez is very adamant in his opinion that these mutilations are the work of the US Government and that it is some clandestine operation either by the CIA or the Department of Energy and in all probability is connected with some type of research into biological warfare.
>
> His main reason for these beliefs is that he feels he was given the 'run around' by Los Alamos Scientific Laboratory and they are attempting to cover up this situation. There are also theories that these are cults (religious) or some type of Indian rituals resulting in these mutilations and the wildest theory advanced is that they have some connection with unidentified flying objects.

On 20 April 1979, the proposed conference came to pass, and was detailed in Bureau memoranda one week later. Such was the concern surrounding the cattle mutilations that nearly two hundred people attended the meeting, which was held at the Albuquerque Public Library.

A report to FBI headquarters from Albuquerque, dated 25 April, outlines the flavour of the meeting, and addresses the various opinions of those in attendance:

> . . . Forrest S. Putman, Special Agent in Charge Albuquerque Office of the FBI, explained to the conference that the Justice Department had given the FBI authority to investigate those cattle mutilations which have occurred on Indian lands. He further explained that the Albuquerque FBI would look at such mutilations in connection with mutilations occurring off Indian lands for the purpose of comparison and control, especially where the same methods of operation are noted . . .
>
> Manuel Gomez addressed the conference and explained he had lost six animals to unexplained deaths which were found in a mutilated condition within the last two years. Further, Gomez

said that he and his family are experiencing fear and mental anguish because of the mutilations . . .

David Perkins, Director of the Department of Research at Libre School in Farasita, exhibited a map of the US which con-

As the mutilations continued, the FBI officially monitored a public conference on the controversy held at Albuquerque in April 1979.

UNITED STATES DEPARTMENT OF JUSTICE

FEDERAL BUREAU OF INVESTIGATION

Albuquerque, New Mexico

April 25, 1979

In Reply, Please Refer to File No.

CATTLE MUTILATIONS

On April 20, 1979, a conference was held at the Albuquerque Public Library at Albuquerque, New Mexico. This conference was chaired by Senator HARRISON SCHMITT, Republican, New Mexico, and United States Attorney R.E. THOMPSON of Albuquerque. The conference convened at 9:00 a.m. The morning session was attended by representatives from various law enforcement agencies, news media representatives, and the general public. Approximately 180 persons attended the conference during the morning session. This session lasted until approximately 12:00 noon.

Senator SCHMITT opened the conference by explaining its purpose. He said, "This hearing is to define the scope of the problem and the basis for federal assistance and to examine how the FBI might be involved." U.S. Attorney R.E. THOMPSON explained to those attending the conference that federal jurisdiction for investigations conducted by the FBI is limited to those areas approved by Congress. U.S. Attorney THOMPSON said there is a possible violation of a federal statute requiring that aircraft be appropriately marked and identified. He explained that this statute might possibly have been violated because of reports that the unidentified aircraft have been observed in the area of cattle mutilations.

Senator SCHMITT explained that his staff and others have searched the federal statutes and have concluded there is possible federal jurisdiction under Title 18, U.S. Code, Sections 7 and 13, having to do with violations of state law on Indian or federal lands. Senator SCHMITT expressed his hope that the FBI could conduct investigation into the cattle mutilations under these statutes. Senator SCHMITT stated to the conference that the FBI would coordinate the investigation of cattle mutilations.

This document contains neither recommendations nor conclusions of the FBI. It is the property of the FBI and is loaned to your agency; it and its contents are not to be distributed outside your agency.

CATTLE MUTILATIONS

        FORREST S. PUTMAN, Special Agent in Charge (SAC),
Albuquerque Office of the FBI, explained to the conference
that the Justice Department had given the FBI authority
to investigate those cattle mutilations which have occurred
or might occur on Indian lands. He further explained that
the Albuquerque FBI would look at such mutilations in connection
with mutilations occurring off Indian lands for the purpose
of comparison and control, especially where the same methods
of operation are noted. SAC PUTMAN said that in order for
this matter to be resolved, the facts surrounding such
mutilations should be gathered and computerized.

        District Attorney ELOY MARTINEZ, Santa Fe, New Mexico,
told the conference that his judicial district had made
application for a $50,000 Law Enforcement Assistance Administratic
(LEAA) Grant for the purpose of investigating the cattle
mutilations. He explained that there is hope that with the
funds from this grant, an investigative unit can be established
for the sole purpose of resolving the mutilation problem. He
said it is his view that such an investigative unit could serve
as a headquarters for all law enforcement officials investigating
the mutilations and, in particular, would serve as a repository
for information developed in order that this information could
be coordinated properly. He said such a unit would not only
coordinate this information, but also handle submissions to
a qualified lab for both evidence and photographs. Mr. MARTINEZ
said a hearing will be held on April 24, 1979, for the purpose
of determining whether this grant will be approved.

        GABE VALDEZ, New Mexico State Police, Dulce, New Mexico,
reported he has investigated the death of 90 cattle during the
past three years, as well as six horses. Officer VALDEZ said
he is convinced that the mutiliations of the animals have not
been the work of predators because of the precise manner of
the cuts.

        Officer VALDEZ said he had investigated mutilations
of several animals which had occurred on the ranch of MANUEL
GOMEZ of Dulce, New Mexico.

        MANUEL GOMEZ addressed the conference and explained
he had lost six animals to unexplained deaths which were found
in a mutilated condition within the last two years. Further,
GOMEZ said that he and his family are experiencing fear and
mental anguish because of the mutilations.

tained hundreds of colored pins identifying mutilation sites. He
commented that he has been making a systematic collection of
data since 1975, and has never met a greater challenge. He said,
'The only thing that makes sense about the mutilations is that
they make no sense at all' . . .

    Tom Adams of Paris, Texas, who has been independently exam-
ining mutilations for six years, said his investigation has shown
that helicopters are almost always observed in the area of the

CATTLE MUTILATIONS

DAVID PERKINS, Director of the Department of Research at Libre School in Farasita, Colorado, exhibited a map of the United States which contained hundreds of colored pins identifying mutilation sites. He commented that he had been making a systematic collection of data since 1975, and has never met a greater challenge. He said, "The only thing that makes sense about the mutilations is that they make no sense at all."

TOM ADAMS of Paris Texas, who has been independently examining mutilations for six years, said his investigation has shown that helicopters are almost always observed in the area of the mutilations. He said that the helicopters do not have identifying markings and they fly at abnormal, unsafe, or illegal altitudes.

Dr. PETER VAN ARSDALE, Ph.D., Assistant Professor, Department of Anthropology, University of Denver, suggested that those investigating the cattle mutilations take a systematic approach and look at all types of evidence is discounting any of the propounded theories such as responsibility by extraterrestrial visitors or Satanic cults.

RICHARD SIGISMUND, Social Scientist, Boulder, Colorado, presented an argument which advanced the theory that the cattle mutilations are possibly related to activity of UFOs. Numerous other persons made similar type presentations expounding on their theories regarding the possibility that the mutilations are the responsibility of extraterrestrial visitors, members of Satanic cults, or some unknown government agency.

Dr. RICHARD PRINE, Forensic Veterinarian, Los Alamos Scientific Laboratory (LASL), Los Alamos, New Mexico, discounted the possibility that the mutilations have been done by anything but predators. He said he had examined six carcasses and in his opinion predators were responsible for the mutiliation of all six.

Dr. CLAIRE HIBBS, a representative of the State Veterinary Diagnostic Laboratory, New Mexico State University, Las Cruces, New Mexico, said he recently came to New Mexico, but that prior to that he examined some mutiliation findings in Kansas and Nebraska. Dr. HIBBS said the mutiliations fell into three categories: animals killed and mutilated by predators and scavengers, animals mutilated after death by "sharp instrument and animals mutilated by pranksters.

mutilations. He said that the helicopters do not have identifying markings and they fly at abnormal, unsafe, or illegal altitudes . . .

Dr Peter Van Arsdale, Ph.D., Assistant Professor, Department of Anthropology, University of Denver, suggested that those investigating the cattle mutilations take a systematic approach and look at all types of evidence is discounting any of the propounded theories such as responsibility by extraterrestrial visitors or Satanic cults . . .

Richard Sigismund, Social Scientist, Boulder, Colorado, presented an argument which advanced the theory that the cattle mutilations are possibly related to activity of UFOs. Numerous other persons made similar type presentations expounding on their theories regarding the possibility that the mutilations are the responsibility of extraterrestrial visitors, members of Satanic cults, or some unknown government agency . . .

Dr Claire Hibbs, a representative of the State Veterinary Diagnostic Laboratory, New Mexico State University, Las Cruces, New Mexico, said he recently came to New Mexico, but that prior to that he examined some mutilation findings in Kansas and Nebraska. Dr Hibbs said the mutilations fell into three categories: animals killed and mutilated by predators and scavengers, animals mutilated after death by 'sharp instruments' and animals mutilated by pranksters . . .

Tommy Blann, Lewisville, Texas, told the conference he has been studying UFO activities for twenty-two years and mutilations for twelve years. He explained that animal mutilations date back to the early 1800's in England and Scotland. He also pointed out that animal mutilations are not confined to cattle, but cited incidents of mutilation of horses, dogs, sheep, and rabbits. He also said that the mutilations are not only nationwide, but international in scope . . .

Chief Raleigh Tafoya, Jicarilla Apache Tribe, and Walter Dasheno, Governor, Santa Clara Pueblo, each spoke briefly to the conference. Both spoke of the cattle which had been found mutilated on their respective Indian lands. Chief Tafoya said some of his people who have lost livestock have been threatened . . .

Carl W. Whiteside, Investigator, Colorado Bureau of Investigation, told the conference that between April and December, 1975, his Bureau investigated 203 reports of cattle mutilations . . .

At the conclusion of the conference, a 'special meeting' was convened in Albuquerque which was attended heavily by the FBI, state law-enforcement officers from New Mexico, and numerous official investigators from Nebraska, Colorado, Montana, and Arkansas. One of the highlights of the meeting, which had not been divulged during the public conference, was the revelation that in Arkansas, the authorities had investigated 28 cases of cattle mutilation, all of which 'were the work of intentional mutilators and not of predators', something with which the investigator from Montana concurred.

As a result, during May 1979, the District Attorney's Office for Santa Fe, New Mexico, received a $50,000 Law Enforcement Assistance Administration (LEAA) grant, to enable a comprehensive review of the evidence to begin in earnest. It was decided, however, that the investigation would be limited to a study of those livestock found solely on Indian land in New Mexico. Oddly, an internal Bureau memorandum of 1 June stated that, following the announcement that an official investigation was to begin, 'there have been no new cattle mutilations in Indian country'.

Four days later, however, the low-profile approach to which the Bureau was hoping to adhere was shattered when the *National Enquirer* devoted one page of its 5 June edition to a discussion of the FBI's involvement in the mutilation issue.

Among those cited by the *Enquirer* was one Henry Monteith, an engineering physicist at Sandia Laboratories. Monteith, having spoken with a number of Indians, had no doubt that the mutilations were the work of extraterrestrials, and went on to disclose that a number of Indians he had spoken with had actually seen 'spaceships land and unload "star people" who chase down animals and take them back to the spaceship'. And in a moment of light relief, District Attorney Eloy Martinez of Espanola, New Mexico, admitting that 'UFOs are a possibility', stated: 'I might be the first district attorney in the country to prosecute an alien from outer space.' Had it come to pass, that would indeed have been a court case worth seeing . . .[1]

Armed with the $50,000 LEAA grant, investigations began in earnest, under the three-person team of Director Kenneth M. Rommel, Jnr (who had served with the FBI for twenty-eight years); Diana S. Moyle, Coordinating Secretary; and an investigator, Cipriano Padilla. Many, however, were critical of the investigation.

In July 1979, the *Rio Grande Sun* reported the finding of 'the county's "freshest" mutilation report so far', which curiously went uninvestigated. 'I was really disgusted,' said Dennis Martinez, a rancher, who had discovered the mutilated carcass within three hundred yards of his Truchas farm. 'The news media said investigators would come as soon as they were called.' For seven hours Martinez waited, but no investigator arrived.

'I don't blame them for being upset,' commented Senator Harrison Schmitt, expressing his concern that the finding on the Martinez ranch remained practically unacknowledged. And when advised that Kenneth Rommel had still to contact Officer Gabe Valdez, whose files were the catalyst that prompted Schmitt to initiate high-level enquiries with the FBI, he responded: 'That doesn't sound like complete investigating.'

There were other stories in circulation, too, concerning the LEAA-funded investigation, as the *Rio Grande Sun* was only too well aware. Citing a number of 'confidential sources', who expressed dissatisfaction with Kenneth Rommel's study, the *Sun* stated: 'Persons who have spoken to the investigator complain he is "brusque," or "too flippant," or he doesn't take their ideas or their reports seriously, and they'd rather not discuss with him further mutilation phenomena.'[2]

This may of course represent nothing more than a marked difference of opinion over the source of the mutilations; however, darker rumours were also in circulation: 'Other persons express fears that not only Rommel, but the District Attorney and the State Police, are working together to cover up whatever is behind the mutilations and rumours are spreading fast.'

Subsequent media coverage was equally damning:

Examination of the first quarterly report submitted in our famous $50,000 cattle mutilation probe would indicate results to date can be described at best disappointing. The worst might be to suggest it's a waste of the taxpayers money. While the public can't expect a solution in the first six weeks of activity, for pete's sake they can expect more than that skimpy one-page report issued last week. And they can expect, for the money they are putting out, for someone to show up to investigate reported mutilations.

But as one optimist remarked cheerfully: 'Look at it this way; it's only $50,000. It could have been half a million.'

On 17 July 1979, Senator Schmitt announced that the Senate Appropriations Committee had directed the FBI to continue its investigations. Such action, said Schmitt, is 'necessary due to the continuing widespread problem of cattle mutilations and the need for federal co-ordination of the investigation. I hope that the Committee's endorsement of this proposal will increase the FBI's investigative activity so that the answer to this bizarre and grisly mystery will be found.'

Within two weeks, however, the Bureau office at Albuquerque noted: 'Since being instructed to investigate this matter, there have been no reports of mutilations on Indian lands in New Mexico . . . In view of this, no investigation is currently being conducted regarding mutilations, and the Albuquerque Office is placing this matter in a closed status.'

Come January 1980, the situation had changed little, as a Bureau report to Washington discloses:

> On January 15, 1980, Kenneth M. Rommel advised [that] his office has pursued numerous investigative leads regarding the possible mutilation of animals in New Mexico. He said that to date, his investigative unit has determined that none of the reported cases has involved what appear to be mutilations by other than common predators. Rommel said he has traveled to other states and conferred with investigators in those areas regarding mutilations, and to date has received no information which would justify the belief that any animals have been intentionally mutilated by human beings. Rommel added that regarding all the dead animals he has examined, the damage to the carcasses has always been consistent with predator action . . .
>
> On January 15, 1980, this matter was discussed with Assistant US Attorney Richard J. Smith, US Attorney's Office, Albuquerque. Assistant US Attorney Smith said that in his opinion there is no Federal interest in continuing an investigation in this matter in the absence of further reports of acts of suspected mutilation of animals on Indian land in New Mexico.

Two months later Rommel's feelings about the mutilations were set forth in a letter to the FBI laboratory at Washington:

> For your information, since approximately 1975, New Mexico and other states, primarily those located in close proximity to New Mexico, have had incidents referred to by many as 'the cattle mutilation phenomena'.
>
> Stock animals, primarily cattle, have been found dead with various parts of the carcass missing such as one eye, one ear, the udder, and normally a cored anus. Most credible sources have attributed this damage to normal predator and scavenger activity. However, certain segments of the population have attributed the damage to many other causes ranging from UFOs to a giant governmental conspiracy, the exact nature of which is never fully explained. No factual data has been supplied supporting these theories.

In writing to the FBI laboratory, Rommel requested that an analysis be carried out on some material (later found to be flakes of enamel paint) which were believed identical to flakes found on the hides of cattle in the Dulce, New Mexico, area.

'. . . I would appreciate it if through the use of a GS Mas spectroscopy test or any other logical test, that these flakes can be identified. This in itself would go a long way to assisting me to discredit the UFO–Cow Mutilation association theory.'

By the summer of 1980, Rommel had prepared a bound report, entitled 'Operation Animal Mutilation', copies of which were circulated within the Bureau. The final entry in the FBI's cattle-mutilation files reads: 'A perusal of this report reflects it adds nothing new in regard to potential investigation by the Albuquerque FBI of alleged mutilations on Indian lands in New Mexico.'

And there matters stand to this day. For all the efforts of Senator Harrison Schmitt, Officer Gabe Valdez and the numerous ranchers, media sources, private and official investigators, the final report generated by the LEAA's $50,000 grant concluded that the mutilations were the work of nothing more than everyday scavengers. A detailed examination of the data set forth in Bureau files, however, clashes acutely with the conclusions of 'Operation Animal Mutilation'.

Firstly, the decision to limit investigations to those cattle found mutilated on Indian land in New Mexico is curious, particularly in view of the fact that, when it was announced that Rommel's study was beginning in earnest, such killings ceased! While individual mutilations outside of Indian land might not technically have been within the Bureau's jurisdiction, surely a detailed comparison with such cases would have been warranted? Indeed it would, and this was something addressed by the special agent in charge at Albuquerque, Forrest S. Putman, in early February 1979:

> If we are merely to investigate and direct our efforts toward the 15 mutilated cattle on the Indian reservation we, I believe, will be in the same position as the other law enforcement agencies at this time and would be seeking to achieve an almost impossible task. It is my belief that if we are to participate in any manner that we should do so fully . . . the sooner we can place this information in the computer bank, the better off we would be and in this regard it would be my recommendation that an expert in the computer field at the Bureau travel to Albuquerque in the very near future so that when the invitation for the April conference is submitted from Senator Schmitt's office that the surrounding States will be aware of the information that is needed to place in the computer . . .

Putman's proposals were certainly laudable, and I admit to being baffled as to why the investigation did not fully address the mutilation issue on a country-wide scale.

There are other anomalies, too. In his letter of 5 March 1980 to the Bureau, Kenneth Rommel wrote that with respect to the claims that the mutilations were the work of UFOs or a 'giant governmental conspiracy': 'No factual data has been supplied supporting these theories.'

Then what of the files of Officer Gabe Valdez? They may not confirm

directly that UFOs are mutilating cattle for reasons best known to themselves; but they do confirm the presence of unidentified aerial vehicles in
the immediate vicinity of mutilation sites. The disturbing report written
up by Valdez on his visit of 14 June 1976 to the ranch of Manuel Gomez
is a perfect example. 'Investigations continued around the area and
revealed that a suspected aircraft of some type had landed twice,' stated
Valdez. And what of the 'pod marks', scorched ground, elevated radiation
readings and 'yellowy oily substance' found at the site? Is this not the
'factual data' Rommel asserted was absent?

Moreover, the reports collected by Valdez in 1978, implying that animals had actually been lifted into the air by some unknown object, are
also convincing evidence of a phenomenon beyond mere predators:
'Both cows were laying on their left side with left front leg and left rear
leg broken which indicates that animals were lifted by their extremities.'

I am also concerned by the fact that investigations in Arkansas had concluded that no fewer than 28 genuine cases of cattle mutilation had been
recorded, and that in Colorado, a phenomenal 203 accounts had surfaced. Yet, the Project sponsored by the Law Enforcement Assistance
Administration considered only the aforementioned fifteen reports,
which emanated from New Mexican Indian reservations.

Is it possible that the *Rio Grande Sun* was close to the truth when it
stated that: 'Other persons express fears that not only Rommel, but the
District Attorney and the State Police, are working to cover up whatever
is behind the mutilations, and rumors are spreading fast'?

Did the Bureau uncover something about the mutilations that was
deemed so shocking that the public had to be kept in the dark at all costs?

Emil P. Moschella, Chief of the Bureau's Freedom of Information/Privacy
Acts Section, has informed me that the FBI has not conducted any investigation of cattle mutilation since 1980, and that all material on the FBI's
involvement in the New Mexican mutilations has been released 'without
any excisions'. A similar assurance has come to me from the Department of
Justice. And yet claims circulate that the Bureau has still to tell the complete
story of what lies behind the livestock killings of the 1970s.

For all the assertions that the cattle mutilations were nothing but the
work of predators, Kenneth Rommel's 297-page 'Operation Animal

Mutilation' report remains closed to the general public in its entirety, which is odd, since such actions on the FBI's part only increase public feeling that something truly macabre is taking place. And a review of additional Bureau files and witness testimony suggests there may be a wealth of untapped material buried within FBI vaults which relates specifically to this topic.

I have referred already to the case of the rancher in Waco, Texas, who in April 1980 came upon two humanoid creatures making off with the body of a calf which was later found horribly mutilated.

It so happens that FBI files from 1973 reflect an unusual incident which may have a bearing on this case. On 9 March 1973, a Sergeant Stigliano of the US Air Force's Recruiting Office at Waco informed the San Antonio Bureau office that an individual (not identified in declassified Bureau documents) had contacted the night-shift supervisor at a Waco-based newspaper, and 'inquired regarding any information [the newspaper] could be able to furnish him concerning any unidentified flying objects observed in the Waco, Texas, area'.

Sergeant Stigliano continued that the individual had identified himself as a captain in the US Air Force, and had in his possession a folder, marked 'Top Secret', which contained photographs of various military installations. 'No specific information concerning these photos could be provided by Sergeant Stigliano,' reported the San Antonio FBI. '. . . [T]he individual did not act in any strange manner, and did not attempt to obtain anything other than information from the newspaper. Sergeant Stigliano advised that this information was being furnished to the proper authorities only for information purposes as they do not suspect any unlawful activity.'

This is a puzzling case, but it is worth noting that the unnamed Air Force captain, seemingly with a 'Top Secret' clearance, was attempting to gather information pertaining to UFO encounters in Waco, Texas, where, seven years later, the actual abduction of a calf by alien entities was witnessed at close quarters by a shocked rancher. Moreover, it was only one month after the experience at the Waco newspaper office that a cluster of mutilations were reported in Iowa. A link, maybe?

* * *

One of the most outrageous claims surrounding the cattle mutilations is that in addition to UFOs and small humanoid creatures, 'Bigfoot'-type animals have also been seen in the same locations. This has led to speculation that Bigfoot itself (if such a creature exists) is some form of extra-terrestrial creature, too!

Newsweek of 30 September 1974, for example, reported that in Madison, Nebraska, a number of residents had reported seeing both UFOs and 'strange creatures resembling bears and gorillas' near to where slaughtered cattle had been found.

In addition, a Bigfoot researcher, Bruce G. Hallenbeck, has told me of a number of mutilation cases in which these creatures have been implicated:

> In 1976, friends and I found dead and mutilated goats in a farmer's field. The peculiar thing is, they did not belong to the farmer who owned the property and nobody knows where they came from. Their horns had been torn off and there was no blood around the bodies. The area where they were found is on the edge of a swamp [called] 'Cushing's Hill', where we believe many of the Bigfoot creatures come from . . .[3]

You may wonder where this is all leading. It may seem unbelievable, but in its files the Bureau does indeed have records relating to creatures fitting the Bigfoot description. In the late 1960s, Frank Hansen, a Minnesota farmer, claimed to have in his possession a hairy, manlike creature which was preserved in a block of ice, having been found floating in the sea off Siberia. Supposedly, the creature had been purchased by an anonymous Californian millionaire, who made arrangements for Hansen to exhibit it.

Investigators Ivan Sanderson and Bernard Heuvelmans made for Hansen's farm in December 1968, and on seeing the creature declared it genuine. Unfortunately, before a scientific study could be undertaken, the corpse was returned to its anonymous owner, and an elaborate latex copy was substituted. And there are, of course, claims that there never was a 'real' body, only the model. But that is hardly the issue.

In 1970, Hansen recalled the tremendous interest that his 'creature' had created, particularly in official circles:

I became extremely nervous when the newspapers in both the US and England pointed out that '. . . if this creature is real, then there may be the question of how and why it was killed . . .' The Federal Bureau of Investigation and hordes of lesser law enforcement officials revealed a sudden, ominous interest in my specimen.[4]

In later years, Frank Hansen expanded on this. Recalling the heady days of the 1960s when his 'specimen' was on display, he stated: '. . . my good friend Sheriff George Ford of Winona County showed up and said: "Frank, would you believe I got an enquiry from Mr Brewer at the FBI office in Rochester who has received a letter from J. Edgar Hoover asking for him to find out what is in this coffin . . . I'll be back tomorrow with a pathologist, I've got to answer this enquiry for Mr Brewer . . ."'

Hansen did not wait around for the authorities to show up: 'The whole world was looking for this thing and we were heading down interstate 94 toward Chicago!'[5] The image of the FBI in hot pursuit of Hansen and his frozen friend boggles the mind, but I use the above to point out that (a) there is testimony available positing a Bigfoot connection with the cattle mutilation mystery; and (b) J. Edgar Hoover's interest in Hansen's very own Bigfoot does not preclude the possibility that other similar accounts of hairy, humanoid creatures roaming the USA had already caught the Bureau's attention.

There is one final issue which must be addressed, however horrific the facts may be. According to some, the mutilators have not limited their activities to the killing and dissection of livestock, but on occasion have also focused their attention on human beings. If only one case of 'human mutilation' by an extraterrestrial entity is proven, then the reasons behind the US government's fifty-year monitoring of the UFO phenomenon become crystal clear. In addition, if the FBI has an awareness that it is not just cattle that are mutilated (and there is evidence to support this hypothesis, as I will now detail), its reluctance to attribute the cattle mutilations to anything other than predators is more than understandable. If nothing else, the Bureau would wish to prevent the truth behind the 'human' aspect of the mystery from surfacing outside of the confines of officialdom.

Don Ecker spent ten years as a police investigator and is now a writer living in Los Angeles. While looking into claims that human beings had been mutilated in a manner similar to that reported in cattle, Ecker contacted an active police detective friend, 'Scot', who had been involved in the investigation of a number of cattle mutilation incidents.

'I relayed my various information on human mutes to [Scot], and asked if he would be willing to send an inquiry through his Department's computer to the National Crime Information Center, operated and maintained by the FBI in Washington, DC.'

Several days later, Scot, sounding troubled, got back in touch with Ecker: 'Someone is sitting on something, big as Hell.' Contact was made with a further source, this time in the Department of Justice, who would only state that 'if all were smart, they would simply leave this issue alone'.[6]

As enigmatic as this certainly was, more was to come. An assistant medical examiner in Westchester County, New York, informed a researcher, Bill Knell, in 1989, that several morgues in the area had been 'hit' in the middle of the night, and fresh human cadavers had been mutilated, which involved partial removal of the face, and total removal of the eyes, thyroid, stomach and genitals. According to the assistant ME, 'the morgues in question wasted no time in putting the mutilations under wraps and out of the public eye'.[7]

It would be comforting if we could relegate accounts such as these to the realm of science fiction; unfortunately, we cannot. You will have noted that, when in 1976 an article published in *Oui* magazine referred to rumours that the cattle mutilations were 'a forerunner for later mutilations of human beings', the FBI special agent in charge at Springfield, Illinois, wasted no time in sending a complete copy of the twelve-page article to Washington. Quite clearly, this was, and still is, an issue that troubles the Bureau greatly.

Perhaps the single positive aspect of this is that, in the 1989 incidents reported by Bill Knell, the mutilators attacked only already deceased persons, rather than living ones. If nothing else, this may indicate a degree of regard for human life.

Trying to come to some form of conclusion concerning the cattle mutilations and associated phenomena is a nigh-on impossible feat. And I sometimes wonder: is this an issue that we should leave well alone? Would it be more beneficial if the official 'scavenger' theory was accepted by one and all?

Admittedly, if the Earth is little more than a gigantic farm for some extraterrestrial species, then this is truly alarming. The official papers released by the FBI, such as those of Police Officer Gabe Valdez, are convincing proof that something is taking place on a huge scale, and the reports cited in the previous chapter suggest that the phenomenon has no intention of curbing its activities.

If the FBI, among other agencies, is aware that alien creatures are systematically mutilating our livestock, and the US government has no connection with the responsible parties, then I can truly sympathise with those who believe earnestly that to withhold this information from the public is in everyone's best interests.

Yet the Bureau, by releasing a significant amount of data from its files, has perhaps taken the first step in informing us that all is not well; that the aliens are not our friends; and that they are not here to 'save' the human race, nor to bestow upon us some universal wisdom. Will the full story ever be told? Only time will tell.

CHAPTER 9

ALIENS OR NAZIS?

OF THE MANY RUMOURS THAT SURROUND THE UFO PUZZLE, ONE HAS long persisted. According to some, UFOs are not extraterrestrial vehicles but highly advanced (and highly classified) earth-based aeroforms modelled on radical German technology captured by American and Soviet forces in the closing stages of World War Two. While there is evidence to support the hypothesis that the Nazis were working to perfect circular and elliptical aircraft during the 1940s, to my mind, the sheer number and diversity of UFO sightings reported throughout the globe since 1947 effectively rules out the possibility that some hidden human hand is responsible for perpetuating this near-impenetrable fifty-year-old mystery.

Nevertheless, a number of accounts do exist which tend to lend credence to the possibility that, had the Nazis succeeded in staving off their defeat in 1945, their burgeoning technology would have dished up a few surprises for the Allied forces. Before addressing the issue of FBI involvement in this matter, let us first acquaint ourselves with those few tantalising facts on this emotive issue. Consider the following, extracted from a Central Intelligence Agency (CIA) report of 27 May 1954:

A German newspaper (not further identified) recently published an interview with George Klein, famous German engineer and aircraft expert, describing the experimental construction of 'flying saucers' carried out by him from 1941 to 1945. Klein stated that he was present when, in 1945, the first piloted 'flying saucer' took off and reached a speed of 1,300 miles per hour within 3 minutes. The experiments resulted in three designs: one designed by Miethe, was a disk-shaped aircraft, 135 feet in diameter, which did not rotate; another, designed by Habermohl and Schreiver, consisted of a large rotating ring, in the center of which was a round, stationary cabin for the crew. When the Soviets occupied Prague, the Germans destroyed every trace of the 'flying saucer' project and nothing more was heard of Habermohl and his assistants. Schriever recently died in Bremen, where he had been living. In Breslau, the Soviets managed to capture one of the saucers built by Miethe, who escaped to France. He is reportedly in the US at present.

A similar account comes from a two-page 1957 paper which originated with the British Air Ministry and was released under the terms of Britain's thirty-year rule. Previously classified at 'Secret' level, the document states: 'A review by the "Daily Worker" of a book recently published on German wartime weapons contained references to a German flying saucer which was flown at a speed of 1,250 mph to a height of 40,000 feet.'[1]

A report dated 3 January 1952 from Brigadier General W.M. Garland, USAF, to General Samford, Air Force Director of Intelligence, also addresses the issue of German involvement in the UFO mystery. Although somewhat speculative, relevant portions of the report confirm that elements of the USAF were of the opinion that some UFOs were of earthly origin:

> The continued reports of unusual flying objects requires positive action to determine the nature and origin of this phenomena . . .
> It is logical to relate the reported sightings to the known development of aircraft, jet propulsion, rockets and range extension capabilities in Germany and the USSR. In this connection, it is to be noted that certain developments by the Germans, particularly the Horton wing, jet propulsion, and refueling, combined with their extensive employment of V-1 and V-2 weapons during World War II, lend credence to the possibility that the flying

objects may be of German and Russian origin. The developments
mentioned above were completed and operational between 1941
and 1944 and subsequently fell into the hands of the Soviets at
the end of the war. There is evidence that the Germans were
working on these projects as far back as 1931 to 1938. Therefore
it may be assumed that the Germans had at least a 7 to 10 year
lead over the United States . . .

Now we'll turn our attention to the FBI. The concern shown by the
Bureau over the possibility that advanced Nazi technology was in the
hands of the Russians is something demonstrated by the following
decades-old Bureau report, which details information related by an
unnamed source. I quote from the relevant section of the paper:

. . . In addition [source] said that more recent reports have been
received from representatives of the Central Intelligence Agency
in Southern Europe and Southern Asia to the effect that the
Russians were experimenting with some type of radical aircraft or
guided missile which could be dispatched for great distances out
over the sea, made to turn in flight and return to the base from
which it was launched. He related that this information was
extremely worthy of notice as experiments in this country have
so far only developed to the point where we are concerned with
delivering a missile to the required point of impact and no consideration has been given to imparting to that missile the ability
to return. [Source] also advised that it is a known fact that the
Russians are attempting to develop some type of nuclear energy,
that they received a wealth of information concerning nuclear
energy at the time of their occupation in Germany, and that they
have at their disposal a limited supply of fissionable materials.
[Source] pointed out that the Russians have some very capable
scientists in the field of atomic energy and that, in addition
thereto, they took into their custody some of the most-advanced
and capable scientists of the German nation.

Another report that may have a bearing on this issue was brought to the attention of the Bureau shortly after the UFOs arrived in force over the USA in the summer of 1947:

> Recently I have heard and read about reports of disc-shaped aircraft, or whatever they are, in our western regions. They reminded me of a nearly-forgotten incident in Germany, after the war. I report this to you because I feel this may be of international scope.
>
> My buddy and I went on pass to see a friend of his. One evening the three of us were driving along some back roads when I sighted a strange-looking object in the sky from eight to ten miles to our front and approximately 5,000 feet high. I immediately stopped the jeep for a better look. The object rapidly came toward us, descending slowly. About a mile away it stopped its horizontal motion but continued a slow oscillating descent, similar to a descending parachute. Then it dropped in a spiral motion.
>
> Immediately I drove over to where it had dropped. It took almost five minutes to reach the place but we saw nothing. After ten minutes of cruising around the area it became too dark to see so we went back to town.
>
> I am not sure my companions saw this because it happened so quickly it could easily have been missed, but I described what I had seen so vividly that they were as excited as I was. My first impression was that it was a cloud, but it was traveling at right-angles to the wind.
>
> The locale of this incident was approximately 120 miles northwest of Habberbishophiem. If necessary, I will swear to the authenticity of this and to the shape of the object.

Also during the summer of 1947, a further report relating to the sighting of unconventional flying objects in the years immediately after World War Two caught the attention of the Bureau. Fortunately, in this particular case, we have the name of the informant, one Edwin M. Bailey of Stamford, Connecticut. Having been interviewed by agents of the FBI office at New Haven, Bailey was the subject of the following memorandum to J. Edgar Hoover:

Bailey prefaced his remarks by stating that he is a scientist by occupation and is currently employed at the American Cyanamid Research Laboratories on West Main Street in Stamford, Connecticut, in the Physics Division. Bailey further indicated that during the war he was employed at MIT, Cambridge, Massachusetts, in the Radiation Laboratory which Laboratory is connected with the Manhattan Project. Bailey advised that he is thirty years of age and is a graduate of the University of Arizona.

Bailey stated that the topic of 'flying saucers' had caused considerable comment and concern to the present day scientists and indicated that he himself had a personal theory concerning the 'flying saucers'. Prior to advancing his own theory, Bailey remarked that immediately after the conclusion of World War II, a friend of his [censored], allegedly observed the 'flying saucers' from an observatory in Milan and Bologna, Italy. He stated that apparently at that time the 'flying saucers' had caused a little comment in Italy but that after some little publicity they immediately died out as public interest. Bailey stated that it is quite possible that actually the 'flying saucers' could be radio controlled germ bombs or atom bombs which are circling the orbit of the earth and which could be controlled by radio and directed to land on any designated target at the specific desire of the agency or country operating the bombs.

Although the FBI was in receipt of this information on 18 July 1947, a full decade was to pass before it received what was probably one of the most convincing reports of Nazi involvement in the UFO issue. Again, the Bureau has chosen to censor various sections of the report, but this in no way detracts from the narrative. According to FBI memoranda of 7–8 November 1957, '. . . news reports of mysterious vehicle in Texas causing engines to stall prompted [witness] to communicate with the United States Government concerning a similar phenomenon observed by him in 1944 in the area of Gut Alt Golssen.'

And the Detroit office of the Bureau related:

[Witness was] born February 19, 1926, in the State of Warsaw,

Poland, [and] was brought from Poland as a Prisoner of War to Gut Alt Golssen approximately 30 miles east of Berlin, Germany, in May, 1942, where he remained until a few weeks after the end of World War II. He spent the following years at Displaced Persons Camps at Kork, Strasburg, Offenburg, Milheim and Freiburg, Germany. He attended a radio technician school at Freiburg and for about a year was employed in a textile mill at

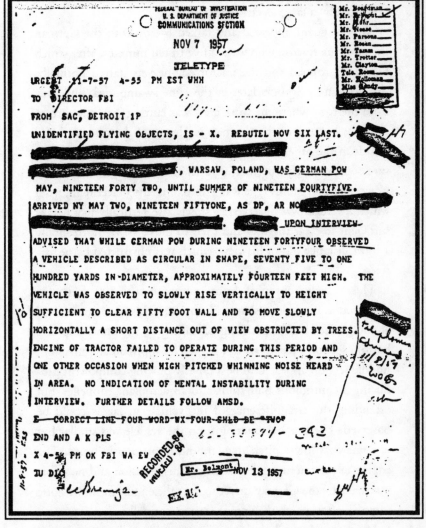

FEDERAL BUREAU OF INVESTIGATION
U. S. DEPARTMENT OF JUSTICE
COMMUNICATIONS SECTION

NOV 7 1957

TELETYPE

URGENT 11-7-57 4-55 PM EST WHH

TO DIRECTOR FBI

FROM SAC, DETROIT 1P

UNIDENTIFIED FLYING OBJECTS, IS - X. REBUTEL NOV SIX LAST.

▓▓▓▓▓▓▓▓▓▓▓, WARSAW, POLAND, WAS GERMAN POW

MAY, NINETEEN FORTY TWO, UNTIL SUMMER OF NINETEEN FOURTYFIVE.

ARRIVED NY MAY TWO, NINETEEN FIFTYONE, AS DP, AR N▓▓▓▓▓▓

▓▓▓▓▓▓▓▓▓▓▓▓▓▓▓▓▓. UPON INTERVIEW

ADVISED THAT WHILE GERMAN POW DURING NINETEEN FORTYFOUR OBSERVED

A VEHICLE DESCRIBED AS CIRCULAR IN SHAPE, SEVENTY FIVE TO ONE

HUNDRED YARDS IN DIAMETER, APPROXIMATELY FOURTEEN FEET HIGH. THE

VEHICLE WAS OBSERVED TO SLOWLY RISE VERTICALLY TO HEIGHT

SUFFICIENT TO CLEAR FIFTY FOOT WALL AND TO MOVE SLOWLY

HORIZONTALLY A SHORT DISTANCE OUT OF VIEW OBSTRUCTED BY TREES.

ENGINE OF TRACTOR FAILED TO OPERATE DURING THIS PERIOD AND

ONE OTHER OCCASION WHEN HIGH PITCHED WHINNING NOISE HEARD

IN AREA. NO INDICATION OF MENTAL INSTABILITY DURING

INTERVIEW. FURTHER DETAILS FOLLOW AMSD.

E CORRECT LINE FOUR WORD WX FOUR SHLD BE TWO

END AND A K PLS

X 4-5½ PM OK FBI WA EW

TU DIO

RECORDED-84

Mr. Belmont NOV 13 1957

Mr. Boardman
Mr. Belmont
Mr. Mohr
Mr. Nease
Mr. Parsons
Mr. Rosen
Mr. Tamm
Mr. Trotter
Mr. Clayton
Tele. Room
Mr. Holloman
Miss Gandy

A Bureau document concerning flying-saucer-type technology developed during World War Two by the Nazis.

Laurachbaden, Germany. He arrived in the United States at New York, May 2, 1951, via the 'SS General Stewart' as a Displaced Person . . .

According to [witness], during 1944, month not recalled, while enroute to work in a field a short distance north of Gut Alt Golssen, their tractor engine stalled on a road through a swamp area. No machinery or other vehicle was then visible although a noise was heard described as a high-pitched whine similar to that produced by a large electric generator.

An 'SS' guard appeared and talked briefly with the German driver of the tractor, who waited five to ten minutes, after which the noise stopped and the tractor engine was started normally. Approximately 3 hours later in the same swamp area, but away from the road where the work crew was cutting 'hay', he surreptitiously, because of the German in charge of the crew and 'SS' guards in the otherwise deserted area, observed a circular enclosure approximately 100 to 150 yards in diameter protected from viewers by a tarpaulin-type wall approximately 50 feet high, from which a vehicle was observed to slowly rise vertically to a height sufficient to clear the wall and then to move slowly horizontally a short distance out of his view, which was obstructed by nearby trees.

This vehicle, observed from approximately 500 feet, was described as circular in shape, 75 to 100 yards in diameter, and about 14 feet high, consisting of dark gray stationary top and bottom sections, five to six feet high. The approximate three foot middle section appeared to be a rapidly moving component producing a continuous blur similar to an aeroplane propeller, but extending the circumference of the vehicle so far as could be observed. The noise emanating from the vehicle was similar but of somewhat lower pitch than the noise previously heard. The engine of the tractor again stalled on this occasion and no effort was made by the German driver to start the engine until the noise stopped, after which the engine started normally.

Uninsulated metal, possibly copper, cables one and one-half inch to two inches in diameter, on and under the surface of the ground, in some places covered by water, were observed on this and previous occasions, apparently running between the enclosure and a small concrete column-like structure between the road and enclosure.

This area was not visited by [witness] again until shortly after the end of World War II, when it was observed the cables had been removed and the previous locations of the concrete structure and the enclosure were covered by water. [Witness] stated he has not been in communication since 1945 with any of the work crew of 16 or 18 men, consisting of Russian, French and Polish POWs, who had discussed this incident among themselves many times. However, of these, [witness] was able to recall by name only [one], no address known, described as then about 50 years of age and presumed to have returned to Poland after 1945.

That this particular report was taken seriously by the Bureau is evidenced by the fact that copies were circulated to the Office of Security at the Department of State; the Director of the Central Intelligence Agency; the Assistant Chief of Staff, Intelligence, Department of the Army; the Director of Naval Intelligence; the Air Force Office of Special Investigations; and the Immigration and Naturalization Service.

On 8 June 1967, a similar story surfaced, this time at the Bureau Office at Miami, Florida. Two pages in length, the report reads:

On April 26, 1967, [source] appeared at the Miami Office and furnished the following information relating to an object, presently referred to as an unidentified flying object, he allegedly photographed during November, 1944.

Sometime during 1943, he graduated from the German Air Academy and was assigned as a member of the Luftwaffe on the Russian Front. Near the end of 1944, he was released from this duty and was assigned as a test pilot to a top secret project in the Black Forest of Austria. During this period he observed the aircraft described above. It was saucer shaped, about twenty-one feet in diameter, radio-controlled, and mounted several jet engines around the exterior portion of the craft. He further described the exterior portion as revolving around the dome in the center which remained stationary. It was [witness's] responsibility to photograph the object while in flight. He asserted he was able to retain a negative of a photograph he made at 7,000 meters (20,000 feet).

From a former member of the Luftwaffe, the FBI office at Miami, Florida, learned of secret Nazi attempts to build flying saucers.

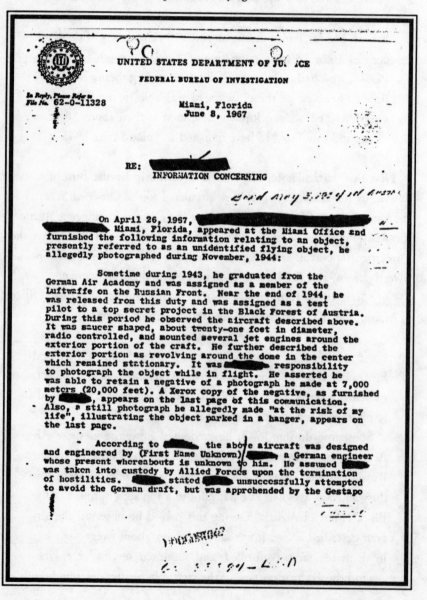

UNITED STATES DEPARTMENT OF JUSTICE

FEDERAL BUREAU OF INVESTIGATION

In Reply, Please Refer to
File No. 62-0-11328

Miami, Florida
June 8, 1967

RE: ▓▓▓▓▓▓▓▓

INFORMATION CONCERNING

good many copies of all known

On April 26, 1967, ▓▓▓▓▓▓▓▓▓▓▓▓▓▓▓▓
▓▓▓▓▓▓▓, Miami, Florida, appeared at the Miami Office and furnished the following information relating to an object, presently referred to as an unidentified flying object, he allegedly photographed during November, 1944:

Sometime during 1943, he graduated from the German Air Academy and was assigned as a member of the Luftwaffe on the Russian Front. Near the end of 1944, he was released from this duty and was assigned as a test pilot to a top secret project in the Black Forest of Austria. During this period he observed the aircraft described above. It was saucer shaped, about twenty-one feet in diameter, radio controlled, and mounted several jet engines around the exterior portion of the craft. He further described the exterior portion as revolving around the dome in the center which remained stationary. It was ▓▓▓▓▓▓▓ responsibility to photograph the object while in flight. He asserted he was able to retain a negative of a photograph he made at 7,000 meters (20,000 feet). A Xerox copy of the negative, as furnished by ▓▓▓▓▓, appears on the last page of this communication. Also, a still photograph he allegedly made "at the risk of my life", illustrating the object parked in a hanger, appears on the last page.

According to ▓▓▓▓▓ the above aircraft was designed and engineered by (First Name Unknown)/▓▓▓▓▓, a German engineer whose present whereabouts is unknown to him. He assumed ▓▓▓▓▓ was taken into custody by Allied Forces upon the termination of hostilities. ▓▓▓▓▓ stated ▓▓▓▓▓ unsuccessfully attempted to avoid the German draft, but was apprehended by the Gestapo

RE: ▆▆▆▆▆▆▆

INFORMATION CONCERNING

in Vienna, Austria, sometime during late 1943 or early 1944.
▆▆▆▆▆ also assumed the secrets pertaining to this aircraft
were captured by Allied Forces. He said this type of aircraft
was responsible for the downing of at least one American B-26
airplane. He furnished the following fuel and engine data:

"....Fuel mixture of N_2H_4O in Methyl Alcohol
(CH_3CH) rather than 'oxygen-holding' mixture of
hydrogen peroxide H_2O_2 in water. 7m 1,3m high two
rocket motors; smooth flow, rotary drive over 2,000
meters per second...."

▆▆▆▆▆ said he copied this data from a board
located in the hanger area.

▆▆▆▆▆ asserted he was shot down by the British
on March 14, 1945, after having been reassigned to the
Western Front. He was held prisoner by the British in
London and later in Brussels until his release in 1946.
He departed for the United States from Bremerhaven, Germany,
on December 26, 1951; entering the United States in New
Jersey on January 7, 1952, and was subsequently naturalized
in Miami during 1958. He is presently employed as a
mechanic at Eastern Airlines, Miami, Florida. He related
he was born May 3, 1924, in Austria.

▆▆▆▆▆ stated he has withheld this information
because he assumed the United States possessed it. He has
become increasingly concerned because of the unconfirmed
reports concerning a similar object and denials the United
States has such an aircraft. He feels such a weapon would
be beneficial in Vietnam and would prevent the further loss
of American lives which was his paramount purpose in contacting
the Federal Bureau of Investigation (FBI).

▆▆▆▆▆ reiterated he has the original negatives
of both photographs. He said the shots were taken at a thirty
second time exposure.

This document contains neither recommendations nor
conclusions of the FBI. It is the property of the FBI and is
loaned to your agency; it and its contents are not to be
distributed outside your agency.

2

According to [witness] the above aircraft was designed and
engineered by a German engineer whose present whereabouts is
unknown to him. [Witness] also assumed the secrets pertaining
to this aircraft were captured by Allied Forces. He said this type
of aircraft was responsible for the downing of at least one
American B-26 airplane.

He has become increasingly concerned because of the unconfirmed reports concerning a similar object and denials the United States has such an aircraft. He feels such a weapon would be beneficial in Vietnam and would prevent the further loss of American lives which was his paramount purpose in contacting the Federal Bureau of Investigation (FBI).

As if that were not astounding enough, there is a distinct possibility that, as far back as the late 1950s, the man may have had direct ties with the Central Intelligence Agency! This may not have had a bearing on his decision to inform the Bureau of his experience in 1944, but a memo of 8 June from Miami to Hoover gives valuable background data on the source of this remarkable account:

A review of the Miami indices revealed information reflecting [that the] subject appeared at the Miami Office on July 24, 1959, and volunteered to return to Austria as an intelligence agent. His expressed motivation was to do something to repay the debt he felt he owed the United States. He was afforded the Washington, DC Headquarters address of the Central Intelligence Agency and told his inquiry should be directed there.

What went on behind the closed doors of the CIA we may never know; however, the Bureau reported that on 4 July 1961, the same source turned up again at the Miami office, this time in a concerned state, and reported that he had been asked to commit a murder on behalf of an unidentified 'individual'.

This is all highly disturbing, but it is noteworthy that the Bureau considered the man a credible source of information: 'During his most recent visit to the Miami Office, [source] seemed genuinely concerned about the existence of the object he allegedly photographed during November, 1944. He exhibited no emotional nor mental disorder and appeared to be rational.'

As these Bureau records show clearly, the probability that the Nazis were working on circular aircraft designs in the 1940s is high. Yet, if that technology did fall into the hands of Russian and American forces at the close of hostilities in 1945, one might ask: where is it now? I have seen no evidence to suggest that such vehicles were deployed in, for example, the wars in Korea, Vietnam, Afghanistan, the Falkland Islands, and the Gulf. And as I have already detailed, on 10 July 1947, the Bureau received an official briefing from General George F. Schulgen, Chief of the Requirements Intelligence Branch of the Air Corps Intelligence, who advised that: '. . . there are no War Department or Navy Department research projects presently being conducted which could in any way be tied up with the flying disks'.

Moreover, there is strong evidence to show that when the Americans did begin to experiment with saucer-like technology in the 1950s, their efforts were an unmitigated disaster. The 'Avrocar', for example, is a perfect case in point. Initially, the prospects for the Avrocar looked good: a circular platform with a diameter of 35.3 feet, the vehicle was designed to have a maximum speed of Mach 3.5, and a range of 1,000 miles. However, as the US Air Force later conceded:

> From 1958 on, Aircraft Lab had many doubts about feasibility as expressed in correspondence and project reviews. On basis of various tests, the Aircraft Lab noted in Feb 1958 that the Avrocar probably would not be capable of supersonic flight. A few months later, Aircraft Lab statements [said] that the concept was feasible, but that much work had to be done before it would ever be operational – serious mechanical problems, engine problems, aerodynamic problems, and flight factors unknown.

Later evaluations revealed that 'wind tunnel tests were unsatisfactory', and the Avrocar project was eventually disbanded.[2] It goes without saying that if, in 1958, circular aircraft were presenting a problem to America's scientific elite, then the possibility that factions of the US military were soaring around the globe in Nazi-built flying saucers a full decade earlier is practically nonexistent.

In addition, the idea that the Soviets were doing likewise evaporates in the light of revelations that, in August 1947, Russian agents were out in force in New Mexico trying to determine if UFOs were an American invention. I hardly need to add that if the saucers were Soviet in origin, such actions on the part of the Russians would have been patently illogical.

I can therefore only conclude that, if the Nazis were working on saucer-like devices during World War Two, they must have carried many of their secrets with them to the grave.

Questions, of course, remain. If, for example, the data related in official FBI memoranda of the 1940s, 1950s and 1960s is accurate, how were the Nazis able to develop technology that, years later, was still defying America's finest? As I will later show, there are firm grounds for believing that a number of extraterrestrial vehicles crashed to earth on US soil in the late 1940s. Is it stretching the bounds of possibility to speculate that a similar event may have occurred on Nazi territory several years previously? If such an event did take place, and the Germans were able to grasp the rudiments of the technology, this would perhaps go a long way towards explaining their pressing desire to perfect a man-made flying saucer. The truth may ultimately turn out to be far stranger than has previously been realised.

CHAPTER 10

INCIDENT AT AZTEC

THE LATE 1980s SAW THE FBI IMPLICATED IN AN INTRIGUING MYSTERY, THE ramifications of which continue to reverberate to this day. The 'MJ-12 Affair', as I have dubbed it, involves incredible tales of crashed UFOs, dead aliens in the possession of the US government, the possible theft and unauthorised release of highly classified official documents, and a shadowy counterintelligence operation, all of which are now inextricably woven into one giant conspiracy – at the heart of which may lie the undeniable evidence that proves that humankind is not alone in the universe.

In 1987, the British investigator and author Timothy Good released his bestselling book, *Above Top Secret*, which provided conclusive evidence that intelligence agencies throughout the world have been keeping a close eye on the UFO puzzle since at least 1947, and possibly since the 1930s. One of the highlights of Good's book (and indeed there were many) was the mention of a top-secret research-and-development group established by the US government in the late 1940s to deal with highly classified UFO data. Variously referred to as 'Majestic 12', 'Majic 12', or simply 'MJ-12', the group was supposedly created following the crash and recovery of an alien spacecraft which had plummeted to earth in the sparse desert of New Mexico in early July 1947. More alarming still, the remains of several strange creatures, referred to as 'Extraterrestrial Biological Entities', or EBEs, were found within the wreckage of the vehicle.[1] I will return to MJ-12 in due course, but for now let us focus our attention on

the many other 'crashed UFO' incidents in which the FBI has been implicated over the last half-century.

According to a letter dated 3 September 1947 from Air Defense
Command Headquarters, New York, for the attention of Assistant Chief
of Staff, A-2:

> It was the original intent of the AC/AS-2, Headquarters, Army
> Air Forces that whereas the ADC Air Forces would interview
> responsible observers whose names would be furnished by AAF,
> the FBI would investigate incidents of so-called 'discs' being
> found on the ground. The services of the FBI were enlisted in
> order to relieve the numbered Air Forces of the task of tracking
> down all the many instances which turned out to be ash can cov-
> ers, toilet seats, and whatnot.

Although there can be no doubt that, in its first weeks and months of
involvement in the UFO subject, the Bureau was certainly confronted
with a number of purported UFO crashes which turned out to have
prosaic explanations, the same cannot be said in every instance. It would
be superfluous of me to discuss all the cases that fall into the former category, but three are worth commenting upon.

What was perhaps the most outlandish (not to mention humorous)
hoaxed account of a downed saucer in which the FBI played a vital role
occurred during the first week of July 1947. As the *Washington Post*
described on 7 July: 'A Catholic priest at Grafton, Wisconsin, said tonight
that a round, metal disc, which might be one of the mysterious "flying
saucers", had crashed into his parish yard and that he is holding it for the
Federal Bureau of Investigation.'

According to the Reverend Joseph Brasky, of St Joseph's Church, earlier
on that same day he had heard a 'swishing and whirring' noise, followed
by a thud and a mild explosion. On investigating his yard, Brasky came
upon a 'sheet metal disc about 18 inches in diameter, resembling a circular saw blade'. In fact, the resemblance to a circular saw blade was hardly
coincidence: that is exactly what it was!

Since the *Washington Post* had revealed that Brasky had intended advising the FBI of what had occurred, Special Agent H.K. Johnson at Milwaukee prepared a memorandum which did not put Father Brasky in a very good light, to say the least.

As Johnson related, at the time of the 'encounter', Brasky had been 'drinking quite heavily', and despite what he had told the *Washington Post*, 'Brasky has never contacted the Milwaukee FBI Office or any Agent concerning his find. In my opinion, this is just another hoax story, since a photograph of Father Brasky with the saw indicates no basis for any investigation by any authority.'

So much for the Wisconsin UFO crash, but there were still other similar cases to come which undoubtedly infuriated the FBI. Consider the following one-page report of 11 July 1947, to the Assistant-to-the-Director, Edward A. Tamm:

> SAC Johnson of the Milwaukee Office called to advise he had just received a telephone call from [a] Reserve Officer with the Civilian Air Patrol, Black River Falls, Wisconsin. [He] reported that at 3:30 p.m., July 10 . . . at Black River Falls a large 17″ disc [was found] which appeared to have been possibly made out of cardboard painted with silver airplane dope. In the center was a tube and a small motor with a propellor attached to the side. Colonel [deleted] expressed the opinion that this disc would not be able to fly by itself. He advised it would be taken to the Air Corps Headquarters.

Again, this case turned out to be nothing more than a crude hoax. While these two cases are noteworthy only for their humour value, the following report is rather more interesting. Despite the fact that the 'debris' referred to was ultimately shown to have no connection with the UFO problem, the steps taken by officialdom to investigate the case reflect the procedures that would undoubtedly follow in the wake of a genuine UFO crash.

A teletype message of 18 July 1947 to FBI headquarters at Washington detailed the report of several individuals who had reported seeing a number of 'small burned spots about one and a half inches in diameter on [their] green lawn'. The teletype continued: 'Also in the long dry grass on both sides of road in a circle approximately two hundred feet in diameter several little blazes had started and the Fire Department was called. Fires were apparently caused by metallic fragmentation which were turned over to [the] Massachusetts Institute of Technology (MIT)'.

According to one source, the fragments resembled the lining of V-2 bombs, 'which he had observed at New Mexico'. However, the Bureau commented that 'a metallurgist at MIT stated that they are possibly the lining from a jet turbo plane'.

A further report, of 29 July, stated that a spectographic examination of the fragments had been undertaken, the conclusion of which was that that they were 'ordinary cast iron which had been subjected to a very high degree of heat'. It was also determined that: 'Measurements of the four pieces examined revealed that they had most likely been originally all part of one hollow cylinder, eight inches in diameter and three-sixteenths of an inch in thickness.'

Although not proven, it was strongly suspected by the staff at MIT that the debris was indeed from a guided missile project based in New Mexico. What is particularly significant, however, is that in this case, MIT was advised that the investigation of the debris was to be considered a 'secret matter', and that 'no publicity has been given and it is not anticipated that any will result'.

For those who would argue that debris from a crashed UFO could not be effectively contained from the public and the media alike, consider the case I have just described: until the Bureau determined that the documentation surrounding the event could be released, no one outside of officialdom had any inkling that unidentified debris had been (a) recovered; (b) classified secret; and (c) examined by leading authorities at the Massachusetts Institute of Technology.

With these three examples of resolved crashed UFO incidents out of the way, let us now examine some of the more tantalising cases that have caught the attention of the Federal Bureau of Investigation.

Next to the so-called 'Roswell Incident' of 1947, perhaps the most talked-about, dissected, criticised, promoted and championed UFO crash is that alleged to have occurred in the vicinity of Aztec, New Mexico, in 1948.

According to information related to the author Frank Scully in the late 1940s, and subsequently published in his 1950 book, *Behind The Flying Saucers*, as a result of a number of separate incidents, the wreckage of four alien spacecraft, and no fewer than 34 alien bodies, had been recovered by US authorities, and were being studied under cover of the utmost secrecy at defence establishments in the United States.

As Scully was willing to admit, the bulk of his information had come from two prime sources, Silas Mason Newton (described in a 1941 FBI report as a 'wholly unethical businessman') and one 'Dr Gee', the name given to protect eight scientists, all of whom had divulged various details of the crashes to both Newton and Scully. As far as the Aztec crash was concerned, Scully's informants had carefully advised him that the saucer had come down at nearby Farmington, whereupon it was found essentially intact, aside from a slight fracture to one of a number of portholes which encompassed the craft.[2]

After access to the UFO was gained via the damaged porthole, inside were found the corpses of no fewer than sixteen small, human-like creatures, all slightly charred. The UFO was then dismantled (after an examination had determined its unique style of manufacture) whereupon it, and the bodies of the crew, were transferred to Wright Field air base.[3]

At the time, Scully's book caused a sensation and it went on to become a bestseller. However, in both 1952 and 1955, J.P. Cahn, a reporter who had previously worked for the *San Francisco Chronicle*, authored two exposés, which cast extreme doubt on the claims of Newton and 'Dr Gee' (identified not as 'eight scientists', but as one Leo A. GeBauer).

Yet, as the years have shown, the Aztec incident refuses to die. In 1974, for example, Professor John Spencer Carr revealed that he had in his possession what was deemed to be credible information on the case, including testimony from a senior Air Force officer who was involved in the retrieval of the Aztec UFO.[4] Twelve months after, however, the case was once again demolished, this time by one Mike McClellan in a persuasive paper titled 'The UFO Crash Of 1948 Is A Hoax'.[5]

In view of this, it was something of a surprise when the researcher William Steinman released a literally massive book in 1987 which asserted that the Aztec crash did occur, and that Frank Scully's original book was in essence factually correct. And just to compound things further, following the release of Steinman's book (co-authored with the researcher Wendelle Stevens), Jerome Clark of *Fate* magazine wrote: '[the Steinman–Stevens book] draws on speculation, rumor, unnamed informants and unbridled paranoia to defend and elaborate on the original story.'[6]

And that is the problem with the Aztec case: much of the original testimony is weak and rests on the shoulders of Newton and GeBauer. But what connection does all this have to the FBI, you may ask? Quite simply, partly as a result of its interest in the UFO issue as a whole, and partly because both Newton and GeBauer were 'known' to the Bureau, a substantial file of data on the Aztec affair was compiled by the FBI, much of which is now in my possession. But first some background on Newton and GeBauer, gleaned from the aforementioned FBI papers.

Born 25 February 1903, Leo Arnold Julius GeBauer is the subject of a huge FBI file totalling 398 pages. Curiously, of that file, fewer than 200 pages have been released to me under the provisions of the Freedom of Information Act. As the available papers demonstrate, GeBauer was, to put it mildly, a somewhat colourful character.

To begin with, he had numerous aliases, including Harry A. Grebauer, Harry A. Gebauer, Harry A. Greybauer, Harry A. Gabauer, Harry A. Barbar, Leo A.J. GeBauer, Leo Arnold Julius GeBauer, and Arnold Julius Leopold Gebauer. And as a confidential Bureau report of 19 December 1941 states, GeBauer had made some disturbing statements seven months previously:

> What this country needs is a man like Hitler; then everybody would have a good job . . . It would be a God's blessing if we had two men in the United States to run this country like Hitler . . . The English people are nothing but a dirty bunch of rats . . . We should stay to home and tend to our own damn business and let Germany give England what they have coming.

More controversially, GeBauer went on to describe Adolf Hitler as 'a swell fellow', adding that 'the guy who shoots President Roosevelt should be given a gold medal'. As Bureau Special Agent J.J. McGuire noted: 'GeBauer is always pointing out the good points of the German

Government over the English and our democratic form of Government.'

To demonstrate that controversy continued to surround GeBauer, a memo dated 14 February 1969 from the Denver office of the FBI referred

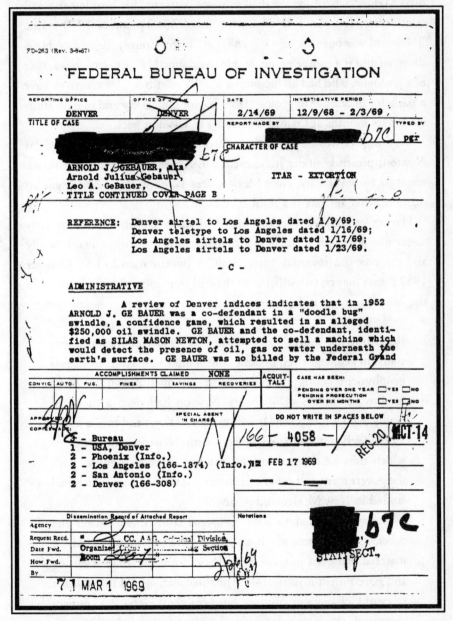

FD-263 (Rev. 3-8-67)

FEDERAL BUREAU OF INVESTIGATION

REPORTING OFFICE	OFFICE OF ORIGIN	DATE	INVESTIGATIVE PERIOD
DENVER	DENVER	2/14/69	12/9/68 - 2/3/69

TITLE OF CASE	REPORT MADE BY	TYPED BY
▓▓▓▓▓▓▓▓ b7C	b7C	pgr

CHARACTER OF CASE

ARNOLD J. GEBAUER, aka
Arnold Julius Gebauer,
Leo A. GeBauer,
TITLE CONTINUED COVER PAGE B

ITAR - EXTORTION

REFERENCE: Denver airtel to Los Angeles dated 1/9/69;
Denver teletype to Los Angeles dated 1/16/69;
Los Angeles airtels to Denver dated 1/17/69;
Los Angeles airtels to Denver dated 1/23/69.

- C -

ADMINISTRATIVE

A review of Denver indices indicates that in 1952 ARNOLD J. GE BAUER was a co-defendant in a "doodle bug" swindle, a confidence game, which resulted in an alleged $250,000 oil swindle. GE BAUER and the co-defendant, identified as SILAS MASON NEWTON, attempted to sell a machine which would detect the presence of oil, gas or water underneath the earth's surface. GE BAUER was no billed by the Federal Grand

		ACCOMPLISHMENTS CLAIMED	NONE			ACQUIT-TALS	CASE HAS BEEN:
CONVIC.	AUTO.	FUG.	FINES	SAVINGS	RECOVERIES		PENDING OVER ONE YEAR ☐YES ☐NO
							PENDING PROSECUTION OVER SIX MONTHS ☐YES ☐NO

APPROVED ▓▓▓ SPECIAL AGENT IN CHARGE

DO NOT WRITE IN SPACES BELOW

COPIES MADE:

3 - Bureau
1 - USA, Denver
2 - Phoenix (Info.)
2 - Los Angeles (166-1874) (Info.)
2 - San Antonio (Info.)
2 - Denver (166-308)

166 - 4058 - REG-20 MCT-14

FEB 17 1969

Dissemination Record of Attached Report		Notations
Agency		b7C
Request Recd.	CC, AAG, Criminal Division,	
Date Fwd.	Organized Crime .... Section	STAT SECT.
How Fwd.	Room	
By	7 1 MAR 1 1969	

A 1969 FBI document confirming that the Bureau was well-acquainted with the activities of both Silas Newton and Leo Gebauer.

to an unnamed source who 'threatened to do bodily harm to GeBauer and demanded $50,000 as part of commissions due him'.

Silas Mason Newton, as we shall now see, attracted his own fair share of controversy, too. An FBI document dated 30 September 1970 states: '[Newton] was born on July 19, 1887, at Shelby County, Kentucky. He is divorced and is a college graduate. He has claimed his occupation was that of a geologist, who had an income of $500 a month . . . He claims to have a Bachelor of Science in geology from Baylor University and to have studied for six months at Oxford University in London [sic].'

Very impressive, but a further Bureau report of 1970 reveals: 'Silas Newton, presently under indictment Los Angeles, California, for fraud, returned to Silver City, New Mexico, area January, 1970, and began to organize what appears as a mining swindle . . .'

Having established Newton and GeBauer's credentials, let us now direct our attention to their involvement with the author Frank Scully and the ever-controversial Aztec crash. A Bureau record of 18 October 1952 shows that certain officials of the FBI were more than well versed in the Aztec story and its background:

Regarding the 'saucer' story . . . in July 1949 GeBauer, as a specialist in geomagnetics, became consultant to Newton, an alleged geophysicist, using instruments of his own design to make microwave surveys of oil pools. Newton had been a friend of Scully, who writes a weekly column for Variety; and in the fall of 1949, GeBauer discussed saucers with Newton and Scully at which time he claimed to have conducted secret inquiries with the government and other scientists on several saucers which had landed in New Mexico and Arizona.

GeBauer claimed to have recovered from these saucers the tubeless radio, some small gears and small disks, all of which material had been secreted by GeBauer from the other scientists and government investigators. The three men agreed to publish a story of GeBauer's discoveries, but because of GeBauer's connections with the matter, he was to be identified only as 'Dr Gee'. To determine the reaction of the public to an authenticated story of the actual existence of flying saucers, on March 8, 1950, Newton, as 'Scientist X' appeared as a guest lecturer before a science class at Denver University.

Newton told of Dr Gee's findings, and the substance of the lecture 'leaked' out to the newspapers. As a result, Scully wrote his book setting forth Dr Gee's discoveries and revelations . . .

[A]fter reading the saucer story, [J.P. Cahn] noted several inconsistencies, and he determined to make an investigation to determine whether the story was based on facts or a hoax. In the beginning he went to Scully, but was unable to obtain the identity of Dr Gee, and Scully was reluctant to produce Newton. [Cahn] met Newton in Scully's home at which time Newton claimed to be a graduate of Baylor University and Yale University, and a post-graduate of the University of Berlin. Newton promised to discuss with Dr Gee the proposition to disclose fully an authenticated announcement that space ships were landing on earth, together with photographs, metals, and other evidence.

Newton exhibited a couple of gears, fine-toothed and about the size of pocket watches, and two disks of unknown metals, all being tied up in Newton's handkerchief. He alleged these items were obtained from one of the saucers. Newton also told [Cahn] of seeing secret detailed plans on the Airflow system of B-26's in Dr Gee's laboratories in Phoenix on which the mysterious Dr Gee was doing research for the government. Dr Gee had developed a magnetic fog, rain and darkness dispelling screen to be fitted on the windshields of airplanes to enable the pilot to see through any weather . . .

Much of the remainder of this document is heavily censored, which in itself is interesting, but a few further sections have been released:

. . . While in Scully's book, Dr Gee was said to have degrees [from] the University of Berlin, GeBauer only claimed electrical engineering degrees from Louis Institute of Technology in Chicago in 1931 or 1932; that while the book claimed from 1943 to 1945 Dr Gee had headed 1,700 scientists doing experi-

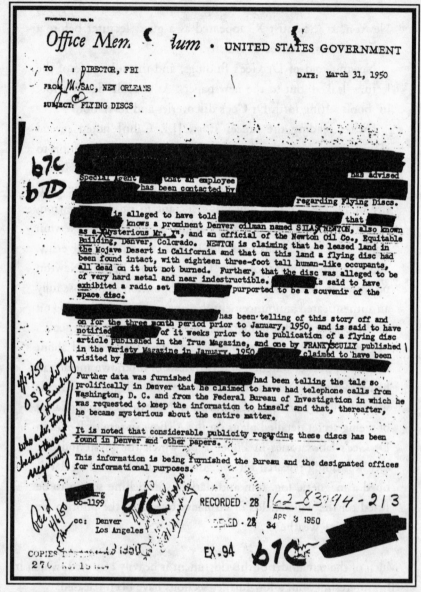

STANDARD FORM NO. 64

Office Mem. (*lum* • UNITED STATES GOVERNMENT

TO   : DIRECTOR, FBI   DATE: March 31, 1950

FROM : SAC, NEW ORLEANS

SUBJECT: FLYING DISCS

b7C
b7D

Special Agent [   ] that an employee [   ] has advised [   ] has been contacted by [   ] regarding Flying Discs.

[   ] is alleged to have told [   ] that [   ] knows a prominent Denver oilman named SILAS NEWTON, also known as a "Mysterious Mr. X", and an official of the Newton Oil Co., Equitable Building, Denver, Colorado. NEWTON is claiming that he leased land in the Mojave Desert in California and that on this land a flying disc had been found intact, with eighteen three-foot tall human-like occupants, all dead on it but not burned. Further, that the disc was alleged to be of very hard metal and near indestructible. [   ] is said to have exhibited a radio set [   ] purported to be a souvenir of the space disc.

[   ] has been telling of this story off and on for the three month period prior to January, 1950, and is said to have notified [   ] of it weeks prior to the publication of a flying disc article published in the True Magazine, and one by FRANK SCULLY published in the Variety Magazine in January, 1950 [   ] claimed to have been visited by [   ]

Further data was furnished [   ] had been telling the tale so prolifically in Denver that he claimed to have had telephone calls from Washington, D. C. and from the Federal Bureau of Investigation in which he was requested to keep the information to himself and that, thereafter, he became mysterious about the entire matter.

It is noted that considerable publicity regarding these discs has been found in Denver and other papers.

This information is being furnished the Bureau and the designated offices for informational purposes.

66-1199

cc: Denver
    Los Angeles

RECORDED - 28   162-83994-213
      D - 28   34 APR 3 1950

COPIES [   ] 1950

EX-94

In 1950, the FBI monitored Silas Newton's involvement in the controversy surrounding the UFO crash at Aztec, New Mexico.

mental work in the secret government magnetic research, GeBauer was merely chief of laboratories of Air Research Company in Phoenix and Los Angeles, mainly in charge of maintenance of equipment.

> [Cahn] talked with GeBauer and obtained a signed statement
> from him denying that he was Dr Gee mentioned in Scully's
> book, and stating that he had no connection with Scully, his
> book, or statements, and had given Scully no authority to infer
> that he was Dr Gee. GeBauer did state that he was acquainted
> with Newton.

Was the Newton–GeBauer–Scully story factually correct? Was
GeBauer the elusive Dr Gee? Or was the entire matter without foundation? Here things become decidely murky. FBI records show that in the
following year, 1953, both GeBauer and Newton received suspended
prison sentences for their part in defrauding Herman Flader, a Colorado
businessman who owned the Stay Put Clamp and Coupling Factory on
the outskirts of Denver, which does not inspire a great deal of confidence
in the Aztec incident as a whole.

And yet, for all the faults of Newton and GeBauer, there are a number
of intriguing pointers which suggest that there may be a degree of fact
behind the story of the UFO crash at Aztec. As far as GeBauer was concerned, it is a proven fact that in the 1940s he most definitely was
employed as chief of laboratories at the Air Research Manufacturing
Company, Phoenix.

It so happens that of the four alleged UFO crashes discussed in Frank
Scully's book, one occurred north of Phoenix, at Paradise Valley in 1947.
That there may be some truth behind this particular case has been
demonstrated by Timothy Good. In his 1996 book, *Beyond Top Secret*,
Good discusses the testimony of a private pilot, Selman E. Graves, who
described witnessing aspects of an operation to retrieve a 'large aluminum dome-shaped thing' in the Paradise Valley area, around which
were 'pitched buildings – tents – and men moving about'.[7]

Speculation it may be, but given the fact that this retrieval occurred
relatively close to where, in the early 1940s, Leo GeBauer had been
employed in the aerospace industry, the possibility that he may have
gleaned details of the crash from former colleagues at Air Research cannot be wholly dismissed.

And with respect to GeBauer, there is one final point which should not
pass without comment. As we have seen, in total the FBI's file on

GeBauer runs to almost 400 pages, of which only half has been declassified. While many of the withheld pages relate to 'personnel and medical files and similar files', others remain exempt from disclosure: (A) 'in the interest of national defense . . . and are in fact properly classified'; and (B) by statute requiring that 'the matters be withheld from the public in such a manner as to leave no discretion on the issue'. There can be no doubt that GeBauer did engage in questionable activities, but they hardly seemed to be the sort of acts that would compromise national defence and require the facts surrounding them to remain 'withheld from the public'. Unless, that is, those FBI papers that *have* been released do not tell the whole story and Frank Scully was essentially correct all along.

With respect to Silas Newton, there are a number of indicators here that perhaps he, too, had latched on to information which he knew pertained to a genuine UFO crash. Although a 1970 FBI file on Newton describes him as 'an accomplished con man of many years standing, who is knowledgable in the field of petroleum and mining, and has exploited this knowledge in swindling people', earlier Bureau papers refer to a statement made by Newton in the 21 October 1952 issue of the *Denver Post*: '. . . Newton had advised that he had never seen a flying saucer nor had he ever pretended to have seen one . . . Newton stated he was merely repeating what he had heard from other sources'. Considering that Newton was 'an accomplished con man', I have to wonder why he seemed curiously intent on playing down his role in the Aztec case. If, however, there was a suspicion on Newton's part that he was possibly in possession of classified information, then all things become clear.

There is another aspect of Newton's role in the Aztec crash that suggests that his information was of interest to elements of the US government. Recall that the FBI document of 18 October 1952 refers to a lecture given on 8 March 1950 by Newton at Denver University, where he was billed as 'Scientist X'.

It so happens that this lecture, if not attended by Bureau officials, was at least monitored by them. An 'Urgent' teletype of 9 March from the Denver FBI office confirms their awareness of Newton's talk: 'Two sources advised today that [Silas Newton] has given at least one and possibly more lectures before classes at Denver University yesterday or today in which he discussed flying saucers which he allegedly personally observed. This person claims to have seen several such objects, one of which allegedly landed in New Mexico. He also claims to have observed occupants of saucers described by him as of human form, but about three feet tall.'

It so happens that Newton had been escorted to the lecture by one George T. Koehler, a staff member of an independent Rocky Mountain radio station. Although Frank Scully confirmed that Koehler never introduced Newton by name (hence 'Scientist X'), Bureau records in my possession make it clear that the FBI knew practically from the outset that 'X' and Newton were one and the same. I therefore have to conclude that whatever the ultimate status of the Aztec case, the FBI took a deep interest in determining who was saying what, when and to whom.

Curiously, in *Behind The Flying Saucers*, Scully reported that within two hours of Newton's lecture, US intelligence agents were asking questions about Newton and the nature of his talk, and what the general concensus of opinion was with respect to his revelations. In addition, there is evidence to show that George Koehler was 'relieved' of certain audio tapes after he had the foresight to surreptitiously record an interview between himself and a representative of the US Army. 'We know you have been recording these interviews,' Koehler was told. 'Now hand them over.'

Matters became even more entangled when, according to a two-page 1950 report released to me by the FBI, Koehler, too, was reported to have actually seen two crashed UFOs held by the US government. In this particular instance the source of the information was revealed to be Rudy Fick, a Kansas City car dealer. In early January 1950, Fick had made a stopover in Denver while returning from Ogden, Utah, and paid a visit to the manager of the Ford agency. According to official records released by the FBI: 'Their conversation was interrupted by some engineers arriving for a meeting; one of whom was named [Koehler]. [Koehler] revealed some startling information,' the report continued, as I shall now show:

[Koehler] stated he 'crashed the gate' at a radar station near New Mexico and Arizona borders, and while there he saw 2 of the highly secret 'Flying Saucers.' Spot report details – the information contained herein was furnished from article which appeared in the Wyandotte Echo newspaper, Kansas City, Kansas, 6 January 1950. Of the two Flying Saucers one was badly damaged and the other almost perfectly intact. They consisted of 2 parts, a cockpit or cabin about 6 feet in diameter. A ring 13 feet across and 2 feet thick surrounded the cabin. The cabin was constructed of metal resembling aluminum, but the actual make of the metal has defied analysis.

[Koehler] showed the group, including Fick, a clock or automatic calendar which was taken from one of the Flying Saucers. This clock or automatic calendar consisted of 2 pieces of metal together with some unusual type of metal. On the face of 1 or 2 pieces of this metal there appeared an indentation which rotated around the disk completing a cycle each 28 days.

According to the information given [Koehler] around 50 of these flying saucers have been found in the United States in a period of 2 years. Of these, 40 are in the 7 US Research Bureau in Los Angeles. Each of the craft had a crew of 3. The bodies in the damaged ship were charred, but the other ship's occupants were in a perfect state of preservation, although dead.

All were uniform height of 3 feet; blond, beardless and their teeth were completely free of fillings or cavities. They wore no under-garments, but had their bodies taped and were dressed in a sort of wire. A quantity of food in tablet form was found in ship. Mr Fick assumed that the reason behind the apparent lack of security was that the Government wanted the information spread from unofficial sources until people are more or less familiar with the facts. Mr Fick feels that the security department of the military fear that the sudden shock of a surprise announcement that interplanetary travel is possible might cause mass hysteria. Fick is well known locally and has a number of friends at the Kansas City Star. OSI District 13 will interview Fick and will make additional inquiries at the Kansas City Star. [Koehler] not otherwise identified, but can be reached through Ford agency in Denver.

Action: Information copies furnished OSI Districts 14 and 17 for action. The editor of the Kansas City Star stated that while they were aware of this story they did not dare publish it in the paper because it is too fantastic.

A partly censored FBI document of 22 March 1950 shows that a story, very similar to that told by Fick, was in circulation in Washington. A one-page report from the Washington special agent in charge, Guy Hottel, to Hoover reads: 'An investigator for the Air Forces stated that three so-

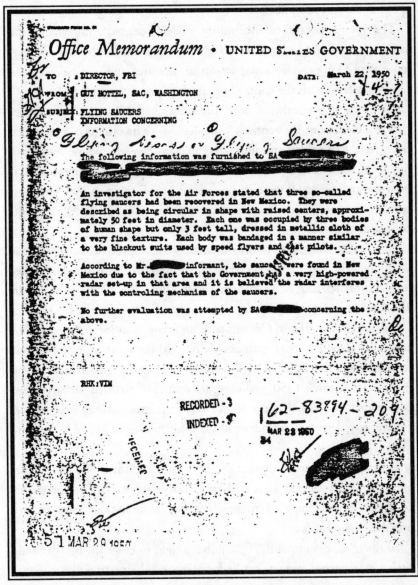

A one-page FBI memorandum of 1950 detailing three UFO crashes in New Mexico.

called flying saucers had been recovered in New Mexico. They were described as being circular in shape with raised centres, approximately 50 feet in diameter. Each one was occupied by three bodies of human shape but only 3 feet tall, dressed in metallic cloth of a very fine texture. Each body was bandaged in a manner similar to the blackout suits used by speed flyers and test pilots.'

The memo continues: 'According to Mr [deleted], informant, the saucers were found in New Mexico due to the fact that the Government has a very high-powered radar set-up in that area and it is believed the radar interferes with the controlling mechanism of the saucers.'

Although it is worthy of note, the researcher William Moore argues that this document is essentially worthless, since its origins can be traced from Fick, to Koehler, and ultimately to Silas Newton, whose testimony has to be examined very carefully. Equally, it could be argued that if Newton and GeBauer were in possession of information that was even remotely accurate, then the provenance of the memo of 22 March 1950 continues to stand.

And I feel obliged to point out that, with respect to this particular document, the FBI has taken extraordinary steps to ensure that no further information relating to its contents enters into the public domain. In 1988, for example, Larry Bryant, a researcher, filed suit in the US District Court for the District of Columbia in an attempt to force the release of additional data. Although ultimately thwarted in his attempt, Bryant put forward a number of valid arguments for the uncensored release of the memo of 22 March 1950, including the fact that 'no documentary proof is provided to show that the source had requested, or had expected to receive, any degree of confidentiality for his having imparted said information'.[8]

Bryant also asserted convincingly: '. . . if those unidentified FBI special agents now are carried as retired from active service, their names and addresses should enjoy no more privacy protection than those of any other federal retirees . . .'

At the time, Bryant said: '[T]he public's right to know the details about such a momentous event as crashed saucers and their retrieved occupants transcends the government's desire to shield agents, witnesses, and informants from public disclosure.' Alas, it all came to naught, and to this day the identities of the 'investigator for the Air Forces' and 'Mr [Deleted]' remain classified, despite the claims of a number of researchers that the document is simply an outgrowth of Silas Newton's original story.[9] And matters do not end there.

In his 1987 book, *UFO Crash at Aztec*, William Steinman related the case of Nicholas Von Poppen, described as 'an Estonian of royal blood', who had perfected the art of close-up metallurgical photography, which led to his being in constant demand by the American aerospace industry. According to Steinman's sources, because of his unique status as a skilled close-up photographer, Von Poppen was drafted into the project that dealt with the analysis of the Aztec saucer, and was given the task of photographing both the interior and exterior of the craft, as well as the corpses of its crew.

Von Poppen's alleged involvement in the Aztec case has surfaced on a number of occasions, the earliest of which I am aware of being in November 1960, when the writer Ray Palmer (himself the subject of a number of FBI papers) published an account submitted by the author and researcher Gray Barker.

Although Von Poppen's involvement in the Aztec affair has often been dismissed, there may be some truth to the reports after all. In 1990, I filed a Freedom of Information request with the FBI in an attempt to obtain any papers that linked Von Poppen with the UFO subject. This prompted a somewhat cryptic reply from J. Kevin O'Brien, the chief of the FOI and Privacy Acts Section within the Information Management Division of the Bureau: 'A search of the indices to our central records system files at FBI Headquarters revealed one reference similar to your request pertaining to Nicholas Von Poppen. However this reference is on microfilm and is illegible. There is nothing more we can do.'

In the final analysis the story of the UFO crash at Aztec is a puzzling and frustrating one. I do not deny that the intimate involvement of both Silas Newton and Leo GeBauer is troubling, and their testimony should be approached with the utmost caution. Yet, if it was a straightforward hoax, the Bureau went to extraordinary lengths to apprise itself of the facts surrounding the alleged Aztec crash, and the 'players' involved. And the fact

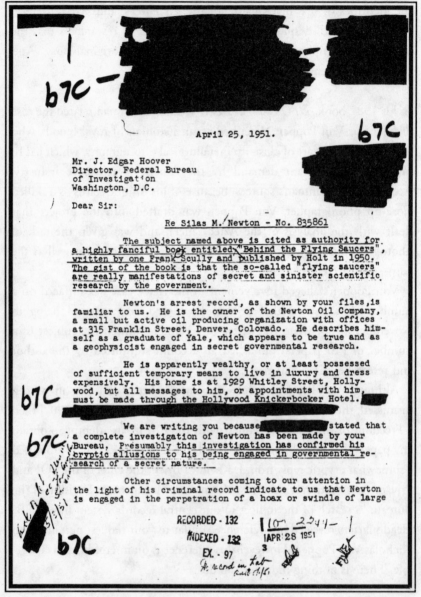

April 25, 1951.

Mr. J. Edgar Hoover
Director, Federal Bureau
of Investigation
Washington, D.C.

Dear Sir:

Re Silas M. Newton - No. 835861

The subject named above is cited as authority for
a highly fanciful book entitled "Behind the Flying Saucers",
written by one Frank Scully and published by Holt in 1950.
The gist of the book is that the so-called "flying saucers"
are really manifestations of secret and sinister scientific
research by the government.

Newton's arrest record, as shown by your files, is
familiar to us. He is the owner of the Newton Oil Company,
a small but active oil producing organization with offices
at 315 Franklin Street, Denver, Colorado. He describes himself as a graduate of Yale, which appears to be true and as
a geophysicist engaged in secret governmental research.

He is apparently wealthy, or at least possessed
of sufficient temporary means to live in luxury and dress
expensively. His home is at 1929 Whitley Street, Hollywood, but all messages to him, or appointments with him,
must be made through the Hollywood Knickerbocker Hotel.

We are writing you because   stated that
a complete investigation of Newton has been made by your
Bureau. Presumably this investigation has confirmed his
cryptic allusions to his being engaged in governmental research of a secret nature.

Other circumstances coming to our attention in
the light of his criminal record indicate to us that Newton
is engaged in the perpetration of a hoax or swindle of large

RECORDED - 132
INDEXED - 132
EX. - 97

A partially censored 1951 letter to the FBI concerning Frank Scully, Silas
Newton and the UFO subject.

that aspects of the Bureau's file on GeBauer remain classified in the interests of national defence cannot be overlooked. In view of the foregoing, I
posit two scenarios:

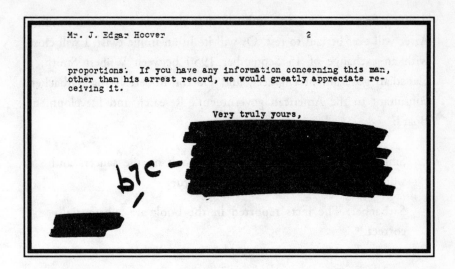

Mr. J. Edgar Hoover   2

proportions. If you have any information concerning this man,
other than his arrest record, we would greatly appreciate receiving it.

Very truly yours,

b7c -

(1) The Aztec crash actually occurred and Newton and GeBauer, having learned of it from sources still unknown, related the facts to Frank Scully, who went on to publish details in *Behind The Flying Saucers*;

(2) the Aztec crash was a complete hoax, but Newton and GeBauer had latched on to the basics of a genuine, albeit distorted, UFO crash incident and promoted Aztec as the crash site in absence of the real location.

Even if one of these a scenarios turns out to be correct, one might be tempted to ask: Why would both Newton and GeBauer agree to confide in Frank Scully, a professional writer, who would (and did) undoubtedly capitalise upon their information? I can only suspect that, given their somewhat questionable business practices, Newton and GeBauer recognised the potential dollar value of the story and hoped to milk it for all its worth.

It is ironic that, if the Aztec UFO crash really did occur, those who inadvertently stumbled across the truth should have been two individuals who, in 1953, were convicted of defrauding a Colorado businessman – hardly the sort of people whose testimony would be accepted at face value.

Fifty years on, short of a government announcement confirming or denying its reality, it seems unlikely that the controversy surrounding Aztec will ever be laid to rest. Or will it? In an ironic twist, I will close with an exchange of 15 September 1950 between Wilbert Smith, a Canadian government engineer, and Doctor Robert Irving Sarbacher, consultant to the American government's Research and Development Board:

Smith: I have read [Frank] Scully's book on the saucers and would like to know how much of it is true.

Sarbacher: The facts reported in the book are substantially correct.[10]

CHAPTER 11

MAJESTIC

THE AZTEC AFFAIR WAS UNDOUBTEDLY THE MOST HIGH-PROFILE UFO crash case in which the FBI was implicated in the 1950s, but it was not the only one.

Leonard Stringfield recalled one such incident: 'In one case in 1952, a New York daily newspaper headlined a crash story in its "bulldog" or 9:00 PM edition. Copies were delivered as usual to newsstands, the first loads going to a neighbourhood in the Bronx. Official reaction was swift. Agents, thought to be the FBI, took the remaining copies at the newsstands and made a door-to-door sweep in all the nearby apartments to round up any of the bulldog strays.'

Confirmation of this event may come from Robert Oliveri, an electronics technician, who learned from his cousin in the Bronx that government agents had been out in force rounding up copies of the offending newspaper.

'Most of the copy about the crash, I've forgotten,' said Oliveri. 'I do remember that three bodies were recovered; two were dead, one injured, still alive. The crash site, too, is not clear. I believe it occurred in New Mexico or Arizona because the terrain was sandy like a desert.'[1]

I do not think it entirely coincidental, either, that Leonard Stringfield was the subject of an extensive FBI file dating back to the 1950s. A 1954 extract from that file reads:

A source of unknown reliability, an acquaintance of Leonard H. Stringfield who is the Director of the captioned organization Civilian Research Interplanetary Flying Objects, in October 1954 advised that Stringfield is the Director of the organization and is assisted by his wife, and that Stringfield writes and publishes monthly the multi-lithographed 'Newsletter' of the organization. He uses the 'Newsletter' to report news pertaining to the sightings of flying saucers and he claims the 'Newsletter' now has a world-wide circulation of about 4,000 copies . . .

The same source furnished a copy of the 'Newsletter' [which] reports that [Stringfield] had a private talk with Lieutenant Colonel John O'Mara, Deputy Commander, Intelligence, United States Air Force, on September 21, 1954, and that in essence Colonel O'Mara told Stringfield that flying saucers do exist and that past contradictions were unfortunate . . .

Stringfield has stated that he believes his home telephone is being monitored, presumably by the Air Force, and that he therefore makes his phone calls to Lieutenant O'Mara at Wright-Patterson Air Force Base . . . from his office . . . Stringfield in talking about the possibility that the US Air Force might stop his operations, made a statement to the effect, 'The Air Force can't do anything to me. I'm claiming saucers are interplanetary.'

As far as official surveillance of Stringfield in later years is concerned, William Moore, a researcher who has known and proven links with the US Intelligence community, wrote in 1989:

Drawing from my own knowledge and experience, I can summarize the individuals and organizations who were the subject of intelligence community interest between 1980 and 1984. It is important to remember here that in some cases, I was not personally involved, but rather only aware of these goings-on through conversations with others . . .

Stringfield remained the subject of some interest through 1983, after which I heard very little about him. The [counter-intelligence] people seemed to know a lot about Len and his sources. The impression I had was that someone else much closer to him than I, was keeping tabs on his activities, but of course, I never knew for certain.[2]

Up until 1991 at least, Stringfield remained the subject of official interest: '. . . I have other sources today who seem to know that I am currently a subject of interest to the intelligence community,' said Stringfield in July 1991. 'If I could draw any conclusions from the travails of my past experiences, then I am also being subjected to both good information and disinformation . . .' Leonard Stringfield died in December 1994.

From the mid-1950s onwards, the FBI's involvement in the issue of crashed UFOs diminished (unless the Bureau has yet to release the relevant files, which is not impossible); however it is interesting to remember that of all the books written in the 1960s on the subject of UFOs, the one that particularly caught the the FBI's attention was *Flying Saucers – Serious Business* by Frank Edwards. A keen supporter of the 'crash' aspect of the UFO mystery, Edwards devoted a complete chapter of his book to accounts of retrieved UFOs, at a time when such stories were largely scoffed at. Moreover, Edwards included the testimony of Wilbert Smith (who displayed a deep interest in the Frank Scully affair), and a brief (not to mention spectacularly garbled) account of the so-called 'Roswell Incident'. As we saw in Chapter 6, an FBI review of the portion of Edward's book which discussed those incidents reads thus:

> Wreckage of crashed saucers has been reportedly recovered on at least three occasions, in one case described as a magnesium alloy, in another as pure magnesium, and in a third case, attributed to an official of the Canadian Government, the material was described as an exceptionally hard unknown metal, actually a matrix of magnesium orthosilicate which contained thousands of 15-micron spheres throughout, and showing evidence of micro-meteorites on its surface.

During the 1970s, the FBI was implicated in at least two incidents involving the reported recovery of crashed UFO technology. From John Ford, head of the Long Island UFO Network, comes the account of a former police officer who recalled such an incident in 1973. Ford's source has requested anonymity; however, the late Leonard Stringfield was permitted to view a video-taped interview in which the officer recalled the event in question. 'After viewing this, which firmly established the former officer's credentials, I reached him by phone for his first-hand story,' said Stringfield.

As Stringfield listened intently, the officer divulged that in 1973 he had attended a special three-day course on 'behavioral science' at the police academy, which was also attended by agents of the FBI.

After a long day's work, he and two of the Bureau agents decided to go out for an evening of dining and much-needed relaxation. During the course of the night, 'the subject of UFOs came up', and to the police officer's surprise one of the FBI man revealed his knowledge of a crashed UFO discovered in Colorado.

'I could tell by his body "English" that he was disturbed,' the officer advised Stringfield, whose account continues: 'As the evening unfolded the FBI agent became more talkative and quietly revealed that a doctor, who had been urgently called upon in the middle of the night to attend to the presumably injured crew of the UFO, died suddenly of "cancer" three weeks later.'

At that stage, the talkative agent was 'booted' under the table by his companion: 'The subject was dropped and nothing was said about the FBI's role in the affair,' Stringfield later stated.[3]

In the following year, a report was brought to the attention of the FBI to the effect that some form of object had come down at Milwaukee. Like many Bureau records already detailed, the released copy of the official report is highly censored, but enough can be gleaned from its contents to determine that an event of sorts did occur.

A report dated 22 August 1974, and titled MILITARY INQUIRY REGARDING UNIDENTIFIED OBJECT THAT FELL FROM SKY AT MILWAUKEE, WISCONSIN 8/21/74, reads:

> At 12:07 a.m. 8/22/74, Security Patrol Clerk (SPC) [name withheld], Intelligence Division received a call via Command Center

telephone from a Major [with the] National Military Command Center. [The] Major asked for any information the FBI might have concerning a report that an unidentified object which fell from the sky at Milwaukee, had been recovered by local police and turned over to the Milwaukee Office of the FBI.

No information available at Intelligence Division. Night Duty Supervisor [name withheld], called Milwaukee Office, who advised an unidentified object had been recovered by [deleted] at about 5:55 p.m. [Source] had called the Milwaukee FBI Office to report the recovery. Very little was known about the object which was described as about 13 x 8 x 5 inches, metallic in substance and color, jagged on one side and had an 'internal heat source'.

In this case, there is a possibility that the debris was terrestrial in origin, but I use it to demonstrate that when unknown objects do crash to earth, the FBI is never far behind.

Let us now turn our attention to what is without doubt the premier crashed UFO event: the so-called 'Roswell Incident' of 1947. Since the late 1970s, a huge amount of testimony has been collected by a variety of researchers which, when viewed as a whole, almost certainly confirms that on a fateful morning in the early part of July 1947, a highly unusual aeroform was recovered by the US Army Air Forces from the desert outside Roswell, New Mexico. A convincing body of evidence also exists which suggests that, in addition to the mystery object, the bodies of a number of strange-looking creatures were also recovered in the same general vicinity.

To date, the Roswell crash has been the subject of at least thirteen full-length books, an inordinate number of newspaper and magazine articles, a government inquiry, and a host of factual and fictionalised television programmes. In view of this, I do not intend to discuss all of the intricacies of the case; rather it is my intention to look at the FBI's involvement in and knowledge of the Roswell UFO crash.

But first a few necessary background details. No one, not even the US government, denies that something crashed on the Foster Ranch, 75 miles northwest of Roswell almost half a century ago. What is in dispute is the nature of the retrieved material. For its part, the US Air Force has two firm opinions:

(a) All available official materials, although they do not directly address Roswell per se, indicate that the most likely source of the wreckage recovered . . . was from one of the Project Mogul balloon trains . . .

(b) The review of Air Force records did not locate even one piece of evidence to indicate that the Air Force has had any part in an 'alien' body recovery operation or continuing cover-up . . .

Others disagree. For those who would contend that the testimony surrounding the Roswell affair is wholly annecdotal and based on the accounts of anonymous, untraceable sources, I relate the following:

With respect to a large quantity of unusual, metallic-looking debris recovered from the Foster Ranch, we have the statement of Major Jesse Marcel, Base Intelligence Officer at Roswell Army Air Field in 1947: '. . . the pieces of metal that we brought back were so thin, just like the tinfoil in a pack of cigarettes . . . [but it] would not bend and you could not tear it or cut it either. We even tried making a dent in it with a sixteen-pound sledgehammer, and there was still no dent in it.'

Of the allegations that, in addition to the field of debris, a semi-intact space vehicle was also found in the area, again the evidence is compelling. Louis Rickett, a counterintelligence corps agent at the time of the incident, has confirmed that the object had a curved front and a wide wing, with a 'batlike' trailing edge; Thomas Gonzalez, who was stationed at Roswell Army Air Field on returning to the US after the end of World War Two, describes the craft as resembling an 'airfoil'; Johnny McBoyle, reporter and part-owner of KSWS radio station in Roswell, recalled seeing a 'big crumpled dishpan'; and according to Frank Kauffman of the 509th Bomb Group, the object recovered was 'heel-shaped'. Quite clearly, none of these people are describing a balloon.

When faced with the most controversial claims, that alien bodies were also recovered, again the information related by on-the-record sources cannot be brushed under the carpet.

Thomas Gonzalez described the bodies as 'little men'; Major Edwin D. Easley, Provost Marshall at Roswell, would only refer to them as 'creatures'; Grady Barnett, a soil conservation engineer with the government, who quite literally stumbled across the bodies while they were still lying strewn on the harsh desert floor, gave a detailed account of seeing a number of small, human-like creatures with large, pear-shaped heads, oddly spaced eyes, skinny arms and legs, and devoid of hair; and Sergeant Melvin E. Brown, also stationed at Roswell, stated firmly that he had seen a number of strange corpses: 'They looked Asian . . . but had larger heads and no hair. They looked a yellowy colour.'

Having digested these quite extraordinary details, let us now address what is, for our purposes, the crux of the matter: the FBI's involvement in the recovery of a crashed extraterrestrial spacecraft.

With the crash as a whole, the Bureau's involvement seems curiously two-sided. On the one hand, there is absolutely no doubt that the FBI played a not insignificant role in the attempt to prevent the story leaking out at the time; yet there is also a good case for arguing that the military did not inform the Bureau precisely what it was that was being 'covered-up'.

In July 1947, Lydia Sleppy was employed as a teletype operator at the KSWS radio station in Roswell. When a reporter, Johnny McBoyle, phoned through his account of seeing a 'big crumpled dishpan' out on the Foster Ranch at 4 p.m. on Monday 7 July 1947, she recognised that this was a 'pretty big story' and proceeded to record the details on the teletype machine. 'The Army is there and they are going to pick it up,' said McBoyle, excitedly, 'and get this – they're saying something about little men being on board.'

As McBoyle dictated, a bell on the teletype rang, signalling an interruption. It was an incoming message from Dallas: 'This is the FBI, you will cease transmitting.' Sleppy duly complied, but continued to take notes as McBoyle told his remarkable story. Unfortunately, the government clampdown had already begun and the story inevitably died a death. Fifty years on, Johnny McBoyle flatly refuses to discuss the Roswell affair. But under what circumstances did the FBI become implicated in Roswell?

On the following day, 8 July, the Bureau office at Dallas forwarded a teletype message to both Hoover and the Cincinnati office concerning the events at Roswell; however it is evident from reading the message that the FBI was in possession of only half of the story. That 'half' had been supplied sometime previously by Major Edwin M. Kirton of Army Air Force Intelligence at Fort Worth. As we now know, Kirton wished the 'crashed saucer' story dead at all costs, but to do so effectively meant calling in the FBI.

Kirton's actions worked (as the McBoyle–Sleppy episode shows), but ever the diligent intelligence officer, he saw no reason for confiding in the FBI what it was that had really been recovered. When it became apparent that the cover story – 'It's just a balloon, honest' – had been accepted by the media, Kirton took the decision that what was good enough for the press was also good enough for the FBI. To illustrate that the Bureau was indeed misled by the Army Air Force, here is the text of the 8 July teletype:

> Flying Disc, information concerning. Major E. Kirton, head-quarters Eighth Air Force, telephonically advised this office that an object purporting to be a flying disc was recovered near Roswell, New Mexico, this date. The disc is hexagonal in shape and was suspended from a balloon by cable, which balloon was approximately twenty feet in diameter. Major Kirton further advised that the object found resembles a high altitude weather balloon with a radar reflector, but that telephonic conversation between their office and Wright Field had not borne out this belief. Disc and balloon being transported to Wright Field by special plane for examination. Information provided this office because of national interest in case and fact that National Broadcasting Company, Associated Press, and others attempting to break story of location of disc today. Major Kirton advised would request Wright Field to advise Cincinnati Office results of examination. No further investigation being conducted.

While this document made it clear to the Bureau that some form of object had been recovered, which might or might not have been a balloon (such tactics are the hallmark of intelligence operatives), it stopped

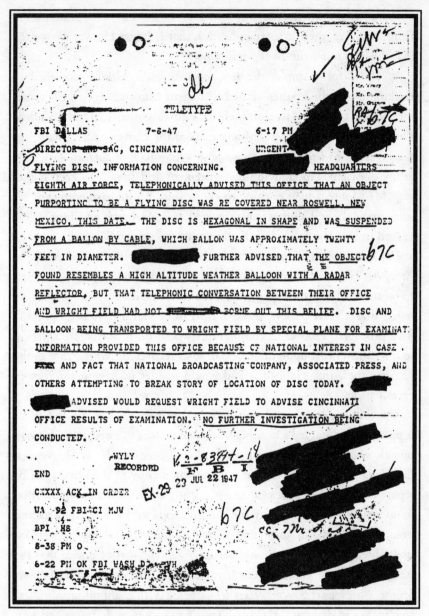

TELETYPE

FBI DALLAS   7-8-47   6-17 PM

DIRECTOR AND SAC, CINCINNATI   URGENT

FLYING DISC, INFORMATION CONCERNING.   HEADQUARTERS

EIGHTH AIR FORCE, TELEPHONICALLY ADVISED THIS OFFICE THAT AN OBJECT

PURPORTING TO BE A FLYING DISC WAS RE COVERED NEAR ROSWELL, NEW

MEXICO, THIS DATE. THE DISC IS HEXAGONAL IN SHAPE AND WAS SUSPENDED

FROM A BALLON BY CABLE, WHICH BALLON WAS APPROXIMATELY TWENTY

FEET IN DIAMETER.   FURTHER ADVISED THAT THE OBJECT

FOUND RESEMBLES A HIGH ALTITUDE WEATHER BALLOON WITH A RADAR

REFLECTOR, BUT THAT TELEPHONIC CONVERSATION BETWEEN THEIR OFFICE

AND WRIGHT FIELD HAD NOT   BORNE OUT THIS BELIEF. DISC AND

BALLOON BEING TRANSPORTED TO WRIGHT FIELD BY SPECIAL PLANE FOR EXAMINAT

INFORMATION PROVIDED THIS OFFICE BECAUSE OF NATIONAL INTEREST IN CASE

     AND FACT THAT NATIONAL BROADCASTING COMPANY, ASSOCIATED PRESS, AND

OTHERS ATTEMPTING TO BREAK STORY OF LOCATION OF DISC TODAY.

     ADVISED WOULD REQUEST WRIGHT FIELD TO ADVISE CINCINNATI

OFFICE RESULTS OF EXAMINATION. NO FURTHER INVESTIGATION BEING

CONDUCTED.

               WYLY
END   RECORDED

CXXXX ACK IN ORDER

UA 92 FBI CI MJW

BPI HS

8-38 PM O

6-22 PM OK FBI WASH D   WH

OK FBI

One of the very few official documents currently available relating to the so-called 'Roswell incident' of July 1947.

short of informing the FBI that in fact what had been retrieved was a heel-shaped aeroform complete with a crew of dwarflike extraterrestrial creatures. A minor omission, to say the least.

For all Major Kirton's attempts to prevent the FBI from learning the truth, however, there is some indication that J. Edgar Hoover recognised that this was not a run-of-the-mill report.

In 1981, for example, the researcher William Moore succeeded in tracking down the by-then-retired FBI agent who transmitted the afore-mentioned teletype. He absolutely refused to consent to an interview. During a July 1988 lecture, Moore recalled the man's words: 'I have had no unexplained fires in my garage, and I have had no men in dark suits at my doorstep. I'm enjoying my retirement and I want to keep it that way, Mr Moore. I have nothing to say to you.' An unusual comment for sure, particularly if all that was recovered at Roswell was a balloon.

And in the days following the receipt of the enigmatic agent's message at FBI headquarters, Hoover was not best pleased with the actions of the Army Air Force. In a Bureau document of 10 July 1947, Agent E.G. Fitch recommended that the FBI should discontinue its investigations, 'it being noted that a great bulk of those alleged discs found have been pranks'. This prompted Hoover to comment: 'I would do it but before agreeing to it we must insist upon full access to discs recovered. For instance in the La. case the Army grabbed it and would not let us have it for cursory examination.'

Was this an allusion to the object found at Roswell? The 'La.' reference is puzzling and has led a number of commentators to assert that Hoover's remark was made in response to another alleged 'crash': at Shreveport, Louisiana. And yet I have in my possession a copy of the one-page FBI report on the Shreveport case and it is quite clear from its contents that in no way did the Army deny the Bureau access to the 'disc'; they had no need to. The records show that what was recovered at Shreveport was undoubtedly another hoax, and certainly not the sort of device that the Army would have 'grabbed'. For anyone having doubts, the official report on the 'Shreveport Saucer' refers to its being a 'thin aluminum disc six-teen inches in diameter. Has small coils two inches in diameter and four inches long at the ends of the diameter. Coils connected by two copper wires to two terminals on each coil and these wires are connected at the crossing in the center of the disc to an object one inch in diameter by two inches long . . . Center object has on upper end – "Made in USA".' Did Hoover confuse Roswell and Shreveport? I do not know, but I can state that the only crashed UFO incident the FBI was effectively kept away from during that time frame was indeed Roswell.

There is a further reason still why Hoover may have recognised that there was more to the Roswell crash than a mere balloon. Two investigators, Kevin Randle and Donald Schmitt, have learned that of those drafted in to work on the autopsies of the dead aliens, one was Dr La June Foster, a renowned expert and authority on the human spinal cord.

Following the crash, Foster was flown to Washington, DC, where she was asked to examine the spinal structures of the retrieved bodies, and reported that it was possible that one of the aliens had survived the crash, albeit in a critically injured state. Foster, too, described the bodies as being short, with oversized heads. Most disturbing of all, Foster was warned that, if she talked, she would be killed.

Crucial to this discussion, Foster was specifically chosen to participate in the autopises because during World War Two she had worked under-cover for the FBI and had a current security clearance. With that fixed firmly in our minds, I have to wonder: Did any of this filter back to Hoover? The phenomenal interest shown by the Bureau in the alleged Aztec crash suggests that someone in the FBI knew that there was some substance behind all the talk of crashed UFOs and dead alien bodies, even if it was not known to the Bureau as a whole.

What of La June Foster's claims that if she spoke openly she would be killed? This is most unsettling, but it is not unprecedented.

Of those with intimate knowledge of the Roswell crash, a number have confirmed they were warned that if they ever discussed their participation in the incident they could count on never seeing their loved ones again. For example, Glenn Dennis, who in 1947 was a mortician at Roswell, learned from a girlfriend, Naomi Maria Seiff, that the bodies had been taken to Roswell Army Air Field for a somewhat ad hoc autopsy. And when it became apparent to the military that Dennis was taking a little bit too much interest in this for his own good, he was tactfully advised by a red-haired captain: 'Somebody will be picking your bones out of the sand'.

A somewhat similar account originates with Frankie Rowe, whose father was with the Roswell Fire Department in 1947. Rowe reports that her father confided in the family that he had seen both debris and bodies, including one live alien: '[T]he one that was walking around was about the size of a 10 year old child, and it didn't have any hair . . . it seemed so scared and lost and afraid . . .'

Several days later, claims Frankie Rowe, three military policemen came to the family home and said that if anyone talked 'they might just take us out to the middle of the desert and shoot all of us and nobody would ever find us'.

Although the military's handling of the Roswell case might not be to all tastes, credit must be given where it is due: there can be no doubt that the Army Air Force's 'Operation Damage Limitation' worked perfectly for decades, and, with the carefully manipulated assistance of the FBI, the story was effectively dead from the off.

So much for the events of July 1947. It would be almost forty years to the day before the FBI became once again embroiled in the mystery of Roswell.[4-10]

A problem that has long beset the Roswell case has been the almost complete lack of official documentation to support the claims that anything (balloon or UFO) crashed there. The aforementioned FBI teletype of 7 July 1947 aside, there are but a few scant pieces of paper from that era that reference the event, and of those the majority prove nothing beyond the fact that something crashed, the Army Air Force recovered 'it', and everything was passed off as a ghastly case of mistaken identity. That all changed in 1987.

As we saw at the beginning of the previous chapter, it was the British investigator Timothy Good who first brought the Majestic 12 documents to the attention of the world in mid-1987. Media and public reaction was intense and Good's book went on to become an international bestseller.

It goes without saying that if any or all of the MJ-12 papers are genuine then there can absolutely no doubt that by July 1947 the US government had in its possession an alien spacecraft and a number of alien bodies. And since the MJ-12 papers had not been declassified in accordance with the American Freedom of Information Act, but had essentially been leaked to Good by a US intelligence source, there were solid grounds for believing that US national security had been compromised. This was to be the central issue of the FBI's investigation of the MJ-12 saga.

Shortly after Timothy Good published copies of the MJ-12 papers in May 1987, additional copies surfaced, this time in the US, having been released by the research team of William Moore (a professional writer), Stanton Friedman (a nuclear physicist), and Jaime Shandera (a television producer).

Moore had been working quietly with a number of intelligence 'insiders' who had contacted him shortly after publication of the 1980 book he co-authored with Charles Berlitz (*The Roswell Incident*) and from time to time various official-looking papers would be passed on to Moore, the implication being that someone in the US government wished to make available to the UFO research community material that would otherwise have remained for ever outside the public domain. It was as a result of Moore's insider dealings that a roll of film negative displaying the documents was quietly delivered to the home of Shandera in December 1984.[11]

Moore, Friedman and Shandera worked carefully for two and a half years in an attempt to determine the authenticity or otherwise of the documents, but, with Timothy Good's release, it was decided the best course of action was to follow suit. As a result, a huge controversy was created which, almost ten years on, continues. But how did the FBI become entangled in the MJ-12 affair?

Howard Blum is an award-winning author and former *New York Times* journalist who was twice nominated by the editors of that newspaper for the Pulitzer Prize in Investigative Reporting. In 1990, Blum's book *Out There* was released, and detailed his investigation of Pentagon involvement in the UFO subject.[12] According to Blum, on 4 June 1987, a UFO sceptic, Philip J. Klass, wrote to William Baker, Assistant Director at the Office of Congressional and Public Affairs within the FBI, thus: 'I am enclosing what purport to be "Top Secret/Eyes Only" documents, which have not been properly declassified, now being circulated . . . by William L. Moore . . . Burbank, California, 91505 . . .' The Bureau swung into action.

A researcher and former principal investigator on Department of

Defense computer networking projects, Jacques Vallee, has stated that the FBI turned away from the MJ-12 documents 'in disgust', and professed no interest in the matter.[13] Papers released to me by the Bureau and the Air Force, however, reflect a totally different scenario.

When the FBI began its analysis of the MJ-12 papers it became apparent immediately that this was no run-of-the-mill hoax. The documents had an air of authenticity about them, and those listed as members of the MJ-12 committee were the sort of people who would have been assigned to just such a group. As papers released to me by the Bureau show, from the outset the FBI–MJ-12 investigation was classified at 'Secret' level, which tends to dismiss the claims that the Bureau maintained no interest in MJ-12. And there is one other issue that greatly concerned the FBI: much of the data contained within the MJ-12 papers tied in directly with information in known-to-be-authentic FBI documents.

Classified 'Top Secret/Majic Eyes Only', the MJ-12 document can essentially be broken down into two definable parts. The first is a 1952 briefing prepared by Admiral Roscoe H. Hillenkoetter for President-elect Eisenhower, informing him of the reality of the Roswell crash and the creation of MJ-12 to deal with the retrieved craft, bodies, and related issues; and the second is a 1947 memorandum from President Harry Truman to Secretary of Defense James Forrestal authorising the establishment of MJ-12.

Were the MJ-12 papers genuine? Was a select group created in the late 1940s to deal with the recovery of an alien spacecraft? The Bureau wanted answers. Aside from the fact that the MJ-12 group was made up of some very prestigious names (including Rear Admiral Roscoe Hillenkoetter, the first Director of the CIA; Rear Admiral Sidney Souers, the first Director of Central Intelligence; General Nathan Twining, Commanding General of Air Materiel Command; and Doctor Vannevar Bush, head of the Joint Research and Development Board), the contents of the papers were of more than passing interest to those FBI agents involved in the investigation. To begin with, the MJ-12 documents give a brief résumé of the status of the Flying Saucer mystery in the summer of 1947: 'On 24 June, 1947, a civilian pilot flying over the Cascade Mountains in the State of Washington observed nine flying disc-shaped aircraft traveling in formation at a high rate of speed . . .'

Although not mentioned by name, this can only be a reference to the now-championed sighting by the pilot Kenneth Arnold, whom we met in the Introduction. The FBI knew that this information was accurate since an extensive file on Arnold's encounter was drawn up by the Bureau at the time of its occurrence. A quote from the FBI's 1947 file on Arnold tells us: 'Arnold is a man of 32 years of age . . . he is well thought of in the community in which he lives . . . It is difficult to believe that a man of Arnold's character and apparent integrity would state that he saw objects and write up a report to the extent that he did if he did not see them . . .'

But as the FBI began to delve further, more and more facts surfaced which tended to suggest that either the MJ-12 documents were what they alleged to be, or, if bogus, they had been put together by an extraordinarily skilled person. On the central theme of MJ-12, the document expanded:

> . . . little of substance was learned about the objects until a local rancher reported that one had crashed in a remote region of New Mexico located approximately seventy-five miles northwest of Roswell Army Air Base (now Walker Field) . . .

Again, the Bureau knew for a fact that something unusual had occurred at Roswell in 1947; the Johnny McBoyle–Lydia Sleppy episode in which the FBI played a direct role was proof of that, as was the one-page Dallas FBI teletype confirming that an object had been recovered and was being shipped to Wright Field Air Base for study. Then there were the subsequent actions of J. Edgar Hoover, complaining at the lack of cooperation afforded the Bureau by the military.

Of the most controversial and sensational aspect of the Roswell event, that alien bodies were also recovered, the MJ-12 papers state:

> On 07 July, 1947, a secret operation was begun to assure recovery of the wreckage of this object for scientific study. During the course of this operation, aerial reconnaissance discovered that four small human-like beings had apparently ejected from the craft at some point before it exploded. These had fallen to earth about two miles east of the wreckage site. All four were dead and

badly decomposed due to action by predators and exposure to the elements during the approximately one week time period which had elapsed before their discovery. A special scientific team took charge of removing these bodies for study.

We have seen that Major Edwin M. Kirton of Army Air Force Intelligence cleverly prevented the FBI from learning the truth about Roswell practically from the word 'go'; however the data related in the MJ-12 document about unusual bodies being found near to the wrecked UFO sounds uncannily like the information collected by the Bureau during the course of its investigations of both Silas Newton and Leo GeBauer. I now begin to wonder if Newton and GeBauer had inadvertently uncovered the bare bones of the Roswell story, and Hoover, frustrated by the Army Air Force in his attempts to get to the bottom of the Roswell case, determined to uncover the truth, distorted as it may have been, from Newton and GeBauer. If for no other reason, this may indicate why around 200 pages of GeBauer's FBI file remains classified.

There were still more pointers that suggested to the Bureau that the MJ-12 document was indeed the real thing. For example, there was apparently a deep debate within MJ-12 about the origin of the aliens found at Roswell:

> Since it is virtually certain that these craft do not originate in any country on earth, considerable speculation has centered around what their point of origin might be and how they get here. Mars was and remains a possibility, although some scientists, most notably Dr [Donald] Menzel, consider it more likely that we are dealing with beings from another solar system.

This in itself is particularly interesting. We might today consider it somewhat quaint that Mars should have been mooted as the aliens' point of origin; however, this document was allegedly prepared in 1952, five years before the first artificial satellite was launched into space. And once again this aspect of MJ-12 receives support from information contained in the FBI's own archives.

As I related in Chapter 5, on 29 July 1952 the FBI's liaison representative with the Air Force, N.W. Philcox, was told by Commander Randall Boyd of the Current Intelligence Branch of the Estimates Division within Air Intelligence that: '. . . it is not entirely impossible that the objects sighted may possibly be ships from another planet such as Mars'. This document is undoubtedly authentic (it was released under the terms of the FOIA), and is absolute proof that, as the MJ-12 papers state, officialdom was of the opinion in 1952 that the aliens were possibly Martian in origin.

There is one further authentic FBI document on UFOs which is supportive of the MJ-12 papers. According to Rear Admiral Hillenkoetter's briefing to President-elect Eisenhower: 'On 06 December, 1950, a second object, probably of similar origin, impacted the earth at high speed in the El Indio–Guerrero area of the Texas–Mexican border after following a long trajectory through the atmosphere. By the time a search team arrived, what remained of the object had been almost totally incinerated. Such material as could be recovered was transported to the [Atomic Energy Commission] facility at Sandia, New Mexico.'

It so happens that on 8 December 1950, two days after the the crash at El Indio, the following teleytype was sent from the FBI Office at Richmond to Washington:

RE FLYING SAUCERS. THIS OFFICE VERY CON-
FIDENTIALLY ADVISED BY ARMY INTELLIGENCE,
RICHMOND, THAT THEY HAVE BEEN PUT ON
IMMEDIATE HIGH ALERT FOR ANY DATA WHATSO-
EVER CONCERNING FLYING SAUCERS. CIC HERE
STATES BACKGROUND OF INSTRUCTIONS NOT
AVAILABLE FROM AIR FORCE INTELLIGENCE, WHO
ARE NOT AWARE OF REASON FOR ALERT LOCAL-
LY, BUT ANY INFORMATION WHATSOEVER MUST BE
TELEPHONED BY THEM IMMEDIATELY TO AIR
FORCE INTELLIGENCE. [Counter-Intelligence
Corps] ADVISES DATA STRICTLY CONFIDENTIAL
AND SHOULD NOT BE DISSEMINATED.

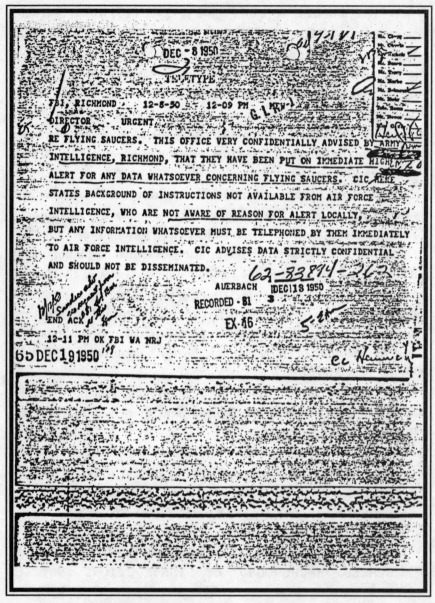

DEC - 8 1950

TELETYPE

FBI, RICHMOND   12-8-50   12-09 PM

DIRECTOR   URGENT

RE FLYING SAUCERS. THIS OFFICE VERY CONFIDENTIALLY ADVISED BY ARMY INTELLIGENCE, RICHMOND, THAT THEY HAVE BEEN PUT ON IMMEDIATE HIGH ALERT FOR ANY DATA WHATSOEVER CONCERNING FLYING SAUCERS. CIC HERE STATES BACKGROUND OF INSTRUCTIONS NOT AVAILABLE FROM AIR FORCE INTELLIGENCE, WHO ARE NOT AWARE OF REASON FOR ALERT LOCALLY, BUT ANY INFORMATION WHATSOEVER MUST BE TELEPHONED BY THEM IMMEDIATELY TO AIR FORCE INTELLIGENCE. CIC ADVISES DATA STRICTLY CONFIDENTIAL AND SHOULD NOT BE DISSEMINATED.

AUERBACH   DEC 13 1950

RECORDED - 81

EX-16

12-11 PM OK FBI WA NRJ

65 DEC 19 1950

A 1950 FBI teletype referenced material contained within the controversial MJ-12 papers.

No further information has come to light suggesting what lay behind this curious report, but a hastily scrawled and practically illegible note at the foot of the document does appear to reference Sandia, where the MJ-

12 papers allege the wreckage from the 1950 crash was taken. And a Bureau teletype of 5 December 1950 shows that twenty-four hours before the El Indio incident the following report was generated by the Bureau:

> Detection of unidentified objects over Oak Ridge area, protection of vital installations. Reurtel December 4 last regarding possible radar jamming at Oak Ridge.
>
> Arrangements should be made to obtain all facts concerning possible radar jamming by ionization of particles in atmosphere. Conduct appropriate investigation to determine whether incident occurring northeast of Oliver Springs, Tennessee, could have had any connection with alleged radar jamming.

These two FBI documents do not of course reference the UFO crash at El Indio, but they do support the notion that something of great importance, directly concerning UFOs, was taking place in the same time frame.

Quite what the FBI thought about all this is unclear, but two things are certain: (1) the high degree of corroboration afforded the MJ-12 papers by authentic Bureau documents was illuminating and did not rule out the possibility that MJ-12 was genuine; and (2), if it *was* genuine, the Bureau was going to have to dig deep to determine where and with whom the papers originated.

Although the FBI initially received a copy of the MJ-12 papers in the summer of 1987, evidence suggests it was not until the latter part of 1988 that it began making tentative enquries with other government and military agencies, as it sought to uncover the identity of the 'whistle-blower' responsible for what appeared to be a very worrying breach of national security.

Howard Blum has stated that of those approached by the FBI 'in the fall of 1988', as it sought to uncover the truth behind MJ-12, one was a 'Working Group' established under the auspices of the Defense Intelligence Agency. Yet even that group, as secret as it may have been, apparently did not have clearance to access the truth behind MJ-12 and the Roswell crash, and was as baffled as the Bureau. In 1990, Blum was interviewed by *UFO Magazine* in the USA, and asked if the Working

Group could possibly have been a 'public' front group for another even more covert investigative body within the US government. Blum's response aptly sums up one of the major problems faced (by those both inside and outside of government) when trying to determine exactly 'who knows what':

> Interestingly, members of [the Working Group] aired that possibility themselves. When looking into the MJ-12 papers, some members of the group said – and not in jest – 'Perhaps we're just a front organization for some sort of MJ-12. Suppose, in effect, we conclude the MJ-12 papers are phony, are counterfeit. Then we've solved the entire mystery for the government, relieving them of the burden in dealing with it, and at the same time, we allow the real secret to remain held by a higher source.' An FBI agent told me there are so many levels within the government that even the government isn't aware of it![14]

Thanks to the Freedom of Information Act, we also know that in addition to an investigation undertaken into MJ-12 by the FBI's Foreign Counter-Intelligence division (which I have been advised operated out of Washington and New York, and was the branch of the Bureau responsible for approaching the DIA Working Group), the FBI office at Dallas, Texas, was also implicated, as Oliver B. Revell, special agent in charge at Dallas, has confirmed to me.

On 15 September 1988, an agent of the US Air Force Office of Special Investigations (AFOSI) contacted Dallas FBI and supplied the Bureau with another copy of the MJ-12 papers, obtained from a source whose identity, according to documentation released to me by the Bureau, AFOSI has deemed must remain classified to this day.

Perhaps unaware of the investigation into MJ-12 undertaken by the Washington office, on 25 October 1988 Dallas transmitted a two-page Secret Airtel to headquarters which read:

> Enclosed for the Bureau is an envelope which contains a possible classified document. Dallas notes that within the last six weeks, there has been local publicity regarding 'OPERATION

MAJESTIC-12' with at least two appearances on a local radio talk show, discussing the MAJESTIC-12 OPERATION, the individuals involved, and the Government's attempt to keep it all secret. It is unknown if this is all part of a publicity campaign.

[Censored] from OSI, advises that 'OPERATION BLUE

In 1988, the FBI's files on Majestic 12 were classified at Secret level.

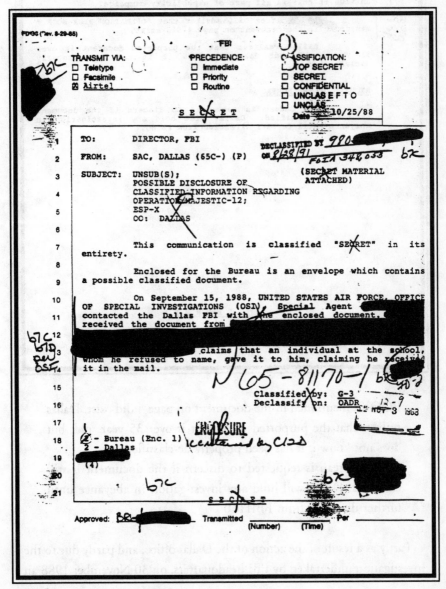

S E C R E T

DL 65C-

Dallas notes that within the last six weeks, there has been local publicity regarding "OPERATION MAJESTIC-12" with at least two appearances on a local radio talk show, discussing the MAJESTIC-12 OPERATION, the individuals involved, and the Government's attempt to keep it all secret. It is unknown if this is all part of a publicity campaign.

_____ from OSI, advises that "OPERATION BLUE BOOK," mentioned in the document on page 4 did exist.

Dallas realizes that the purported document is over 35 years old, but does not know if it has been properly declassified.

REQUEST OF THE BUREAU

The Bureau is requested to discern if the document is still classified. Dallas will hold any investigation in abeyance until further direction from FBIHQ.

S E C R E T

2*

BOOK,' mentioned in the document on page 4 did exist. Dallas realizes that the purported document is over 35 years old, but does not know if it has been properly de-classified.

The Bureau is requested to discern if the document is still classified. Dallas will hold any investigation in abeyance until further direction from FBIHQ.

Partly as a result of the action of the Dallas office, and partly due to the investigation undertaken by FBI headquarters, on 30 November 1988 an arranged meeting took place between agents of the Bureau and those of AFOSI in Washington, DC, during which the FBI requested that if the Air Force had any information on MJ-12, the Bureau would like to know.

A 'Secret' communication back to the Dallas office from Washington on 2 December 1988 read: 'This communication is classified "Secret" in its entirety. Reference Dallas Airtel dated October 25 1988. Referenced Airtel requested that FBIHQ determine if the document enclosed by referenced Airtel was classified or not. The Office of Special Investigations, US Air Force, advised on November 30, 1988, that the document was fabricated. Copies of that document have been distributed to various parts of the United States. The document is completely bogus. Dallas is to close captioned investigation.'

At first glance that would seem to lay matters to rest once and for all. Unfortunately, it does not. There can be no dispute that the Air Force has played a most strange game with respect to MJ-12. Although the FBI was assured by AFOSI that the MJ-12 papers were fabricated, Special Agent Frank Batten Jnr, chief of the Information Release Division at the Investigative Operations Centre with the USAF, has admitted to me that AFOSI is maintaining no records pertaining to MJ-12, or any investigation thereof, which begs the question: How was AFOSI able to determine that the papers were faked? Batten has also advised me that, while AFOSI did 'discuss' the MJ-12 documents with the FBI, incredibly they made absolutely no written reference to that meeting in any shape or form. This I find most odd: if nothing else government and military departments are methodical when it comes to documenting possible breaches of security.[15]

Richard L. Weaver, one-time Deputy for Security and Investigative Programs with the US Air Force, has also advised me that, 'the Air Force considers the "MJ-12" (both the group described and the purported documents) to be bogus'. He, too, conceded, however, that there were 'no documents responsive' to my request for Air Force files on how just such a determination was reached.[16]

Moreover, there is the fact that AFOSI informed the Bureau that 'copies of that document have been distributed to various parts of the United States'. To make such a statement AFOSI simply had to have conducted some form of investigation, however informal or unofficial. On the other hand, if AFOSI truly did not undertake any such investigation into MJ-12, then its statement to the FBI decrying the value of the documents is essentially worthless, since it is based on personal opinion rather than sound evaluation.

If the Bureau learned anything further about MJ-12 in the post-1989 period, then that information has not surfaced under the Freedom of Information Act. Perhaps the Bureau, unable to satisfactorily get a straight answer from the military and the intelligence community, simply gave up the chase; I do not know. I do know, thanks to Richard L. Huff, Bureau Co-Director within the Office of Information and Privacy, that MJ-12 remains the subject of an FBI headquarters Main File titled 'Espionage'. Today, that file is in 'closed status'. As Howard Blum was advised by a Bureau source: 'It wouldn't surprise me if we never know if the papers are genuine or not.'

The Bureau may not have received the required answers from the Intelligence community with respect to MJ-12 and Roswell, but there were other ways and means. If the government wouldn't talk, then the Bureau would turn its attention to those outside government: the civilian UFO researchers who were responsible for circulating the MJ-12 documents in the first instance!

As far as Timothy Good is concerned, evidence of direct surveillance by the FBI has not been forthcoming; however, I am able to show that in 1987, when the controversy surrounding MJ-12 was at its peak, the British Ministry of Defence was aware of the contents of Good's book. In a letter of 3 September 1987 from the Defence Minister Roger Freeman to a Labour MP, Stan Crowther, it was stated that with respect to MJ-12, 'the only information we have on this subject is that contained in Timothy Good's book and related press articles. If the operation exists it would appear to have been a US national one, of which we in the UK had no knowledge'.

However, there is clear proof that both Stanton Friedman and William Moore have been the subjects of FBI investigations.

On 16 October 1988, Larry Bryant (who had worked hard to force the Bureau to release an unexpurgated copy of its memo of 22 March 1950, concerning three crashed UFOs found in Arizona and New

Mexico) wrote to Ms Hope Nakamura of the Center for National Security Studies and advised her that in a then-recent conversation with William Moore, he had been informed of Moore's efforts to secure the release of the FBI's dossier on his unidentified-flying-object research activities. The vast bulk of that dossier – which amounted to no less than fifty-five pages of official documentation – was being withheld by the Bureau for reasons directly affecting the national security of the United States of America.

Bryant went on to explain that Moore was attempting to find legal assistance in challenging the nondisclosure of the vast bulk of the FBI's file on him. In a determined effort to lend assistance to Moore, Bryant drafted a lengthy and detailed advertisement which he proposed submitting to a number of military newspapers for future publication.

Titled 'UFO SECRECY/CONGRESS-WATCH', the advertisement (which was one of a number Bryant submitted to newspapers on the issue of UFOs in the late 1980s) specifically addressed the eye-opening fact that the Bureau's file on Moore was classified at no less than 'Secret' level, and that at least one other (unnamed) US government agency was also keeping tabs on Moore and his UFO pursuits – in particular those pursuits relating to certain 'whistle-blower testimony' which Moore had acquired from a variety of sources within the American government and military.

Courageously, Bryant signed off urging those reading the advertisement to contact their local congressman and to press for nothing less than a full-scale inquiry into the issue of UFOs.

Bryant's advert was ultimately published (in the 23 November 1988 issue of the *Pentagram*, a publication of the US Army); yet as spirited as this was it failed to force the Bureau to relinquish its files on Moore. By 1993, the FBI's dossier on Moore was running at 61 pages, of which Moore had succeeded in gaining access to only six.

In 1989, Bryant, mindful of the FBI's surveillance of William Moore, attempted to force the Bureau to release any or all records on Moore's research partner, Stanton Friedman. On 2 August of that year, Bryant received the following response from Richard L. Huff: 'Mr Friedman is the subject of one Headquarters main file. This file is classified in its entirety and I am affirming the denial of access to it . . .'

On 28 August 1989, Bryant filed suit in the District Court for the Eastern District of Virginia.

'My complaint,' explained Bryant, 'seeks full disclosure of the UFO-related content of the FBI dossier on Stan Friedman. Neither Stan nor I have been able to convince the US Federal Bureau of Investigation to loosen its grasp on that dossier, which Bureau officials assert bears a security classification.'

Fortunately, in Friedman's case, a 'small portion' of the FBI's file pertaining to him was eventually released (on 13 November 1989) as a result of Bryant's actions.

What are we to make of all this? The intense surveillance of both Moore and Friedman, both of whom were (and still are) at the forefront of research into the Roswell crash and MJ-12, inclines me to believe that the Bureau has learned infinitely more about both issues than it is willing to admit.

You might be forgiven for thinking that by now FBI involvement in the Roswell crash would have been thoroughly exhausted. Not so.

In the spring of 1993, United States Congressman Steven Schiff began to make enquiries with the Defense Department in an attempt to determine exactly what it was that occurred at Roswell in 1947. After having received several responses from DoD officials and the National Archives, all of which suggested that he was being given 'the runaround', Schiff approached the investigative arm of Congress, the General Accounting Office, who agreed to look into the matter.

Perhaps the most significant finding of the GAO was that detailed in a press release from Schiff's staff on 28 July 1995:

> Congressman Steve Schiff today released the General Accounting Office (GAO) report detailing results of a records audit related to events surrounding a crash in 1947, near Roswell, New Mexico, and the military response . . . Schiff said important documents, which may have shed more light on what happened at Roswell, are missing. The GAO report states that the outgoing messages from Roswell Army Air Field (RAAF) for this period of time were destroyed without proper authority.

This was certainly of great significance, but it was largely ignored by the media, primarily because, ten months earlier, the US Air Force had issued its own report on Roswell (which it was not mandated to do by the GAO), suggesting that what crashed at Roswell was a balloon from Project Mogul – a top-secret operation designed to monitor nuclear weapons research undertaken by the former Soviet Union.

In 1995, the Air Force followed this initial release with yet another report – 'The Roswell Report, Fact Vs. Fiction In The New Mexico Desert' – once again asserting firmly that Mogul debris was responsible for the Roswell story. A massive tome, almost one thousand pages in length, it contains the results of numerous interviews, reproductions of fifty-year-old diaries, documents, and a host of other material previously unseen. As impressive as it seems on first inspection, the report has its flaws.

The issue of 'alien bodies', for example, is passed swiftly over: '. . . the recovered wreckage was from a Project MOGUL balloon. There were no "alien" passengers therein'. This is, quite frankly, outrageous and a discourtesy to those retired military persons who have been willing to risk their reputations and assert that bodies were recovered. Perhaps recognising that this statement would provoke controversy, the Air Force added: '. . . persons who have come forward and provided their names and made claims may have, in good faith but in the "fog of time," misinterpreted past events'. Quite.

There is also the problem of the nature of the Mogul balloons. It is quite true that Project Mogul was a top-secret operation; however, the balloons used were wholly conventional, which hardly explains the debris recovered by Major Jesse Marcel: 'We even tried making a dent in [the debris] with a sixteen-pound sledgehammer, and there was still no dent in it.'

And what of the death threats made to innocent civilians by the government at the time? It has been suggested that, given the very real military threat posed by Russia in the late 1940s, the crash of a Mogul balloon at Roswell prompted an overinflated degree of 'Cold War nerves' on the part of the Army Air Force, which led them to issue rash warnings to those with intimate knowledge of what occurred. This particular hypothesis is entirely possible, and we should not be quick to

judge those who were tasked with maintaining the security of the free
world in the period after World War Two.

Unfortunately, this theory is belied by the facts. Once again we turn to
the FBI. On 23 September 1947, the Bureau drew up a one-page memorandum concerning its acquisition of an 'Instrument found on farm near
Danforth, Illinois'. Initially, it was not known what this object was; however, the FBI made it available to a Mrs Whedon of the Army Engineers,
who postulated that 'the instrument had been used by the Air Forces on
tests which were classified as "Top Secret".'

Special Agent S.W. Reynolds of the Bureau's Liaison Section made
additional enquiries and contacted the Intelligence Division of the Air
Force, who informed him: 'Mrs Whedon alluded that the instrument was
used in "Operation Mogul".'

Further enquiries showed the entire matter to be a hoax, and the
'object' was in actuality a part of an old-style radio loudspeaker. Initially,
however, it was believed to have been Mogul-based debris. And, faced
with the possibility that debris from a top-secret project had come down
on an Illinois farm, what did the Air Force do? Did they dispatch military
police to the farm and request the silence of the owner? Did they issue
stark threats of death? No, the material was simply forwarded with the
minimum of fuss to Wright Field for inspection, and it was they who
determined that it was unconnected to Project Mogul.

For proponents of the theory that the object found at Roswell was a
Mogul balloon, this presents a major problem. We have two incidents,
one in New Mexico, one in Illinois. In the first instance, the Air Force
assert that a Mogul balloon was recovered; in the second instance,
Mogul was suspected. Yet the procedures undertaken to deal with the
recovery and analysis of both objects were entirely different. More
importantly, the overwhelming security afforded the Roswell case was
absent in the incident at Illinois. Had the two events occurred in different time spans, say over the space of three or four years, it could be
argued that the secrecy surrounding Mogul had been downgraded. Yet
Roswell occurred in early July 1947, and the finding at the Danforth,
Illinois, farm occurred only weeks later. For the sake of clarification, the
Air Force's analysis of the debris found at Darnforth (released to me in
unedited form by the FBI) follows. Prepared for the Commanding

General, Army Air Forces, Washington 25, DC, the two-page report reads:

1. The specimens of an alleged 'Flying Saucer' brought to this Command by Colonel H.M. McCoy, which were obtained by the FBI and given to Lieutenant Colonel Garrett, were examined to determine their connection, if any, with the so-called 'Flying Saucers', or any project at HQ Air Materiel Command, Wright Field. The specimens were carefully examined by both technicians of the Analysis Division (T-2) and Electronics Sub-division (T-3). The latter organization stated that these specimens definitely had no connection whatsoever with the 'Mogul' project nor with any other research and development project of this Command.

2. It is also the opinion of this Command that these specimens have no connection with the so-called 'Flying Saucer' or 'Disc'. These specimens, therefore, are considered as part of a hoax that could be perpetrated by most anyone seeking publicity or for any other reasons.

3. The specimens shown in the attached photograph include fragments of an undertermined shape made from plaster of paris or similar ceramic and containing some electrical resistance wire for measurement or heating purposes. The condition of the ceramic indicates that the resistance wire was heated electrically at one time or another. These fragments could not be connected with any AMC project. The other articles at the top of the photograph reading from left to right are identified as follows:

(a) An outmoded type of magnetic speaker diaphragm made of aluminum alloy, manufactured by the Nathaniel Baldwin Company of Salt Lake City, Utah, which was first patented May 1, 1910. This article cannot be connected with any AMC project.

(b) The second and third articles are bakelite coil forms wrapped with ordinary thin enameled copper wire. These coils indicate that they were skillfully made at one time but were crudely rewrapped by one not familiar with the art of making a coil. These coils also have no connection with any AMC project.

(c) The fourth article is a metallic box which is the remains of an electronic filter condenser made by the Polymet Manufacturing Company of New York, NY. This article also has no connection with any AMC project.

(d) The fifth article is the remains of a metallic magnetic ring that could not be identified as any part of any device used at this command.

(4) This information and attached photograph may be transmitted to the FBI to inform various agencies throughout the United States as to what action to take in the event other similar specimens are found.

Faced with the evidence presented in this Air Force report (which was only classified at 'Confidential' level), I have to conclude that, whatever was recovered at Roswell, the all-encompassing blanket of secrecy surrounding the entire affair extended to something far more important than a mere Mogul balloon.

Any serious attempt on our part to try to ascertain what exactly the FBI knows about the recovery of crashed UFOs and their seemingly alien crews, is inevitably predetermined by the amount of data the Bureau has been willing to release. Nevertheless, we can make some judgements.

For example, the Bureau's interest in the Newton–GeBauer–Scully affair as it related to the alleged crash of an alien spacecraft at Aztec was more than passing, as was (and possibly still is) its interest in the Majestic 12 controversy and the activities of its premier researchers: Stanton Friedman and William Moore.

Then there is the matter of the Bureau's surveillance in the 1950s of the 'crash-retrieval' expert Leonard Stringfield – who perhaps more than any other researcher was responsible for demonstrating that the issue of crashed UFOs was one worthy of study. If the FBI's monitoring of Stringfield continued into the 1970s and 1980s (when his investigations into this aspect of the UFO mystery were at a peak), there is a likelihood that a truly substantial amount of unseen data on this topic exists at FBI headquarters in Washington, DC.

Yet we should not forget that, with respect to the most credible of all the many alleged UFO retrievals – the Roswell event of July 1947 – the Army Air Force almost certainly prevented the FBI from learning the real facts behind what was actually retrieved. This seems to suggest that whatever the United States Department of Defense has learned from the study of recovered UFOs, it does not feel that fully informing the FBI of those conclusions is warranted.

The final word I will leave to one of Howard Blum's confidential Bureau sources: 'All we're finding out is that the government doesn't know what it knows. There are too many secret levels.'

CHAPTER 12

CONTACT!

WHEN PEOPLE CONTEMPLATE THE POSSIBILITY OF A MEETING BETWEEN the human race and the representatives of an alien species, there is a tendency to imagine that any visiting extraterrestrial beings are going to be manifestly different in appearance and character from ourselves.

In 1974, the author Jack Stoneley and Anthony T. Lawton, a key member of a research team headed by Sir Barnes Wallis in the 1950s, which worked on the principle of swing-wing aircraft, made an astute observation:

> The extreme heat and gaseous surface of a planet like Jupiter might produce a creature that would float beneath its own built-in balloon, feeding off organic compounds produced in electrical discharges in the upper atmosphere. The intelligences we may one day encounter could have two legs or two hundred; they might be flat or round, they may walk, swim, fly, roll, slide, crawl, hop, or squirm. They may be hairy or bald, transparent or solid. They may have one eye, a thousand eyes or, though rather unlikely, no eyes at all. They may even be just shapeless masses suspended in an atmosphere.[1]

In 1995, the science writer and author Edward Ashpole put forward his beliefs regarding the physicality of alien beings: 'Any technological species visiting us from a far-away biosphere would not look like us. We are vertebrates, and vertebrates have a long history of evolution going back to a certain group of fishes. The bones which form the human skeleton can be traced back through that evolutionary history and are not going to be duplicated in another planetary biology. Statistically it would be impossible.'[2]

For all the arguments that alien visitors to our planet would look, appropriately enough, like 'nothing on Earth', there are numerous accounts from across the globe which, when examined as a whole, offer the very real possibility that some of our cosmic counterparts resemble the human race to a striking degree. Moreover, there is the comforting fact that they also appear to be concerned by our somewhat warlike nature and are attempting to steer us towards a more peaceful future. That said, this may be nothing more than a deceptive trap designed to lull us into a false sense of security before zapping us into infinity!

Whatever the intent of this particular band of visitor, the FBI has on its files the claims of numerous persons who asserted that in the 1950s and 1960s they were in covert contact with benevolent alien beings of human appearance. Thus was born the cult of the 'contactee'. But before addressing the issue of the Bureau's involvement in the contactee puzzle, I wish to draw your attention to a number of cases that support my belief that not all our alien visitors are bug-eyed, two-headed, six-armed monsters.

If human-like extraterrestrials are operating, and perhaps even living, on Earth, the likelihood is that in some capacity a number of governments are aware that this is the case.

In early 1994, the investigator Don Berliner received a roll of film from an anonymous source which, when developed, showed what appeared to be pages of highly classified US government documents concerning Majestic 12 and its findings on UFOs, alien beings and the procedures for dealing with extraterrestrial technology and biology.

According to the document (which was allegedly prepared in April 1954), the US government had determined that 'two distinct categories' of alien were visiting our planet, one of which was three and a half to four feet tall, with a large head and 'very large, slanted' eyes; while the other appeared extraordinarily human-like in outward form. An extract from the document concerning this particular race of creature states:

These entities are humanoid and might be mistaken for human beings of the Oriental race if seen from a distance. They are bi-pedal, 5–5 feet 4 inches in height and weigh 80–100 pounds. Proportionally they are similar to humans, although the cranium is somewhat larger and more rounded. The skin is a pale, chalky-yellow in color, thick, and slightly pebbled in appearance. The eyes are small, wide-set, almond-shaped, with brownish-black irises with very large pupils. The whites of the eyes are not like that of humans, but have a pale gray cast. The ears are small and set low on the skull. The nose is thin and long, and the mouth is wider than in humans, and nearly lipless. There is no apparent facial hair and very little body hair. The body is thin and without apparent body fat, but the muscles are well-developed. The hands are small, with four long digits but no opposable thumb. The outside digit is jointed in a manner as to be nearly opposable, and there is no webbing between the fingers as in humans. The legs are slightly but noticeably bowed, and the feet are somewhat splayed and proportionally large.[3]

Further support that 'humanoid aliens' are among us comes from Robert Dean, a retired US Army command sergeant major, who maintains that in the early 1960s the North Atlantic Treaty Organisation (NATO) conducted an in-depth study of the entire UFO problem. Dean maintains further that he had access to a huge report generated as a result of the NATO inquiry, and learned that:

. . . part of the study stated that [NATO] had come to the conclusion that we had four different civilizations – cultures – intelligences – that were present here on Earth and that were visiting us and interacting with us. One of the most interesting conclusions, and one which struck me most, was that one of the groups – one of the civilizations or cultures that were here on this Planet – was identical with us – or rather, that we were identical with them! And that made a vast impression on the people involved in the investigation.[4]

The late Leonard Stringfield, who was probably the world's leading authority on the subject of UFO crashes and retrievals, learned in 1981 from a certain French professor that at Wright-Patterson Air Force Base in the USA the bodies of at least two humanoid extraterrestrials were held following their recovery from a presumed crash or accident:

> They were very tall (2.30 meter or so, or 7 feet, 3 inches – the height of an American basketball player), and bore hideous mutilations on their bodies, as if they had been the victims of a road accident! The heads of these two creatures were intact. The forehead high and broad. Very long blond hair. The eyes were stretched towards the temples which gave them an Asiatic look. The nose and mouth were small. The lips were thin, perfectly delineated. The chin was small and slightly pointed. The two faces were beardless. Despite slight differences in their facial appearances, the two humanoids looked like twins.[5]

The description of the aliens' hair ('Very long [and] blond') is interesting and appears time and time again in contactee accounts. And so prevalent are such accounts that I firmly believe beyond any shadow of a doubt that our planet does harbour extraterrestrial beings who could pass for members of the human race – on first inspection, at least.

One area of the world that has had more than its fair share of contactee-type encounters is Latin America. On 9 December 1954, Olmira da Costa e Rosa, a farmer, of Rio Grande do Sol, Brazil, was tending his crop of French beans and maize when he was stunned to see a cream-coloured object (described as resembling an explorer's hat) hovering over a nearby field.

As the panic-stricken Rosa watched, he saw three unusual-looking 'men': one in the craft; one examining a barbed-wire fence; and, most alarming, one approaching Rosa himself.

Awestruck by what he was seeing, Rosa dropped his hoe and could only stand in stark terror as the being came closer. But Rosa had nothing to fear: the 'man' simply smiled, picked up the hoe, and handed it back to the farmer. After doing so, he bent down and tugged out of the ground a few plants and returned to the craft in the adjacent field. At that point the object rose into the air and accelerated suddenly away from the area.

As with the bodies at Wright-Patterson Air Force Base, the beings were described by Rosa as broad-shouldered, with long blond hair. Rosa added that their eyes were somewhat slanted and their skin extremely pale. It had been a terrifying experience for the near-illiterate farmer, who had not even the merest awareness of the subject of unidentified flying objects.[6]

For decades UFO literature has been filled with literally dozens of accounts where, as in the case of Olmira da Costa e Rosa, the aliens have been reported taking soil and plant 'samples' – the presumption being that this is done for biological research purposes. This I find a wholly untenable theory.

In all probability any civilisation that is sufficiently advanced to navigate from star to star (if not galaxy to galaxy) would be more than capable of conducting an intensive study of Earth's plant life, animal life, oceans and land masses in a relatively short space of time – perhaps no more than a few months. So why the apparent ongoing need to make hasty touch-downs (almost always in full view of one or two isolated witnesses), during which they repeatedly grab handfuls of plants, soil and leaves before departing quickly?

I am certain that these actions are little more than an elaborate 'game', played out largely for our own benefit. Two theories spring to mind:

- The aliens are benevolent, and wish to present themselves to us in a manner that is acceptable and non-threatening, i.e. as interplanetary scientists undertaking routine research of the Earth. Presumably when we are fully acclimatised to this scenario, meaningful liaison between our two (or more) species can begin.
- The aliens are wholly deceptive creatures who are promoting the image of the 'interplanetary scientist' to mask their true intent – the exploitation of the Earth.

A contact with similar beings to those seen by Rosa occurred in Argentina in October 1973. During the early hours of 28 October,

Dionisio Llanca, a lorry driver, was negotiating Highway 3 near Bahia Blanca when he was forced to stop his lorry, which for several hours had been suffering from a slow puncture.

As he began to jack up the lorry to change its tyre, Llanca was suddenly enveloped in a yellow beam of light which emanated from a saucer-shaped object hovering some fifteen to twenty feet from the ground. Semi-paralysed by the light beam, Llanca was amazed to see behind him three humanoids, all of whom were staring at him intently.

All three, two men and one woman, were about five foot six and wore tight-fitting, grey, one-piece outfits and three-quarter-length boots. Again they looked very human and had the now-familiar long blond hair.

Suddenly Llanca was forcibly grabbed, and a device was placed on the index finger of his left hand. Llanca then became disorientated and fainted.

Later he recalled that the beings had informed him that they had been present on Earth since 1950 and had warned him: '[Your] planet is bound to suffer very grave catastrophes if [your] behaviour continues as it is at present'.[7]

Concern over our development of atomic weapons and our misuse of the environment are staple parts of countless contactee cases, and, as will soon become clear, are two of the reasons why the FBI took such a keen interest in the subject.

Moving to England, an encounter occurred in August 1992 very much like that at Rio Grande do Sol, Brazil, in December 1954. The setting was Cannock Chase – a large area of forest in Staffordshire, which has been the site of numerous UFO sightings since the 1940s.

In this instance, at around 9.30 p.m. in the evening, the witness was walking through the woods and came across an area of mist within which was a 'metallic, shining object' surrounded by a display of coloured lights.

As the witness approached he was confronted by two 'people' in light-coloured overalls who informed him that they were taking samples and that he would not understand. Suddenly the figures began to glow slightly and the witness began to grow drowsy, almost as if he were being hypnotised. As he watched in a somewhat groggy state the beings walked into the mist and promptly vanished into thin air!

In virtually all respects the beings looked human: slightly shorter in stature than an average adult male, with dark-brown or black hair and a Latin appearance.[8]

Is it really feasible that, forty years after the Brazilian encounter, there was still a need on the part of some advanced alien intelligence to gather samples of terrestrial biology from an area of British woodland? My feelings on this matter I have already spelled out, and I suggest that if anyone reading this has a similar experience, you do your utmost to keep out of the clutches of our elusive visitors! Friendly they may be, but I am certain there is deception at work.

In 1994, Robert Dean gave a talk before an audience at the Civic Theatre, Leeds, during which he elaborated on his knowledge of the more human-like aliens present in our environment. As the audience listened, Dean revealed that so similar to us was at least one race of extraterrestrial that 'they could sit next to you in an airplane or in a restaurant in a coat and tie or a dress and you would never know. They could be sitting next to you in a theatre like this . . .'

More alarming were the ramifications that this had within NATO. 'Back in 1964,' said Dean, 'this was a matter of great concern to the admirals and generals at SHAPE Headquarters in Paris. Some of the discussions which went on in the War Room were kind of frightening and some of them were rather amusing. One officer said: "My God, man, do you realise that these could be walking up and down the corridors of SHAPE Headquarters and we wouldn't know who the hell they were?"'[9]

Perhaps Dean's revelations go some way towards explaining the FBI's deep desire to keep under watch the many and varied contractees who surfaced in the USA in the 1950s.

Born 12 March 1910 at Jefferson County, Ohio, George Wellington Van Tassel claimed deep involvement with human-like extraterrestrial intelligences following an encounter in August 1953 near his home in Yucca Valley, California – an encounter that resulted in his being the subject of an extensive FBI surveillance operation which lasted from 1954 until well into the 1960s.

The full story surrounding Van Tassel's alleged encounters is a strange one, involving wild accounts of meetings with imaginatively named aliens including 'Numa of Uni', 'Ah-Ming of Tarr', 'Rondolla of the Fourth Density', and 'Zolton, the Highest Authority and Commandant of all spacecraft in the Sector System of Vela'. Coupled with the remarkable fact that Van Tassel and his family actually lived in a cave under a huge rock in the middle of the desert, you may wonder why I have even bothered to make a mention of the man and his claimed experiences with beings from other worlds.

Whether we like it or not, Van Tassel's accounts do tally to an astonishing degree with a number of those I have cited earlier in this chapter, and, faced with the fact that there is circumstantial evidence to show that some of the human-like beings visiting our planet are deceptive in nature, perhaps we should not dismiss out of hand the seemingly unbelievable information imparted by Van Tassel.

According to the Bureau's records, prior to moving to Yucca Valley in 1947, Van Tassel had worked for the Douglas Aircraft Corporation in Santa Monica; Hughes Aircraft, where he was employed in an assistance capacity to Howard Hughes; Universal Airlines; and Lockheed.

Quite what prompted him to relocate to Yucca Valley is unclear, but, along with his wife and children, Van Tassel soon settled into his new, if somewhat odd, surroundings: his famous 'cave' under Giant Rock – an area leased from the government.

To the uninitiated, the thought of a family living in a cave situated beneath a sixty-foot-high rock 28 miles from Joshua Tree, California, must seem more than a little strange, and surely conjures up scenes of some prehistoric family struggling to survive in less-than-friendly conditions.

Initially, day-to-day living was more than a little taxing for the Van Tassels, but, ever resourceful, the family soon began to make ends meet via an airstrip they rented (the 'Giant Rock Airport') and a small, but hospitable, restaurant.

As time went on, Van Tassel began to improve the family's living facilities and the cave became a cosy environment: fully furnished, equipped with electricity, its own water supply, an impressive library of books and, as the journalist Ed Ritter noted in 1954, 'a comfortable living room where [Van Tassel] studies and entertains guests'.

But what prompted the Federal Bureau of Investigation to take such an overwhelming interest in the affairs of George W. Van Tassel?

As a result of his August 1953 encounter, Van Tassel established the grandly titled 'College of Universal Wisdom', which, according to the man himself, '. . . will be devoted to interplanetary communications and a diffusion of universal wisdom gained through the medium of space beings'.

Within two months, Van Tassel had compiled the first issue of the *Proceedings of the College of Universal Wisdom*, an eight-page journal which served as a mouthpiece for not only Van Tassel but his cosmic communicators, too. In the opening edition, 'Desca', like Rondolla also of the Fourth Density, urged Van Tassel's followers (whose number would soon reach almost one thousand) to 'remove the binding chains of limit on your minds . . . throw out the barriers of fear [and] dissipate the selfishness of individual desire to attain physical and material things'.

In the edition of the *Proceedings* dated 1 December 1953, Van Tassel revealed that on 6 November a 'message was received from the beings who operate the spacecraft', with orders from Ashtar, the Commandant of Space Station Schare (pronounced Share-ee) to contact the office of Air Force Intelligence at Wright-Patterson Air Force Base, Dayton, Ohio, to advise that: 'The present destructive plans formulated for offensive and defensive war are known to us in their entirety . . . the present trend toward destructive war will not be interfered with by us, unless the condition warrants our interference in order to secure this solar system. This is a friendly warning.'

Were Van Tassel's contacts genuinely of alien origin? Were they merely the ravings of a deluded mind? Or were they possibly a part of some sophisticated Communist-inspired intelligence operation designed to disrupt the internal security of the United States? This final theory was certainly of concern to a Yucca Valley resident who, on 5 August 1954, wrote to the Bureau suggesting that Van Tassel be investigated to determine if he was working undercover as a Soviet spy. The identity of the woman who prompted the Bureau to undertake its investigation of Van Tassel remains unknown; however, there is a distinct possibility that she may have had access to Van Tassel's *Proceedings* at some time.

On 1 June 1954, only two months before the Bureau received the woman's letter, a number of statements were made in Van Tassel's newsletter which certainly suggested that this third theory could not be dismissed: 'Secrecy under the phoney word 'Security' has permitted some of the authorities to take advantages, with the taxpayers money, to violate our God given constitution under 'National Emergency Laws' . . . the collapse of the world money system may forestall a reason for another world war . . . the space people who understand God and the subtle forces of His creation, and use these forces for many things – besides space travel – are not limited by established brain theories. They do things that are astounding to the multitudes here because they are not limited by rules of class, authority, money or dogma'. And copies of Van Tassel's *Proceedings* in the possession of the Bureau show that all of the extracts I have noted above had been carefully 'circled' by someone who was clearly interested in some of the more politically extreme comments of both Van Tassel and his purported alien contacts.

Naturally concerned that Van Tassel was possibly a witting or unwitting player in a subversive Communist plot, the FBI determined to ascertain the facts.

On 12 November 1954, Major S. Avner of the Air Force's Office of Special Investigations met with the Bureau's liaison with the Air Force, N.W. Philcox, and advised that OSI and Air Intelligence files reflected no knowledge of Van Tassel, but further checks were being made with the Air Technical Intelligence Center at Wright-Patterson Air Force Base.

Three days later, Avner re-established contact with Philcox, informing him that ATIC 'has information on Van Tassel indicating that he has corresponded with them regarding flying saucers'. Almost certainly this was a reference to the letter Van Tassel wrote to ATIC at the request of the mysterious Ashtar, who it will be recalled offered a 'friendly warning' with respect to 'plans formulated for offensive and defensive war'. Perhaps more aware of Van Tassel than has previously been thought, the Air Force added: '. . . it would be possible to furnish the Bureau with more detailed information if it is so desired'.

Whether or not the Bureau accepted the Air Force's offer of 'more detailed information' on Van Tassel is unclear, and those papers declassified under the provisions of the Freedom of Information Act by the FBI do not reflect this; however, there is a wealth of fascinating documentation at our disposal which shows that the Bureau was more than capable of conducting its own investigations.

One day after Major Avner of AFOSI spoke with Philcox two Special Agents of the Los Angeles FBI office met with Van Tassel at his Giant Rock home. 'Van Tassel declared that he moved from Los Angeles to Giant Rock seven years ago and purchased a ranch near this area and subsequently leased land near Giant Rock from the Government,' the Los Angeles office advised Hoover. 'He stated that this newly acquired land is known as Giant Rock Airport. He pointed out that the airport was acquired under the "Airport Act" and is a certified CAA emergency landing strip.' But Van Tassel had much more to impart, as is amply shown from the following memorandum drawn up by the FBI on 16 November 1954:

> Relative to spacemen and space craft, VAN TASSEL declared that a year ago last August, while sleeping out of doors with his wife in the Giant Rock area, and at about 2:00 a.m. he was awakened by a man from space. This individual spoke English and was dressed in a gray one piece suit similar to a sweat suit in that it did not have any buttons, pockets, and noticeable seams. This person, according to VAN TASSEL, invited him to inspect a space craft or flying saucer, which had landed on Giant Rock air strip. VAN TASSEL claimed the craft was bell shaped resembling a saucer. He further described the ship as approximately 35 feet in diameter and is now known as the scout type craft. Aboard this craft was located three other male individuals wearing the same type of dress and identical in every respect with earth people.
>
> VAN TASSEL claims that the three individuals aboard the craft were mutes in that they could not talk. He claimed they conversed through thought transfers, and also operated the flight of the craft through thought control. He stated that the spokesman for the group claimed he could talk because he was trained by his family to speak. The spokesman stated that earth men are using too much metal in their everyday work and are

fouling up radio frequencies and thought transfers because of this
over use of metal. According to VAN TASSEL, these individuals
came from Venus and are by no means hostile nor do they intend
to harm this country or inhabitants in any manner. He declared

An early example of the FBI's involvement in the 'Contactee' controversy.

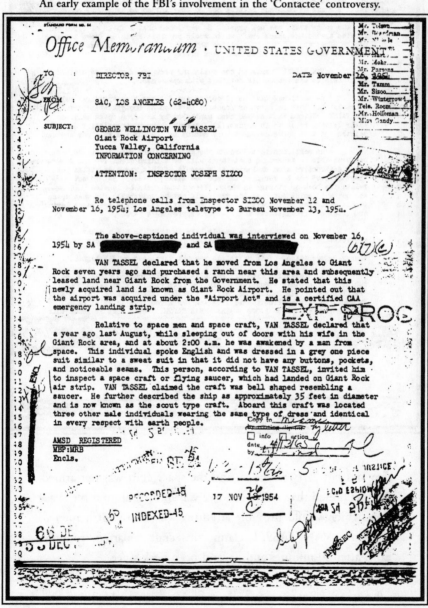

LA 62-4080

　　　　VAN TASSEL claims that the three individuals aboard the craft were mutes in that they could not talk. He claimed they conversed through thought transfers, and also operated the flight of the craft through thought control. He stated that the spokesman for the group claimed he could talk because he was trained by his family to speak. The spokesman stated that earth men are using too much metal in their everyday work and are fowling up radio frequencies and thought transfers because of this over use of metal. According to VAN TASSEL, these individuals came from Venus and are by no means hostile nor do they intend to harm this country or inhabitants in any manner. He declared they did not carry weapons, and the space craft was not armed. He mentioned that a field of force was located around the space craft which would prohibit anything known to earth men to penetrate. VAN TASSEL claims this craft departed from the earth after 20 minutes and has not been back since.

　　　　VAN TASSEL furnished the following background which he claimed might help to understand his dealings with space men.

　　　　He mentioned that he advocates and follows a metaphysical religion or research. This religion or research is based on thought transfers. VAN TASSEL claimed that he had been contacted by men from space prior to their landing on earth in August, 1953 through thought transfers. He again pointed out that space men used this medium to communicate with one another.

　　　　He mentioned that through thought transfers with space men, he has been able to ascertain that there will be a third world war and a large destructive atom explosion as a result of this war. He stated that these "facts" can be verified through the Bible; however, he did not relate the book or passage in which these facts could be located. He was quick to point out that the war would not be universal, and that space people would not be involved. He stated that space people are peace loving and under no circumstances would enter or provoke a war.

　　　　He claims that space people have imparted to him a means of rejuvenating earth peoples' life expectancy from what it is today to 300 - 1500 years. He claimed this is done through a principle of light energy rejuvenation. This principle was not developed by VAN TASSEL.

　　　　In connection with his metaphysical religion and research, he publishes bi-monthly a publication in the form of a booklet called "PROCEEDINGS OF THE COLLEGE OF UNIVERSAL WISDOM, YUCCA VALLEY, CALIFORNIA." He declared this publication is free and has grown from an original mailing list of 250 to 1,000 copies. VAN TASSEL stated that he sends this

- 2 -

they did not carry weapons, and the space craft was not armed. He mentioned that a field of force was located around the space craft which would prohibit anything known to earth men to penetrate. VAN TASSEL claims this craft departed from the earth after 20 minutes and has not been back since.

As the amazed Bureau agents listened, Van Tassel added that 'through

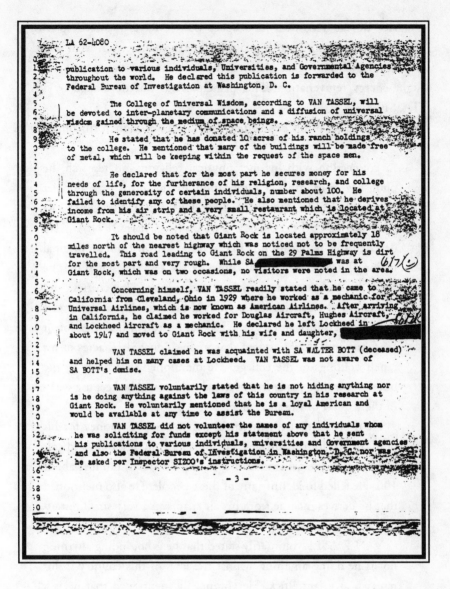

LA 62-4080

publication to various individuals, Universities, and Governmental Agencies throughout the world. He declared this publication is forwarded to the Federal Bureau of Investigation at Washington, D. C.

The College of Universal Wisdom, according to VAN TASSEL, will be devoted to inter-planetary communications and a diffusion of universal wisdom gained through the medium of space beings.

He stated that he has donated 10 acres of his ranch holdings to the college. He mentioned that many of the buildings will be made free of metal, which will be keeping within the request of the space men.

He declared that for the most part he secures money for his needs of life, for the furtherance of his religion, research, and college through the generosity of certain individuals, number about 100. He failed to identify any of these people. He also mentioned that he derives income from his air strip and a very small restaurant which is located at Giant Rock.

It should be noted that Giant Rock is located approximately 18 miles north of the nearest highway which was noticed not to be frequently travelled. This road leading to Giant Rock on the 29 Palms Highway is dirt for the most part and very rough. While SA   was at Giant Rock, which was on two occasions, no visitors were noted in the area.

Concerning himself, VAN TASSEL readily stated that he came to California from Cleveland, Ohio in 1929 where he worked as a mechanic for Universal Airlines, which is now known as American Airlines. After arriving in California, he claimed he worked for Douglas Aircraft, Hughes Aircraft, and Lockheed Aircraft as a mechanic. He declared he left Lockheed in about 1947 and moved to Giant Rock with his wife and daughter,

VAN TASSEL claimed he was acquainted with SA WALTER BOTT (deceased) and helped him on many cases at Lockheed. VAN TASSEL was not aware of SA BOTT's demise.

VAN TASSEL voluntarily stated that he is not hiding anything nor is he doing anything against the laws of this country in his research at Giant Rock. He voluntarily mentioned that he is a loyal American and would be available at any time to assist the Bureau.

VAN TASSEL did not volunteer the names of any individuals whom he was soliciting for funds except his statement above that he sent his publications to various individuals, universities and Government agencies and also the Federal Bureau of Investigation in Washington, D. C., nor was he asked per Inspector SIZOO's instructions.

- 3 -

thought transfers with space men', he had been able to ascertain that a third world war was on the horizon, which was likely to be 'large' and 'destructive'; that much of this correlated directly with certain biblical passages; that the war would not be 'universal'; and that the 'space people are peace loving and under no circumstances would enter or provoke a war'. And to illustrate their benevolence towards mankind, the aliens had bestowed upon Van Tassel some remarkable data: 'He claims,' the Los

Angeles Bureau recorded, 'that space people have imparted to him a means of rejuvenating earth people's life expectancy from what is today to 300–1,500 years. He claimed this is done through a principle of light energy rejuvenation. This principle was not developed by VAN TASSEL.'

On the matter of his newsletter, Van Tassel was more forthcoming:

> In connection with his metaphysical religion and research, he publishes bi-monthly a publication in the form of a booklet called 'PROCEEDINGS OF THE COLLEGE OF UNIVERSAL WISDOM, YUCCA VALLEY, CALIFORNIA.' He declared this publication is free and has grown from an original mailing list of 250 to 1,000 copies. VAN TASSEL stated that he sends his publication to various individuals, Universities, and Government Agencies throughout the world. He declared this publication is forwarded to the Federal Bureau of Investigation at Washington, DC. He stated that he has donated 10 acres of his ranch holdings to the college. He mentioned that many of the buildings will be made free of metal, which will be keeping within the request of the spacemen.
>
> He declared that for the most part he secures money for his needs of life, for the furtherance of his religion, research, and college through the generosity of certain individuals, number about 100. He failed to identify any of these people. He also mentioned that he derives income from his air strip and a very small restaurant which is located at Giant Rock.
>
> VAN TASSEL voluntarily stated that he is not hiding anything nor is he doing anything against the laws of this country in his research at Giant Rock. He voluntarily mentioned that he is a loyal American and would be available at any time to assist the Bureau.
>
> VAN TASSEL did not volunteer the names of any individuals whom he was soliciting for funds except his statement above that he sent his publications to various individuals, universitites and Government agencies and also the Federal Bureau of Investigation in Washington, DC . . .

At the conclusion of the interview, the two agents obtained various copies of Van Tassel's *Proceedings*, which were dispatched to Washington for scrutiny, and became the subject of a confidential report, which in part stated: 'One of the pamphlets contains an article by Van Tassel claiming that Jesus Christ was born of space men and that the Star of Bethlehem was a space craft that stood by while Jesus was born.' Today, such claims are part and parcel of much of the UFO lore, and attract a great deal of interest and controversy; forty years ago, however, in some US states, to postulate that Jesus Christ was of extraterrestrial descent was akin to signing one's own death warrant. And it's worth remarking, too, that Van Tassel's claims preceded the famed writer Erich Von Däniken's books on the issue of ancient astronauts by more than fifteen years. If nothing else, Van Tassel was a remarkable setter of trends.

As a result of his ever-growing reputation as someone with intimate knowledge of alien intelligences, Van Tassel found himself increasingly in demand at public meetings and conventions, where he would espouse at length on his dealings with the aliens, their intentions for mankind, and their general philosophy as a whole. Van Tassel may or may not have been aware of it, but it was not just the general public who were turning out for his appearances . . .

On 17 April 1960, Van Tassel gave a lengthy speech at the Phipps Auditorium, City Park, Denver, Colorado, having been invited by the Denver Unidentified Flying Objects Investigative Society, whose 'executive officer' acted as the Master of Ceremonies.

To ensure that the lecture was a success, advertising time was taken out on local radio, which, not surprisingly, caught the attention of the Denver FBI, who subsequently directed a special agent to attend and report back the details of Van Tassel's talk.

A comprehensive document on that lecture, some four pages in total, was generated by the Bureau and is so detailed that I suspect a surreptitious tape recording may have been made in the auditorium to ensure that nothing was omitted from the Denver office's report to Hoover, of which relevant extracts follow:

The program consisted of a 45 minute movie which included

several shots of things purported to be flying saucers, and then a number of interviews with people from all walks of life regarding sightings they had made of such unidentified flying objects. After the movie GEORGE W. VAN TASSEL gave a lecture which was more of a religious-economics lecture rather than one of unidentified flying objects.

VAN TASSEL stated that he had been in the 'flying game' for over 30 years and currently operates a private Civil Aeronautics Authority approved airfield in California. He said he has personally observed a good many sightings and has talked to hundreds of people who have also seen flying saucers. He said that he has also been visited by the people from outer space and has taken up the cause of bringing the facts of these people to the American people. He said it is a crusade which he has undertaken because he is more or less retired, his family is grown and gone from home, and he feels he might be doing some good by this work.

Van Tassel then began a detailed examination of the highly contentious claims that there is a biblical link to the UFO mystery:

The major part of his lecture was devoted to explaining the occurrences in the Bible as they related to the space people. He said that the only mention of God in the Bible is in the beginning when the universe was being made. He said that after that all references are to 'out of the sky' or 'out of heaven.'

He said that this is due to the fact that man, space people, was made by God and that in the beginning of the world the space people came to the earth and left animals here. These were the prehistoric animals which existed at a body temperature of 105 degrees; however, a polar tilt occurred whereby the poles shifted and the tropical climates became covered with ice and vice versa.

The Bureau noted that Van Tassel duly postulated that, to ensure life on Earth continued following the Ice Age, the aliens populated the planet with other species of animals, and it was this action that led to the legend of Noah's Ark.

'. . . [A]fter the polar tilt the temperature to sustain life was 98.6 degrees, which was suitable for space people,' continued Van Tassel, 'so they established a colony and left only males here, intending to bring females at a later date on supply ships. This is reflected in Adam not having a wife . . . Adam was not an individual but a race of men . . .' The Denver FBI office further added:

[Van Tassel] said that this race then inter-married with 'intelligent, upright walking animals,' which race was EVE. Then when the space people came back in the supply ships they saw what had happened and did not land but ever since due to the origin of ADAM, they have watched over the people on earth.

He said that this is recorded in the Bible many times, such as MOSES receiving the Ten Commandments. He said the Ten Commandments are the laws of the space people and men on earth only give them lip service. Also, the manna from heaven was bread supplied by the space people.

[Van Tassel] also stated that this can be seen from the native stories such as the Indians in America saying that corn and potatoes, unknown in Europe, were brought here by a 'flaming canoe.' He said this can be shown also by the old stories of Winged Chariots and Winged White Horses, which came from out of the sky.

He said that JESUS was born of MARY, who was a space person sent here already pregnant in order to show the earth people the proper way to live. He said the space people have watched over us through the years and have tried to help us. He said they have sent their agents to the earth and they appear just as we do; however, they have the power to know your thoughts just as JESUS did. He said this is their means of communication and many of the space people are mute, but they train a certain number of them to speak earth languages.

Bringing matters up to date, Van Tassel went on to proffer an ingenious explanation for so-called poltergeist and spectral phenomena: '[Van Tassel] said that the space people here on earth are equipped with

a "crystal battery" which generates a magnetic field about them which
bends light waves so that they, the space people, appear invisible. He said
this has resulted in ghost stories such as footsteps, doors opening, and
other such phenomena.'

Nineteen sixty saw the FBI dispatch an agent to monitor a public lecture
given by contactee George Van Tassel.

UNITED STATES DEPARTMENT OF JUSTICE

FEDERAL BUREAU OF INVESTIGATION

In Reply, Please Refer to
File No.

Denver, Colorado
April 26, 1960

Re: UNIDENTIFIED FLYING OBJECTS,
INVESTIGATIVE SOCIETY;
GEORGE W. VAN TASSEL

      On April 17, 1960, a lecture was given by GEORGE
W. VAN TASSEL at Phipps Auditorium, City Park, Denver,
Colorado, which was advertised to be a lecture, movie film,
and discussion of unidentified flying objects. The audience
was comprised of a majority of older individuals and also
a majority of the audience was female. There were few
young people, although some family groups.

      The program was sponsored by the Denver Unidenti-
fied Flying Objects Investigative Societies, one of which
meets monthly at the Jefferson County Bank, Lakewood,
Colorado, whose executive officer was the Master of Ceremonies.
The program consisted of a 45 minute movie which included
several shots of things purported to be flying saucers, and
then a number of interviews with people from all walks of
life regarding sightings they had made of such unidentified
flying objects. After the movie GEORGE W. VAN TASSEL gave a
lecture which was more of a religious-economics lecture
rather than one of unidentified flying objects.

      VAN TASSEL stated that he had been in the "flying
game" for over 30 years and currently operates a private
Civil Aeronautics Authority approved airfield in California.
He said he has personally observed a good many sightings and
has talked to hundreds of people who have also seen flying
saucers. He said that he has also been visited by the people
from outer space and has taken up the cause of bringing the
facts of these people to the American people. He said it
is a crusade which he has undertaken because he is more or
less retired, his family is grown and gone from home, and
he feels he might be doing some good by this work.

      PROPERTY OF FBI - This memorandum is loaned to you by the
FBI, and neither it nor its contents are to be distributed
outside the agency to which loaned.

62-83894-418

ENCLOSURE

As radical as Van Tassel's biblical claims certainly were, what was possibly the FBI's main concern was the effect that his warnings about atomic destruction would have on the American populace: the world of 1960 was a very different place from that of today, and under no circumstances could the Western Alliance have been expected to relax its attitude towards the Soviet Union. If enough of his followers expressed a desire for

RE: UNIDENTIFIED FLYING OBJECTS,
INVESTIGATIVE SOCIETY;
GEORGE W. VAN TASSEL

The major part of his lecture was devoted to explaining the occurrences in the Bible as they related to the space people. He said that the only mention of God in the Bible is in the beginning when the universe was being made. He said that after that all references are to "out of the sky" or "out of heaven." He said that this is due to the fact that man, space people, was made by God and that in the beginning of the world the space people came to the earth and left animals here. These were the pre-historic animals which existed at a body temperature of 105 degrees; however, a polar tilt occurred whereby the poles shifted and the tropical climates became covered with ice and vice versa. He said that then the space people again put animals on the earth and this is depicted in the Bible as Noah's Ark. He said that after the polar tilt the temperature to sustain life was 98.6 degrees, which was suitable for space people, so they established a colony and left only males here, intending to bring females at a later date on supply ships. This is reflected in ADAM's not having a wife. He said that ADAM was not an individual but a race of men. He said that this race then inter-married with "intelligent, upright walking animals," which race was EVE. Then when the space people came back in the supply ships they saw what had happened and did not land but ever since due to the origin of ADAM, they have watched over the people on earth. He said that this is recorded in the Bible many times, such as MOSES receiving the Ten Commandments. He said the Ten Commandments are the laws of the space people and men on earth only give them lip service. Also, the manna from heaven was bread supplied by the space people. He also stated that this can be seen from the native stories such as the Indians in America saying that corn and potatoes, unknown in Europe, were brought here by a "flaming canoe." He said this refers to a space ship and the Indians' highest form of transportation was the canoe, so they likened it unto that. He said this can be shown also by the old stories of Winged Chariots and Winged White Horses, which came from out of the sky. He said that JESUS was born of MARY, who was a space person sent here already pregnant in order to show the earth people the proper way to live. He said the space people have watched over us through the years and have tried to help us. He said they have sent their agents to the earth and they appear just as we do; however,

- 2 -

they have the power to know your thoughts just as JESUS did. He said this is their means of communication and many of the space people are mute, but they train a certain number of them to speak earth languages.

He said that the space people here on earth are equipped with a "crystal battery" which generates a magnetic field about them which bends light waves so that they, the space people, appear invisible. He said this has resulted in ghost stories such as footsteps, doors opening, and other such phenomena.

He stated that the space people are now gravely concerned with our atom bombs. He said that the explosions of these bombs have upset the earth's rotation and, as in the instance of the French bomb explosion in North Africa, have actually caused earthquakes. He said that the officials on earth are aware of this and this was the reason for the recent Geophysical Year in order to try to determine just what can be done. He said these explosions are forcing the earth toward another polar tilt, which will endanger all man-kind. He said that the space people are prepared to evacuate those earth people who have abided by the "Golden Rule" when the polar tilt occurs, but will leave the rest to perish.

He advised that the space people have contacted the officials on earth and have advised them of their concern but this has not been made public. He also said that the radioactive fallout has become extremely dangerous and officials are worried but each power is so greedy of their own power they will not agree to make peace.

VAN TASSEL also spent some time saying that the U. S. Air Force, who are responsible for investigations on unidentified flying objects, has surpressed information; and as they are responsible only to the Administration, not to the public, as elected officials are, they can get away with this. He said that also the Air Force is afraid that they will be outmoded and disbanded if such information gets out.

He said that the Administration's main concern in not making public any information is that the economy will be

- 3 -

an end to the arms race, there was a very real possibility that Van Tassel, a relatively minor figure within the canon of UFOs as a whole, would mutate into a major national security problem. Consider what Van Tassel imparted to the audience at the Phipps Auditorium:

. . . the space people are now gravely concerned with our atom bombs. He said that the explosions of these bombs have upset the

RE: UNIDENTIFIED FLYING OBJECTS,
     INVESTIGATIVE SOCIETY;
     GEORGE W. VAN TASSEL

ruined, not because of any fear that would be engendered
in the public. He said this is due to the number of scientific discoveries already made and that will be made which
are labor saving and of almost permanency so that replacements
would not be needed.

        In summation, VAN TASSEL's speech was on these
subjects:

        (1) Space people related to occurrences in
             Bible.

        (2) Atom Bomb detrimental to earth and universe.

        (3) Economy is poor and would collapse under
             ideas brought by space people.

        Throughout his lecture, VAN TASSEL mentioned only
the U. S. economy and Government and the U. S. Air Force. He
did refer to the human race numerous times but all references
to Government and economy could only be taken as meaning the
U. S. One question put to him was whether sightings had been
made in Russia or China. He answered this by saying sightings
had been reported all over the world, but then specifically
mentioned only the U. S., Australia, New Zealand, and New
Guinea.

        He also mentioned that he was not advocating or
asking for any action on the part of the audience because he
said evil has a way of destroying itself. He did say that
he felt that the audience, of about 250 persons, were the
only intelligent people in Denver and he knew they had not
come out of curiosity but because they wanted to do the right
thing. He said that they were above the average in intelligence
and when the critical time came, the world would need people
such as this to think and guide.

        An application blank was distributed
for membership in the Denver society of this

                        - 4 -

earth's rotation and, as in the instance of the French bomb explosion in North Africa, have actually caused earthquakes. He said
that the officials on earth are aware of this and this was the reason for the recent Geophysical Year in order to try to determine
just what can be done. He said these explosions are forcing the
earth toward another polar tilt, which will endanger all mankind.
He said that the space people are prepared to evacuate those earth

people who have abided by the 'Golden Rule' when the polar tilt occurs, but will leave the rest to perish.

He advised that the space people have contacted the officials on earth and have advised them of their concern but this has not been made public. He also said that the radioactive fallout has become extremely dangerous and officials are worried but each power is so greedy of their own power they will not agree to make peace.

It was not only with world governments that Van Tassel had an argument: he vehemently criticised the US Air Force's entire handling of the UFO problem. The following will show why, in addition to forwarding a copy of its final report on Van Tassel to J. Edgar Hoover, the Denver Bureau office also made the facts known to the Air Force Office of Special Investigations at Lowry Air Force Base, Denver: 'Van Tassel also spent some time saying that the US Air Force, who are responsible for investigations on unidentified flying objects, has suppressed information; and as they are responsible only to the Administration, not to the public, as elected officials are, they can get away with this. [Van Tassel] said that also the Air Force is afraid that they will be outmoded and disbanded if such information gets out.'

Again commenting on areas that almost certainly led the Bureau to determine that he had potentially subversive tendencies, Van Tassel concluded his talk by assuring the audience that: '. . . the Administration's main concern in not making public any information is that the economy will be ruined, not because of any fear that would be engendered in the public . . . this is due to the number of scientific discoveries already made and that will be made which are labor saving and of almost permanency so that replacements would not be needed.'

In its final comment on the lecture, the Denver Office noted:

Throughout his lecture, VAN TASSEL mentioned only the US economy and Government and the US Air Force. He did refer to the human race numerous times but all references to Government and economy could only be taken as meaning the US.

One question put to him was whether sightings had been made in Russia or China. He answered this by saying sightings had been reported all over the world, but then specifically mentioned only the US, Australia, New Zealand, and New Guinea.

He also mentioned that he was not advocating or asking for any action on the part of the audience because he said evil has a way of destroying itself. He did say that he felt that the audience, of about 250 persons, were the only intelligent people in Denver and he knew they had not come out of curiosity but because they wanted to do the right thing. He said that they were above the average in intelligence and when the critical time came, the world would need people such as this to think and guide.

If anyone reading this book is considering giving a public lecture on the UFO subject, you might be wise to take a close look at your audience; in view of the above, you never know who may be sitting in front of you, carefully noting your every word . . .

Perhaps the most interesting aspect of Van Tassel's character was his love of all manner of weird and wonderful electronic knick-knacks, the most famous being his imaginatively titled 'Integratron'. With a name like that, the Integratron sounds like it would have been at home in some 1950s science-fiction film, blasting into oblivion marauding radioactive monsters.

The truth, though by no means inconsequential, was a little more low-key. For years Van Tassel worked on his machine, the purpose of which was to enhance mankind's latent psychic powers and considerably extend the human life span. Regrettably, Van Tassel never had the opportunity to see his project come to fruition, but his reputation as someone with a deep fascination of advanced technology was not lost on his followers – nor was it lost on the FBI.

In April 1965, rumours flew around the Bureau office at Miami that Van Tassel had succeeded in perfecting a weapon which could be used to blind people, and that the production and utilisation of this weapon was somehow related to an acquaintance of Van Tassel's described in Bureau memoranda as 'an ultra-rightist with tendency toward violence'.

The earliest documented indication that the Miami office had an inkling of this came on 9 April, when, in a two-page teletype to FBI headquarters, the basics of the story were related:

A source, who has furnished reliable information in the past,
and in addition has furnished information which could not be

UNITED STATES DEPARTMENT OF JUSTICE

FEDERAL BUREAU OF INVESTIGATION

Los Angeles, California
April 12, 1965

*In Reply, Please Refer to
File No.*

GEORGE WELLINGTON VAN TASSEL
GIANT ROCK AIRPORT,
YUCCA VALLEY, CALIFORNIA

VAN TASSEL has been known to the Los Angeles FBI
Office since 1954. He is reported to be owner and operator
of the Giant Rock Airport, which is located approximately
18 miles from Yucca Valley, California. He has also been
reported to be a director of the College of Universal Wisdom,
Yucca Valley, California. Numerous complaints have been
received by the Los Angeles Office concerning VAN TASSEL
and his activities surrounding "flying saucers", "spacemen"
and "space craft."

VAN TASSEL was interviewed by Special Agents of
the FBI on November 16, 1954, and advised that he had purchased a ranch in the vicinity of Giant Rock about seven
years prior to the interview and subsequently had leased
land from the government. He stated that the newly acquired
land was then known as Giant Rock Airport, having been
acquired under the "Airport Act", and was a certified Civil
Aeronautics Authority (CAA) emergency landing strip.

VAN TASSEL advised that in August 1954 he had been
awakened by a man from space. The spaceman had allegedly
invited VAN TASSEL to inspect a space craft, or flying
saucer, which was manned by three other male individuals
who were identical in every respect with earth people. VAN
TASSEL furnished detailed descriptions of an unarmed, bell-
shaped flying saucer and claimed the spacemen were mutes who
conversed with him through thought transfers.

VAN TASSEL stated that he advocates and follows a
metaphysical religion and research which is based on thought
transfers, and that through the thought transfer media he
has ascertained that there will be a third world war with a
destructive atomic explosion. He further stated the above
facts could be verified through the Bible, and that the peace-
loving space people would not enter or provoke a war.

62-1566-12

ENCLOSURE

One of the final enclosures in the FBI's file on George Van Tassel.

verified or corroborated, advised . . . that a secret device, which can be carried on a person and used to blind people, has recently been perfected. This device, also referred to by [censored] as a weapon, formerly developed to keep others from seeing operator of weapon. [Censored] reports no other details regarding description and use of device. However, he said his information was second hand.

The source states that it has been determined the alleged device was developed by GEORGE W. VAN TASSEL, Giant Rock, Yucca Valley, California, who reportedly owns or operates an airport some 20 miles from Yucca Valley in the desert area . . .

Source stated VAN TASSEL claimed he worked over seven years in research and development of this device and the machine to make it. The weapon reportedly is of an electrical type, not further described. Any additional information can be obtained only by individuals who purchase the device and must be present at the time it is made . . .

Five days later, having examined the claims and counterclaims concerning Van Tassel's machine, the Miami FBI office determined that further investigation was unwarranted:

Because of Van Tassel's apparent mental condition, as evidenced by his statements and apparent beliefs concerning interplanetary travel by men from Venus, and in view of his other highly imaginative and incredible statements concerning space travel and population, it is believed that no further inquiries need be conducted by the Miami or Los Angeles Offices concerning Van Tassel.

The final entry in the FBI's file on Van Tassel is a copy of a letter dated 17 August 1965, from a member of the American public, to the Information Office of the Air Force's UFO programme, Project Blue Book. As was the case in 1954, the letter-writer expressed concern that Van Tassel's claims were of detriment to the wellbeing of the US: 'In my opinion, it is quite subversive and in conflict with the interests of the

United States the way this gentleman uses the demoralizing of religion and also his accusations against our Government.'

The Bureau evidently took no action with respect to this letter beyond filing it, and until his death on 9 February 1978 aged 67, Van Tassel never again crossed paths with the FBI.

It is quite clear that up until 1960 at least, the Bureau was deeply interested in Van Tassel's activities and his comments on UFOs, the structure of government, and the issue of nuclear weapons. By 1965, however, that interest had waned: a 12 April Bureau Airtel refers to Van Tassel as 'an eccentric, self-ordained minister of a quasi-religious organization', while a three-page document forwarded to Washington from the Bureau at Los Angeles comes straight to the point, describing him as 'a mental case'.

We could speculate endlessly upon Van Tassel's claims of alien contact. And, while many of his purported extraterrestrial friends (Rondolla, Zolton and Ah-Ming, in particular) sound like they would have been more at home on a cheap science-fiction television series, similar accounts abound, as we saw earlier in this chapter.

In the pages that follow, I will detail the many other so-called contactees investigated by the FBI, and reveal some intriguing facts which may throw new light on this enduring mystery.

CHAPTER 13

THE ADAMSKI CONNECTION

GEORGE VAN TASSEL WAS PERHAPS THE CONTACTEE INVESTIGATED MOST thoroughly by the FBI in the 1950s, but his was not an isolated case. Declassified papers show that others including Truman Bethurum, George Hunt Williamson, Daniel Fry, and George Adamski had all come under the scrutiny of the Bureau.

As with Van Tassel, many of the claims of these individuals sounded incredible. Truman Bethurum, for example, stated that he had liaised with human-like aliens (though of smaller stature and of darker skin) from 'Clarion', a planet in our solar system hidden from the Earth as a result of its orbit around the sun. Of all the contactees, Bethurum was perhaps the most envied among his circle of colleagues, since during his experience aboard a UFO he was introduced to its female captain, 'Aura Rhanes', who came across like some spectacularly attractive 'Space Babe'! 'Tops in shapeliness and beauty' were the words the lucky Bethurum used. Of course, today we might find Bethurum's story little more than an amusing aside, but again the Bureau felt obligated to look into the man's account.[1]

In December 1954, the Palm Springs Republican Club contacted the FBI as its president had both spoken with Bethurum and read his then recently published book, *Aboard a Flying Saucer*.

' . . . I am always skeptical and I have been wondering if he could be trying to put over any propaganda,' stated the club president in a letter to J. Edgar Hoover.

'Although I would like to be of service,' replied Hoover, 'information in FBI files is confidential and available for official use only. I would like to point out also that this Bureau is strictly a fact-finding agency and does not make evaluations or draw conclusions as to the character or integrity of any individual, publication or organization.'

Nevertheless, Bureau files do reflect knowledge of Bethurum's activities: 'In June, 1954, an inquiry was made by the Cincinnati Office concerning Bethurum and his flying disk lectures since that office had received a complaint similar to current correspondents,' it was recorded by FBI headquarters on 17 December 1954. 'No other references were located which might be identical with subject of current inquiry.'

It may not be surprising that, although known to the Bureau, Bethurum's activities were of less concern than those of Van Tassel. He was not as outwardly political as Van Tassel, and his dealings with Aura Rhanes seemed to almost border on the farcial. On several occasions during the middle of the night, the gorgeous Aura actually materialised in Bethurum's bedroom, which did not exactly please his wife, who later divorced him, evidently unable to compete with a woman of Aura's galactic charms!

George Hunt Williamson (whose real name was Michel d'Obrenovic) had an equally strange story to tell.[2] Not only did he write a book detailing his encounters, *The Saucers Speak*, co-written with Alfred C. Bailey, he also imparted details to Edward J. Ruppelt, former head of Project Blue Book, as Ruppelt recalled in 1955:

> George Williamson . . . said the story started back in the summer of 1952 when he and a few other people who believed that flying saucers weren't hallucinations got together with a ham radio operator in Arizona. On the night of August 26, they were playing around with the radio receiver when they picked up a strange signal. They listened to the signal and soon found that it was international code coming in at a 'fantastically fast and powerful rate' from a spaceship hovering off the earth.[3]

Over a period of time up until February 1953 the contacts continued, and a wealth of technological and philosophical data were imparted, after which time Williamson was advised to go out and 'spread the word' to like-minded persons – something he did until he retired from the scene in the 1960s. And again, during the 1950s the FBI had been monitoring Williamson's career as a contactee. A Bureau document of 2 June 1961 asserts:

> Bufiles indicate that George Hunt Williamson [has] come to the Bureau's attention in the past in connection with allegations that flying disks exist. In 1954, Williamson was connected with a program to be presented in Cincinnati which was entitled 'The Real Flying Saucer Story'.

In 1949, Daniel Fry was employed in an engineering capacity with the Aerojet General Corporation at White Sands Missile Range, New Mexico. On 4 July of that year, Fry claimed that he had made initial contact with an advanced extraterrestrial being ('A-lan') who 'wants everyone in this world to understand the truth about our existence and how we can spiritually profit from the beneficence of extraterrestrial contact'.[4]

Six years later, Fry was referenced in Bureau memoranda following an investigation of the Detroit Flying Saucer Club, which planned to have Fry speak at one of its meetings. As the club was co-directed by a cousin of Fry's, the Bureau was able to glean detailed information about his alleged experiences, inlcuding the fact that, according to the club, 'Daniel Fry . . . has actually flown in a saucer from Sandia Base to New York City, the round trip requiring only 30 minutes'. A memorandum says:

> FRY CLAIMS SAUCER CLUBS HAVE ACTUALLY RECEIVED MESSAGES FROM OUTER SPACE AND ALTHOUGH [HE] SAYS HE DOES NOT KNOW, HE FEELS THEY DO EXIST: HAVE BEEN SEEN BY MANY PEOPLE AND CLAIMS HE HAS SEEN THEM HIMSELF. HE FEELS THE PURPOSE OF CONTACTS WITH EARTH IS LIMITED AT THIS TIME TO PREPARING PEOPLE TO RECEIVE LANDINGS FROM OUTER SPACE. HE SAID THE SAUCERS ARE

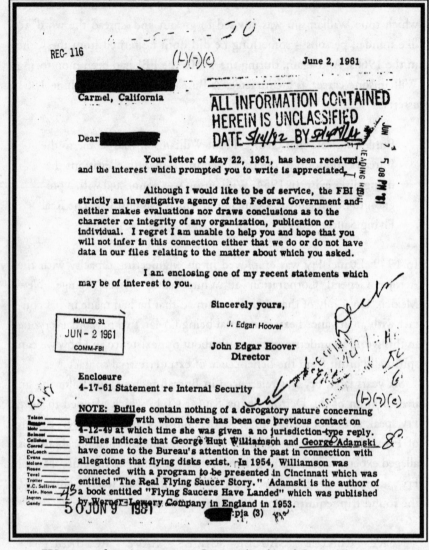

REC-116

(h)(7)(c)

June 2, 1961

Carmel, California

ALL INFORMATION CONTAINED
HEREIN IS UNCLASSIFIED
DATE 5/4/92 BY 5/4/91/4

Dear

> Your letter of May 22, 1961, has been received and the interest which prompted you to write is appreciated.

> Although I would like to be of service, the FBI is strictly an investigative agency of the Federal Government and neither makes evaluations nor draws conclusions as to the character or integrity of any organization, publication or individual. I regret I am unable to help you and hope that you will not infer in this connection either that we do or do not have data in our files relating to the matter about which you asked.

> I am enclosing one of my recent statements which may be of interest to you.

Sincerely yours,

J. Edgar Hoover

MAILED 31
JUN - 2 1961
COMM-FBI

John Edgar Hoover
Director

Enclosure
4-17-61 Statement re Internal Security

NOTE: Bufiles contain nothing of a derogatory nature concerning _____ with whom there has been one previous contact on 4-12-49 at which time she was given a no jurisdiction-type reply. Bufiles indicate that George Hunt Williamson and George Adamski have come to the Bureau's attention in the past in connection with allegations that flying disks exist. In 1954, Williamson was connected with a program to be presented in Cincinnati which was entitled "The Real Flying Saucer Story." Adamski is the author of a book entitled "Flying Saucers Have Landed" which was published by Werner-Lowery Company in England in 1953.

Tolson
Belmont
Mohr
Callahan
Conrad
DeLoach
Evans
Malone
Rosen
Tavel
Trotter
W.C. Sullivan
Tele. Room
Ingram
Gandy

50 JUN 9 1961

(h)(7)(c)

:pja (3)

FBI papers referencing contactees George Adamski and George Hunt Williamson.

FRIENDLY TO U.S. HE SAID MESSAGES RECEIVED INDICATE ALL PLANETS BUT EARTH HAVE CONQUERED OUTER SPACE. OUTER SPACE PEOPLE CONSIDER THOSE ON EARTH THE LOWEST FORM OF UNIVERSAL EXISTENCE.

Other persons implicated in the contactee mystery were the subject of FBI files, too. Heavily censored August 1954 memoranda refer to an unnamed woman who claimed repeated contact with nonhuman entities in the mid-1950s.

> According to [censored] stated that there were two spaceships from which she had been receiving messages. They were described as 150 miles wide, 200 miles in length, and 100 miles in depth . . . these ships are designated as M-4 and L-11 and they also contain mother ships which measure approximately 150 to 200 feet in length . . . there were approximately 5,000 of these mother ships . . . 'Affa' is the Manager or the Commander of the ship M-4 which is from the planet Uranus and 'Ponnar' is the Manager or the Commander of the ship L-11 which is from the planet Hatann . . .
>
> These contacts with 'Affa' and 'Ponnar' were for the purpose of protecting our own earth from destruction caused by the explosion of the atom bomb, hydrogen bomb, and wars of various kinds which they, 'Affa' and 'Ponnar', say disrupt the magnetic field of force which surrounds the earth . . . 'Affa' and 'Ponnar' are presently working the area of the Pacific Ocean repairing 'fault lines' which are in danger of breaking . . .

Having examined the cases of George Van Tassel, Daniel Fry, Truman Bethurum and George Hunt Williamson, let us now look at the FBI's relationship with the man who will surely go down in history as the definitive contactee: George Adamski.

Born in Poland on 17 April 1891, Adamski emigrated to the US with his family several years later and went on to become the most widely supported (and criticised) of the contactees. While there are those who claim that Adamski was nothing but an outright fraud, in my opinion enough circumstantial data exists which leads me to believe that the man's claims are not completely without merit.

In the authoritative *George Adamski: The Untold Story*, its co-writer, Timothy Good, presents a number of convincing reasons why Adamski should not be rejected outright.

One of Adamski's more sensational claims was that on 18 February 1953 he was taken aboard a UFO which then journeyed into space. Placing his thoughts on record, Adamski later said of his flight: 'I was amazed to see that the background of space is totally dark. Yet there were manifestations taking place all around us, as though billions upon billions of fireflies were flickering everywhere, as fireflies do . . .'

Nine years later, the astronaut John Glenn reported something similar while orbiting the Earth in his Mercury space capsule: '. . . a lot of the little things that I thought were stars were actually a bright yellowish green about the size and intensity as looking at a firefly on a real dark night . . . there were literally thousands of them'.

Additional testimony comes from three Soviet cosmonauts, Vladimir Komarov, Konstantin Feoktistov and Boris Yegorov, who saw much the same thing during their October 1964 flight aboard Voskhod One: 'We were very much interested in the shining particles we saw. We had heard about these mysterious particles . . . from the reports of John Glenn and our astronauts . . . The general feeling was that these tiny particles came from our ship; apparently, they are simply dust particles that are found everywhere, even in the cosmos.'[5]

Was Adamski's description simply a lucky guess or was it based on a genuine outer-space encounter? In cases such as these, it is difficult to ascertain the facts, but Adamski's claimed viewing of the 'firefly effect' tallies remarkably with the accounts of both US and Soviet astronauts. Moreover, Adamski cannot be accused of having based his story on the accounts of genuine visits into space by Earth-based space crews, since his alleged visit preceded that of the first man in space, Yuri Gagarin, by eight years.

Timothy Good also presents further intriguing data which tends to put some of Adamski's other claims in a favourable light, and anyone wishing to learn of Adamski's experiences would do well to consult Good's book, which does not shirk from reporting both the pros and the cons of the entire affair. And now to the FBI.

To many not fully conversant with the facts, the Adamski story begins on 20 November 1952, when along with six other people (George Hunt Williamson maintained that he was one of the six) he witnessed the landing of a UFO in the Californian desert, and subsequently made contact with its pilot.[6] FBI documentation, however, shows that Adamski's interest in UFOs preceded the 1952 date by at least two years, and Timothy Good has learned that Adamski claimed to have been contacted by extraterrestrials as a child, and to have later received instruction from them in Tibet (hence his 1936 book, *Wisdom of the Masters of the Far East*, published by 'The Royal Order of Tibet').

At the outset of its surveillance of George Adamski, the Bureau was seemingly unaware of his early contacts, but memoranda of 28 May 1952 reference his 1950 experiences, and also reveal some interesting facts which suggest, as with George Van Tassel, the Bureau considered Adamski a potentially subversive character.

A study of the documentation at issue shows that much of the FBI's initial data on Adamski had come from a source (whose name the Bureau declines to reveal) who imparted details to the San Diego office on 5 September 1950:

> . . . [Source] advised the San Diego Office that he first met Adamski about three months ago at the cafe which is named the Palomar Gardens Cafe, owned and operated by Adamski, at the road junction, five miles East of Rincon, California, at a point where the highway branches off leading to Mount Palomar Observatory . . .
>
> [Source] became involved in a lengthy conversation with Adamski during which Adamski told them at great length of his findings of flying saucers and so forth. He told them of a spaceship which he said he saw between the earth and the moon, which he estimated to be approximately three miles in length, which was flying so fast that he had to take about eighty photographs before he could get three of them to turn out . . .

Adamski then went on to reveal his knowledge of covert interaction between representatives of the US government and the aliens:

> According to [source] Adamski stated that the Federal Communications Commission, under the direction of the

'Military Government' of the United States, has established communication with the people from other worlds, and has learned that they are so much more advanced than the inhabitants of this earth that they have deciphered the languages used here.

In 1952, the FBI took a keen interest in George Adamski's activities.

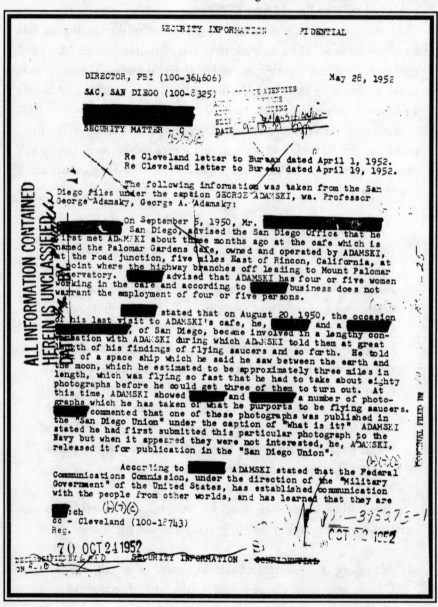

SECURITY INFORMATION . . FIDENTIAL

DIRECTOR, FBI (100-364606)   May 28, 1952
SAC, SAN DIEGO (100-8325)

SECURITY MATTER - C

Re Cleveland letter to Bureau dated April 1, 1952.
Re Cleveland letter to Bureau dated April 19, 1952.

The following information was taken from the San Diego files under the caption GEORGE ADAMSKI, wa. Professor George Adamsky, George A. Adamsky:

On September 5, 1950, Mr. ▮▮▮▮▮ San Diego, advised the San Diego Office that he first met ADAMSKI about three months ago at the cafe which is named the Palomar Gardens Cafe, owned and operated by ADAMSKI, at the road junction, five miles East of Rincon, California, at a point where the highway branches off leading to Mount Palomar Observatory. ▮▮▮▮▮ advised that ADAMSKI has four or five women working in the cafe and according to ▮▮▮▮▮ business does not warrant the employment of four or five persons.

▮▮▮▮▮ stated that on August 20, 1950, the occasion of his last visit to ADAMSKI's cafe, he, ▮▮▮▮▮ and a ▮▮▮▮▮, of San Diego, became involved in a lengthy conversation with ADAMSKI during which ADAMSKI told them at great length of his findings of flying saucers and so forth. He told ▮▮▮ of a space ship which he said he saw between the earth and the moon, which he estimated to be approximately three miles in length, which was flying so fast that he had to take about eighty photographs before he could get three of them to turn out. At this time, ADAMSKI showed ▮▮▮▮ and ▮▮▮▮▮ a number of photographs which he has taken of what he purports to be flying saucers. ▮▮▮▮▮ commented that one of these photographs was published in the "San Diego Union" under the caption of "What is it?" ADAMSKI stated he had first submitted this particular photograph to the Navy but when it appeared they were not interested, he, ADAMSKI, released it for publication in the "San Diego Union".

According to ▮▮▮▮▮ ADAMSKI stated that the Federal Communications Commission, under the direction of the "Military Government" of the United States, has established communication with the people from other worlds, and has learned that they are

:ch (b)(7)(c)
cc - Cleveland (100-18743)
Reg.

70 OCT 24 1952

SECURITY INFORMATION - CONFIDENTIAL

Adamski stated that in this interplanetary communication, the Federal Communications Commission asked the inhabitants of the other planet concerning the type of government they had there and the reply indicated that it was very different from the democracy of the United States. Adamski stated that his answer was kept secret by the United States Government, but he added, 'If you ask me they probably have a Communist form of government and our American government wouldn't release that kind of thing, naturally.

That is a thing of the future – more advanced.

TO: DIRECTOR, FBI   5-28-52
   3D 100- 8325

so much more advanced than the inhabitants of this earth that
they have deciphered the languages used here. ADAMSKI stated
that in this interplanetary communication, the Federal Communications Commission asked the inhabitants of the other planet concerning the type of government they had there and the reply indicated that it was very different from the democracy of the
United States. ADAMSKI stated that his answer was kept secret
by the United States Government, but he added, "If you ask me
they probably have a Communist form of government and our
American government wouldn't release that kind of thing, naturally.
That is a thing of the future - more advanced.'

    ADAMSKI advised ▮▮▮▮ that he wants to set up his
own radio station in order to communicate with the inhabitants
of other planets, but that to do so would cost him approximately
$5,000. Commenting on observation and study at Palomar Observa-
torn, ADAMSKI stated "Everything is bottlenecked" at the Observa-
torn, and "they won't let anybody know of their findings with
their lar   scope because it would make all the textbooks
obsolete".

    ADAMSKI, during this conversation, made the prediction
that Russia will dominate the world and we will then have an era
of peace for 1000 years. He stated that Russia already has the
atom bomb and the hydrogen bomb and that the great earthquake
which was reported behind the Iron Curtain recently was actually
a hydrogen bomb explosion being tried out by the Russians.
ADAMSKI states this "earthquake" broke seismograph machines and
he added that no normal earthquake can do that.

    ADAMSKI stated that within the next twelve months,
San Diego will be bombed. ADAMSKI stated that it does not make
any difference if the United States has more atom bombs than
Russia inasmuch as Russia needs only ten atom bombs to cripple
the United States by placing these simultaneously on such spots
as Chicago and other vital centers of this country.

    ADAMSKI further stated that the United States today
is in the same state of deterioration as was the Roman empire
prior to its collapse and it will fall just as the Roman empire
did. He stated the Government in this country is a corrupt form
of government and capitalists are enslaving the labor.

- 2 -

```
TO:  DIRECTOR, FBI                                    5-28-52
     SD 100- 325
```

███████ advised that when ADAMSKI left the group
for a brief period, one of the women working in the cafe came
over and entered into the conversation. She stated that some
of our servicemen who stopped there to have drinks during
World War II and subsequent thereto, told "Professor" ADAMSKI
of the atrocities which they were forced to commit, murdering
women and children on orders of their superior officers. ███████
stated that while this woman was making these statements, ███
exhibited a great deal of animosity against the United States,
stating the United States committed more atrocities during
World War II than did the Japanese but since the Japanese were
the ones who lost the war, they were the ones who were tried
as war criminals.

          This woman added that a friend of hers who recently
returned from Russia stated he was very pleased with everything
he found there. He stated to her that the people in Russia
received seven tickets per month for the opera and cinema.
These tickets are free, being issued by the government. The
woman added "The people there (in Russia) don't have to be
worrying about where their next meal is coming from Everything
is fine in Russia a   in the United States we have to fight for
everything we get."

          ███████ advised that ADAMSKI returned to continue his
conversation stating that the United States will soon be in the
same condition that Europe was in during the last war. He added
that "It is a good idea to be quiet now. Right now if you talk
in favor of Communism you will be spotted as a Communist and if
you talk against Communism you will be spotted by the Communist,
so it's best to just shut up". ADAMSKI stated to ███████ that
"The United States hasn't a chance to win the war. Russia will
take over the United States."

                                              Valley Center,
California, ████████████████████████ advised that ADAMSKI
has lived in the vicinity for approximately ten years and is the
owner of the Palomar Gardens Cafe. ███████ advised that
ADAMSKI also operates a small telescope on the premises and is
noted for giving lectures on "Space Ships". ███████ advised
that ADAMSKI recently appeared on a television program in San Diego
and gave a lecture on "Space Ships". ███████ could furnish

                              - 3 -

Adamski's comment that the aliens had a communist type of government certainly caused raised eyebrows within the Bureau, and was indis-
putably one of the foremost reasons behind its continued surveillance of
him. With the Cold War at its peak, this was more than understandable.
Additional data supplied by the Bureau's source elaborates on this aspect
of Adamski's activities and statements:

Adamski, during this conversation, made the prediction that
Russia will dominate the world and we will then have an era of
peace for 1,000 years. He stated that Russia already has the

atom bomb and the hydrogen bomb and that the great earth-quake which was reported behind the Iron Curtain recently was actually a hydrogen bomb explosion being tried out by the Russians. Adamski states this 'earthquake' broke seismograph machines and he added that no normal earthquake can do that.

Adamski stated that within the next twelve months, San Diego will be bombed. Adamski stated that it does not make any difference if the United States has more atom bombs than Russia inasmuch as Russia needs only ten atom bombs to cripple the United States by placing these simultaneously on such spots as Chicago and other vital centers of this country.

Turning his attention to the status of American society, Adamski added: '. . . the United States today is in the same state of deterioration as was the Roman empire prior to its collapse and it will fall just as the Roman empire did . . . the Government in this country is a corrupt form of government and capitalists are enslaving the poor.'

The document continues in similar vein, to such an extent that in the Bureau's eyes Adamski was thereafter considered officially a 'security matter'.

In January 1953, Adamski was once again the subject of FBI interest when word got back to the San Diego office that: 'Adamski had in his possession a machine which could draw "flying saucers" and airplanes down from the sky.'

Despite his statements of 1952 apparently lauding the Soviets, Adamski was concerned that the device (which supposedly operated on the principle of 'cutting magnetic lines of force') could be used against US aircraft, and requested a meeting with representatives of both the FBI and the Air Force Office of Special Investigations. On 12 January 1953, that meeting took place.

At the outset, Adamski maintained that the machine was in fact the brainchild of another individual, and that despite what the Bureau had been told, he (Adamski) had yet to see it, but knew enough of both it and its operator to suggest that production of the device might not be in the best interests of the US government, since the person concerned 'was not entirely loyal'.

On this matter Adamski seemingly cooperated to the full, and supplied the Bureau and the Air Force with enough data to allow a formal investigation of the machine's 'inventor' to begin. Adamski also divulged details of his celebrated encounter of 20 November 1952 in the California desert with nonhuman beings:

> . . . at a point ten and two-tenths miles from Desert Center on the road to Parker and Needles, Arizona, [Adamski] made contact with a space craft and had talked to a space man. Adamski stated that he, [deleted] and his wife Mary, had been out in the desert and that he and the persons with him had seen the craft come down to the earth. Adamski stated that a small stairway in the bottom of the craft, which appeared to be a round disc, opened and a space man came down the steps. Adamski stated he believed there were other space men in the ship because the ship appeared translucent and could see the shadows of the space men.

As in many of the examples already cited, Adamski continued that the alien was 'over 5 feet in height, having long hair like a woman's and garbed in a suit similar to the space suits or web suits worn by the US Air Force Men'.

Echoing the claims of George Van Tassel that many of the human-like aliens visiting the Earth are mute, Adamski related to the Bureau and OSI agents that he conversed with the entity by means of sign language, but felt that his mind was being 'read'. To back up this belief, Adamski stated that when he was about to take a photograph of the UFO, the alien 'motioned' to him to cease. Perhaps at some risk to his personal safety, Adamski ignored the actions of the extraterrestrial and took his photograph regardless. This did not go down too well with the camera-shy space traveller, who duly snatched the incriminating evidence out of Adamski's hands, and departed. Adamski's experiences were not over, however, as the Bureau noted:

Adamski further advised that he had obtained plaster casts of the footprints of the space man and stated that the casts indicated the footprints had designs on them similar to the signs of the Zodiac.

On January 12, 1953, Adamski advised that on December 13, 1952, the space ship returned to the Palomar Gardens and came low enough to drop the [film negative] which the space man had

FBI files pertaining to George Adamski's dealings with alien creatures.

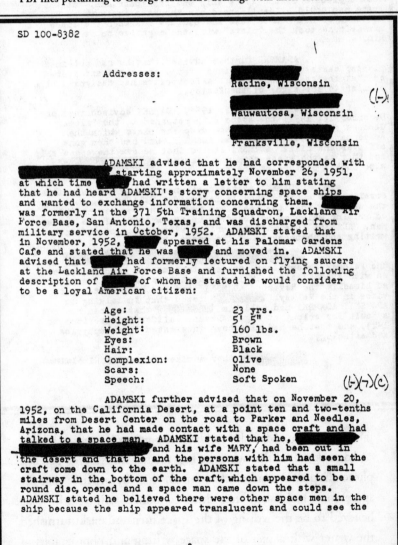

SD 100-8382

Addresses:

███████ Racine, Wisconsin

(L-)

███████ Wauwautosa, Wisconsin

███████ Franksville, Wisconsin

███ ADAMSKI advised that he had corresponded with ███ starting approximately November 26, 1951, at which time ███ had written a letter to him stating that he had heard ADAMSKI's story concerning space ships and wanted to exchange information concerning them. ███ was formerly in the 371 5th Training Squadron, Lackland Air Force Base, San Antonio, Texas, and was discharged from military service in October, 1952. ADAMSKI stated that in November, 1952, ███ appeared at his Palomar Gardens Cafe and stated that he was ███ and moved in. ADAMSKI advised that ███ had formerly lectured on flying saucers at the Lackland Air Force Base and furnished the following description of ███ of whom he stated he would consider to be a loyal American citizen:

Age:	23 yrs.
Height:	5' 5"
Weight:	160 lbs.
Eyes:	Brown
Hair:	Black
Complexion:	Olive
Scars:	None
Speech:	Soft Spoken

(L-)(7)(c)

ADAMSKI further advised that on November 20, 1952, on the California Desert, at a point ten and two-tenths miles from Desert Center on the road to Parker and Needles, Arizona, that he had made contact with a space craft and had talked to a space man. ADAMSKI stated that he, ███ ███ and his wife MARY, had been out in the desert and that he and the persons with him had seen the craft come down to the earth. ADAMSKI stated that a small stairway in the bottom of the craft, which appeared to be a round disc, opened and a space man came down the steps. ADAMSKI stated he believed there were other space men in the ship because the ship appeared translucent and could see the

- 3 -

SD 100-8382

shadows of the space men. ADAMSKI described the space man
as being over 5' in height, having long hair like a woman's
and garbed in a suit similar to the space suits or web suits
worn by the U. S. Air Force Men. ADAMSKI stated that he
and the space man conversed by signs and that there appeared to be a certain area around the space ship which consisted of magnetic or electric lines of force, inasmuch as when
he got too close, some of the lines went through his arm
and momentarily paralyzed his arm. ADAMSKI stated that he
took a picture of the space ship and the space man, but the
space man could evidently read his thoughts inasmuch as he
motioned to him not to take the picture and when the space
man left he took the "plate" with the negative on it with
him.

ADAMSKI further advised that he had obtained
plaster casts of the footprints of the space man and stated that the casts indicated the footprints had designs on them
similar to the signs of the Zodiac,.

On January 12, 1953, ADAMSKI advised that on $(b)(7)(c)$
December 13, 1952, the space ship returned to the Palomar
Gardens and came low enough to drop the plate which the
space man had taken from him, ADAMSKI, and had then gone
off over the hill. ADAMSKI stated that he saw the space ship
and that as the space ship was leaving, ███████████
also took a picture of the ship.

ADAMSKI stated that when he had the negatives
developed at a photo shop in Escondido, California, that
the negative that the space man had taken from him contained writing which he believed to be the writing of the space
men. ADAMSKI furnished the writer with copies of the space
writing and photographs of the space ship.

$(b)(7)(c):(b$
███████████████████████████████ at
the Palomar Observatory, advised that he had been acquainted with ADAMSKI since 1943, at which time ADAMSKI had called himself "the Reverend ADAMSKI" and had held Easter Services in the Valley. ████████ stated that in talking to
ADAMSKI, ADAMSKI had told him, ████████ that he had had
a "cult" or colony at Laguna Beach, California, previous to
1943, and that he had also been interested in metaphysics
and astrology.

$(b)(7)(c):$
████████ further advised that ADAMSKI claimed

- · -

taken from him, Adamski, and had then gone off over the hill . . .

Adamski stated that when he had the negatives developed at a
photo shop in Escondido, California, that the negative that the
space man had taken from him contained writing which he
believed to be the writing of the space men. Adamski furnished
the writer with copies of the space writing and photographs of
the space ship.

SD 100-6332

to have worked at the Observatory at Mount Palomar, but stated that ADAMSKI had never been employed at the Observatory.
███████ stated that ADAMSKI also claims to have been associated with ████████████, formerly with the Observatory at Mount Palomar, but now located in Pasadena, California. ███████ stated that ████████ had known ADAMSKI
for quite some time and that ████████ address was:

          ███████████████████████████

          Pasadena, California

          Telephone: Sycamore █████

          ████████ stated he considered ADAMSKI to be
more qualified in astrology than astronomy. He continued
that he had never viewed any space ship and believed ADAMSKI
to be an opportunist.

          Copies of the letters of ████████ and prints
of the space writing and flying saucers, are being enclosed
to the Bureau, for informational purposes only.

          Copies are also being enclosed to the Cleveland
Office for any action that they may desire to take.

          This information is not being furnished to
the U. S. Air Force inasmuch as ████████████ OSI, was along
at the time of the interview, and is cognizant of all facts
contained herein.

          ADAMSKI furnished the following information
concerning himself:

Born:	4-17-1891
Place:	Poland
Father:	JOSEPH ADAMSKI (deceased)
Mother:	FRANCES ADAMSKI (deceased)
Sister:	██████████████
	(phonetic)
Address:	Lackawana, New York
Sister:	Mrs. ████ (_____),
Address:	Dunkirk, New York
Sister:	Mrs. █████████████
Address:	Dunkirk, New York

- 5 -

Not everyone was convinced by the photographs, however, with one
source informing the Bureau of his belief that 'the photographs were
taken by setting the camera lens at infinity, which would sharpen the
background of mountains and trees and blurs the saucer, which was probably strung on a thin wire. [Source] advised that if the camera were set at
infinity the wire would not show.'

I would not disagree that Adamski's photographs have long been a contentious issue, with one piece of evidence, Adamski's famous 1965 'Silver Spring' film, being particulary notorious. Although the film has been widely panned by critics of Adamski and his claimed contacts with alien beings, in *George Adamski: The Untold Story*, Timothy Good devotes a whole chapter to a discussion of this controversial 8 mm film, which purports to show a UFO in flight, and presents some interesting data in support of its authenticity, including the extraordinary fact that the UFO appears to 'distort' in shape (a result, some postulate, of the craft's gravitational force field).

From 23 March 1953 onwards, much of the FBI's dealings with Adamski were relative to what was, or what was not, said by Adamski during a talk given by him before the Californian Lions Club, on 12 March of that year. According to the San Diego office, Adamski had prefaced his talk with a statement to the effect that, and I quote the Bureau here, 'his material had all been cleared with the Federal Bureau of Investigation and Air Force Intelligence'.

Certain that no such clearance had been afforded Adamski, representatives of both the Bureau and the Air Force visited him at his Palomar Gardens Cafe, and 'severely admonished' him for making any statement alluding to his material having FBI and Air Force blessing. For the record, however, Adamski denied making any such claims and it has to be said no audio recording of the alleged statement exists. Indeed, the only documented reference to this matter appeared in the 13 March edition of a local newspaper: the *Riverside Enterprise*.

Regardless of whether or not Adamski did make such a statement (and with media people present would he have been so reckless?), he was obliged to sign an official document for both the Bureau and the Air Force to the effect that his material did not have official clearance. With one copy of the statement retained by Adamski, additional copies were circulated to Hoover and the FBI offices at Dallas, Los Angeles and Cleveland, since 'these offices have received previous communications concerning [Adamski]'.

On 10 December 1953, matters took a decidedly downward turn for Adamski when a representative of the Los Angeles-based Better Business

Bureau (BBB) turned up at the Los Angeles FBI office and advised that it was investigating Adamski's 1953 book, *Flying Saucers Have Landed*, to determine if it was a fraud.

The BBB advised the Bureau that to ascertain the facts surrounding Adamski he had been interviewed by one of its staff, and during the course of the interview Adamski had produced a document 'having a blue seal in the lower left corner, at the top of which appeared the names of three Government agents' – one from the FBI and two from the Air Force. Once again, the implication was that Adamski's material had the official clearance of both the Air Force and the FBI.

'[The Better Business Bureau] is interested in whether or not this document is authentic and whether your organization is making an endorsement of [Adamski's] book,' the FBI was advised.

The document was not authentic. Investigations undertaken by Special Agent Willis of the San Diego FBI revealed that the document displayed by Adamski to the Better Business Bureau as evidence of his having the official sanction of the FBI, was nothing less than a doctored copy of the statement he had been obliged to sign for both the FBI and the Air Force months earlier. A Bureau report of 16 December 1953 from Louis B. Nichols, head of the Bureau's public relations department, to Clyde Tolson, records the events surrounding this blow to Adamski's credibility:

[Deleted] instructed Willis to call on Adamski at the Palomar Gardens Cafe, Valley Center, California. (This is located five miles east of Rincon, California, near the Mount Palomar Observatory.) Willis was told to have the San Diego Agents, accompanied by representatives of OSI if they care to go along, call on Adamski and read the riot act in no uncertain terms pointing out he has used this document in a fraudulent, improper manner, that this Bureau has not endorsed, approved, or cleared his speeches or book, that he knows it, and the Bureau will simply not tolerate any further foolishness, misrepresentations, and falsity on his part. Willis was told to instruct the Agents to diplomatically retrieve, if possible, the document in issue from Adamski. Willis said he would do this and send in a report at once.

Despite threats of prosecution, the Bureau took no further action against Adamski on the matter of the falsified document. Yet Adamski's actions were foolish in the extreme and do have a bearing on his credibility and accounts of meetings with extraterrestrial beings.

Documentation declassified under the terms of the Freedom of Information Act reveals that the Bureau's active interest in Adamski tailed off in the mid-1950s, but by 1959 that interest had been revived.

In February 1959, Adamski toured New Zealand and gave a series of lectures before audiences in both Wellington and Auckland.[7] This was evidently of some concern to the US intelligence community and his talks were monitored heavily. For example, a one-page Foreign Service Dispatch from the American Embassy in New Zealand to the Department of State in Washington, detailing the main points of what Adamski had to say, was circulated to the FBI, the CIA, the Army, the Air Force and the Navy. Titled: 'FLYING SAUCER' EXPERT LECTURING IN NEW ZEALAND, the document gives more than a brief account of Adamski's activities while in New Zealand:

Mr George ADAMSKI, the California 'flying saucer expert' and author of the book Flying Saucers Have Landed and others, has been visiting New Zealand for the last two weeks. He has given well-attended public lectures in Auckland and Wellington as well as meetings with smaller groups of 'saucer' enthusiasts. In Wellington his lecture filled the 2,200 seats in the Town Hall. He was not permitted to charge for admission as the meeting was held on a Sunday night, but a 'silver coin' collection was taken up and this would more than recoup his expenses.

Adamski's lectures appear to cover the usual mass of sighting reports, pseudo-scientific arguments in support of his theories and his previously well-publicized 'contacts' with saucers and men from Venus. He is repeating his contention that men from other planets are living anonymously on the earth and, according to the press, said in Auckland that there may be as many as 40,000,000 of these in total. He is also making references to security restrictions and saying that the US authorities know a lot more than they will tell.

The report of Adamski's lecture in Wellington in The Dominion was flanked by an article by Dr I.L. THOMSEN, Director of the Carter Observatory, vigorously refuting Adamski on a number of scientific points. However, the news report of the lecture called it 'the best Sunday night's entertainment Wellington has seen for quite a time.'

Interest in flying saucers in New Zealand seems to be roughly comparable to that in the United States. There is a small but active organization which enthusiasts have supported for some years. This organization publishes a small paper and receives and circulates stories of sightings. At the Adamski lecture in Wellington, approximately 40 members of the 'Adamski Corresponding Society' wore blue ribbons and sat in reserved seats in the front row. Press reports suggest that Adamski probably is making no new converts to saucer credence in his current tour. His audiences have given forth with a certain amount of 'incredulous murmuring' and are said to be totally unimpressed with his pictures of saucers.

Ten months later Adamski was again the subject of FBI interest when, as had been the case previously, a member of the public contacted the Bureau to express concern that Adamski was promoting pro-Soviet ideas:

[Censored] said that in recent weeks she and her husband had begun to wonder if Adamski is subtly spreading Russian propaganda. She said that, according to Adamski, the 'space people' are much better people than those on earth; that they have told him the earth is in extreme danger from nuclear tests and that they must be stopped; that they have found peace under a system in which churches, schools, individual governments, money, and private property were abolished in favor of a central governing council, and nationalism and patriotism have been done away with; that the 'space people' want nuclear tests stopped immediately and that never should people on earth fight; if attacked, they should lay down their arms and welcome their attackers . . .

[Censored] said the particular thing that first made her and her husband wonder about Adamski was a letter they received from him dated 10/12/59, in which it was hinted that the Russians receive help in their outer space programs from the 'space people,' and that the 'space people' will not help any nation unless such nation has peaceful intent . . .

It occurred to them that the desires and recommendations of the 'space people' whom Adamski quotes are quite similar to Russia's approach, particularly as to the ending of nuclear testing, and it was for this reason she decided to call the FBI . . .

A few scant documents aside, thus ends the FBI's file on George Adamski. Right up to the time of his death on 23 April 1965, Adamski continued to proclaim that his accounts of interaction with alien beings were genuine, and, more than thirty years on, the debate continues. But what lies behind the claims of the contactees? Having examined the subject at length, I suggest there are but five possibilities:

- There are no human-like extra terrestrials visiting our planet, and those proclaiming contact with such were simply hoaxers, opportunists, and persons suffering from overactive imaginations and/or delusions;

- all of those individuals who can be described in general terms as contactees did have genuine experiences with alien beings, and related the details of those experiences with unswerving accuracy;

- although having been genuinely in communication with extraterrestrial beings, the contactees were repeatedly lied to concerning the nature of the aliens and their point of origin;

- the contactees were unwitting players in a Soviet intelligence operation designed to adversely affect US morale by convincing 1950s America that its superior alien visitors were Communists;

- the contactees were witting or unwitting players in a disinformation campaign orchestrated by the US government to promote to the populace the image of peace-loving, human-like aliens, which in reality was at variance with the facts.

Can any one theory, or indeed a combination of all five, go some way towards gauging the truth? One can never entirely rule out the possibility that some of the contactees were spreading untruths of their own making; however, the fact that reports similar to those of Van Tassel, Bethurum, Fry and Adamski have surfaced throughout the entire planet over the course of the last fifty years convinces me that, overall, the 'hoax' theory is in no way sufficiently valid to lay the matter to rest.

The notion that the contactees were given one-hundred-percent-accurate information by their cosmic informants is something else I reject outright. Not for one moment do I believe that George Adamski had contact with alien creatures from Venus. Nor do I accept that George Van Tassel had dealings with Ah-Ming of Tarr, and Zolton, the Highest Authority and Commandant of all spacecraft in the Sector System of Vela. Likewise, I have similar feelings with respect to Truman Bethurum's dealings with Captain Aura Rhanes of Clarion, and those of Daniel Fry.

I do, however, consider it highly probable that in the early 1950s, at least one species of human-like extraterrestrial was interested in making covert contact with elements of the human race. And that, to do so in a fashion that would not create undue and unwelcome attention, the visitors concocted improbable and far-fetched stories concerning their 'names' and point of origin. The account of Harry Barnes, Senior Controller at Washington International Airport, who put forward a theory that the aliens are able to monitor our radio transmissions, may be relevant here. If our radio transmissions are monitored by beings from beyond our solar system, then it may be the case that the structure of our entire society has also come in for scrutiny. That being so, to avoid the possibility of 'culture shock', the aliens may have deemed it more suitable to promote themselves as spacefaring near-neighbours (hence the promotion of Venus and Mars as their point of origin), rather than as intergalactic supermen with mind-numbingly advanced technology. The decision on their part to adopt familiar titles such as 'Commandant' and 'Captain', may also have been a subtle way of impressing upon the human race that their civilisation was little different from our own.

The theory that the contactees may have been given genuine (albeit to a degree distorted) data, which was to be expanded upon when the human race had become acclimatised to the idea of alien visitation, was something allegedly conferred upon Daniel Fry by 'A-lan': 'One of the purposes of this visit is to determine the basic adaptability of the Earth's peoples, particularly your adaptability to adjust your minds quickly to conditions and concepts completely foreign to your customary modes of thoughts.'

There is also the disturbing possibility that the contactees were guilty of spreading alien-originated disinformation which was not in the best interests of humankind. I may be guilty of thinking negatively here, but the repeated pleas of the aliens that we lay down our nuclear arms strike me as being very suspicious. What better way to render the Earth open to attack than to lull the human race into believing in the existence of friendly 'space cousins'? Again, Daniel Fry's source of information may have inadvertently divulged aspects of some nefarious alien plot to exploit our home: '. . . the purpose of this visit is not entirely philanthropic, since there are some materials upon your planet which we could use to the advantage of both our peoples, material which you have in great abundance but which are rather scarce elsewhere in this solar system.'

For all the evidence suggesting that the contactee mystery is connected to the activities of extraterrestrial creatures, what of the theory that many of the accounts of meetings with human-like aliens have their origin in a Soviet-sponsored intelligence operation? As outrageous as this sounds, it cannot be entirely discounted.

Particularly in the late 1940s and early to mid-1950s, there was more than a passing concern on the part of the American military and intelligence services that the Soviets were to a degree implicated in the saucer mystery. And there is no doubt that many of the contactees of the 1950s were either pro-Russian, or had made statements that indicated they were Communist sympathisers. For example, in 1952, George Adamski suggested that the aliens most likely were communist-like in nature, and openly asserted that: 'Russia will dominate the world and we will then have an era of peace for 1,000 years . . . the Government in [the USA] is in the same state of deterioration as was the Roman empire prior to its collapse . . . the Government in this country is a corrupt form of government and capitalists are enslaving the poor.'

Likewise, no later than 5 August 1954, the FBI had in its possession information from a resident of Yucca Valley, California, who expressed concern that George Van Tassel was a Soviet spy. His predilection for attacking the US government's handling of the UFO issue; his warnings (and those of his alleged alien contacts) concerning the proliferation of atomic weapons; and his lecture of 17 April 1960, described by the Bureau as 'more of a religious-economics lecture rather than one of unidentified flying objects', all convince me that the Bureau recognised that Van Tassel's activities were not in keeping with the wellbeing of the United States.

Similarly, in December 1954, the Palm Springs Republican Club contacted the Bureau to enquire if Truman Bethurum was guilty of 'trying to put over any propaganda'. Finally there was that mysterious cosmic couple 'Affa' and 'Ponnar' who, it was recorded in a Bureau memorandum of August 1954, were making contact 'for the purpose of protecting our own earth from destruction caused by the explosion of the atom bomb, hydrogen bomb, and wars of various kinds . . .'

You may consider it quite unbelievable that the Soviets would be in any way implicated in the contactee mystery, but consider this: practically all of those 1950s contactees who came under the watchful eye of the FBI openly championed the cause of peace-loving, communist-like aliens who desired an end to the arms race. And as time went on, their status grew and grew and they garnered support from all around the world. If the Soviets wished to manipulate a percentage of the US public into believing that the disarmament of America's nuclear stockpile was warranted (as the aliens repeatedly stated it was), their efforts were somewhat successful.

In 1954, George Van Tassel's newsletter, originally mailed to around 250 people, soon had a circulation of no less than one thousand. In addition, having made enquiries as to how Van Tassel funded his operations, the Bureau noted: '[Van Tassel[secures money . . . through the generosity of certain individuals, number about 100. He failed to identify any of these people.' Who were Van Tassel's mysterious paymasters? Today, that is a question still being asked.

On the issue of George Adamski, a Bureau document of 10 December 1953 notes that his first book, *Flying Saucers Have Landed*, 'has sold over 100,000 copies and Adamski is getting a great deal of publicity'. On 13

November 1954, the Bureau noted that still more organisations and persons of Adamski's and Van Tassel's ilk were surfacing in the US: 'As the Bureau is aware, there are numerous individuals operating in Southern California under the guise of religion or religious cults with a prophet or director who have a certain emotional appeal.'

It was not just the FBI who recognised the possibility that the Soviets were in a position to exploit facets of the UFO mystery. On 19 August 1952, the CIA prepared a report which addressed this entire matter:

> With world-wide sightings [of UFOs] reported, we have found not one report or comment, even satirical, in the Russian press. This could result only from an official policy decision and of course raises the question of why and of whether or not these sightings could be used from a psychological warfare point of view either offensively or defensively. Air Force is aware of this and has investigated a number of the civilian groups that have sprung up to follow the subject. One – the Civilian Saucer Committee in California has substantial funds, strongly influences the editorial policy of a number of newspapers and has leaders whose connections may be questionable. Air Force is watching this organization because of its power to touch off mass hysteria and panic. Perhaps we, from an intelligence point of view, should watch for any indication of Russian efforts to capitalize upon this American credulity.

Were the contactees witting or unwitting players in a subtle Soviet intelligence operation, the intent of which was to promote in the US public pro-disarmament and anticapitalist feelings? We may never know, but I feel sure the Soviets would not have looked upon the claims of Van Tassel, Adamski and the many other contactees adversely.

Finally, we come to what may be the most controversial theory of all. A variation on the 'foreign intelligence operation' is one that attributes the contactee legend to a US government-inspired programme designed to instil in the public the image of humanoid, freedom-loving beings whose only purpose in coming to our planet was to bestow upon us their worldly wisdom. Some may consider this theory too outlandish for words; in the world of the UFO, however, nothing is as it seems . . .

Aside from the similarity of their accounts, there is another issue which binds the early contactees of the 1950s: their ties with government and political bodies in the 1940s. Let us start with George Van Tassel.

The Bureau of the 1950s may not have been overly enamoured of Van Tassel's activities, but, as the Freedom of Information Act has shown, in previous years the man had what could be termed 'quasi-official' links with the Bureau which were not frowned upon. A document of 16 November 1954, for example, references Van Tassel as having been 'acquainted' with FBI Special Agent Walter Bott (who had then recently died), and that furthermore Van Tassel 'helped [Bott] on many cases at Lockheed'.

In addition to that startling revelation, you will remember that, while employed with Hughes Aircraft, Van Tassel acted in an assistance capacity to Howard Hughes himself. In 1977, an astonishing book, *The Hughes Papers* by Elaine Davenport, Paul Eddy and Mark Hurwitz, was published, and disclosed a wealth of hitherto unknown material pertaining to Hughes, including his connections with the CIA. This does not of course link Van Tassel with the CIA in any capacity (the Agency was not officially formed until 1947), but it is food for thought, nevertheless.[8]

It may therefore not be entirely coincidental that Howard Hughes's name crops up in a further Bureau document relating to UFOs. Dated 31 July 1950, and captioned 'Flying Discs', the 'Air Mail, Special Delivery' memo for J. Edgar Hoover's attention had come from the Bureau's Chicago office and dealt with the following letter, a copy of which the Bureau had obtained from a Chicago-based newspaper – its original recipient:

Since we are on the brink of a third world conflict, the world is more air conscious than ever. Aviation in some phases is yet in its pioneering days. Much talk goes on about the flying saucers or discs. The saucer we speak about is not a military secret, and is not yet owned by any government. The flying saucer which was seen over south Chicago last April is a large fuel tank with crystal glass wings. It has two large jet engines on both sides. It is radio controlled. It resembles a saucer very much when in flight. The wings cannot be seen on a clear day. This is so it is a most difficult target for anti aircraft gunners. The reason for the large flat gas or fuel tank is to give the ship a long range for atomic bombing. The ship was financed by HOWARD HUGHES, millionaire aviation enthusiast. It is now being tested by the Glen F. Martin Aircraft Co., makers of the Martin Marauder. The craft is only made for one way trips. It has a range of 4,000 miles, ceiling of 25,000 feet, and a speed of 750 miles per hour. So far only a few of these craft have been made, and they usually are pitched in the lake or ocean as they cannot be landed. They are merely to carry a bomb of high destruction to enemy country. They have no wheels, but small steel rails on the bottom from which they take off. All other mechanism can be explained in detail. The man who welded the ship says it is by far the best long range bombing instrument he has ever seen. The name of the ship is the 'Danse Macabre'.

Bureau files reveal that the newspaper did not wish to publish the letter, since it was felt that 'the Army desired that the matter be kept confidential'. The Bureau took little action beyond filing the letter for future reference purposes, but the reference to Howard Hughes is interesting in light of George Van Tassel's pre-1950s acquaintances with the man. But Van Tassel was not the only contactee with rumoured connections of a somewhat 'interesting' nature, as the researcher George C. Andrews has noted:

People who traveled with [George] Adamski noticed that he had been issued a special passport, such as is usually reserved for diplomats and high government officials. It is entirely possible that he may have been a CIA disinformation agent, who successfully fulfilled the mission of making the subject of UFOs seem so absurd that no independent in-depth investigation would be made by qualified academics.[9]

And there is more to come. In 1954, a group of West Coast contactees, including both Truman Bethurum and George Hunt Williamson, gave a series of lectures at the Hotel Gibson in Cincinnati. As this was also the home town of the researcher Leonard Stringfield, paths inevitably crossed. Hoping to get Stringfield to endorse their talks, Bethurum, Williamson and their flock called at his home and introduced themselves.

Stringfield flatly refused to lend his support, but had an interesting experience which is worth recording:

> After their departure I began to wonder about their causes. At one point during the evenings many tete-a-tetes, I chanced to overhear two 'members' discussing the FBI. Pretending aloofness, I tried to overhear more. It seemed that one person was puzzling over the presence of an 'agent' in the group. When I was caught standing too close, the FBI talk stopped. Whether or not I had reason to be suspicious, it was not difficult for me to believe that some of the contactees behind all this costly showmanship were official 'plants'.[10]

Officialdom aside, many of the contactees were connected by their affiliations with a variety of right-wing political bodies.

In the early years of the 1930s, William Dudley Pelley was the leader of an American Nazi association known as the Silver Shirts, an association that was linked closely with a similar organisation: Guy Ballard's I AM movement. Indeed, such was the affiliation that the membership of both groups overlapped.

Following the end of the World War Two (during which he was interned for sedition), Pelley formed an occult-based group known as Soulcraft, and it so happens that direct ties can be found to link those contactees investigated by the FBI in the 1950s and persons affiliated to I AM, the Silver Shirts and Soulcraft.

The researcher and astrophysicist Jacques Vallee had learned that George Adamski had pre-war connections with Pelley, as did George Hunt Williamson in 1950 when he began working for Soulcraft's office in Noblesville, Indiana. It was Williamson who, two years later, witnessed Adamski's meeting with an extra-terrestrial in the Californian desert.

Moreover, George Van Tassel's 'Integratron' was adorned with prominent I AM designs, including portraits of Saint Germain and Jesus, which had been commissioned by the aforementioned Guy Ballard, who was well known to William Dudley Pelley.[11,12]

George Hunt Williamson was also an acquaintance of Ray and Rex Stanford, two researchers who in the 1950s wrote a small, privately published book which recorded their dealings with, among others, George Van Tassel.[13]

All of the above may be nothing more than mere coincidence. But remember: the majority of the seminal contactees had direct and unquestionable ties to radical, right-wing political bodies in the 1940s and early 1950s. Moreover, the testimony of Leonard Stringfield is illuminating to say the least, as are the revelations concerning George Van Tassel's pre-1950s work with FBI Special Agent Walter Bott, and his association with Howard Hughes – himself a character who moved within very high circles.

Quite reasonably, however, one might ask: if the contactee movement was indeed the brainchild of some US government (or at least 'para-government') disinformation operation, then why the desire to instil in the public the idea that the aliens were almost communist-like in nature?

The contactees may have been criticised for the ever-present political overtones that beset their claims, but they also subtly fostered in the US public the image of kindly, human-like beings with whom it was possible to cultivate a degree of meaningful contact on a one-to-one basis.

If, when saucer hysteria was at its height, the American government had absolutely no parity with the aliens (which I believe to be the case) it may have been deemed wise by officialdom to steer those with a passion for the UFO subject into carefully controlled avenues (i.e. those avenues in which the 'kindly alien' dominated), rather than risk troublesome investigators from discovering the US government's absolute ignorance of (a) who the visitors were and (b) their intent with regard to the human race. I would add, however, that if any or all of the contactees did have official sanction to promote their claims, it seems unlikely that the FBI of the 1950s and 1960s had any awareness that this was the case. This should not be considered surprising, since the US intelligence community thrives on the policy of 'need to know'.

One final piece of evidence in favour of this particular theory comes from the investigator John Keel. Commenting on the experiences of one contactee, Howard Menger (a well-known figure much in the spotlight in the 1950s and 1960s, and author of *From Outer Space To You*, a book that described his dealings with human-like alien beings), Keel says:

> . . . in letters to [the researcher] Gray Barker and Saucer News editor Jim Moseley, Menger termed his book 'fiction-fact' and implied that the Pentagon had asked him to participate in an experiment to test the public's reaction to extra-terrestrial contact.[14]

Will we eventually uncover the truth that lies behind the contactee mystery? And, if so, will that truth be found to lie somewhere within one (if not a combination of all) of the five theories I have presented? Perhaps in time we will know the answer. For now, the unique documentation generated by the FBI on this difficult topic establishes that something remarkable was taking place in 1950s America. The question that remains is: what?

CHAPTER 14

BEWARE THE MEN IN BLACK

'THE DOOR BANGED REALLY SLOWLY BUT HARD, LIKE SOMEONE WAS HITTING it with their fist instead of knocking, [and] when I opened it there was this horrible little man about five feet tall. He was dressed in a black suit and tie and had a funny little black hat on. His face was really strange: he looked like someone with anorexia, you know? His cheeks were all gaunt; his eyes were dark and his skin was almost white.

'I didn't know what to do and just stared; it was really frightening. Then he suddenly gave me this horrible grin, and I could tell his lips had been coloured, like with make-up or something. He took off his hat and had this really bad wig on. You know, he looked about sixty but the wig was jet black.

'All he said was: "We would ask you cease your studies." I said, "What?" Then he repeated it, exactly the same and I had to ask what he meant. "The sky lights; always the sky lights," he said. Then it dawned on me. I'd seen a UFO late at night about a week before when me and my husband had been driving home and we both had a really weird dream after about some little men standing around our car on the edge of the woods.

'Then he said something like "Cease and dream easy." I think that was it, and he gave me a really long stare like he was going to attack me or something. But he just walked away down the drive. I started to feel dizzy and slammed the door. I just crawled to the bed, and fell asleep for about three hours. But when I woke up there was this horrible smell like burning rubber all through the house. We had to have the windows wide open for days and get the carpets and furniture cleaned to get rid of [the smell].

'It really shook me up, and apart from telling you I haven't really talked about it to anyone – and I don't really want to!'

That account was related to me in 1994 by a British housewife who lives in a small English village near to the previously referred-to Cannock Chase, and is a classic description of a meeting with what has become popularly known as a 'Man in Black'.

Since the early part of the 1950s, the Men in Black (I use the plural since they generally are reported in groups of three) have been a persistent part of the UFO lore – as the FBI is more than well aware. In the following pages I will detail what the Bureau knows about this peculiar phenomenon, but to fully appreciate the enormity of the MIB mystery I relate the following:

In 1952, Albert K. Bender, a resident of Bridgeport, Connecticut, established a UFO investigative society known as the International Flying Saucer Bureau. Bender's group was warmly received by researchers both in the USA and abroad, and soon blossomed into an impressive body with a network of investigators.

In 1953, however, without warning Bender disbanded the IFSB, alluding to an unusual experience in which three men in black suits had entrusted in him the true facts surrounding the UFO mystery. Supposedly, Bender had himself stumbled across the truth and the MIBs wished him to remain silent – which he did for a number of years – and to ensure that silence, Bender was given the full, uncensored facts pertaining to the aliens' mission on Earth.

According to Bender, like the houswife whose account I have already cited, on one particular occasion he was overcome with a sensation of dizziness and retired to his bedroom when he suddenly became aware of

> . . . three shadowy figures in the room. The figures became clearer. All of them were dressed in black clothes. They looked like clergymen, but wore hats similar to Homburg style. The faces were not clearly discernible, for the hats partly hid and shaded

them. Feelings of fear left me. The eyes of all three figures suddenly lit up like flash-light bulbs, and all these were focussed upon me. They seemed to burn into my very soul as the pains above my eyes became almost unbearable. It was then I sensed that they were conveying a message to me by telepathy . . .

The three men did indeed convey a message, but such was Bender's terror that he stayed silent for years, conveying only the basic facts of the 'visit', and only to trusted colleagues. Of those, one was Gray Barker, who went on to write the definitive exposé of the Men in Black in 1956: *They Knew Too Much About Flying Saucers*.[1]

A full decade after he had retired from the UFO scene, Bender's uncensored story surfaced in the form of *Flying Saucers and the Three Men* – a rather unusual book published privately by Gray Barker. Having read the book, I can advise that its contents are truly bizarre and chronicle Bender's alleged experiences with the Men in Black, his knowledge of a secret UFO base in Antarctica, and the MIBs' mission to obtain a unique element from the Earth's oceans. Bender's account also touches on a host of 'fringe' topics including the occult, black magic, spiritualism and demonology. As a result, many of the seminal UFO researchers in the USA largely ignored Bender's book when it was first published.[2] A mistake, in my view.

If Bender's account was isolated, there would be acceptable grounds for believing that his claims were solely those of a disturbed mind. But quite literally hundreds of similar stories have surfaced across the planet.

Typically, those who attract the MIBs are either (a) UFO researchers who have perhaps uncovered details of something a little too sensitive for their own good or (b) witnesses to UFO phenomena. More often than not the person concerned is visited at their home (invariably by MIBs in groups of three) and ordered not to discuss their experiences with outsiders.

Time after time, the Men in Black are described as being dressed in black suits, black hats, black ties, and white shirts. They are often short in stature, painfully thin, with slightly oriental or, on occasion, Spanish features. They also seem to have a tenuous grasp of the English language, and are glaringly unaware of our most basic customs and conventions. The

Spanish reference is particularly interesting since in November 1947 the FBI office at Pittsburgh was informed by a letter-writer in Port Allegany, that 'the saucers reported as seen in various parts of the country, were actually from Spain . . . this had been ascertained by the Government in Washington, but it was not being made known'.

One of the most learned scholars in the field of the Men in Black is John Keel. The author of numerous books on unexplained phenomena, Keel has devoted much of his time to chronicling the accounts of MIB activity, and presents a strong case for the reality of the mystery. Keel, too, has had his run-ins with one particular type of MIB which he terms 'the cadavers':

> . . . these are people who look like they've been dead a long time. Their clothes hang on them; their flesh is pasty white and they look like maybe somebody's dug them up from a cemetery. This cadaverous type has turned up in strange places: England, Sweden. [The writer and investigator] Brad Steiger saw one. I saw one in the early '60's. And we have no idea what these fellows are about. They're very elusive when you approach them, and hurry away [and] they do have a habit of turning up in UFO areas and following UFO investigators around.[3]

The MIBs do not always dress exclusively in black, however. In the 1960s in particular, the Men in Black changed their tactics and, to ensure the silence of witnesses to UFO encounters, began to pass themselves off as military and government personnel. With reports mounting even the US Air Force was plunged into the MIB controversy, as a widely circulated memo of 1 March 1967 from Lieutenant General Hewitt, Assistant Vice Chief of Staff, shows:

> Information, not verifiable, has reached Hq USAF that persons claiming to represent the Air Force or other Defense establishments have contacted citizens who have sighted unidentified flying objects. In one reported case an individual in civilian clothes, who represented himself as a member of NORAD, demanded and received photos belonging to a private citizen. In another, a

person in an Air Force uniform approached local police and other citizens who had sighted a UFO, assembled them in a school room and told them that they did not see what they thought they saw and that they should not talk to anyone about the sighting. All military and civilian personnel and particularly Information Officers and UFO investigating Officers who hear of such reports should immediately notify their local OSI offices.

In 1979, the Men in Black were still out in force, and still masquerading as representatives of the military. One researcher, Richard D. Seifried, recalls an incident during that year when two MIBs were present at a UFO lecture in Ohio. According to Seifried, both were dressed in 'very neat, dark suits, sported GI haircuts and what looked like Air Force regulation dress shoes'.

At the end of the lecture, Seifried and his friends left the hall and, while walking along a long corridor towards the car park, saw the two men directly in front of them. 'They rounded the corner,' recalled Seifried. 'Although we were probably no more than forty or fifty feet behind them by the time we turned the corner the two men had disappeared . . . what they did was inhuman.'[4]

I am also conversant with the facts surrounding a doctor's experience with the Men in Black in the 1970s. In this instance the doctor was asked to conduct an examination of a young boy's arm which was marked with an unusual abrasion.

'I asked him how he got the strange marks, and what created them,' said the doctor. 'He replied, "The space doctors!"' As the doctor listened the boy related seeing a 'low-flying plane' enter a secluded area of woodland near his home. Curious as to what was going on the boy ventured into the woods and came across a group of strange people who, said the doctor, captured him', transferred him to some form of craft, and subjected him to 'countless medical and intelligence tests'.

All of this could be considered nothing more than the result of an overactive imagination on the part of the boy. However, five years later, the doctor was at home watching television when there was a knock at the door.

There before him were two men dressed in 'black jumpsuits, black shoes, and black gloves and even sunglasses'. Only one spoke, and enquired as to whether or not the doctor 'had known of the boy'.

The doctor asked why the man wanted to know, and the response was that he was simply 'curious'. Naturally suspicious, the doctor related only part of the story, after which one of the MIBs 'managed a slight emotionless smile' before leaving. Again, the experience sounds incredible, but such accounts proliferate.

Despite the large body of evidence suggesting that the MIBs are of nonhuman origin, not everyone is convinced that this is the case.

The researcher William Moore is convinced that at least some of the Men in Black are 'really government people in disguise' who originate with a 'rather bizarre unit of Air Force Intelligence known currently as the Air Force Special Activities Center'.

Moore relates that the history of the AFSAC can be traced back to the 1127th Field Activities Group – 'an oddball unit, a composite of special intelligence groups . . . The men of the 1127th were con artists. Their job was to get people to talk.'

Recruited into the group were 'safe-crackers, cat burglars, lock-pickers . . . impersonators, assorted masters of deception . . . and useful flakes of all types'. Moore, I am quite sure, is on to something here and it would be a relatively easy task for an experienced field operative to exploit the Men in Black phenomenon for various US intelligence-related purposes, such as procuring photographs of UFOs in flight from witnesses, soliciting the silence of those who have viewed UFOs – particularly if those masquerading as MIBs wished to disguise their true point of origin.[5]

I cannot accept that every encounter with the Men in Black falls into this category, however. For example, there are the accounts of MIBs appearing and disappearing at will (as described by Albert Bender and numerous others), which are extraordinarily difficult to explain. In addition, encounters with the MIBs are not limited to the USA, as we saw at the beginning of this chapter.

In 1994, I conducted an interview with Nick Pope, a serving member of Britain's Ministry of Defence who for three years worked in one particular office of the MOD which dealt with UFO reports. A firm believer that some UFOs are extraterrestrial, in 1996 Pope wrote an extraordinarily important book chronicling his time in the MOD's UFO division and relating a number of previously unheard-of cases.

During the course of my interview with Pope, I advised him that on a number of occasions I had spoken with UFO witnesses who claimed (very often in complete confidence, which effectively rules out the possibility of hoax) to have been warned by supposed MOD sources not to talk about their UFO encounters. What is Pope's opinion of this?

> Men in Black stories? From what I understand some of these UFO conferences, the front rows are taken up by 'Walter Mitty'-type characters who dress in black with sunglasses and take notes on everything. If there was one thing that anyone who was trying to be inobtrusive would not do, it would be that. I think any allegations about people turning up and wanting to know about sightings, what you're dealing with is either people who are lying, and saying it happened when it didn't; or perhaps more likely, people who have genuinely been visited by someone, but where that someone is some Walter Mitty-type character who likes to think he's some sort of 'James Bond' secret agent. If anyone's going around saying: 'You must keep quiet about that', it's the opposite of what we do. So it's nothing to do with us . . .[6]

As with William Moore, I am quite certain that Pope's theory does explain some of the MIB accounts that have surfaced in the UK over the past half-century; however, in my previous book, *A Covert Agenda*, I presented convincing proof that the division of the MOD in which Pope worked was only one of a number that are tasked with investigating the UFO problem, and it would therefore be unwise to assume that Pope has complete 'need to know' with respect to UFOs.

And now to the FBI.

In 1953, the author Harold T. Wilkins was apprised of the facts pertaining to an unusual FBI-related Men-in-Black-type encounter which occurred in Los Angeles in 1953. Wilkins's source of the story insisted on anonymity at the time but it appears that the basics of the account can be traced back to an official in a Los Angeles-based attorney's office concerned with tracing missing persons.

In a letter to Wilkins it was revealed that in the latter part of January 1953 two 'emaciated'-looking men, at least six and a half feet in height, arrived in Los Angeles and were given temporary work by the director of the attorney's office. Wilkins recorded later: 'They were so efficient that they astonished other investigators by tracing missing persons in a fraction of the customary time.'

Whoever the two men were has never been made clear, but they were certainly not run-of-the-mill individuals. For example, Wilkins's informant advised him that the bone structure present in the hands of the two men differed from that seen in humans, to the extent that their wrists and hands appeared jointless, and at least one of the men was possessed of remarkable strength: 'It is also alleged that, one day, one of these two men leaned over the steel top of a filing cabinet, and, with his curiously curved hand, scored an indentation in the steel at least one-half inch deep!'

Moreover, the men asserted that they were not of the Earth, but had 'landed from a small flying saucer, in the Mojave Desert, some 200 miles east of Los Angeles, and learned to speak English by listening to broadcasts of radio and TV!'

It transpired that someone had informed the FBI of this and agents were dispatched to investigate the entire affair. In mid-February, however, with the Bureau closing in, the two men vanished without trace and were never again seen. But that was not the end of the matter.

The Bureau supposedly sequestered the damaged filing cabinet and turned it over to a metallurgical chemist who determined that, to produce the indentations present where one of the two men had 'leaned' on the cabinet, it would have taken a force of some 2,000 pounds or more! And contained within the dented area were traces of more than a dozen unknown elements. Somewhat alarmed by this the FBI forwarded a 'secret report' to Washington, where it resides to this day.[7]

But is there any truth to this account? Harold T. Wilkins was seemingly satisfied that his source of the story was genuine, and in abbreviated form it appeared in Wilkins's 1954 classic, *Flying Saucers on the Attack*. In addition, the story appeared in a number of other publications throughout the 1950s, including the August 1954 issue of *Mystic* magazine.[8]

On 7 August 1954, a resident of Lanesville, Ohio, who had read the issue of *Mystic* in question, wrote to J. Edgar Hoover and enquired if there was any truth behind the alleged incident.

In response Hoover stated: 'I would like to advise you that the article you mentioned is entirely incorrect with reference to the FBI, and there is no information on the matter which I can give you.'

Hoover's carefully prepared reply may tell us more than the Bureau would have liked. Note that Hoover did not deny the authenticity of the alleged incident; he merely stated that, with respect to the FBI, *Mystic*'s article was in error. Secondly, Hoover's statement, 'there is no information on the matter which I can give you', is odd. If the entire matter was nothing but a hoax, why not simply say so? Instead, Hoover's letter had the effect of actually prolonging the controversy! And there is firm evidence to show that when the *Mystic* article first appeared Hoover was quick to inform the editor that only with respect to the Bureau was the story false, and that a retraction should appear in the next issue. To expand on this, I refer you to the following Bureau 'note' of 12 August 1954:

> This article was previously brought to our attention, and the field advised the magazine editor that the story was not true as far as the Bureau's part was concerned. The editor stated he regretted the error and he would publish a retraction in the next issue, which is not due for several months yet.

Two years later, a similar letter reached Hoover, which again received a similar response from the Bureau. But perhaps the most interesting development occurred in 1964. On 9 November of that year a UFO researcher from Orange, Texas, wrote to Hoover and specifically requested a copy of the FBI's report on the two mystery men: 'If the story is true and or if the FBI has a report on this case in its files, I would appreciate a copy of that report . . . I realize this story sounds fantastic but I would appreciate a reply, since it is actually supposed to have occurred.'

This particular letter prompted what was probably the most guarded response from the Bureau: 'While I would like to be of assistance in connection with your inquiry, I must advise that information contained in the files of the FBI is confidential and available only for official use, persuant to regulations of the Department of Justice. Please do not infer either that we do or do not have information of the type you mentioned. I hope you will understand my inability to be of aid.'

Again, why the couched response from Hoover? Had the Bureau put out an authoritative statement wholly decrying the validity of the affair, this would have firmly laid the matter to rest once and for all. The fact that Hoover chose not to, it seems, is of some lasting importance.

On 28 August 1953, only months after the Los Angeles incident, Gray Barker, who was largely responsible for chronicling the early exploits of the Men in Black, was visited by an agent of the Bureau who put to him a number of questions concerning Albert Bender's International Flying Saucer Bureau.

It turns out that Bender had forwarded to Barker a number of 'business cards' which he had printed identifying Barker as 'Chief Investigator' for the IFSB. In his 1956 book, *They Knew Too Much About Flying Saucers*, Barker admitted giving 'four or five [of the cards] to close friends, who still had them when I checked with them one week later'. It was therefore something of a surprise when the FBI turned up on Barker's doorstep with one of the aforementioned business cards. 'I have always been puzzled about just how the Federal Bureau of Investigation got hold of one of them,' Barker later said.

'What's this all about?' asked the agent. A little nervously, Barker explained that the IFSB was simply an organisation formed to investigate 'flying saucer phenomena', and the business cards were a means by which IFSB investigators could be identified.

The Bureau man then proceeded to ask Barker if he knew a certain individual (whose name Barker later could not recall) who lived in Florida. Barker replied that he did not. This prompted the agent to advise Barker that the man had suffered an epileptic fit and had been taken to the nearby St Mary's Hospital. Among his belongings was one of Barker's cards.

Satisfied that Barker was not acquainted with the man, the Bureau agent thanked him and departed. 'Then it struck me,' recalled Barker. 'How in the world had anyone from Florida come into possession of one of my business cards?'

Barker began to wonder if there really had been an epileptic man, or if this had simply been a ruse to allow the Bureau to covertly check out Barker, Bender and the IFSB. Barker voiced these concerns in a report to Bender, who wrote back: 'I cannot for the life of me see why [the FBI] would be checking up. It certainly proves one thing – the government is more interested in the Saucers than we realize.'

Five years later, both Barker and Bender were once again the subject of Bureau interest. On 22 November 1958, an enquiring citizen of Oklahoma city contacted Hoover thus:

> Recently many rumors have been printed in UFO periodicals, concerning reports that Special Agents of the Federal Bureau of Investigation have discouraged certain saucer investigators, particularly Mr Albert Bender of Bridgeport, Connecticut, from further research into the secret of these elusive discs. Since you are the Director of the FBI, I would like to know whether or not these reports are factual or whether they are just rumors.

Hoover's response was swift: 'I am instructing a Special Agent of our Oklahoma City Office to contact you concerning the matter you mentioned.' A note from Hoover to the special agent in charge at Oklahoma City added: 'An Agent of your office should contact [letter writer] immediately and secure copies of or information concerning the periodicals described.'

In a memorandum to Hoover on 9 December 1958, the Oklahoma office reported that the periodical in question was the *Saucerian Bulletin* published by Gray Barker, in which it was stated that the 'three men' responsible for silencing Albert Bender were from 'the FBI, Air Force Intelligence, and the Central Intelligence Agency'.

A report of 12 December continues: '. . . Bender formed the International Flying Saucer Bureau in Bridgeport, Connecticut, in 1952 to look into the flying saucer mystery. In 1953 Bender allegedly stated that he knew what the saucers are. Then . . . "three men in black suits" silenced Bender to the extent that even today Bender will not discuss the matter of his "hush-up" with anyone.'

Such was the interest in the claims of both Barker and Bender that on 22 January 1959 Hoover instructed the Chicago office: 'The Bureau desires to obtain a copy of the book written by Gray Barker entitled "They Knew Too Much About Flying Saucers." Reportedly, this book was

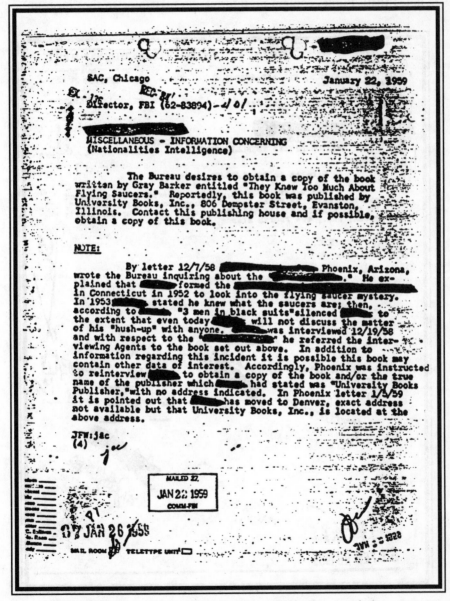

A 1959 FBI document concerning Albert Bender's experiences with the Men in Black.

published by University Books, Inc . . . Illinois. Contact this publishing
house and if possible, obtain a copy of this book.'

Three weeks later a copy of Barker's book was in Hoover's hands, as
were copies of Bender's *Space Review* magazine. The Bureau subsequently
noted that: 'Bufiles contain no information pertaining to the "hush-up"

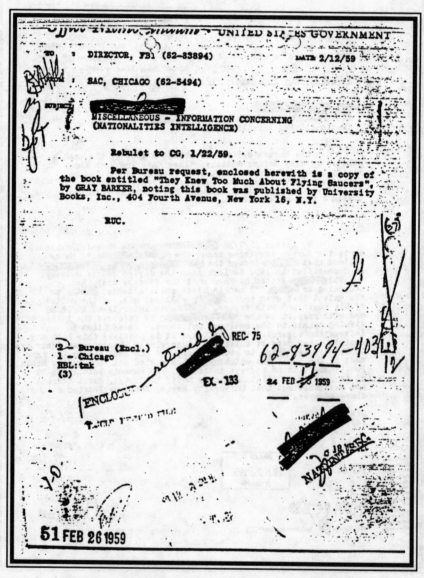

Confirmation that the FBI had in its possession a copy of Gray Barker's
classic Men in Black book, *They Knew Too Much About Flying Saucers*.

of Bender', and that with respect to his *Space Review* journal: 'This magazine contains numerous articles and squibs concerning the sighting of flying saucers throughout the world. It does not appear to have any security significance.' This would seem to imply that whoever Bender's mysterious visitors were, they were not Bureau agents; however, it is curious that nowhere in the released papers is there any mention of the FBI's 1953 interview with Gray Barker. Was this simply an off-the-record interview, or does the Bureau have its reasons for not releasing its files on the matter?

On 14 May 1969, the Bureau was in receipt of yet another letter from a member of the public who had latched on to the stories surrounding the Men in Black:

> There currently are rumors over the grapevine and in print that suggest men with oriental features wearing dark clothes go around terrorizing people who have had close-up views of UFOs. It is also rumored these creatures have impersonated armed forces officers and FBI investigators. They are supposed to ride around in black or dark automobiles that either have old license tags or none at all. Several are reported to have attempted to run down witnesses of UFO sightings, made disturbing almost macabre phone calls, silenced several investigators who were supposed to have learned some dark secret about extra-terrestrial craft or mission plans and opened mail, tapped telephones and even taken pictures of several homes where UFO witnesses lived.
>
> Can you give me any information on such rumors?

In light of the fact that both Albert Bender and Gray Barker were known to the Bureau (not to mention the glaring fact that the Bureau had in its possession a copy of Barker's book), it is rather amusing to note that the Bureau responded by assuring the letter-writer that it was completely ignorant of the Men in Black mystery, and therefore had no information in its possession that related to rumours of MIB activity!

Patricia Hyde is a former employee of the FBI who in July 1972 had an experience that brought her into direct contact with one of our mystery men. At around nine o'clock on a summer's evening Hyde witnessed a strange object, described as 'batlike', flying over Arcadia, Florida. As is often the case following UFO encounters, Hyde naturally wished to find out more about what she had seen and dug deep into the UFO mystery.

Shortly after, while still employed by the FBI, she was confronted at her apartment by an unusual-looking 'Oriental man' dressed in dark clothing, who had 'deeply slanting eyes': 'Miss Hyde,' he said, 'you will stop investigating flying saucers!' Further similar events occurred and Patricia Hyde eventually tendered her resignation with the Bureau and gave up her UFO research. Such is the effect that encounters with the Men in Black can have on a person.[9]

Nineteen ninety-six saw the FBI once again implicated in the MIB mystery when an intriguing report was posted on the Internet. Although bizarre in nature, the report contains many of the key elements of the Men in Black encounters which we have already examined. It reads thus:

I AM THE LEAD VOCAL FOR A TOP-40 COVER BAND IN SOUTHERN CALIFORNIA. DURING A LATE NIGHT JAM SESSION WITH MY BAND (THIS WAS LATE JANUARY [1996]), WE TOOK A CIGARETTE BREAK. WE SAT AROUND, TALKING ABOUT NOTHING, REAL-LY. THE NIGHT AIR WAS WARM, AND THE SKY WAS PRETTY CLEAR. I DON'T REMEMBER WHAT HAPPENED NEXT, ONLY THAT THE NEXT THING I KNEW, IT WAS MID-AFTERNOON, TWO DAYS LATER! NOW BEFORE YOU GO ON AND ASSUME THAT BECAUSE WE'RE MUSICIANS WE MUST BE DRUG USERS, ALCO-HOLICS, ETC., LET ME JUST SAY THAT I AM NOT A DRUG USER OR A DRINKER. AND THAT NIGHT WAS NO EXCEPTION TO MY OWN PERSONAL RULE.
LITTLE BITS AND PIECES COME BACK TO ME. I BELIEVE THAT I WAS ABDUCTED BY ALIENS. FOR ONE, THERE IS A LITTLE SCAR, NOW, ON MY RIGHT FOREARM. IT'S BARELY VISBLE. THE FINGERS ON

MY RIGHT HAND ARE NOT AS AGILE AS THEY ONCE WERE. ALONG THE SCAR LINE, THERE IS NO HAIR (I AM A VERY HAIRY PERSON). THERE ARE OTHER SUCH SCARS ON MY CHEST, NECK AND LEGS, ALTHOUGH MY MUSCLES IN THESE AREAS ARE JUST FINE. SINCE THAT NIGHT, I'VE BEEN HAVING RECURRING VISIONS OF HUMAN-LIKE BEINGS STICKING HUGE NEEDLES INTO ME, DRAWING OUT FLUIDS AND BEING CUT UP AND SEWN BACK TOGETHER. THIS HAS NOT BEEN VERY PLEASANT.

MY FELLOW BAND MEMBERS DO NOT REMEMBER A THING ABOUT ME DISAPPEARING. THEY, TOO, BLACKED OUT, BUT REMEMBER WAKING UP 10 MINUTES LATER. THEY DID NOT KNOW WHERE I WENT. THEY WERE COMPLETELY BAFFLED. COULD YOU IMAGINE THEIR SURPRISE WHEN THEY FOUND ME TWO DAYS LATER, LYING DOWN NAKED ON OUR PORCH?

LUCKILY, WE HAVE A HOUSE IN A VERY SECLUDED AREA AND NO ONE SAW ME IN THE STATE I WAS. I WENT TO MY DOCTOR, AND HE COULD NOT EXPLAIN THE SCARS. I TALKED TO THE POLICE, AND THEY BLEW ME OFF. WHAT THE HECK, I'M JUST A LONG HAIRED BAR MUSICIAN, RIGHT? IT'S BEEN VERY FRUSTRATING. I'VE EVEN TRIED TALKING TO SOME FRIENDS. NO ONE BUT MY FRIENDS IN OUR BAND SEEM TO BELIEVE ME.

DURING THE THIRD WEEK OF FEBRUARY [1996] I HAD A STRANGE VISIT BY THREE VERY PALE, VERY BALD MEN IN BLACK SUITS. AT FIRST GLANCE, THEY KIND OF LOOKED ORIENTAL, BUT A CLOSER LOOK LET ME KNOW THAT THEY WERE NOT ORIENTAL AT ALL. I WAS SITTING ON OUR PORCH, SIPPING ON A SODA. IT WAS A SATURDAY AFTERNOON. A BLACK, LATE MODEL CADILLAC PULLED UP IN FRONT OF OUR HOUSE, AND THE THREE GUYS GOT OUT OF THE CAR. THEY MOVED RATHER SLOWLY AND

METHODICALLY. THEY WERE STIFF AND EMOTION-
LESS, ALMOST LIKE ROBOTS. THE LEAD MAN
BLURTED OUT MY NAME. I REPLIED, 'YES?' THE
SECOND MAN TOLD ME THAT THEY WERE WITH THE
FBI AND THAT I HAD TO ACCOMPANY THEM TO
THEIR OFFICE TO ANSWER A FEW QUESTIONS. THEY
PRODUCED SOME ID AND BADGES.

I GOT INTO THE CADILLAC, HESITANTLY. THE
FIRST THING I NOTICED WAS THAT EVEN THOUGH
IT WAS A '78 MODEL, THE DAMN CAR SMELLED
BRAND NEW! THE LEAD MAN DROVE, WHILE I SAT
IN THE BACK SEAT, WITH ONE MAN ON EITHER
SIDE OF ME. THEY BASICALLY DROVE ME UP
TOWARD LOS ANGELES AND THEN BACK DOWN TO
WHERE I LIVE. ONE BIG CIRCLE. DURING THE
RIDE, I WAS WARNED NOT TO CONTINUE TALKING
ABOUT MY ALIEN ABDUCTION. THEY SHOWED ME
PICTURE AFTER PICTURE OF WHAT HAPPENS TO
PEOPLE WHO DO NOT COMPLY. EACH PICTURE WAS
A GRISLY DISPLAY OF DISMEMBERED CORPSES,
DECAPITATED HEADS AND SO FORTH. THEY ALSO
HAD A SMALL TELEVISION IN THE CAR, AND
SHOWED ME SOME SICK VIDEO FOOTAGE OF THEM
KILLING PEOPLE, SUPPOSEDLY PEOPLE WHO DID
NOT HEED THEIR WARNING. I TRIED TO FORCE MY
WAY OUT OF THE CAR AT A STOPLIGHT, BUT ONE
GUY PUT A GRIP ON ME THAT A BEAR COULD NOT
BREAK OUT OF. HIS HANDS WERE COLD.

'YOU'LL BE OUT OF THIS CAR IN DUE TIME,'
HE TOLD ME. 'BE PATIENT.' AFTER HALF AN HOUR
OF WARNINGS AND SHOW AND TELL PICTURES, THEY
DROPPED ME BACK OFF AT MY HOUSE. BY THAT
TIME, MY BANDMATES HAD COME BACK HOME. THEY
SAW THE CAR PULL UP, AND SAW ME GET OUT. BY
THE TIME THEY RAN OUT OF THE HOUSE, THE CAR
WAS PULLING AWAY. THEY CAUGHT THE LICENSE
PLATE NUMBER.

WE CALLED THE POLICE, AND THE FBI, BUT
THEY SAY THAT NO SUCH PLATE IS REGISTERED IN
CALIFORNIA OR WITH THE FBI. I'M TRYING TO
SPREAD THIS STORY AROUND ANONYMOUSLY, HOPING
THAT THOSE GUYS WON'T COME BACK. I DON'T
KNOW WHAT TO DO. MY LIFE HASN'T BEEN THE
SAME EVER SINCE. SHOULD I JUST SHUT UP?
WHERE SHOULD I TURN?

There ends the strange account. Genuine Men in Black, or FBI agents working to silence those implicated in the alien abduction puzzle? The mystery remains unresolved.

But who are the MIBs? Are they, as the MOD official Nick Pope suggests, merely 'Walter Mitty' characters acting out their fantasies? Are they intelligence operatives as suggested by William Moore? Or are they the denizens of some other world or reality which does not wish us to learn the true and apparently shocking facts that lie behind the entire UFO puzzle?

Unfortunately, the UFO subject does on occasion attract the mentally deranged who see government spies on every street corner. And I have to say, it is those same persons who gain some form of personal gratification from passing themselves off as 'secret agents'.

Equally, I am convinced that the US intelligence community is not above exploiting the legend of the Men in Black for its own purposes; however, I cannot accept that either of these two theories explains to a sufficient degree the many truly unusual MIB cases involving nonhuman beings who, if the accounts are to be believed, have the ability to appear and disappear almost at will, are able to manipulate the thought process-es of those who witness UFOs, and have acutely different physical characteristics from those of the human species.

I do not pretend to have even the slightest idea who the genuine Men in Black are, but if you are one day in a position to see a UFO, and you later hear a slow banging on your front door, be careful: they may be coming for you!

CHAPTER 15

SUMMING UP

HAVING NOW DIGESTED THOROUGHLY THE FEDERAL BUREAU OF Investigation's very own 'X-Files', what can be determined from the material currently at our disposal?

The significant number of UFO reports filed with the Bureau by highly credible sources, such as both military and civilian pilots (whose statements pertaining to the sighting of structured UFOs it is very difficult to dismiss), leads me to believe firmly that our planet has had in its midst since at least 1947, infinitely advanced creatures from other worlds who display a technology far ahead of our own. But are our alien visitors friendly, hostile, or simply following an agenda that requires them to refrain from making any form of open contact with the human species?

From reading the Bureau's files relating to Project Twinkle, I can see demonstrable evidence to show that, since the late 1940s, the UFO intelligences have displayed a deep interest in monitoring both our development and utilisation of atomic energy. Indeed, such was the concentration of sightings of unusual aerial phenomena in the vicinity of atomic energy installations in New Mexico in 1948 and 1949, that Bureau files reflect that 'an organized plan of reporting these observations should be undertaken'. And as Dr Lincoln La Paz of the University of New Mexico observed, there was an unmistakable connection between the 'green fireballs' seen near the Los Alamos atomic facility and the many and varied UFO encounters reported throughout the rest of the state.

Moreover, Bureau files confirm that in 1952 the UFOnauts were still exhibiting concern over the US government's use of atomic power: 'Savannah River Plant. Atomic Energy Commission . . . Four employees of DuPont Co., employed on Savannah River Plant near Ellention . . . saw four disc shaped objects approaching the Four Hundred area . . .'

For all this interest, however, there was no appreciable degree of enmity noted. This would seem to imply that either (a) the aliens are truly benign and are concerned that our misuse of atomic energy will have a detrimental effect on both our species and our planet; or (b) the aliens are devious beings and are undertaking a lengthy, and on going, programme to ascertain whether or not we are sufficently advanced (technologically) to withstand an all-out planetary assault.

My gut instinct suggests that, of the two, the former scenario is more likely. Consider: between 1947 and 1952 the FBI received an exceptional number of UFO reports detailing incidents where pilots had attempted to intercept UFOs in flight. More often than not, the result was that the UFOs would simply streak away, leaving the aircraft floundering. Nowhere in those Bureau documents declassified to date is there any evidence to show that a UFO has ever seriously engaged a military aircraft in an air-to-air 'dogfight'.

Certainly, Bureau files reflect that on occasion pilots have felt concerned in the vicinity of UFOs. Take the encounters of 22 and 23 January 1950, for example, in which it was reported: 'The object was observed to open out somewhat, then to turn to the left and came up on Smith's quarter. Smith considered this to be a highly threatening gesture, and turned out all lights in the aircraft.'

Again, however, the encounter passed by without further incident. Similarly, as Commander Randall Boyd of the US Air Force advised N.W. Philcox, the FBI's Air Force Liaison Representative, in 1952:

. . . the Air Force is attempting in each instance to send up jet interceptor planes in order to obtain a better view of these objects. However, recent attempts in this regard have indicated that when the pilot in the jet approaches the object it invariably fades from view . . .

Boyd's statement seems to indicate that it was also the Air Force's conclusion that, even if the saucers were not overly friendly in nature, they were not overly hostile, either. Perhaps I should at this stage point out that, while there are accounts where UFOs have acted aggressively, this is often in response to actions of our own instigation. Under such circumstances one can hardly blame those piloting the saucers for taking extreme defensive countermeasures.

But if the extermination of the human species is not a part of the alien mission on Earth, can we consider our cosmic visitors friendly?

In my judgement the friend-or-foe question is far too simplistic. A takeover of our planet may not be imminent, but there is evidence to show that at least some of the extraterretrials operating on our planet do not have a high regard for Earth-based life forms.

The Bureau's files on the disturbing cattle mutilations of the 1970s are a perfect case in point. One can only guess at the type of intelligence which, seemingly without conscience, violates to a horrifying degree defenceless animals for its own purposes – purposes which, I should point out, are still unclear.

In addition, the rumoured mutilation of human beings is a very worrying issue, and suggests to me that on a universal scale, the human race is considered a rather lowly creature. But do we not have a somewhat low regard for the animal kingdom of our world? Perhaps to the aliens we are little more than farm produce, ready for exploiting . . .

Keeping this in mind, how can this scenario be reconciled with the many FBI records relating to the benevolent aliens cited by the contactees of the 1950s and the 1960s? As you will by now be aware, the whole contactee issue is one of deep mystery.

If there are human-like extraterrestrials journeying to (and even living on) our world, I have to conclude that they are either benevolent and unconnected with the nonhuman beings involved in the cattle mutilations, or working to subvert the human race by passing themselves off as friendly creatures, when in truth they are completely ruthless beings to be avoided at all costs. While I have shown that there is evidence of deception on the part of the 'human aliens', I hope sincerely that the former scenario is the correct one.

For all the data held by the FBI on the subjects of UFO sightings, cattle mutilations and the contactees, what of the truly sensational allegation that in its possession the US government has the remains of a number of alien spacecraft and their dead crews?

Having studied the available documentation I have come to the conclusion that, like the general public, the FBI is kept largely in the dark by the US intelligence community when it comes to the 'crashed UFO' issue: the Bureau's inability to uncover the truth surrounding the MJ-12 papers, the Air Force's careful manipulation of the FBI in 1947 to hide the truth behind the incident at Roswell, and J. Edgar Hoover's interest in the Aztec affair of 1948 all suggest to me the FBI is aware that this matter is valid, even if it is one that remains tantalisingly unresolved. In time, one hopes, both the Bureau and the populace at large will be entrusted with the full facts. And this now brings me on to my final point.

Are we, the general public, entitled to know that our planet is not the only one in the universe to harbour intelligent life forms? Do we have the right to know that some of those life forms are actively visiting our home on a regular basis? Am I right to argue that, if in its possession the US government has a crashed UFO, then a public announcement confirming this is long overdue? And most important of all, if some of the aliens are not friendly, should we not be warned?

To all of the above, my answer is: Yes. The Cold War is over and there is now a welcome degree of unity on our planet where hostility once reigned. If as a species we face a future in which overt interaction with an alien civilisation is likely to play an integral part, I firmly believe the general public on the threshold of the twenty-first century is in a position to accept that reality.

The FBI has seen fit to make available its files on the subject of unidentified flying objects – files that both astound and alarm. In time, other governmental and intelligence agencies throughout the world will follow suit (as some are now indeed doing), and the full facts will be made known to us; of that I am certain. Until that day arrives, the unique documentation collated by the Bureau since 1947 will serve as a crucial pointer towards what has long been suspected: Planet Earth has extraterrestrial visitors. I leave you to muse upon the words of the pioneering investigator Donald E. Keyhoe: 'It is my earnest hope that there will prove to be no danger behind the UFO surveillance of our world. But as long as such a possibility remains, the facts should be frankly revealed.

'The public has a right to know – and to be prepared for whatever is to come.'[1]

REFERENCES

The following references aside, all of the material related herein is extracted directly from official documentation released to the author by the Federal Bureau of Investigation under the terms of the United States' Freedom of Information Act.

INTRODUCTION

1. 'Conducting Research in FBI Records', FBI, 1990.
2. 'Analysis of Flying Object Incidents in the US', US Air Force, 1948.

CHAPTER ONE: THE ALIENS ARRIVE

1. 'Soviet UFO Secrets', by Bryan Gresh, published in the *MUFON Journal*, October 1993 (copyright 1993 by the Mutual UFO Network, 103 Oldtowne Road, Seguin, Texas, 78155, USA).
2. *The Flying Saucers Are Real*, Donald E. Keyhoe, Fawcett Publications Inc., 1950.

CHAPTER TWO: ENCOUNTERING THE UNKNOWN

1. *The Report on Unidentified Flying Objects*, Edward J. Ruppelt, Ace Books, Inc., 1956.
2. 'Analysis of Flying Object Incidents in the US', US Air Force, 1948.

CHAPTER THREE: PROJECT TWINKLE

1. *The FBI–KGB War*, Robert J. Lamphere and Tom Shachtman, Random House, Inc., 1986.
2. 'Project Twinkle Final Report,' US Air Force, 1951.
3. *UFO*, Vol. 5, No. 3, 1990.
4. Public Record Office file: AIR 2/16918; Crown copyright exists.
5. Interview with Simon Miller, 22 December 1995; letter to the author from Simon Miller, 15 December 1995.

CHAPTER FOUR: THE OAK RIDGE INVASION

1. *The Flying Saucers Are Real*, Donald Keyhoe, Fawcett Publications Inc., 1950.
2. *Crash at Corona*, Stanton T. Friedman and Don Berliner, Paragon House, 1992.
3. Majestic 12 Group Special Operations Manual, April 1954.
4. *A Covert Agenda*, Nicholas Redfern, Simon and Schuster, 1997.

CHAPTER FIVE: THE UFOs TARGET WASHINGTON

1. *The Coming of the Saucers*, Kenneth Arnold and Ray Palmer, Amherst Press, 1952.
2. Various US Air Force Intelligence files, July 1952.
3. *Aliens from Space*, Donald E. Keyhoe, Panther, 1975.
4. *Alien Update*, Timothy Good, Arrow, 1993.
5. *The FBI–KGB War*, Robert J. Lamphere and Tom Shachtman, Random House Inc., 1986.
6. *A Covert Agenda*, Nicholas Redfern, Simon & Schuster, 1997.

CHAPTER SIX: SOCORRO AND BEYOND

1. *Socorro Saucer in a Pentagon Pantry*, Ray Stanford, Blueapple Books, 1976.
2. Undated Central Intelligence Agency report, circa April 1964.
3. *An Alien Harvest*, Linda Moulton Howe, Linda Moulton Howe Productions, 1989.
4. Ohio *UFO Notebook*, No. 4, 1996.
5. 'Studies In Intelligence', CIA, 1966.

6. *Citizens Against UFO Secrecy* bulletin, 1990.

7. *UFO*, Vol. 8, No. 5, 1993.

8. *Saga UFO Special*, No. 3, 1972.

9. *Secrecy and Power*, Richard Gid Powers, Arrow Books, 1989.

10. Statements by John Lear, 29 December 1987 and 25 March 1988.

11. *A Covert Agenda*, Nicholas Redfern, Simon & Schuster, 1997.

12. *The UFO Crash/Retrieval Syndrome*, Leonard H. Stringfield, the Mutual UFO Network, 1980.

13. *UFO Crash/Retrievals: Amassing the Evidence*, Leonard H. Stringfield, privately published 1982.

14. *Just Cause*, No. 25, 1990.

15. *Clear Intent*, Lawrence Fawcett and Barry J. Greenwood, Prentice-Hall, 1984.

16. *Just Cause*, No. 28, 1991.

17. *Just Cause*, No. 29, 1991.

18. *Defence Electronics*, July, 1993.

CHAPTER SEVEN: COSMIC PREDATORS

1. *Pueblo Chieftain*, 7 October 1967.

2. *An Alien Harvest*, Linda Moulton Howe, Linda Moulton Howe Productions, 1989.

3. *Argus Leader*, 30 August 1974.

4. *Idaho Statesman*, 6 July 1975.

5. *Elsberry Democrat*, 22 June 1978.

6. *Greeley Tribune*, 18 September 1980.

7. *Arizona Republic*, 15 August 1991.

8. *Leading Edge*, No. 66, 1994.

9. *UFOs and the Alien Presence*, Michael Lindemann, the 2020 Group, 1991.

10. *The Bennewitz Papers*, Christa Tilton, 1992.

11. Letter to the author from Christa Tilton, 23 January 1992.

12. United States Air Force Intelligence papers, 1975/6.

13. *The MJ-12 Documents: An Analytical Report*, William L. Moore and Jaime H. Shandera, 1990.

CHAPTER EIGHT: OPERATION ANIMAL MUTILATION

1. *National Enquirer*, 5 June 1979.

2. *Rio Grande Sun*, various editions July 1979.

3. Letter to the author from Bruce G. Hallenbeck, 26 August 1992.
4. *Saga*, July 1970.
5. *Fortean Times*, No. 83.
6. *UFO*, Vol. 4, No. 3.
7. *UFO*, Vol. 5, No. 2.

CHAPTER NINE: ALIENS OR NAZIS?

1. Public Record Office file: AIR 20/9321; Crown copyright exists.
2. Information relating to the Avrocar released to the author by Ron Scherrill, Archives Technician, Wright-Patterson Air Force Base, 18 September 1990.

CHAPTER TEN: INCIDENT AT AZTEC

1. *Above Top Secret*, Timothy Good, Sidgwick and Jackson, 1987.
2. *Behind the Flying Saucers*, Frank Scully, Henry Holt, 1950.
3. *UFO Crash at Aztec*, William Steinman and Wendelle Stevens, UFO Photo Archives, 1987.
4. *Clearwater Sun*, 27 October 1974.
5. *Official UFO*, December 1975.
6. *Fate*, February 1988.
7. *Beyond Top Secret*, Timothy Good, Sidgwick and Jackson, 1996.
8. Larry W. Bryant Versus Department of Justice, United States District Court for the District of Columbia, 24 August 1988.
9. *Citizens Against UFO Secrecy*. 'Bryant v. Justice: Another Step Toward Revealing the "Ultimate Secret"', 1988.
10. Canadian Department of Transport memorandum, 21 November 1950.

CHAPTER ELEVEN: MAJESTIC

1. *UFO Crash/Retrievals: Search for Proof in a Hall of Mirrors*, Leonard Stringfield, privately published, 1994.
2. *Focus*, September 30, 1989.
3. *UFO Crash/Retrievals: Is the Cover-Up Lid Lifting?*, Leonard Stringfield, privately published, 1989.
4. *The Roswell Incident*, Charles Berlitz and William Moore, Granada, 1980.
5. *UFO* Vol. 9, No. 5.

6. *Crash at Corona*, Stanton T. Friedman and Don Berliner, Paragon House, 1992.
7. *Alien Liaison*, Timothy Good, Century, 1991.
8. *The Truth About the UFO Crash at Roswell*, Kevin D. Randle and Donald R. Schmitt, M. Evans, 1994.
9. *Roswell in Perspective*, Karl Pflock, the Fund for UFO Research, 1994.
10. *UFO Crash at Roswell*, Kevin D. Randle and Donald R. Schmitt, Avon, 1991.
11. 'The MJ-12 Documents: An Analytical Report', by William L. Moore and Jaime H. Shandera, 1990.
12. *Out There*, by Howard Blum, Simon & Schuster, 1990.
13. *Revelations*, by Jacques Vallee, Ballantine, 1991.
14. *UFO*, Vol. 5, No. 5.
15. Letter to the author from Frank H. Batten, Jnr, Chief, Information Operations Center, Bolling Air Force Base, 30 April, 1993.
16. Letter to the author from Colonel Richard L. Weaver, USAF, 12 October 1993.

CHAPTER TWELVE: CONTACT!

1. *Is Anyone Out There?* by Jack Stoneley and A.T. Lawton, Star Books, 1975.
2. *The UFO Phenomena*, Edward Ashpole, Headline, 1995.
3. Majestic Twelve Group Special Operations Manual, April 1954.
4. *Flying Saucer Review*, Vol. 39, No. 3.
5. *Preuves Scientifiques OVNI*, J.C. Fumoux, 1981. (extract translated and published in *UFO Crash/Retrievals: Amassing the Evidence*, Leonard Stringfield, privately published, 1982).
6. *The Humanoids*, Charles Bowen, Neville Spearman, 1969.
7. *Flying Saucer Review*, Vol. 26, No. 4.
8. *UFO Magazine*, Vol. 12, issue 4, September/October 1993.
9. Lecture given by Robert Dean at the Civic Theatre, Leeds, 24 September 1994.

CHAPTER THIRTEEN: THE ADAMSKI CONNECTION

1. *Aboard A Flying Saucer*, Truman Bethurum and Mary Kay Tennison, DeVorss and Co., 1954.
2. *The Saucers Speak!*, George Hunt Williamson and Alfred C. Bailey, New Age, 1954.
3. *UFO Magazine*, September/October 1995.

4. *The White Sands Incident*, Daniel Fry, Horus House Press, Inc., 1992.
5. *George Adamski – The Untold Story*, Lou Zinsstag and Timothy Good, Ceti Publications, 1983.
6. *Flying Saucers Have Landed*, Desmond Leslie and George Adamski, Werner Laurie, 1953.
7. *Behind the Flying Saucer Mystery*, George Adamski, Paperback Library, Inc., 1967.
8. *The Hughes Papers*, Elaine Davenport and Paul Eddy with Mark Hurwitz, Sphere Books Ltd, 1977.
9. *Extra-Terrestrials Among Us*, George C. Andrews, Llewellyn Publications, 1986.
10. *Situation Red: The UFO Siege*, Leonard H. Stringfield, Sphere Books Ltd, 1978.
11. *Messengers of Deception*, Jacques Vallee, Berkeley, 1979.
12. *Dimensions*, Jacques Vallee, Souvenir Press, 1988.
13. *Look Up*, Ray and Rex Stanford, privately published, 1958.
14. *UFOs: Operation Trojan Horse*, John Keel, Souvenir Press Ltd, 1971.

CHAPTER FOURTEEN: BEWARE THE MEN IN BLACK

1. *They Knew Too Much About Flying Saucers*, Gray Barker, University Books, Inc., 1956.
2. *Flying Saucers and the Three Men*, Albert K. Bender, Saucerian Books, 1962.
3. Lecture given by John Keel, 1988.
4. 'Those Mysterious MIBs', Richard D. Seifried, Oklahoma *MUFONEWS*, April 1993.
5. *Far Out*, Vol. 2, No. 6.
6. Interview with Nick Pope, MOD, 29 March 1994.
7. *Flying Saucers on the Attack*, Harold T. Wilkins, Ace Books, Inc., 1954.
8. *Mystic*, August 1954.
9. *The UFO Silencers*, Timothy Green Beckley, Inner Light Publications, 1990.

CHAPTER FIFTEEN: SUMMING UP

1. *Flying Saucers – Top Secret*, Donald E. Keyhoe, G.P. Putnam's Sons, 1960.

© Photograph Credits:

© Popperfoto
© Timothy Good
© Federal Bureau of Investigation
© Quest Picture Library
© Quest Picture Library
© Quest Picture Library
© Quest Picture Library
© Quest Picture Library
© Quest Picture Library
© Quest Picture Library
© Staffordshire UFO Group
© Quest Picture Library
© Quest Picture Library
© Quest Picture Library
© Christa Tilton
© Christa Tilton

INDEX